Families and Law

The *Marriage & Family Review* series:

Families and Law

Lisa J. McIntyre
Marvin B. Sussman
Editors

The Haworth Press, Inc.
New York • London • Norwood (Australia)

Families and Law has also been published as *Marriage & Family Review*, Volume 21, Numbers 3/4 1995.

The development, preparation, and publication of this work has been undertaken with great care. However, the publisher, employees, editors, and agents of The Haworth Press and all imprints of The Haworth Press, Inc., including The Haworth Medical Press and Pharmaceutical Products Press, are not responsible for any errors contained herein or for consequences that may ensue from use of materials or information contained in this work. Opinions expressed by the author(s) are not necessarily those of The Haworth Press, Inc.

Paperback edition published in 1997.

Cover design by Becky Salsgiver.

Library of Congress Cataloging-in-Publication Data

Families and law / Lisa J. McIntyre, Marvin B. Sussman, editors.
    p.   cm.
    Published as Marriage & family review, volume 21, numbers 3/4, 1995–Verso t.p.
    Includes bibliographical reference and index.
    ISBN 0-7890-0215-9 (acid-free paper)
    1. Domestic relations–United States. I. McIntyre, Lisa J. II.Sussman, Marvin B.
KF505.A2F35 1995
346.7301'5–dc20   94-45052
[347.30615]   CIP

INDEXING & ABSTRACTING

Contributions to this publication are selectively indexed or abstracted in print, electronic, online, or CD-ROM version(s) of the reference tools and information services listed below. This list is current as of the copyright date of this publication. See the end of this section for additional notes.

- *Abstracts in Social Gerontology: Current Literature on Aging,* National Council on the Aging, Library, 409 Third Street SW, 2nd Floor, Washington, DC 20024

- *Abstracts of Research in Pastoral Care & Counseling,* Loyola College, 7135 Minstrel Way, Suite 101, Columbia, MD 21045

- *Academic Abstracts/CD-ROM,* EBSCO Publishing, P.O. Box 2250, Peabody, MA 01960-7250

- *AGRICOLA Database,* National Agricultural Library, 10301 Baltimore Boulevard, Room 002, Beltsville, MD 20705

- *Applied Social Sciences Index & Abstracts (ASSIA) (Online: ASSI via Data-Star) (CDRom: ASSIA Plus),* Bowker-Saur Limited, Maypole House, Maypole Road, East Grinstead, West Sussex RH19 1HH, England

- *Current Contents: Clinical Medicine/Life Sciences (CC:CM/LS) (weekly Table of Contents Service), and Social Science Citation Index. Articles also searchable through Social SciSearch, ISI's online database and in ISI's Research Alert current awareness service,* Institute for Scientific Information, 3501 Market Street, Philadelphia, PA 19104-3302 (USA)

- *Family Life Educator "Abstracts Section,"* ETR Associates, P.O. Box 1830, Santa Cruz, CA 95061-1830

- *Family Violence & Sexual Assault Bulletin,* Family Violence & Sexual Assault Institute, 1310 Clinic Drive, Tyler, TX 75701

- *Guide to Social Science & Religion in Periodical Literature,* National Periodical Library, P.O. Box 3278, Clearwater, FL 34630

- *Index to Periodical Articles Related to Law,* University of Texas, 727 East 26th Street, Austin, TX 78705

- *Inventory of Marriage and Family Literature (online and hard copy),* National Council on Family Relations, 3989 Central Avenue NE, Suite 550, Minneapolis, MN 55421

(continued)

- *PASCAL International Bibliography T205: Sciences de l'information Documentation,* INIST/CNRS-Service Gestion des Documents Primaires, 2, allee du Parc de Brabois, F-54514 Vandoeuvre-les-Nancy, Cedex, France

- *Periodical Abstracts, Research I (general & basic reference indexing & abstracting data-base from University Microfilms International (UMI), 300 North Zeeb Road, PO Box 1346, Ann Arbor, MI 48106-1346),* UMI Data Courier, P.O. Box 32770, Louisville, KY 40232-2770

- *Periodical Abstracts, Research II (broad coverage indexing & abstracting data-base from University Microfilms International (UMI), 300 North Zeeb Road, PO Box 1346, Ann Arbor, MI 48106-1346),* UMI Data Courier, P.O. Box 32770, Louisville, KY 40232-2770

- *Population Index,* Princeton University Office Population, 21 Prospect Avenue, Princeton, NJ 08544-2091

- *Psychological Abstracts (PsycINFO),* American Psychological Association, P.O. Box 91600, Washington, DC 20090-1600

- *Sage Family Studies Abstracts (SFSA),* Sage Publications, Inc., 2455 Teller Road, Newbury Park, CA 91320

- *Social Planning/Policy & Development Abstracts (SOPODA),* Sociological Abstracts, Inc., P.O. Box 22206, San Diego, CA 92192-0206

- *Social Sciences Index (from Volume 1 & continuing),* The H.W. Wilson Company, 950 University Avenue, Bronx, NY 10452

- *Social Work Abstracts,* National Association of Social Workers, 750 First Street NW, 8th Floor, Washington, DC 20002

- *Sociological Abstracts (SA),* Sociological Abstracts, Inc., P.O. Box 22206, San Diego, CA 92192-0206

- *Special Educational Needs Abstracts,* Carfax Information Systems, P.O. Box 25, Abingdon, Oxfordshire OX14 3UE, United Kingdom

- *Studies on Women Abstracts,* Carfax Publishing Company, P.O. Box 25, Abingdon, Oxfordshire OX14 3UE, United Kingdom

- *Violence and Abuse Abstracts: A Review of Current Literature on Interpersonal Violence (VAA),* Sage Publications, Inc., 2455 Teller Road, Newbury Park, CA 91320

(continued)

SPECIAL BIBLIOGRAPHIC NOTES

related to special journal issues (separates)
and indexing/abstracting

☐ indexing/abstracting services in this list will also cover material in any "separate" that is co-published simultaneously with Haworth's special thematic journal issue or DocuSerial. Indexing/abstracting usually covers material at the article/chapter level.

☐ monographic co-editions are intended for either non-subscribers or libraries which intend to purchase a second copy for their circulating collections.

☐ monographic co-editions are reported to all jobbers/wholesalers/approval plans. The source journal is listed as the "series" to assist the prevention of duplicate purchasing in the same manner utilized for books-in-series.

☐ to facilitate user/access services all indexing/abstracting services are encouraged to utilize the co-indexing entry note indicated at the bottom of the first page of each article/chapter/contribution.

☐ this is intended to assist a library user of any reference tool (whether print, electronic, online, or CD-ROM) to locate the monographic version if the library has purchased this version but not a subscription to the source journal.

☐ individual articles/chapters in any Haworth publication are also available through the Haworth Document Delivery Services (HDDS).

Families and Law

CONTENTS

ABOUT THE EDITORS

Lisa J. McIntyre, PhD, is Associate Professor of Sociology at Washington State University in Pullman, Washington. She received her Doctorate in Sociology from the University of Chicago in 1985. Her research and writings have contributed significantly to the Sociology of Law. In 1987, she published *The Public Defender: The Practice of Law in the Shadows of Repute* which received recognition from a number of legal and sociological professional societies. In 1992, she published the article "Family Law" in the *Encyclopedia of Sociology* and currently is completing a volume entitled *Law in the Sociological Enterprise: A Reconstruction.* Her major fields of interest in addition to the Sociology of Law are: sociology of work, social theory, quantitative research methods and complex organizations. Her professional memberships include the American Society of Criminology, American Sociological Association, Law and Society Association, Pacific Sociological Association, and Sociologists for Women in Society.

Marvin B. Sussman, PhD, is UNIDEL Professor of Human Behavior Emeritus at the College of Human Resources, University of Delaware; and Member of the CORE Faculty, Union Graduate School, Union Institute, Cincinnati, Ohio. A member of many professional organizations, he was awarded the 1980 Ernest W. Burgess Award of the National Council on Family Relations. In 1983, he was elected to the prestigious Academy of Groves for scholarly contributions to the field, as well as awarded a life-long membership for services to the Groves Conference on Marriage and the Family in 1984. Dr. Sussman received the Distinguished Family Award of the Society for the Study of Social Problems (1985) and the Lee Founders Award (1992), SSSP's highest Professional Award. Also in 1992 he was the recipient of the State of Delaware Gerontological Society Award for contributions to research and education in the family and aging fields. Dr. Sussman has published over 250 articles and books on family, community, rehabilitation, organizations, health and aging.

Fantasy Fulfillment

Marvin B. Sussman

This special volume on Families and Law is the fulfillment of one of my most cherished fantasies. In 1981 in the Ernest W. Burgess address on "Law and legal systems: The family connection" (Sussman, 1983), I was polemical and beat on myself for not using law and its attendant systems in family research.

Not too many years before with colleagues I completed a basic empirical study on family inheritance patterns (Sussman, Cates, Smith, 1970). The conceptual framework was derived from previous studies of generational continuity and transfers; and exchanges of goods and services among members of extended kin networks.

A sociological over a legal perspective was used in the inheritance transfer study. This was a natural outcome of studies which had established the existence of urban kin networks and their various patterns of interaction, exchange of goods and services. The lesson to be learned was the intricate nexus between law and societal systems and structures; the power of legal precepts. Even those established in times of antiquity and perceived today to be outdated, were regulating virtually the most intimate, private and complex of human relationships.

The laws, procedures, and regulations of the inheritance system based on historic precedents governing the distribution of assets and naming of heirs and legatees upon the death of an individual with a will (testate) or without one (intestate) are adhered to universally. The legal system regarding inheritance transfers establishes the boundaries for appropriate behav-

---

Marvin B. Sussman is UNIDEL Professor of Human Behavior, Emeritus, University of Delaware.

[Haworth co-indexing entry note]: "Fantasy Fulfillment." Sussman, Marvin B. Co-published simultaneously in *Marriage & Family Review* (The Haworth Press, Inc.) Vol. 21, No. 3/4, 1995, pp. 1-4; and: *Families and Law* (ed: Lisa J. McIntyre, and Marvin B. Sussman) The Haworth Press, Inc., 1995, pp. 1-4. Multiple copies of this article/chapter may be purchased from The Haworth Document Delivery Center [1-800-3-HAWORTH; 9:00 a.m. - 5:00 p.m. (EST)].

ior which may not be in consonance with one's perceptions of reality or those of the Testator.

To some of our citizens the laws are more invasive than protective and facilitative of individual and family goals. The impact and power of the law becomes evident when "you run into it or it runs into you."

Assume for a moment that you are called to jury duty. For years you have been excused because of your important work. This time you decide to serve if you are selected; you feel a strong need to express your citizenship. You are given a prospective juror questionnaire and you are astounded to discover that the questions asked are very personal. You are being demographically and sociologically profiled. In addition to ascertaining your mental status there are questions regarding your religion and religiosity; political affiliation, income, make of car; books and magazines read; TV programs watched; radio programs listened to; and other queries into your personal and private life. For some decades it has been reputed, perhaps a myth, that respondents to a survey are more willing to give details regarding their sex life than to reveal their income. A cardinal blunder is made in this inquiry, asking about income.

You are emotionally distraught and cannot comply with this imposed reality. You felt safe, empowered and just "good" before this protocol was given to you. Your anger and distress increases and you begin to view this effort to intrude on your privacy as a loathsome act.

You refuse to answer most of the questions, marking these personal ones as non-applicable. You are arrested, booked, fingerprinted, and jailed. A hurried call to a family member and your lawyer prevents an overnight stay in the county jail. Bond is posted and you are released. You appear in court accompanied by your lawyers to answer to the contempt citation. The judge rules against you. You are deemed in contempt, fined $200 and sentenced to three days in jail. You appeal the verdict. You have two lawyers, your family lawyer and a specialist on Bill of Rights issues, one highly recommended by a colleague. The costs are high and will become astronomical if you carry the appeal to higher courts unless the Civil Liberties Union or some other Bill of Rights organization rallies to your cause. A number of individuals who learned about your plight have taken on your cause. They are present when you arrive at the courthouse; they express their indignation regarding your treatment, and give you their moral support.

It could happen to you. It happened to Dianna Bradborg, a resident of Denton County, Texas (*Tampa Tribune*, 1994). A supporter of Bradborg in the news article describing this happening is reported to have said "Where did we (citizens) lose control? . . . We have an injustice system, instead of a justice system." The objective of these questions, according to the past president of the Tarrant County Trial Lawyers Association, is that "questions about cars and political affiliations help lawyers to better represent their cause." The power of the law and its functionaries is awesome in its impact upon individuals and families. There is little need to formulate the scenario of your family's life if you had Mrs. Bradborg's experience.

Another example of the pervasiveness of law and legal action in a suing culture is the frivolous lawsuit when one exercises first amendment rights in the course of engaging in public activities. The appropriate acronym for these spurious lawsuits is SLAPP, "strategic lawsuits against public participation." Most of these lawsuits are groundless and their aim is to annoy, punish and decimate the defendant's and family's financial resources and destroy their psychic well-being.

Legislative efforts to curb this wanton behavior, such as requiring plaintiffs to present evidence quickly that the case has merit, have not been successful (*Tampa Tribune*, 1994). Such legislation is not intended to eliminate lawsuits for just cause but rather to determine which are meritorious or frivolous; and to manage threats of lawsuits and fears of violence and retribution.

You may become a recipient of a SLAPP suit by participation in social or political activities. "The victims included people sued by developers for testifying against a project; environmentalists sued for reporting pollution; parents sued for criticizing a teacher; people sued for reporting police brutality; businesses sued for trying to get an advantage over competitors; humane societies and animal welfare advocates sued for urging protection of animals; and representatives of labor unions and activists in other causes sued by political opponents, and even by government for lobbying for changes in government policies" (ibid., p. 8).

Both of these examples illustrate the power of law and its endemic frustrations, chaos, and unintended consequences for innocent victims and their families.

In 1981 (Sussman, op. cit., p. 19) I wrote "Family theorists, researchers and watchers should incorporate into their repertoire of conceptual approaches and methodological tools the accounting of law and legal systems in formulating issues and developing problems for family studies. It is critical that we internalize this law and legal system dimension in our diagnostic and conceptual frameworks. We are missing reality, the true state of being, if we examine a behavioral issue or problem and ignore the possible explanatory power which may be attributed to the law and its endemic legal systems." . . . "The legal system should become a focused area of study by workers in the family field. Such studies should not be left solely to the psychologists, sociologists, historians, and anthropologists of occupational systems. Divorce has become a multibillion dollar industry, and there are enough creative alternative mechanisms for handling the dissolution of marriage–which can be done less expensively and even with less trauma–through disavowal of the adversary process in effecting such separations. This is only one example of the power of the legal system in family matters. The power and influence extends beyond profit taking; it includes interpretation of the law. Because of inexperience and insensitivity to law and how it functions (until there is a problem like separation and divorce or abuse in the family), family members are almost completely controlled. Suggested is consideration of the treatment of law and the family in any course or family training program."

Since 1981 some of these concerns have been addressed. There is a growing group of scholars becoming increasingly involved and invested in family, law, and legal systems research. This special collection with its coverage of a wide range of theoretical and substantive issues will increase the prevalence and incidence of family and law studies. In 1981, I implored sociologists to become involved in such studies similar to the engagement of scholars from other disciplines. At the same time, I urged the development of cross and interdisciplinary research programs. My position was and still is: ". . . The family and law and its attendant legal systems share a pervasive connectedness. As family academicians and scholars, we have been negligent in our advocacy role relevant to increasing the family's position in relation to the law and legal system and in making ourselves and our constituents aware of the expressiveness and power of the laws and of the ways in which we can influence it. This can be readily corrected by legal- and family-oriented behavioral scholars developing cross-professional and disciplinary research programs. This requires hard work, increasing use of the right side of the brain, and conceptual development of a legiofamiliobehavioral science, an interdisciplinary approach to understanding human behavior. The yeasting, green, and harvesting of this wasteland can only occur if such an ecumenical development takes place" (ibid., p. 20).

We are in the beginnings of this process.

REFERENCES

Sussman, M.B., Cates, J., & Smith, D. (1970) *The Family and Inheritance,* New York: Russell Sage Foundation.

Sussman, M.B. (1983) "Law and legal systems: The law family connection," *Journal of Marriage and the Family,* vol. 9-21.

the *Tampa Tribune* (1994) "Editorials," March 15, p. 8.

the *Tampa Tribune* (1994) "People: She chose jail over personal questions," March 11, Section C, p. 2.

Law and the Family
in Historical Perspective:
Issues and Antecedents

Lisa J. McIntyre

INTRODUCTION

Law, family. The words evoke very different images: law is formal, cold and impersonal; families are informal, warm and affectionate. Ideally, legal relationships are detached, restrained and sober; familial relationships, demonstrative, effusive and exuberant. On the surface, at least, the law and the family are antagonistic and belong to separate domains within society–the law to the public and the family to the private. Yet, as the essays in this volume illustrate vividly, law and family have a great deal to do with one another these days. It almost seems as if at every turn the family unit encounters the law.

What is easy to overlook is that the ties that exist between the family and legal order are not uniquely modern. Looking back, one finds that the law has long been twined to family concerns. However, as I will show in this essay, the nature of law's impact on the family has changed a great deal in the recent past. Moreover, it is surprising to learn that, notwithstanding the apparent conflict between law and family, to the degree that in modern society the family remains a private institution, a sanctuary from the world of the market and the political arena, a great deal of this state of affairs is owed to the law.

Lisa J. McIntyre is Associate Professor of Sociology at Washington State University, Pullman, WA.

[Haworth co-indexing entry note]: "Law and the Family in Historical Perspective: Issues and Antecedents." McIntyre, Lisa J. Co-published simultaneously in *Marriage & Family Review* (The Haworth Press, Inc.) Vol. 21, No. 3/4, 1995, pp. 5-30; and: *Families and Law* (ed: Lisa J. McIntyre, and Marvin B. Sussman) The Haworth Press, Inc., 1995, pp. 5-30. Multiple copies of this article/chapter may be purchased from The Haworth Document Delivery Center [1-800-3-HAWORTH; 9:00 a.m. - 5:00 p.m. (EST)].

The nature of law's relationship with the modern American family is best understood by looking back to the beginnings of this relationship, where it took root first in England.

ENGLISH ROOTS

In England, from the twelfth until the mid-nineteenth century, the laws respecting marriage and family life were of two principal sorts: secular or common law and church or ecclesiastical law. In the main, the regulation of marriage per se was left to ecclesiastical courts which had jurisdiction over such matters as who could marry whom and under what circumstances husbands and wives could separate. Similarly, adultery, fornication and incest, as well as "any uncleanness and wickedness of life" (Ingram 1987, 239) were not crimes but spiritual offenses to be dealt with as church, not temporal courts, dictated (Blackstone *IV* 1769, 64-65).

Guided, perhaps, by the Biblical injunction that it is better to marry than to burn, a valid marriage was easily contracted according to early ecclesiastical law. As far as the Church was concerned, the essence of marriage was a private contract. Thus, a valid union could be created simply by the man and woman consenting to marriage in words of the present tense (*sponsalia per verba de praesenti*) (Menefee 1981, 10).[1] Although ministers preached the importance of sanctified marriage and exhorted those wishing to marry to submit to a church wedding, all that was needed was the mutual consent of the couple: "Neither solemnisation in church, nor the use of specially prescribed phrases, nor even the presence of witnesses, was essential to an act of marriage" (Ingram, 132). The truly private nature of such marriages, however, meant that doubt could exist about whether a valid marriage had ever been contracted. This, in turn, led to a number of disputes about property: to the degree that there was doubt about the validity of marriage, so, too, was there doubt about whether widows and children could inherit. Such doubts and disputes were put to an end in 1753, when Lord Hardwicke's Marriage Act mandated that no marriage was valid unless solemnized in the Anglican church after proper publication of banns or a license had been obtained.[2]

If creating a valid marriage was historically a relatively simple matter, ending one was not. In post-Reformation England, divorce *a vinculo matrimonii* (absolute divorce) was prohibited. Couples could win divorce *a mensa et thoro* (from bed and board)–akin to a modern legal separation– for sufficient cause (adultery or extreme cruelty), but this did not permit either spouse to remarry. Winning a decree of divorce *a mensa et thoro*, however, did allow an innocent wife to sue for alimony. For a few couples, annulment (a decree that the union had never been a valid marriage) provided an avenue for escape, but this required proof that specific impediments to marriage existed. The grounds for annulment were few: if it could be proved that the pair were related within a prohibited degree–either by blood (consanguinity) or marriage (affinity)–then the marriage might be annulled. A marriage might likewise be declared void if it could be proved that husband or wife was permanently incapable of consummating the union. Sexual incapacity, however, was not an easy way out, for as Martin Ingram has noted, "however common such incapacity may have been, it was extremely difficult to prove. The law demanded evidence that the condition was permanent and had prevented consummation" (173). Such evidence was not easy to produce.[3]

In any case, annulment was not an altogether satisfactory substitute for absolute divorce. Although it allowed for remarriage, it cut off the woman's rights to support and to inherit a share (generally a third) of her former husband's estate (the so-called dower portion) and made bastards of any children born to the couple during the lifetime of the marriage.

After 1700, divorce *a vinculo matrimonii* or absolute divorce began to be granted–but only by a private act of Parliament. This procedure was time consuming and very expensive, and hence, was out of the reach of all but the very rich and influential (Stone 1977, 38). (It would not be until the *Matrimonial Clauses Act of 1857* that judicial–as opposed to Parliamentary–divorce was permitted in England even on a limited basis.)

Once a marriage had been created, the law, both ecclesiastical and temporal–for most intents and purposes–lost interest. Despite the assertion by English historians Pollock and Maitland that "to the canonist there was nothing so sacred that it might not be expressed in definite rules" (*II* 1898, 436) church courts tended not to concern themselves with purely personal relations within intact families. The courts, for example, "made virtually no effort to punish autoerotic activities and sexual irregularities which took place between husband and wife in the marriage bed" (Ingram, 239-40). This does not mean, however, that family relations were not subject to social control. What it does mean is that infringements of conventional morality were left to the rude, but no doubt effective justice of the community. One means of informal punishment was known as skimmington, a process in which the wrong-doer was "paraded around the village seated backwards on a donkey" (Stone 1977, 145). Martin Ingram, in his study *Church Courts, Sex and Marriage in England*, described other ways in which the community might express its disapproval: "Notorious fornicators or adulterers were sometimes visited with the discordant din of 'rough music,' made by the beating of pots and pans and other household utensils. In 1586, for example, a certain Thomas Atkyns was 'rung about the town of Purton with basins for that he did live with the wife of Robert Pearce.' Cuckolds (husbands whose wives had been unfaithful) were often savagely mocked: horns or antlers were hung up on their houses, or neighbors grimaced or made horn signs at them with their fingers." In other cases, adulterers or cuckolds would be made the subject of mocking rhymes and satire, as was the case of one sorry husband in Bremhill, England in 1816:

> *Woe to thee, Michael Robins, that ever thou wert born*
> *For Blancute makes thee cuckold, and thou must wear the horn.*
> *He fetcheth the nurse, to give the child suck,*
> *That he may have time, thy wife to fuck.*

And so it continued, Ingram reports, "for a further ten scurrilous verses"[4] (173).

This is not to say that marital matters were not litigated in the ecclesiastical courts; indeed, anticipating their American descendants, English folks proved themselves notoriously litigious in the sixteenth and seventeenth centuries. Yet, many of these cases were not instigated to punish sexual offenders, but rather were begun at the behest of those informally accused of prurient misbehavior. The best way to regain one's reputation after such an allegation was to bring suit for sexual slander (Ingram, chapter 10). In this fashion, the ecclesiastical law could be invoked to check communal normative control; the church courts, then, afforded some degree of protection from malevolent or overly zealous neighbors.

Notwithstanding the centrality of ecclesiastical law, the effect of *secular* law on family dynamics cannot be ignored for it was English common law that most specifically defined men's and women's places in society. Common law made the husband and father the head of the family. Although his powers were no match for those of the patriarch of ancient Rome (who, according to the doctrine of *patria potestas*, literally held the power of life and death over his wife, children and servants) the English father and husband was clearly master of the domestic domain. While it is not original to him, the conventional phrasing of the main legal effect of marriage is Blackstone's: "By marriage the husband and wife are one person in law" (Blackstone *I*, 430).[5] The modern gloss on this is more telling: Husband and wife are one—and that one is the husband (*United States v. Yazell*, 382 U.S. 341 [1966] Black, J. *dis.*).[6] Upon marriage the woman came under the doctrine, expressed in Law French,[7] of *coverture*; she ceased to exist as a person in her own right for her legal identity was subsumed under the cover of her husband's person. As a married woman, or *feme covert*, she could not be sued in her own right, nor could she bring action for suit "without her husband's concurrence" (Blackstone *I*, 430). While the husband was prohibited from selling or otherwise alienating property in any way that jeopardized his wife's dower rights without her consent, under common law the married woman effectively lost control over all of her possessions; whatever property she had brought to, or might acquire during the marriage was subject to her husband's control. The husband was, moreover, legally responsible for his wife's behavior–for her torts (or civil wrongs, that is, non-criminal legal wrongs) and even for any crimes she committed in his presence, excepting the most "atrocious" crimes of treason, murder or robbery (*The Laws Respecting Women*, 1777). Coupled with this, the husband had the right (or, more accurately, the duty) to moderately chastise his wife when she acted contrary to his wishes or the rules of decorum. Most telling of the political relation of husband and wife was the law that stipulated–in early times–that the husband's murder of his wife was treated as ordinary murder, while a wife who killed her husband was guilty of petite treason. The principal difference between the two acts was how they were sanctioned–murder was punishable by hanging, petite treason was punishable by burning at the stake.

To an extent, the laws of England provided some relief for wives who became the victims of gross abuses by their husbands. The common law, as Blackstone noted, would marshal its police powers to protect wives when life and limb were in jeopardy from physically abusive husbands. When less drastic action was required, as for example, when a woman's property rights were at issue, she might find some relief in English Courts of Equity.

Beginning in the fourteenth and fifteen centuries, courts of equity developed in parallel with common law courts, and served to an extent to alleviate the defects of common law which was viewed by many as overly formalistic. While common law courts decided cases according to the strict rules of law, cases brought before equity courts were decided according to the maxims of equity–a series of principles established to help ensure that the law was not used to unfair ends: "equity will not suffer a wrong to be without a remedy"; "equity looks to the intent rather than to the form." As legal historian Stanley Katz noted, in a legal system that grew up in the spirit of formalism, equity "was an attempt to make law supple enough to do substantial justice" (1971, 259). Persons under various legal disabilities–including married women–could make special appeals to equity courts to protect their rights; especially important in equity were rights established by trusts and settlements, devices that were intended to protect married women from the excesses of profligate spouses:

"Beginning in the late sixteenth century in England a woman or her relatives and friends could arrange a contract under which she or her trustee would retain full managerial rights over her separate property. Either personal or real property placed in such a trust could not be touched by the woman's husband or his creditors. Women with separate estates gained protection under the rules of equity, and their husbands lost traditional common law marital rights under which they had access to all their wives' property" (Salmon 1986, 7-8).

Diversity of Common Law

It is important to note that the idea that England was served by a "common law" is misleading to the degree that this invokes an image of a uniform body of law that everywhere applied in England. Typically, common law is distinguished as being that law which, unlike statutory law that is enacted by legislators, is the "unwritten law announced by judges and only when disputes are brought before them" (Rembar 1980, 59). In England, the actual substance of much of the common law varied throughout the numerous jurisdictions within its borders; "rules on widows' dower rights, conveyancing [i.e., transferring lands] practices, and femme sole [i.e., single women] trader actions shifted between counties and boroughs in seventeenth and eighteenth century England. London had many standards of its own" (Salmon 1986, 2). Primogeniture–inheritance of land by the eldest son–"was the common-law rule," but not one observed everywhere in England. For example, in Kent, all sons inherited equally under a rule known as gavelkind tenure (Friedman 1985, 25).

THE COLONIAL EXPERIENCE

The diversity of English common law, and its differential impact on families was amplified in the newly founded American colonies by two important factors. In the first place, those who settled in the new world were neither lawyers nor aristocrats; hence, they were not learned in the complexities of law as it was practiced in English Royal Courts. Indeed, to many of the early colonists, the English law was a bewildering and "intricate mass" of statutes and cases written in Latin and Law French. Eschewing the "loquacity and prolixity" of English law, their leaders sought reform (Chapin 1983, 4). Colonial laws, then, were often simplified versions of remembered English common law coupled with a mixture of local customs and practices.

The tendency to diversity was augmented by differences in colonists' circumstances. Some colonies (notably those in New England) were settled originally by men and women seeking religious freedom; others (e.g., many Southern colonies) were settled by those whose motives were primarily economic. The diversity of settlers' goals was reflected in early colonial codes. Especially noteworthy, as Marylynn Salmon in her study of property law points out, is the fact that "no one ever envisioned a single colonial code of laws. From the earliest days of settlement, legislative bodies in the colonies held the power to create laws suited to New World conditions. Contemporaries accepted the fact that life in America required the institution of rules unknown at home, and life everywhere in America was not the same. Chattel slavery, the need to promote clearing of wilderness lands, and the creation of a new religious leadership in New England and Pennsylvania all but demanded innovation among American lawmakers" (1986, 3-4). As George Haskins notes, even at the end of the eighteenth century, by which time the substantial reception of much common-law doctrine had brought a degree of uniformity to the American legal scene, Thomas Jefferson, writing in Virginia, could "properly refer to the law of Massachusetts, along with that of Bermuda and Barbados, as 'Foreign law'" (1960, 6-7).

Nonetheless, it does not do too much of a disservice to the diversity of colonial law to generalize about the law's impact on families–for the nature of that impact was fairly straightforward: the law held that the husband and father was master of the domestic domain. While southern colonial laws retained those English rules that protected married women's rights in her property (or at least the dower share), married women in the northern colonies tended to lose these safeguards. All of the colonies were hostile to equity courts, the traditional protectors of the rights of women wealthy enough to make use of them. As a result, there was a "virtual absence of equity" courts in seventeenth century America (Katz, 263). In the New England colonies, the husband's authority was augmented by religious precepts. The good Christian woman trusted and obeyed her husband and any technicalities that existed solely to protect her were unnecessary complications. In any case, the "central tenet of Puritanism" was "the wife's submission to her husband's will." As William Gouge asserted in *Of Domestical Duties*, the husband and wife are "yoak-fellows in mutuall familaritie, not in equall authoritie. . . . If therefore he will one thing, and she another, she must not thinke to have an equall right and power. She must give place and yeeld" (Salmon, 8).

As in England, however, the day-to-day relationships within intact families were unlikely to come under the scrutiny of the courts. Again, however, this does not mean that individuals within families acted autonomously and were not subject to interference from outsiders. The community closely watched over courtship, husband and wife relations, child-rearing practices and other domestic matters. In other words, there was a great deal of control exercised, but it was normative, not legal.

For example, as historians have noted of Puritan communities, "Neighbors were expected to watch each other so that the sins of a few would not jeopardize the standing of the entire community in God's eyes" (Pleck 1987, 18). While the church elders had ultimate responsibility for supervising people's conduct, they were assisted "by the members of the congregation, who exercised mutual inspection, or 'holy watching,' over one another's lives, and reported delinquencies that came to their attention. . . . John Cotton had preached to the Winthrop group as they left England, 'goe forth, every man that goeth, with a publicke spirit, looking not on your owne things onely, but also on the things of others' " (Haskins 1960, 91). Even after it ceased to be a strict religious duty, many continued to take seriously the obligation to keep holy watch. Nancy Cott's study of divorce records in the eighteenth century found that what many of us would consider to be the most private areas of life were routinely intruded upon by "neighbors, lodgers, and kin." In one case, for example, Mary Angel and Abigail Galloway of Boston, out for a walk, saw through an open window their neighbor Adam Air, "in the Act of Copulation" with Pamela Brichford. Testimony about what happened next conveys a sense of their zeal for "overseership":

> on Seeing this We went into the House, & stood behind them as they lay on the Floor, and after observing them some time, the said Abigail Galloway spoke, & asked him if he was not Ashamed to act so when he had a Wife at home, he got up & answered, one Woman was as good to him as another he then put up his nakedness before our faces, & went away, and she on his getting off her, jumped up & ran away into another part of the House. (Cott 1976, 22)

THE REPUBLICAN FAMILY

In the immediate post-Revolutionary America, the laws respecting family, like most laws, entered a period of transition. With independence came the need to rethink the entire legal system and in the Anglophobia of Revolutionary America continued reliance on English law seemed anathema. Yet, as the leaders of the New United States set about to create a system of laws that was distinctly American, they found they could not abandon entirely their English heritage if only because, as legal historian Grant Gilmore put it, "English law was the only law that post-Revolutionary American lawyers knew anything about" (Gilmore 1977, 19). The same presumably was true of American judges and legislators. In the main, then, English law–without its ecclesiastical overtones–was kept as the basis of law in the new states. Yet English law was not received wholesale, even early American law contained some important novelties.

There was no thought that the new American states would adopt laws common to the entire country. This was particularly true with respect to family law. The Tenth Amendment to the Constitution provided that "the powers not delegated to the United States . . . are reserved to the States, respectively, or to the people." Because the power to regulate domestic life was not one of the powers assigned to the federal government by the Constitution, family law was to be "a virtually exclusive province of the states" (*Sosna v. Iowa*, 419 U.S. 393 [1975]).

One important difference between English law and the laws of most American states had to do with divorce. Prior to the Revolution the legal codes in some New England colonies had provided for divorce–this despite the fact that absolute divorce was not generally permitted in England. Thus, as Linda Kerber points out, a colony that passed laws legalizing divorce "was always vulnerable to reprisal" from England. However, it was not until the very eve of the Revolution that England did in fact take official notice of colonial disobedience in this respect. One result was that "freedom to regulate colonial marriages, like freedom to regulate colonial taxation became a Revolutionary issue" (Kerber 1986, 160). After the Revolution, all states except South Carolina passed laws allowing absolute divorce.

The nineteenth century was a period of tremendous growth and change in this country. Two sorts of changes were particularly relevant to the development of family law. The first of these changes was essentially ideological: the same liberal ideals used to justify the break with England remained to have an impact on the everyday lives of American citizens. The second had to do with shifting economic conditions. In the nineteenth century the country's economic system moved from having an agricultural to a commercial and later to a full-blown industrial base.

Ideological Change

Abigail Adams is best remembered for the letter she sent to her husband John as he toiled to draft a new legal code for the soon-to-be-created country. In that letter she invoked the language of revolutionary ideals and enjoined the future president to "Remember the ladies and be more generous and favourable to them than your ancestors. Do not put such unlimited powers into the hands of Husbands. Remember all Men would be tyrants if they could. If particular care and attention is not paid to the Laidies we are determined to foment a Rebelion. . . ." John Adams' response to his wife's suggestion that women be recognized in the new code of laws is perhaps not so well known, but it is telling: "As to your extraordinary Code of Laws, I cannot but laugh. . . . Depend on it, We know better than to repeal our Masculine systems" (Kurland and Lerner *I* 1987, 518-519).

To give Abigail Adams her due, however, in many important respects, hers was the more prophetic missive. Although, true to his word, Adams and his colleagues indeed, did not "Remember the Ladies" in a kindly fashion, one of the more significant effects of the War was the degree to which it provoked a rethinking of women's roles in society and in the family. The Enlightenment ideals which had justified Revolution in the face of tyranny and lack of representation did not work well as legitimating formulae to undergird a society that relegated women to subordinate status. Women had supported the war effort by making great personal sacrifices (including, in some cases, actually fighting alongside men). Republican ideals demanded that the contributions of all citizens be recognized (Norton 1984, 616). So, what was to be woman's place in the new republic?

The resounding answer was that in the new social order women were to be given official charge of the domestic arena. In an enlightened political climate in which individualism was paramount and in an economic order in which work took men further from the domestic hearth, women were charged with maintaining the morality of the American civilization; with nurturing their children–especially their sons–so that they would grow into citizens who would preserve the republic and its high moral character.

As it turned out, then, the woman's place in the new order was not all that different from her place in the old order. A cynic might observe that all that had changed was the rhetoric justifying her station in life. But the new rhetoric was compelling and it caught the imagination of the American public.

> Frequent biographies of "mothers of the wise and good" in the domestic literature connoted that the chief aim of women's vocation was the rearing of moral, trustworthy, statesmanlike citizens. George Washington's mother became a favored model. The story of her training George to be "a good boy" showed in a stroke that mothers were crucial influences, that women's social and political contribution consisted purely in their domestic vocation, and that the nation could not do without their service. (Cott 1977, 94)

This rhetoric, which in time enlarged to become the basis of a "cult of domesticity" so often noted as characteristic of nineteenth century American society, actually contained not one, but two important messages. The first, as noted above, was the idea that women's place was in the home; her highest ambition was to manage the domestic world and raise her children to be fit to participate in the country's life. The second one, often overlooked, was no less important: families existed for the good of society as they were the basis of civilization and our hope for the future. This message, a reiteration of the basic Puritan notion that the family was what held society together–"the root whence church and Commonwealth Cometh" (Haskins 1960, 80)–though not entirely novel–did emphasize the idea that society had a stake in the family. These themes were to prove important in the development of American family law.

Economic Changes

As the country moved away from its agrarian roots, those facets of English laws that were better suited to a social organization based on feudal ties and stable land ownership were abandoned. The English system of primogeniture, for example, was particularly ill-suited to a country in which fortunes could be made in land speculation and after the Revolution it was rejected everywhere in the new states.

Similarly, the married women's dower rights were affected by changing economic conditions. Under the English common law, a husband had acquired full rights to manage his wife's property; once the couple had a child, the husband's control strengthened for he became–for his lifetime–"tenant by courtesy" of his wife's estates. Yet, while the husband enjoyed full rights to profit from the use of his wife's estates, he could not sell or otherwise alienate them without her consent. Moreover, owing to the right of the wife to inherit a share of her husband's estate should he leave her a widow, the husband could not sell or convey any portion of his own estates that risked his wife's dower portion. Even should a husband disregard his wife's interests and attempt to sell her property, buyers would be difficult to find for the law allowed the widow to sue to regain her property. Hence, anyone foolish enough to purchase property pledged to dower portions could never be sure of retaining title. In short, one of the effects of coverture and dower rights was that a significant amount of property was kept "outside the normal operations of the market economy" (Kerber 1986, 144).

After the Revolution, many states acted to mitigate the effects of such constraints. In some places, the result was to abolish dower rights almost entirely, in other places, dower remained but was watered down.

However, in a fluid, if not downright risky economic environment, the loss of dower rights put families at risk, for this meant that an unlucky husband's creditors could reach all of the family's property. In many states, legislators responded by passing Married Women's Property Acts. Beginning in the late 1830s, states began to pass laws which, in effect, undid most of the legal constraints of coverture. In consequence, married women gained some rights to own their own property; in many cases placing it out of reach of their husband's creditors.

The passing of coverture, however, was not to be the undoing of women's legal disabilities that many had hoped (or, in many cases, feared)–mostly because judges interpreted the Married Women's Property Acts in a very narrow fashion. In court decisions, the Married Women's Property Acts were deemed not to erode the husband's right to control the family assets, nor did they provide married women the right to control their own earnings or to contract without their husbands' consent.

> Statutory reforms abolishing coverture forced the judiciary to recognize women as separate, but not necessarily as equal. By viewing the disabilities of married women as "general" and the capabilities created by statute as "exceptional," courts not only stemmed the flow of marketplace Amazons, but also severely impaired women's ability to obtain economic independence. For example, statutes recognizing women's right to their separate earnings were typically interpreted to exclude domestic tasks, such as operating a boarding house or selling home products and services. The apparent theory was that such work was performed by the male head of the household through his spouse. In addition, since the husband was entitled to determine the household's needs, his wife's separate property could be charged for his purchases, even if the items were for his exclusive use. (Rhode 1989, 25-26)

The Emergence of American Family Law

This combination of economic and ideological currents gave rise to what was, in many respects, a new family. It was smaller, more mobile and at its basis was a "companionate" marriage, a partnership between man and woman each charged with separate spheres of life. Legally this partnership was a contractual one. In some respects this harkened back to the early Christian ideal of marriage as contract–but, absent its religious trappings, marriage as contract took on new meanings.

The idea of marriage as contract led to official recognition of informal as well as formal marriage. This informal union, the so-called common law marriage, was effected by the simple express agreement of a man and a woman to be married, followed by their cohabitation. (Contrary to popular myth, common law marriages did not require a specific number of years to go into effect, but could be established instantly.) While today they are only recognized in a minority of jurisdictions (thirteen states plus the District of Columbia), until the twentieth century common law marriages were as valid as formal marriages in most states (Wardle, Blakesley and Parker 1988, §3:17). Recognition of common law marriage meant that settlers on the geographic fringes of society, without access to officials, could enjoy the same protection of their property rights and their children's legitimacy as was afforded in formal marriages. In 1833, Chief Justice Gibson of Pennsylvania ruled that rigid marriage laws were "ill adapted to the habits and customs of society as it now exists." Pragmatically, the court also noted that refusing to recognize common law marriages would "bastardize the vast majority of children which have been born within the state for half a century" (*Rodenbaugh v. Sanks*, 2 Watts 9).

Marriage as contract rather than sacrament, also helped lawmakers in many jurisdictions to justify liberalizing divorce laws to an unprecedented extent. While by modern standards divorce was not all that easy to obtain, it was possible and growing easier. A few states even allowed divorce simply where the cause seemed "just and reasonable." Connecticut, for example, permitted divorce for conduct that "permanently destroys the happiness of the petitioner and defeats the purpose of the marriage relation" (Clark 1968, 283).

The laws' diffidence with respect to marriage and families left a void that could not easily be filled by either parental or communal control in an increasingly heterogeneous and mobile society. In the early nineteenth century, the new American family, moreso than at any point in its history, emerged as an autonomous unit, little subject to either legal or normative control.

The notion of companionate marriage, insofar as it stressed marriage as a partnership between husband and wife, had some important consequences. Until the nineteenth century, the legal system had not really treated the family as a unit. "Family autonomy," heretofore had meant, for all intents and purposes, "paternal autonomy." The father was more than head of household, he was the only one with a complete legal personality; all others in the household were under his "cover" and hence had no immediate relation to the law. In effect, the wife, children and servants were the patriarch's concern and did not come under the purview of law (unless and until the male head of household failed in his duty to control his charges).

Yet, the stress placed on women's role in the republican family and the growing sentimental attachment to children (particularly with respect to their status as the future of our country) caused a rethinking of the father's role in the family, and in consequence, the law's role vis-à-vis the family.

While a great deal of attention has been paid by historians to the elevation of woman to domestic saint, what is typically overlooked is the concomitant demotion of man to domestic lout. As Norma Basch shows in her study of women and property law in New York, legislators debating the need to pass Married Women's Property Acts often invoked the image of husbands as intemperate, inept and morally degenerate, likely to squander their wives' property by "extravagant and stylish living," or in "riot, drunkenness, and other homogeneous dissipation" (1982, 115-116). Elizabeth Pleck, in her study of domestic violence, suggests that the temperance movement added fuel to the flames: for example, lecturers described "with characteristic hyperbole the husband who, under the influence of cider alone, savaged with an axe his loving wife and the baby nursing at her breast" (1987, 50).

In the mid-nineteenth century judges took notice of society's attachment to children and women's superiority in the domestic arena and began to rethink the relationship of children to their parents--especially with respect to the issue of custody. Under common law, children had "belonged" to their fathers. By the mid-nineteenth century, courts in many American jurisdictions began to recognize that mothers had equal rights in their children. In many cases, this reevaluation of parental roles was tied to an emphasis on the importance of children to the society as a whole. Jamil Zainaldin's study of the emergence of modem custody law traces the point of origins to a judicial decision handed down by Senator Paige (writing for the New York Court for the Correction of Errors). In the state of nature, said Senator Paige, the father was indeed the sovereign and supreme head of the family. But once the family entered into civil society, this sovereignty was passed to the "chief or government of the nation." Yet, because the nation could not care for all the children on its own, the sovereign transferred to the parents "the duty of education and maintenance and a right of guardianship." This transferral of rights, however, was limited for sovereignty remained with the state: "The moment a child is born . . . it owes its allegiance to the government of the country of its birth, and is entitled to the protection of the government." For its part, the government is obliged to "consult the welfare, comfort and interests of such child in regulating its custody during the period of its minority." Paige concluded that there could be "no inequality between the father and mother," because the parents' rights to the child's custody were delegated to them both by the state (*Mercein v. People, ex rel. Barry*, 25 Wend. 65 [N.Y. 1840], quoted in Zainaldin 1979, 1071).

If the parents' rights with respect to their children were equal, on what basis would the state make custody decisions? According to the "child's best interests." And, given the popularly accepted natural superior of the mother as nurturers, this generally meant that the mother would be granted custody of the children. "Any attempt to deprive the able mother of the care of her child 'would violate the law of nature' and would not be a proper exercise of discretion" (*Mercein v. People*, in Zainaldin 1979, 1073).

It has been observed that this historical novelty of granting women custody of their children was not the boom to women's status in society that it first had appeared. As Michael Grossberg notes, "the judicially inspired changes in custody and guardianship shifted the locus of patriarchal authority much more than they challenged the subordinate status of women" (1983, 246-247). Yes, married women tended to receive custody of their children, but this was not automatic; whether the woman would be granted custody of her children depended, for one thing, on whether she conformed to the judge's idea of a good mother. Thus, "the decline of paternal rights did not automatically increase maternal ones. On the contrary, the law reduced the rights of parenthood itself." Grossberg thus concludes that the decline in paternal authority gave rise not to maternal authority but rather to a novel form of judicial patriarchy.

In most respects, this is a fair characterization. But what it glosses over is the degree to which traditional patriarchal control as exercised by fathers had been subject to the control of the community. In a sense, the increasing legal intervention in the mid-nineteenth century was a revival of community control. However, the "community" had grown into society, and especially white middle class society writ large; the law tended to represent the values of that portion of society who wished to maintain control but could only do so through the machinery of the law.

The legal system would come to play an increasingly important role as the fruits of laissez faire family law and familial autonomy came to be apparent. Most disturbing was what was seen as an appalling rise in divorce rates. While the rate was small by modern standards, it was increasing and "to some self-appointed guardians of national morals, it was an alarming fire bell in the night, a symptom of moral dry rot, and a cause itself of still further moral decay. President Timothy Dwight of Yale, in 1816, called the rise of divorces 'dreadful beyond conception.'" Connecticut, he prophesied, faced "stalking, barefaced, pollution" (Friedman 1985, 206).

Divorce was not the only sign of what was seen as imminent social collapse; equally troubling to many was a declining birth rate among whites. "In 1800, a married couple had an average of slightly over seven children. A generation later, in 1825, the marital fertility rate had fallen to under six children. By the 1850s, married women were bearing on average only 5.42 children, and by 1880, only 4.24" (D'Emilio and Freeman 1988, 58).

In response to these troubles, after the civil war there came a movement to strengthen state regulation of marriage. Many of the liberal divorce laws that had been passed early in the century were repealed. The laws that remained allowed divorce only in response to specific types of fault, usually, adultery, desertion, extreme cruelty or long-term imprisonment. States also tightened entrance to marriage. Already, most states required marriage licenses, but in antebellum America, courts had treated these licenses as a way "to register, not to restrict marriage" (Grossberg 1985, 78). By the end of the nineteenth century, however, marriage licenses had clearly become a means of social control. Because the process of acquiring a marriage license brought the couple under scrutiny of some official, licensing requirements helped states prevent marriages of people who were too young, or too closely related, either by a consanguinity or affinity. Official scrutiny of those seeking to wed also helped to enforce laws against bigamy and polygamy. Again, in important respects, the law provided resources for social control in communities where traditional, normative-based means of social control (shaming, ridicule and other manifestations of disapproval) were proving ineffectual in the increasingly pluralistic and mobile society.

But legislators, encouraged by eugenicists who believed that crime, mental illness, and other social ills could be traced to hereditary biological factors, also enacted laws enumerating other kinds of forbidden marriages. For example, marriage was prohibited to those not mentally capable of contracting owing to conditions variously labeled as insanity, lunacy, idiocy, feeblemindedness, imbecility, or unsound mind (Clark 1968, 95-96). Marriage was also prohibited to those physically incapable of performing the "marriage essentials." Generally, this latter criterion involved only the capacity to have "normal" or "successful" sexual intercourse, and not necessarily the ability to procreate. As one author explained it, "Copula, not fruitfulness, is the test" (Tiffany 1921, 29).

Eugenics also justified, scientifically, laws that prohibited people with certain diseases (e.g., epilepsy, tuberculosis, and venereal disease) and statuses (e.g., habitual criminal, rapist, pauper) from marrying. In most cases, such obstacles could only be overcome if the person consented to sterilization. Many believed such statutes were necessary to "prevent the demise of civilized society" (Linn and Bowers 1978, 629). Even some of the most respected legal thinkers joined the eugenicists. Justice Oliver

Wendell Holmes of the United States Supreme Court, for example, wrote that it would be "better for all the world, if instead of waiting to execute degenerate offspring for crimes, or to let them starve for their imbecility, society can prevent those who are manifestly unfit from continuing their kind" (*Buck v. Bell*, 274 U.S. 200 [1927]). By way of example, here is a summary of the relevant Washington State Statutes:

> No woman under forty-five years of age or man of any age, unless marrying a woman over forty-five shall marry or intermarry within this state who is a common drunkard, habitual criminal, epileptic, imbecile, feeble-minded, idiot, or insane person, or who has heretofore been afflicted with hereditary insanity or is afflicted with pulmonary tuberculosis in its advanced stages or any contagious venereal disease, the county auditor requiring before license issuance an affidavit, sworn to before nay person authorized to administer oaths, of the male applicant showing that he is not afflicted with any contagious venereal disease, an affidavit of some disinterested credible person that neither party is a habitual criminal, and an affidavit of each applicant that he is not within the other named conditions. (May 1929, 441)

The most notorious marriage impediment was race. As slaves, African Americans had no legally recognizable relationships: "By law the slave had no brother or sister, no husband or wife, no son or daughter, no ancestors and no prosperity. This 'kinlessness' and 'natal alienation' meant that among slaves spouses had no legal obligations to one another and parents could exercise no formal responsibilities toward their children" (Oakes 1990, 4).

After the civil war, African Americans had been able to legitimate (in most cases, for the first time) their marriage and kinship relations. And, during the brief Reconstruction era in which African Americans actually gained a voice in the southern political system, laws were passed that provided some relief to African American women whose children had white fathers by making these fathers provide for the offspring. But, the legal abilities of African Americans proved short-lived. Within a few decades, not only were the bastardy laws repealed, but a new form of law had appeared: miscegenation statutes.[8] In the post-Reconstruction era laws were passed that forbade marriages between whites and blacks. By 1930, thirty states had enacted statutes prohibiting interracial marriages (Clark 1968, 91 [see Figure 1]). In several cases, the prohibition of interracial marriage was extended to, for example, whites and Malays, whites and Mongolians, whites and Native Americans, and blacks and Native Ameri-

FIGURE 1. Distribution of Anti-Miscegenation Laws in 1929

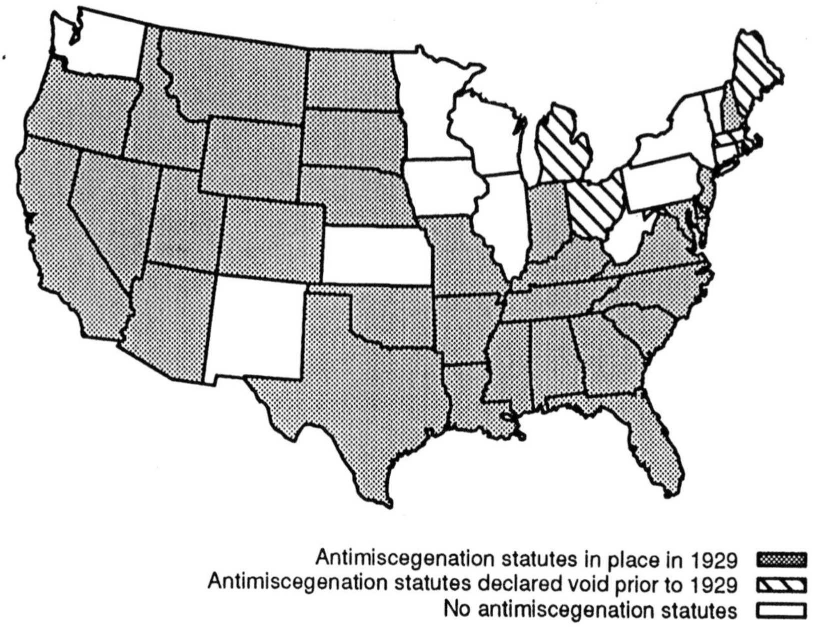

Antimiscegenation statutes in place in 1929
Antimiscegenation statutes declared void prior to 1929
No antimiscegenation statutes

Compiled from Geoffrey May, *Marriage Laws and Decisions in the United States*, 1929.

cans (Kennedy 1959, 59-69). For example, the laws of Oregon forbade "the marriage of a white person with a person of one-fourth or more Negroe or mulatto blood." Further, the Oregon statutes said that "it shall be unlawful for any white person hereafter to intermarry with any person having one-fourth or more Negro, Chinese, or Kanaka blood, or any person having more than one half Indian blood" (May 1929, 356).[9]

Early cases that challenged the constitutionality of antimiscegenation statutes in state courts failed. Then, in 1879, the United States Supreme Court ruled that such laws did not violate the freedom of contract clause of the Constitution (Article 1 § 10) or the Fourteenth Amendment. Marriage, according to the Court, was not a "right" of United States citizens (*Ex parte Kinney*, 3 Hughes 9).

Throughout the late nineteenth century, judges and legislators justified the law's intrusion into the private world with references to society's stake in the family as the seedbed of its civilization. In *Maynard v. Hill*, for example, Mr. Justice Field of the United States Supreme Court put it this way:

Marriage, as creating the most important relation in life, as having more to do with the morals and civilization of the people than any other institution, has always been subject to the control of the legislature. . . . [Marriage] is an institution, in the maintenance of which in its purity the public is deeply interested, for it is the foundation of the family and of society, without which there would be neither civilization nor progress. (125 U.S. 190 [1888])

Nonetheless, with few exceptions the law's intrusion into the domestic arena was limited to regulating entry to and exit from marriage. With respect to intact families the courts and legislators maintained a hands off approach and the activities of and relations between husbands and wives and their children in intact marriages were generally protected from legal scrutiny.[10]

Well into the twentieth century, the principle of nonintervention remained so strong that neither husbands nor wives *could* invoke the law to resolve marital disputes even when they wished to. In one case, for example, the sixty-year-old wife of a well-to-do, but stingy, eighty-year-old husband, asked the Nebraska courts to require him to pay for indoor plumbing and to provide a reasonable allowance to her. The court agreed that, given the husband's "wealth and circumstances" (he owned a farm valued at $90,000 and additional assets of $117,000) the husband's attitude "leaves little to be said in his behalf." But, said the court, "the living standards of a family are a matter of concern to the household and not for the courts to determine" (*McGuire v. McGuire*, 157 Neb. 226, 59 N.W.2d 336 [1953]).

The extent of the courts' reluctance to intervene in family matters or, as it was sometimes put, to "disrupt family harmony," was shown in the rule that spouses could not sue one another for personal torts or injuries. If, for example, a husband assaulted or battered his wife, she was enjoined from taking legal action against him in civil court (Keeton, Dobbs, Keeton, and Owen 1984, 901-902).[11]

The practice of nonintervention was carried a step further at the turn of the century when the courts invented the doctrine of "parental immunity." Owing to reasons of "sound public policy, designed to subserve the repose of families and the best interests of society" (*Hewellette v. George*, 68 Miss. 703, 9 So. 885 [1891]), an unemancipated minor was barred by the Mississippi Supreme Court from suing her parents for personal injuries. The capstone of parental immunity came in *Roller v. Roller* (37 Wash. 242, 70 P. 788 [1905]) when the Supreme Court of Washington State enjoined a daughter from suing for personal injuries received as a result of being raped by her father. The court ruled that society has an important interest in preserving domestic harmony, an interest not served by allowing children to sue their parents. The Washington court rejected the daughter's assertion that there was little harmony to protect when a father raped his own daughter.

MODERN FAMILY LAW

In the twentieth century, the state has enhanced the amount of protection afforded the family unit to be free from interference from both state and community control with respect to marital intimacy, procreation and childrearing and education. Such protection is typically justified on the principle of "family privacy." In *Prince v. Commonwealth of Massachusetts* (321 U.S. 158 [1944]) the Supreme Court of the United States put it this way: "It is cardinal with us that the custody, care and nurture of the child reside first in the parents, whose primary function and freedom include preparation for obligations the state can neither supply nor hinder . . . And it is in recognition of this that these decisions have respected the private realm of family life which the state cannot enter." Some twenty years later, in a case involving contraception, the Supreme Court reiterated the point: "we deal with a right of privacy older than the Bill of Rights" (*Griswold v. Connecticut*, 381 U.S. 479).

At the same time, beginning in the 1960s, strict regulation of entrance to and exit from marriage began to unravel. In the 1967 case of *Loving v. Virginia*, the United States Supreme Court held antimiscegenation laws to be unconstitutional. According to the Court, the states had no right to "prevent marriages between persons solely on the basis of racial classification." Mere decades after it had held that marriage was not a right, the United States Supreme Court reversed itself: "Marriage," said the Court, "is one of the 'basic civil rights of man,' fundamental to our very existence and survival" (388 U.S. 1; quoting *Skinner v. Oklahoma*, 316 U.S. 535 [1942]). Since *Loving*, many other marriage restrictions have been repealed or eased. Age requirements in many states have been lowered; the mental ability needed to contract marriage has been ruled to be less than that required for other sorts of contracts; and the necessary mental competency is presumed to be present unless there is "clear and definite" proof to the contrary. Moreover, "there is a trend in modern times to abolish affinity restrictions" (Wardle et al., § 2:09); only one state (Missouri) still prohibits epileptics to marry (Wardle et al., § 2:47); and in many states, even prison inmates are deemed to have a right to marry (*In re Carrafa*, 77 Cal. App.3d 788 [1978]). The decision to marry, according to the Supreme Court of the United States, is among "the personal decisions protected by the right to privacy" (*Zablocki v. Redhail*, 434 U.S. 374 [1978]).

Recent changes in divorce laws have been, if anything, even more dramatic than changes in marriage laws. Implicitly accepting the principle that there is a right to divorce, the Supreme Court ruled in 1971 that welfare recipients could not be denied access to divorce courts because they could not afford to pay court costs and fees (*Boddie v. Connecticut*, 401 U.S. 371). By the mid-1980s, every state had either replaced fault based divorce laws with no-fault laws, or added no-fault grounds to existing laws (Freed and Walker 1986, 444). No longer, then, must there be a "guilty" and an "innocent" party in a divorce. Instead, one spouse simply needs to assert that the marriage has ended, or that the couple has been living apart for a certain amount of time.

Yet, notwithstanding the courts' designation of the family as a "private realm into which the state cannot enter," as regulations governing entrance to and exit from marriage and family life have decreased, there has been a concomitant *increase* in laws potentially affecting relations in ongoing families. In the late twentieth century there has been, in fact, a virtual explosion of such laws.

Today, for example, we not only speak of custody law with respect to parents, but step-parents; another burgeoning area of law concerns the rights of grandparents. Spousal immunity has been abrogated (or abolished) in most states (*Heino v. Harper*, 306 Or. 347, 759 P.2d 253 [1988]) and as a result, there has been an increase in case law on "domestic torts"–husbands and wives suing one another for noncriminal wrongs (including "intentional infliction of emotional distress," assault, battery, intentional and negligent transmission of sexually transmitted disease, etc.). Moreover, in many states the law recognizes the crime of "marital rape." Similarly, children now have rights that can be asserted against their parents. For example, minors have the right to obtain information about and to use birth control without a parent's consent (*Carey v. Population Services International*, 431 U.S. 678 [1977]); to receive psychiatric care (*In re Alyne E.*, 113 Misc. 2d 307, 448 N.Y.S.2d 984 [1982]); and perhaps even to separate from their parents should the parents and children prove "incompatible" (*In re Snyder*, 85 Wash. 2d 182, 532 P.2d 278 [1975]). Increasingly, states are abrogating laws affording parents immunity from suits (Beal 1984) and in many sorts of cases children may seek redress in the civil courts from intentional and negligent harms done by parents. At base, says the U.S. Supreme Court, children "are 'persons' under the Constitution" and have rights that should be protected by the state (*Tinker v. Des Moines Independent School District*, 393 U.S. 503 [1969]).

We have arrived in the late twentieth century to face a confusing situation. On the one hand, the law tends to say to outsiders, "hands off the family–families have a right to do as they see fit." On the other hand, the law now allows itself to be invoked such that wives may sue husbands and children may sue parents. Thus, while law has seemingly strengthened the family's ability to proceed as it wishes with respect to private life, more and more sorts of family squabbles are showing up in the courts.

These seemingly contradictory trends reflect the increasing willingness of courts and legislators to protect the rights of individuals to make their own choices about marriage and related matters. The idea of family autonomy and privacy, and hence, the policy of nonintervention, was traditionally based on "paternal" authority; the authority of the family patriarch. But family autonomy that is based on paternal power is viable only when other members of the family are unable to invoke the power of the state against the father. Things are much different today: while children still have many "legal disabilities," they can no longer be regarded as chattel and women have achieved at least technical legal equality.

Some mourn the loss of near total family autonomy; the family, they say, has lost its integrity (Peirce 1988). And, there is no doubt that the notion of nonintervention served an important function. It has been, "a convenient way for dealing with a problem . . . [that is] especially acute in the United States–that of devising family law which is suited to the needs and desires of persons with different ethnic and religious backgrounds, different social status, and different standards of living" (Glendon 1989, 95). At the same time, however, in many instances the policy of nonintervention created private Hobbesian jungles in which the strong ruled and the weak could not call upon the law for help.

The major impact of law on family life these days is that it provides a set of resources upon which family members may draw when they do not believe their interests are being served by other members of the family group. Today when the courts tend to speak of "family privacy" it is clear that such privacy is based on family members' individual rights, and exists only as long as family members are not in serious conflict about how they wish to assert those rights.

FAMILY AND LAW IN THE TWENTY-FIRST CENTURY

Families continue to play important roles in American society, and there can be little doubt that family relations will continue to be regarded as legally different and worthy of special protection. The big question is, to whom is the law's protection to be extended in domestic matters as we embark upon the twenty-first century? Traditionally, the courts have extended this protection to a limited variety of relationships–the two-parent household surrounded by a picket fence comes to mind here. Yet, as individuals within society, freed from normative and legal controls to an unprecedented degree, continue to explore new ways of constituting family life, new and complex issues of law emerge. As the other essays in this volume illustrate, the principal challenge seems to be this: will the law allow itself to be invoked to protect those arrangements which favor traditional family *forms* or those which favor traditional family *functions*?

CASES

Boddie v. Connecticut, 401 U.S. 371 (1971)
Buck v. Bell, 274 U.S. 200 (1927)
Carey v. Population Services International, 431 U.S. 678 (1977)
Griswold v. Connecticut, 381 U.S. 479 (1965)
Ex parte Kinney, 3 Hughes 9 (1879)
Heino v. Harper, 306 Or. 347, 759 P.2d 253 (1988)
Hewellette v. George, 68 Miss. 703, 9 So. 885 (1891)
In re Alyne E., 113 Misc. 2d 307, 448 N.Y.S.2d 984 (1982)
In re Carrafa, 77 Cal. App.3d 788 (1978)
In re Snyder, 85 Wash. 2d 182, 532 P.2d 278 (1975)
Loving v. Virginia, 388 U.S. 1 (1967)
Maynard v. Hill, 125 U.S. 190 (1888)
McGuire v. McGuire, 157 Neb. 226, 59 N.W.2d 336 (1953)
Mercein v. People, ex rel. Barry, 25 Wend. 65 (N.Y. 1840)
Prince v. Commonwealth of Massachusetts, 321 U.S. 158 (1944)
Rodenbaugh v. Sanks, 2 Watts 9 (1933)
Roller v. Roller, 37 Wash. 242, 70 P. 788 (1905)
Skinner v. Oklahoma, 316 U.S. 535 (1942)
Sosna v. Iowa, 419 U.S. 393 (1975)
Tinker v. Des Moines Independent School District, 393 U.S. 503 (1969)
United States v. Yazell, 382 U.S. 341 (1966)
Zablocki v. Redhail, 434 U.S. 374 (1978)

NOTES

1. A second form of informal marriage, *sponsalia per verba de futuro*, was created when a man and woman pledged to marry and later consummated the union.
2. Lord Hardwicke's Act put an end to "irregular" or informal marriages, but the requirement that unions be solemnized in the Anglican Church also invalidated the marriages of Protestant dissenters and Roman Catholics.

3. Ingram further notes that, owing to the difficulty of proving sexual incapacity, some "English courts in the fifteenth century had adopted the bizarre and apparently uncanonical practice of subjecting allegedly impotent males to the attention of a group of women, whose task it was to try to excite their passion" (173).

4. The *OED* relates the origins of the term cuckold to the cuckoo's habit of laying its egg in the nest of another bird. The idea that cuckolds wore horns on their brows dates back to the ancient practice engrafting the spurs of a castrated cock on the root of the excised comb. Apparently, the spurs thus attached grew and became horns, sometimes several inches in length.

5. Writing in the late nineteenth century, Pollock and Maitland take issue with Blackstone's conception of the unity of husband and wife, calling it an "impracticable proposition." The real working principle, they argue, was that the husband was a guardian of the wife and her property (Pollock and Maitland, 1898, *II* 405-406). Indeed, in many respects the wife's legal status was akin to that of a minor—if she did contract with a "stranger," she could disavow that contract but the stranger, like anyone foolish enough to contract with a legal "infant," could be held to the bargain. Similarly, a wife had the right to pledge her husband's money for "necessaries" if he failed to provide them to her. Minor children had the right to do the same.

6. For the uninitiated, case citations are decoded this way: *United States v. Yazell*—involved the United States as plaintiff (or the one who brings suit) and Yazell as defendant; 382 U.S. 341 (1966)—the Supreme Court of the United States decided the case in 1966 and the opinion begins at page 341 of volume 382 of the *United States Reports* (the official record of the Supreme Court's decisions since 1875). The actual quote is from Justice Black's dissent from the majority opinion.

Citations to state appellate court decisions tend to look much more complex, but that is only because alternate sources for the decisions are generally included in the citation. Appellate court decisions are published in volumes called "case reporters." The largest publisher of these is West Publishing Company. Each published opinion will appear in one of seven regional reporters, depending upon which state's court decided the case: *North Eastern* (N.E.), *Atlantic* (A.), *Pacific* (P.), *South Eastern* (S.E.), *South Western* (S.W.), *North Western* (N.W.) and *Southern* (So.). More recent citations will refer to the second series of a reporter. This is indicated by the initials "2d."

McGuire v. McGuire, 157 Neb. 226, 59 N.W. 2d 336 (1953), may be decoded as follows: the first set of numbers (157 Neb. 226) refers to the version of the decision that is published in the official Nebraska reports. The second series of numbers (59 N.W. 2d 336) refers to the opinion's location in the *North Western Reporter*, second series. The decision may be found in volume 59 at page 336.

7. Law French was one of the last remnants of the influence of the Norman Conquest in England. Until about 1400, French was the language of choice among England's educated upperclass; Law French as a highly technical language of art retained its influence on the law well into modern times.

8. Miscegenation—from the Latin *Miscere*, to mix, and *genus*, race. Forrest Wood, in *Black Scare: The Racist Response to Emancipation and Reconstruction*,

traces the origins of the term to a pamphlet published anonymously in 1864. The authors of the pamphlet, purporting to support interracial marriage by extolling its benefits, Wood suggests, were actually Democrats trying to stir up white fears of racial mixing and "mongrelization" and thereby discredit Republican Party attempts to promote Emancipation (1968, 54).

9. Kanaka refers to those of Hawaiian or South Sea Islands ancestry.

10. The most notable of these exceptions was the passage of the Comstock Act in 1873–this forbade the delivery of birth control information through the mails.

11. In theory, the husband could be prosecuted in criminal court, but police and criminal courts, too, were reluctant to interfere in domestic matters (Pleck 1987, 187).

REFERENCES

Basch, N. (1982). *In the Eyes of the Law: Marriage and Property in Nineteenth-Century New York*. Ithaca, NY: Cornell University Press.

Beal, R. (1984). "Can I sue mommy?" An analysis of a woman's tort liability for prenatal injuries to her child born alive. *San Diego Law Review, 21*, 325-370.

Blackstone, W. (1769/1979). *Commentaries on the Laws of England*. Four volumes. Chicago: The University of Chicago Press.

Chapin, B. (1983). *Criminal Justice in Colonial America, 1606-1660*. Athens, GA: University of Georgia Press.

Clark, H. H., Jr. (1968). *Law of Domestic Relations*. St Paul, MN: West.

Cott, N. (1977). *The Bonds of Womanhood: "Women's Sphere" in New England, 1780-1835*. New Haven, CT: Yale University Press.

Cott, N. (1976). Eighteenth century family and social life revealed in Massachusetts divorce records. *Journal of Social History, 10*, 20-43.

D'Emilio, J. & Freeman, E. B. (1988). *Intimate Matters: A History of Sexuality in America*. New York: Harper and Row.

Freed, D. J. & Walker, T. B. (1986). Family Law in the Fifty States: An Overview. *Family Law Quarterly, 20*, 439-587.

Friedman, L. M. (1985). *A History of American Law, 2nd ed.* New York: Simon & Schuster.

Gilmore, G. (1977). *The Ages of American Law*. New Haven, CT: Yale University Press.

Glendon, M. A. (1989). *The Transformation of Family Law, State, Law and Family in the United States and Western Europe*. Chicago: The University of Chicago Press.

Grossberg, M. (1985). *Governing the Hearth: Law and Family in Nineteenth Century America*. Chapel Hill, NC: University of North Carolina.

Grossberg, M. (1983). Who gets the child? Custody, guardianship, and the rise of a judicial patriarchy in nineteenth-century America. *Feminist Studies, 9*, 235-260.

Haskins, G. (1960). *Law and Authority in Early Massachusetts: A Study in Tradition and Design*. New York: The Macmillan Company.

Ingram, M. (1987). *Church Courts, Sex and Marriage in England, 1570-1640*. New York: Cambridge University Press.

Katz, S. N. (1977). The politics of law in colonial America: Controversies over chancery courts and equity law in the eighteenth century. *Perspectives in American History, 5*, 257-284.

Keeton, W. P., Dobbs, D. B., Keeton, R. E. & Owen, D. G. (1984). *Prosser and Keeton on the Law of Torts, 5th Edition.* St. Paul, MN: West.

Kennedy, S. (1959). *The Jim Crow Guide to the USA.* London: Lawrence and Wishart.

Kerber, L. K. (1986). *Women of the Republic: Intellect and Ideology in Revolutionary America.* New York: W.W. Norton & Company.

Kurland, P. B. & Lerner, R. (1987). *The Founders' Constitution,* Five volumes. Chicago: The University of Chicago Press.

Linn, B. J. & Bowers, L. A. (1978). The historical fallacies behind legal prohibitions of marriages involving mentally retarded persons–the eternal child grows up. *Gonzaga Law Review, 13,* 625-690.

May, G. 1929. *Marriage Laws and Decisions in the United States.* New York: Russell Sage Foundation.

Menefee, S. P. (1981). *Wives for Sale: An Ethnographic Study of British Popular Divorce.* New York: St. Martin's Press.

Norton, M. B. (1984). The evolution of white women's experience in early America. *The American Historical Review, 89,* 593-619.

Oakes, James. (1990). *Slavery and Freedom.* New York: Vintage Books.

Peirce, D. S. (1988). *BRI v. Leonard:* The role of the courts in preserving family integrity. *New England Law Review, 23,*185-219.

Pleck, E. (1987). *Domestic Violence: The Making of American Social Policy Against Family Violence from Colonial Times to the Present.* NY: Oxford University Press.

Pollock, F. & Maitland, F. W. (1898). *The History of English Law Before the Time of Edward I.* Two volumes. Cambridge: Cambridge University Press.

Rembar, C. (1980). *The Law of the Land.* New York: Simon and Schuster.

Rhode, D. L. (1989). *Justice and Gender.* Cambridge: Harvard University Press.

Salmon, M. (1986). *Women and the Law of Property in Early America.* Chapel Hill, NC: The University of North Carolina Press.

Stone, L. (1977). *Sex and Marriage in England 1500-1800.* New York: Harper and Row.

The Laws Respecting Women. (1777/1974). London: J. Johnson Edition. Reprinted, Dobbs Ferry, NY: Oceana Publications.

Tiffany, W. C. (1921). *Handbook on the Law of Personal and Domestic Relations, 3rd Edition.* St Paul, MN: West.

Wardle, L. D., Blakesley, C. L. & Parker, J. Y. (1988). *Contemporary Family Law: Principles, Policy and Practice.* Four volumes. Deerfield, IL: Callaghan.

Wood, F. G. (1968). *Black Scare: The Racist Response to Emancipation and Reconstruction.* Berkeley, CA: The University of California Press.

Zainaldin, J. S. (1979). The emergence of a modern American family law: Child custody, adoption, and the courts, 1796-1851. *Northwestern University Law Review, 73,* 1038-1089.

Men and Family Law:
From Patriarchy to Partnership

Rebecca J. Erickson
Ginna M. Babcock

Family law represents the intersection of two of the most pervasive and fundamental institutions in our society. Not surprisingly then, the confusions and contradictions that characterize contemporary family life, including those that relate to men's and women's "proper" familial roles, tend to be reflected in family law. Moreover, because legislative statutes and judicial decisions reflect the particular culture from which they arise, a thorough understanding of men's legal rights and responsibilities within the family requires not only an appreciation of the family and legal systems in relation to one another, but also in relation to their broader socio-historical context. As such, the legal institution has become a prime testing ground for the ever-evolving cultural definitions of marriage, parenthood, and family.

This review of the role of law in the family life of men brings together a number of divergent state and federal laws, as well as court decisions. Such diversity in the sources of family law has left it open to a number of conflicting interpretations by legal professionals and others. Given this great latitude of interpretation, gender bias has become entrenched as one of family law's most prominent governing influences (Fineman, 1989; Smart & Sevenhuijsen, 1989; Grossberg, 1985; Sachs & Wilson, 1978).

Rebecca J. Erickson is Associate Professor, Department of Sociology at the University of Akron. Ginna M. Babcock is with the Department of Sociology at the University of Idaho.

[Haworth co-indexing entry note]: "Men and Family Law: From Patriarchy to Partnership." Erickson, Rebecca J., and Ginna M. Babcock. Co-published simultaneously in *Marriage & Family Review* (The Haworth Press, Inc.) Vol. 21, No. 3/4, 1995, pp. 31-54; and: *Families and Law* (ed: Lisa J. McIntyre, and Marvin B. Sussman) The Haworth Press, Inc., 1995, pp. 31-54. Multiple copies of this article/chapter may be purchased from The Haworth Document Delivery Center [1-800-3-HAWORTH; 9:00 a.m. - 5:00 p.m. (EST)].

Contributing to the perpetuation of gendered law is the adversarial nature of the courtroom. Despite reform efforts (as in no-fault divorce), the very nature of the legal system tends to place men and women on opposite sides. One outcome of this adversarial relationship has been a tendency to view men's legal rights and responsibilities as contrary to those of women. Hence, investigation into how the legal system's treatment of men's family roles has changed inevitably must recount how women's legal status has changed as well. Similarly, cases viewed as primarily affecting women, e.g., *Roe v. Wade* (410 U.S. 113 [1973]), have also had important effects on men's legal rights and duties (e.g., Does a woman's decision to bear a child against the will of the father reduce the father's legal responsibility to support that child?).

Making sense of the various trends and transitions in family law as it relates to men is made even more difficult because of the broad-based cultural assumption that family life is private and personal, not public and political. As Hanisch (1971) recognized, however, today the personal has become political–and in the past three decades this is perhaps nowhere more evident than among the range of gender-based issues that emerge within the domain of family law.

Following a brief discussion of the recent Supreme Court decisions that have influenced men's familial rights and responsibilities, and a short history of the changes in men's legal standing in the family, we review more recent trends in family law regarding paternity, artificial insemination and other reproductive technologies, illegitimacy and the rights of unwed fathers, abortion and paternal rights, spouse abuse and marital rape, marital and parenting rights of gay men, child custody, and divorce and spousal support.

Two caveats are in order here. First, although federal courts have heard a number of significant family-related cases over the past three decades, most family law continues to fall under the purview of the states. In light of the variety of state law (Salt, 1986), we have chosen to outline basic legal trends, over time and across states, rather than attempt to provide a complete catalog of rulings and statutes. Second, because family law has traditionally focused on the concerns and values of white, middle class, Americans (Glendon, 1989; Sachs & Wilson, 1978), the ensuing discussion may not reflect the specific legal experiences of either the lower class or racial-ethnic minorities (see Krause, 1986; also see Walters & Chapman, 1991 for a review of the interconnections between race, ethnicity, and family law).

INDIVIDUAL RIGHTS, GENDER NEUTRALITY,
AND THE SUPREME COURT

While the states continue to decide a majority of cases related to family life, the growing number of decisions handed down by the Supreme Court over the past three decades have had an enormous impact on men's familial rights and obligations. In the 1960s and 70s, the high court specifically began to hear an increasing number of gender and family related cases pertaining to issues of equality and individual liberty (e.g., *Hoyt v. Florida*, 368 U.S. 57 [1961]; *Griswold v. Connecticut*, 381 U.S. 479 [1965]; *Levy v. Louisiana*, 391 U.S. 68 [1968]; *Reed v. Reed*, 404 U.S. 71 [1971]; *Stanley v. Illinois*, 405 U.S. 645 [1972]; *Roe v. Wade*, 410 U.S. 113 [1973]).

The points raised in these cases have been treated as "federal" issues (and hence, subject to Supreme Court review) because one party claims that she or he has been denied rights accorded to individuals by the Fourteenth Amendment's Due Process and/or Equal Protection clauses. Although state law must fit within federal constitutional parameters, contradictions between the two (as well as with people's lived experience) continue to flourish, and consistency in family law remains the exception rather than the rule. For example, Glendon (1989) notes the contradiction between the attempt to formulate gender-neutral laws and the unequal status of men and women in our society. Moreover, LaRossa (1988) observes a clear contradiction between contemporary beliefs about fatherhood and the actual conduct of fathers. Rotundo (1987) echoes this theme by pointing out that while more men enjoy joint and single custody of their children, there are also more men who fail to meet their child support payments. Finally, a fundamental contradiction underlies the continued questioning of whether the family should be understood in terms of the functions it serves for society or in terms of the benefits it provides for its individual members.

One explanation for this wealth of contradiction between family reality and family law is noted by Fineman (1989). She observes that, at base, we now suffer from contradictory visions of marriage, seeing it both as a partnership between equals and as a means of taking care of the historically-based structural dependency of women and children. The following review of men's legal standing within the family reflects many of these underlying confusions and contradictions–just some of the cultural artifacts accompanying our transition from a family system based in patriarchy, toward one increasingly (though perhaps inappropriately; see Smith, 1990) characterized by the concept of partnership.

TRANSFORMATION OF MEN'S RIGHTS
AND RESPONSIBILITIES

At the beginning of the nineteenth century, American law, being firmly rooted in English common law (Grossberg, 1985; Glendon, 1989), gave men complete control over the family, its assets, and its members. This unquestioned patriarchal authority was intimately tied to the agriculturally-based economy in which the family was the primary economic unit, and property the principle form of wealth (Rotundo, 1987; Foster & Freed, 1978). Although men held absolute rights as far as their wives and children were concerned, they also bore the responsibility of their lifelong support. This reciprocal relationship fostered men's interest in the regulation of female sexuality and in the concept of legitimacy. As a result, the male-dominated legal system sought to ensure that women's infidelity was punished and that birth within a stable (i.e., marital) institution served as the sole basis of children's inheritance claims against their biological fathers (Grossberg, 1985; Krause, 1986).

As the industrial era began to take hold in the mid-1800s, men's power and authority within the family began to change (Rotundo, 1987; Dizard & Gadlin, 1990). First, as the economy became centered around industry rather than agriculture, property ownership no longer held such a prominent place in regard to familial wealth. Second, the resulting industrial division of labor removed men from the home for much of the day, thereby diminishing their ability to control the daily functioning of the household. Influenced by these sociohistorical transformations, men's control of their children's lives began to diminish.

Accompanying this economic change was the first women's movement and the dissemination of social scientific research that proclaimed women's "natural" or "instinctual" proficiency in the care and nurturance of children (Foster & Freed, 1978). Such movements reflected the growing cultural ideology that the family's primary function was one of nurturance rather than economic productivity (Rotundo, 1987). Family law began to reflect this set of beliefs and further erode men's direct control over their children by taking on a maternal custody presumption best exemplified in the "tender years" doctrine. While the male was still regarded as *the* provider for the family, his absolute control over the family realm eroded as the primacy of maternal custody became an almost unquestioned assumption.

In the 1930s, this erosion continued as men's economic role was jeopardized as well (Rotundo, 1987). Soon, however, postwar growth restored men's tremendous economic advantage, and reinstated them as "heads" of the household. Yet, beginning in the 1960s, a changing global economy and the second organized women's movement drew more and more women into the paid labor force; leading once again to an increase in men's confusion about their familial rights and responsibilities (Glendon, 1987).

Due to both general acceptance of the idea that women were "naturally superior" parents, and to a legal system that required men seeking custody to prove that the mother was clearly unfit, it took until the cultural upheaval of the last few decades for fathers to mount a serious challenge against the traditional doctrine that women are best suited to care for children of "tender years." The movement of women into the labor force has helped in this regard in that it has served to lessen some of the culturally perceived differences between men's and women's abilities. Technological advancement in reproductive control and the trend toward egalitarian values (if not always behavior) that emerged out of the women's movement has further influenced men's orientation toward their familial roles. Once again, social science has played a significant role in this newest ideological transformation, as recent studies consistently demonstrate that while men may parent in a way different from women, it is no less appropriate or successful (Lamb, 1986; Orthner & Lewis, 1979). Clearly, there is no inherent reason for women to be the preferred primary caretakers of children.

In sum, men's legal domination of family life has not remained static. The industrial revolution eroded men's control over children through the separation of home and work and the accompanying cult of motherhood. From that point until the last few decades, men have primarily been equated with the family's economic function. Recently, however, as more men have begun to actively participate in their children's lives (Lamb, 1986; Russell, 1986), and as the blurring of gender lines continues, men's legal rights and responsibilities (especially in regard to child custody and support) are changing accordingly.

It should be noted, however, that not all men are of one mind on these issues. As Smart and Sevenhuijsen (1989) point out, fathers' advocacy groups differ quite sharply in their perspectives on men's roles within the family. Those taking the "New Fatherhood" orientation encourage men's participation in those duties associated with the traditional view of motherhood: caretaking, nurturance, and day-to-day responsibility (Lamb, 1986). In contrast, "Fathers' Rights" groups concentrate on obtaining greater legal control for men outside the institution of marriage (e.g., on divorce, support, visitation, and custody issues). Finally, those who consider themselves members of the "New Right" work to restore both fathers and mothers to their traditional places within the family system.

Establishing Paternity

Historically, any child born to a married couple was assumed to be the husband's biological child, and conversely, any child born out of wedlock was considered to have no father in the eyes of the law (Krause, 1971). More recently, however, increases in the rates of desertion, divorce, and out-of-wedlock births, combined with the advent of the welfare system, have led mothers (and the state) to become increasingly interested in requiring fathers to share the responsibility for raising their children. Because the concept of "responsibility" has traditionally referred to economic responsibility, paternity suits have been made civil cases, rather than criminal, and often involve little more than an order for the father to pay child support.

Technological advancement has aided the state in its investigation of paternity through the increasingly sophisticated use of human leukocyte antigen (H.L.A.) blood testing and DNA fingerprinting. These tests are now able to accurately exclude potential fathers 99 percent of the time (see 253 *J.A.M.A.*, 3298 [1985] for guidelines). While courts in some states were slow to adopt this new technology, by 1988 only South Dakota had yet to enact a statute allowing for the admissability of some sort of genetic testing (*King v. Tanner,* 15 Fam. L. Rep. 1236 N.Y. S.Ct. [1989]); and of the others, all but Connecticut used tests to demonstrate the inclusion of the putative father rather than merely his possible exclusion (Kaye & Kanwischer, 1988).

Under the Uniform Putative and Unknown Fathers Act (1988) any man who claims to be, or is named as, the biological father can now bring a legal action to determine the verity of the claim. Moreover, proof of paternity currently needs only a "preponderance of evidence" (*Rivera v. Minnich*, 483 U.S. 574 [1987]) rather than the "clear and convincing" evidence required when paternity suits were considered criminal cases (Krause, 1986). Further, *Little v. Streater* (452 U.S. 1 [1981]) made the use of such testing available to fathers who wish to establish (or deny) their paternity but are not able to pay for the requisite tests. While these changes indicate an improvement in men's legal rights in comparison to the days when only mothers and the state could initiate paternity actions, the Uniform Parentage Act (1973, sec. 14(a)) still allows the putative father to present "evidence regarding another man's sexual relationship with the mother only if blood tests do not exclude the other man" (Krause, 1986: 157). Finally, except in cases of assisted conception, judges continue to presume that the husband of the biological mother is the father of the child.

Artificial Insemination and Assisted Conception

A 1987 survey by the Office of Technology Assessment of the U.S. Congress found that approximately 172,000 women underwent artificial insemination and more than 30,000 babies had been conceived using anonymous donors (Wadlington, 1990). In light of this new and evolving technology, practitioners of family law have been called upon to rethink a number of legal issues regarding paternity and legitimacy. Specifically: (1) who is to be seen as the legal father: the sperm donor or the mother's husband; and (2) what are the child's rights in relation to each of the these men? Historically, the courts have sent mixed messages. Some decisions have labelled children born as a result of artificial insemination as bastards and their mothers as adulteresses (*Doornbos v. Doornbos*, 23 U.S.L.W. 2308, Super. Ct. Cook County, Ill., Dec. 13 [1954]; *Gursky v. Gursky*, 39 Misc. 2d 1083, 242 N.Y.S.2d 406, Sup. Ct. [1963]); others have held that such children are legitimately the husbands' (*Strnad v. Strnad*, 190 Misc. 786, 78 N.Y.S.2d 390, Sup. Ct. [1948]; *People v. Sorenson*, 68 Cal. 2d 285, 66 Cal. Rptr. 7, 437 P.2d 495 [1968]).

In the early cases, because the children were conceived in adultery, and thus illegitimate, the father had no legal rights over them, nor did the children have any legal claims on the father. In 1964, however, Georgia enacted a statute declaring that a child born to a woman and her husband through heterologous artificial insemination is the legitimate child of the married couple if both partners have consented to the procedure in writing and the insemination is performed by a licensed physician (Ga. Code Ann. tit. 74 sec. 101.1 [1968]). Other states soon followed suit and this reasoning was incorporated into the Uniform Parentage Act (sec. 5, [1973]). By 1985, half the states had instituted statutes absolving the sperm donor of legal responsibility for the child. However, where statutes do not provide for status of the donor, there remains a technical possibility that he could be legally responsible for support (Krause, 1986). While most are comfortable with the wording of the Georgia statute, Oakley (1974) argues that if the father/husband receives the child into his home and holds him or her out to the world as being his own, the child should legitimately be considered the father's/husband's, regardless of his prior written consent.

There remain two further issues that interrelate the legal interests of men and the process of artificial insemination. First, if the insemination is done without the husband's consent, he nonetheless is presumed responsible for supporting a child born to his wife. Because of this accountability, Oakley (1974) suggests that the physician should be civilly liable to the nonconsenting spouse (see Comment, *Artificial Insemination and the Law*, Ill. L.F. 203, 229 [1968]). Second, if the mother does not use a licensed physician for the insemination and personally knows the donor, it is possible for the donor to be declared the legal father in a paternity action (*Jhordan C. v. Mary K.*, 179 Cal.App.3d 386, 224 CalRptr 530 [1986]; Colorado supported *In re R.C.*, 15 F.L.R. 1404 [1989]).

One sort of case regarding assisted conception that we are likely to see more of as technology advances, is the recent battle between a separating husband and wife over the custody of eight frozen embryos produced through in vitro fertilization (*Davis v. Davis*, 15 Fam.L.R. 2097, 2103, 2104 [1989]). Finding that "human life begins at conception" and that the embryos were "human" not mere "property," the Tennessee Appellate court invoked the common law doctrine of *parens patriae* and gave the wife custody of the embryos for the purpose of implantation. The court added that matters related to support, visitation, and final custody would be considered later, if/when the embryos resulted in a live birth. Mr. Davis appealed and the decision was reversed, finding that "there is no compelling state interest to justify ordering implantation against the will of either party." The appellate court awarded joint control of the embryos to both parties. In June of 1992, Ms. Davis decided not to have the embryos implanted but wished to donate them to another couple. She also objected to the appellate court's analysis and sought review from the Tennessee state supreme court. In a landmark decision, the court found that there is no compelling state interest in the embryos and that in the absence of a prior written agreement between the parents, the interests of the father are greater and should prevail. This represents the nation's first state supreme court decision regarding the disposition of frozen embryos upon the divorce of the parents.

Legitimacy and the Rights of Unwed Fathers

Traditionally, children born out of wedlock were labelled bastards having no father in the eyes of the law; technically, they were *filius nullius*. Similarly, in common law, fathers of illegitimate children did not have to recognize such children's existence nor support them. It is true, however, that the English poor laws, early on, protected the public from the burden of support by allowing a father to be charged for the support of a bastard child (Krause, 1986). As mentioned above, however, when out-of-wedlock births began to increase, and the state was faced with having to support the growing number of children born to unwed mothers, its interest in locating the biological father, and making him financially responsible for his children, grew as well.

This change in the state's conception of its interests resulted in a stark legal contradiction: while fathers became financially responsible for their children born both in and out of wedlock, unwed fathers remained unable to claim any legal rights of visitation or custody. In response to the state's expanding search for unwed fathers and its effort to make them contribute to child support, men began to demand that their custody rights be equalized (Rubin, 1986).

Both the social climate of the 1960s and court decisions at the federal level were again pivotal in transforming the legal precedents regarding the rights of unwed fathers (Leashore, 1979). Citing the Equal Protection Clause of the Fourteenth Amendment, the Supreme Court has, in a number of related cases, granted all children, regardless of the circumstances of their birth, the right to legal equality (*Levy v. Louisiana*, 391 U.S. 68 [1968]; *Gomez v. Perez*, 409 U.S. 535 [1973]). Invoking the Due Process Clause as well as the Equal Protection Clause of the Fourteenth Amendment, the court has also ruled that an unwed father could not be deprived of his children, upon the death of their mother, without a hearing on his parental fitness or proof of his neglect (*Stanley v. Illinois*, 405 U.S. 645 [1972]).

Stanley's widest influence has been on an unwed father's right to be notified when his parental rights are to be terminated, as in the case of a pending adoption (Barron, 1975). The *Stanley* case signified an end to constitutional indifference toward unwed fathers, and gave them the same legal rights over their children as unwed mothers and married couples. By overturning the "irrebuttable presumption" that all unwed fathers are unfit parents, *Stanley* shifted the emphasis in legitimacy cases from equal rights for all children to equal rights for unwed parents (Rubin, 1986). Rubin goes on to explain that declaring all unwed fathers to be incapable is unconstitutional because it denies individual men the opportunity to rebut the charges, thus violating their constitutional rights to due process. At the same time, the case also involves issues of equal protection. Specifically, by denying unwed fathers the same procedural rights as any other marital or gender categories, the state denies them equal protection under the law. At base, said the Supreme Court, the state was discriminating against unwed fathers solely on the basis of their gender classification.

While *Stanley v. Illinois* clearly broadened the rights of unwed fathers in regard to adoption, these rights are not as fundamental as they are for unwed mothers (Salt, 1986). Instead, an unwed father's rights to his children are conditioned on his behavior toward both his children and their mother during pregnancy. For example, the Uniform Putative and Unknown Fathers Act (sec. 5, [1988]) lists fourteen factors that the court is to consider in determining the parental rights of the father. Of these fourteen, twelve concern either the father's relationship history with or toward the child (e.g., financial, emotional, or physical), or his behavior toward the mother before, during and after the child's birth. Such concerns have been of critical importance in cases where the father's behavior toward the child was a primary factor in determining custody. For example, in *Quilloin v. Walcott* (434 U.S. 246 [1978]) it became clear that the Equal Protection Clause did not require the court to treat all unmarried fathers similarly (Rubin, 1986). In *Quilloin,* the court allowed a woman's second husband to adopt her children over the objections of the biological father. Unlike the case in *Stanley,* the father had developed no personal relationship with the child nor showed much interest in the child until notified about the pending adoption.

In *Lehr v. Robertson* (103 S. Ct. 2985 [1983]) the court imposed similarly stringent qualifications on the father's right to be notified of an impending adoption. Although Lehr, unaware of the adoption proceedings, filed a petition of paternity and an order of support within the month, the court ruled that he had failed to take on "tangible and affirmative responsibilities" toward his children (*Lehr,* 103 S. Ct. at 2993). Never before had a court relied on the substantial-relationship-with-the-child test as a prerequisite for the basic procedural rights of notice sought by Lehr. One disquieting result of this decision is that by denying him the right of notice, the decision enabled the judge to determine the best interests of the child without benefit of any information Lehr might have been able to provide concerning either the family situation or his daughter's needs (Raab, 1984).

However, in *Caban v. Mohammed* (441 U.S. 380 [1979]) the Court ruled in favor of the biological father. Here again, however, the behavior of the father was decisive. Caban, largely due to the long-term caring relationship he had established with his children, was able to block his children's pending adoption claiming gender discrimination.

In sum, these cases indicate that while the father's biological relationship is important, it alone is not sufficient for the court to decide in his favor; the existence of a social and economic parent-child relationship outweighs biological ties (Rubin, 1986). It seems that in terms of paternal rights, men's behavior toward or *within* the family system is now legally scrutinized and evaluated in ways that, historically, women's behavior *outside* the family has been. Clearly, there are still important and recognized distinctions regarding paternal rights, if not responsibilities, between married and unmarried men.

Abortion and Father Rights

The majority in *Roe v. Wade* (410 U.S. 113 [1973]) argued that a woman's decision whether to terminate her pregnancy (during the first trimester) is protected by her right to personal privacy–as contained under the Fourteenth Amendment's concept of personal liberty or the Ninth Amendment's reservation of rights to the people. Moreover, the court held that this decision is solely a matter between the pregnant woman and her physician.

To be sure, *Roe* has had an extremely consequential legacy for women. Not to be overlooked, however, is the fact that the court's decision to leave the matter wholly in the woman's hands has at least two consequences for men. First is the question raised by *Planned Parenthood of Central Missouri v. Danforth* (428 U.S. 52 [1976]) concerning the right of spousal consent to an abortion. Ruling again on the basis of individual rights, the court overturned the provisions of the 1974 Missouri statute requiring the husband's consent before an abortion could be performed. In dissent, a minority of the court argued that abortion was a "family" issue and that the father has an important stake in the life of the child, a right that the state should protect. The majority, while recognizing that "family" interests were involved, argued that because of the physical involvement of the mother, her interests deserve a greater degree of protection. They further noted that legislating such "involvement" by other family members was unlikely to strengthen family ties (Rubin, 1986).

Reflecting cultural ambivalence to the abortion issue, and despite the precedent set in *Danforth,* a recent Supreme Court decision has increased states' power to restrict abortions (*Webster v. Reproductive Health Services,* 492 U.S. 490 [1989]). As a result, this decision opened the door for renewed court challenges concerning, among other issues, spousal and parental consent. Take, for example, the newly enacted Pennsylvania statute. As one of the first states to take advantage of the modification in power implied by *Webster,* Pennsylvania wanted to require a minor to notify one of her parents and have her/him provide informed consent before obtaining an abortion, and to require women to notify their husbands of the planned abortion (*Planned Parenthood of Southeastern Pennsylvania v. Casey,* 744 U.S. 902 [1991]). In June of 1992, the Supreme Court upheld the Pennsylvania law *except* in regard to women having to notify their husbands. The court continues to protect the interests of pregnant women over those of putative fathers.

The second of men's legal concerns in the wake of *Roe v. Wade* has been whether a father should be relieved of his support responsibilities if the mother refuses his request to have an abortion. The logic underlying this argument is that such refusals break the assumed nexus between conception and birth. According to some, because the woman's voluntary decision to bear the child intervenes between intercourse and birth, the male in such a case should be considered no more of a parent to the resulting child "than is a sperm donor in a case of artificial insemination" (Levy & Duncan, 1976, p. 185). Because the biological father no longer voluntarily assumed the status of parent–that choice now being the mother's alone–she alone should be responsible for the child's support.

Although cases that deny fathers a legal voice in the abortion decision tend to corroborate this reasoning (e.g., *Jones v. Smith*, 278 So.2d 339, Fla.Ct.App. [1973]; *Doe v. Rampton,* 335 F.Supp. 189, D. Utah [1973]; *Doe v. Doe,* 314 N.E.2d 128, Mass. [1974]), they have not been successful in arguing against paternal support liability (*People in Interest of S.P.B.,* 651 P.2d 1213, Colo. [1982]; see Levy and Duncan, 1976 for an explanation of the reasoning's failure through the use of analogies to both contract and criminal law).

Abuse and Marital Rape

As with most other family laws, those regarding battering and marital rape were originally developed to protect the interests of men (Freeman, 1981). While reforming such laws is a process that appeals to such disparate groups as ardent conservatives and radical feminists, reform has been slow in coming (Gelles & Straus, 1988; Freeman, 1981). One reason for this lag is that, although there have been significant changes in men's social roles since the time these legal doctrines were enacted, they nonetheless continue to protect men's interests. It therefore comes as little surprise that it was due primarily to the Women's Movement of the late 1960s and 1970s that renewed interest in domestic violence and abuse arose. In addition, Gelles and Straus (1988) note that the recent move toward mandatory reporting, arrest, prosecution and incarceration of abusers reflects the broader societal emphasis on the strict and severe control of all forms of crime, not just family violence.

The legacy underlying spouse abuse and marital rape laws harken back to English common law and the patriarchal system that gave husbands and fathers complete and legitimate control over their family members' behavior. These laws provided the foundation for such cultural guidelines as the "rule of thumb." According to this "rule," the beating of one's wife was deemed acceptable and appropriate as long as the implement used was no larger than the husband's thumb (Dobash & Dobash, 1979). Husbands have also been immune from the prosecution of marital rape. The foundation of this legal tradition is the Hale doctrine (Hale, 1736) which states that "the husband cannot be guilty of rape committed by himself upon his lawful wife, for by their mutual matrimonial consent and contract, the wife hath given up herself in this kind unto her husband which she cannot retract" (quoted in Freeman, 1981, p. 10).

Such common law orientations have consistently been upheld by the courts over the years. In fact, only recently has it been legally possible for a man to rape his wife. Michigan took the lead in this regard in 1974 when it enacted its Criminal Sexual Conduct Law (Mich. Comp. Laws Ann. sec. 750.5201, Supp. [1977-1978]). Yet the wording of even this statute represents only a marginal improvement: "A person does not commit sexual assault under this act if the victim is his or her legal spouse, unless the couple are living apart and one of them has filed for separate maintenance or divorce" (quoted in Freeman, 1981). In 1975, South Dakota became the first state to completely remove spousal immunity from its rape statute. But it was not until 1978 and the case of *State v. Rideout* (Or. Cir. Ct.; see 5 Fam. L. Rep. 2164 [1978] for a discussion) that the issue of marital rape gained attention. Despite the recent increases in awareness, state laws have been slow to change and remain far from consistent (see Freeman 1977, 1981; Clark 1988). As recently as 1977, for example, a New Jersey court upheld the common law exempting husbands from prosecution for marital rape (*State v. Smith*, 372 A.2d 386 [1977])–though in handing down its ruling the court attacked the Hale doctrine on which the law was based.

Yet, a few years later, a New York court of appeals struck down both the marital and gender exemptions in the state's criminal rape statutes, thereby legally allowing for men's potential victimization as well as women's (*People v. Liberta*, 6 N.Y.2d 152m 485 N.Y.S.2d 207, 474 N.E.2d 567). In 1985, a Georgia decision also overturned *Hale* (*Warren v. State*, 255 GA 151, 336 S.E.2d 221) and enforced a conviction of marital rape. Laws in other states vary from the total abolishment of the marital exemption rule (New Jersey, Oregon), to the granting of spousal immunity only when the force used by the perpetrator is not considered deadly (Iowa), to other forms of limited immunity (see Freeman, 1981; Clark, 1988, p. 307). Although there are many more reforms to be made before family violence laws are applied equally to both sexes, there does seem to be a consistent trend away from the legal system's concern with protecting men from spurious accusations, and toward a greater emphasis on victim protection (Freeman, 1981). Clearly, men's coercive behavior no longer falls outside the purview of the law.

Marital and Parenting Rights of Gay Men

In today's America, there exists no single family prototype. Commensurate with a rise in the variety of extant family forms has been the expansion of the state's interest in family life. In regard to gay and lesbian families, however, many jurisdictions remain ambivalent. It seems that for some legislators and judges, there is more concern with preserving the traditional American family structure than with addressing the needs of all types of families (see McIntyre's discussion elsewhere in this volume).

Although it is impossible to collect accurate statistics on the incidence of gay men in America, data suggest that approximately ten percent of the adult male population of the United States is homosexual (Kinsey, Pomeroy & Martin, 1948). While homosexuality is not a recent phenomenon, in the wake of the sexual revolution of the 1960s, the gay lifestyle emerged as one of a number of alternative family structures now recognized in contemporary society.

While some gay couples have sought to marry, they have met with no success. A few jurisdictions state that marriage may only take place between a man and a woman (Md.Code, Family Law, art. 2-201 Supp. [1984]; also Uniform Marriage and Divorce Act 201, 9A Unif.L. Ann 106 Supp. [1979]). More often, the prohibition of gay marriage is not expressed in statute but is rather an application of custom (*Jones v. Hallahan*, 501 S.W. 2d 588 Ky. [1973]).

Gay men have challenged the constitutionality of the laws prohibiting same sex marriage with the argument that such prohibition is grounded in religion and reflects the Christian attitude that homosexuality is sinful (Bailey, 1975). This, it is argued, constitutes an infringement of First Amendment rights. Since forbidding these marriages embodies discrimination based on sex (*Baker v. Nelson,* 291 Minn. 310, 191 N.W.2d 185 [1971]), others contend that the prohibition of same-sex marriage is in violation of the Due Process Clause of the Fourteenth Amendment. To date, gay men enjoy no standing in federal law. In terms of the recognition of homosexuality, gay men have probably lost ground at the national level over the past few years.

Despite these setbacks, fathering is one of the areas where gay men have gained considerable legal support. There has been a decided increase in court cases holding that a man cannot be denied child custody simply because of his homosexuality (*Bezio v. Patenaude,* 381 Mass. 563, 410 NE 2d 1207 [1980]; *Matter of J. S. & C.,* 129 N.J.Super. 486, 324 A.2d 90 [1974]). As a result, more and more gay fathers are winning custody of their natural children. Many gay men are also experiencing fatherhood through adoption or foster parenting (Bozett, 1985), though this trend continues to provoke significant debate (Uhl, 1986-1987).

CHILD CUSTODY

Custody law has a long and convoluted history. In Roman law, and later in English common law, the father literally owned his children, so paternal custody went unquestioned (Foster & Freed, 1978a). Despite this legacy, the United States experienced a shift toward maternal custody preference in the mid-1800s through the combined effect of the first organized Women's Movement and a widespread acceptance of child development theories of the time (Folberg, 1991). The maternal preference came to be extolled in the "tender years doctrine" (*Commonwealth v. Addicks*, 5 Binn. 520, 521 Pa. [1813]) and was soon described as a "best-interest-of-the-child test." At the time, however, this "test" merely reinforced the maternal care presumption (Roth, 1977). From the latter part of the nineteenth century and into the twentieth, paternal custody cases was rarely awarded except in cases where the mother was shown to be unfit (Oster, 1965). While courts continued to favor mothers in custody cases until the latter half of the twentieth century (Roth, 1977), many questions about the validity of a maternal presumption emerged as early as the 1920s (Luepnitz, 1991).

It was not until the 1960s and 70s, however, that custody law underwent a second wave of reform. Similar to changes occurring during the nineteenth century, recent reforms were prompted by an organized Women's Movement and the dissemination of social research. Beyond this similarity in origin, recent transformations reflect women's pursuit of goals outside the family which have led to greater child care involvement by fathers and others (Folberg, 1991).

In addition to fathers' willingness to play a more comprehensive role in their children's lives, this change was supported by scientific investigations that emphasized the significant role fathers play in their children's development as well as the importance of both parents' active involvement in their children's lives (Roth, 1977).

Even though custody reform during the 1970s brought fathers back into the picture, physical custody continued to be awarded overwhelmingly to mothers (Cochran, 1991). One reason for the continued custody problems of fathers might be attributable to claims made in the study, *Beyond the Best Interests of the Child* (Goldstein, Freud, & Solnit, 1973). The authors emphasized the importance of preserving the "stability and continuity" of the child's life following divorce. The legal system adopted this position in awarding custody to the "primary caretaker" of the children, that is, the parent who had primary responsibility for child care before the divorce (Folberg, 1991). Notwithstanding the gender neutrality of the wording, the application of the primary caretaker rule to actual custody cases preserved the maternal preference (Cochran, 1991).

As child custody continued to be awarded to mothers, fathers' interest groups formed to challenge the array of gender biases they perceived in the legal system (Morgenbesser & Nehls, 1991). In turn, fathers began seeking custody in greater numbers, disputing the tender years presumption, and pursuing legislative changes to make the best interest of the child test more explicitly gender neutral (Quinn, 1976; Folberg, 1991).

In response to pressure from fathers' interest groups, many states amended their statutes to decide custody based on the best interests of the child regardless of the sex of the parent (*Ex parte Devine*, 398 So.2d 686 Ala. [1981]). In most jurisdictions the mother and father are therefore statutorily equal in their rights to custody (Foster & Freed, 1978b).

Although the move to a best-interest-of-the-child test explicitly included fathers in post-divorce parenting, it left the courts with incredible discretionary power in the adjudication of child custody. In the absence of clear and precise guidelines, the presence of two fit parents has made it increasingly difficult for judges to determine custody with any sense of consistency. As a result, custody was being determined on a case-by-case basis. Cochran (1991) notes that the adoption of the case-by-case best-interests rule strengthened the bargaining position of fathers, especially when compared to the maternal or primary caretaker preference.

In 1980, the California legislature[1] declared a public policy encouraging parents to continue sharing child care responsibilities after divorce (S.B. 1306, Cal. Leg. Re. Sess. [1980]). Motivation for such action came from social scientific data that suggested the maternal preference rule did not serve the children's best interests (Roth, 1977) and from the prevailing belief that the maternal preference rule discriminated against fathers (Cochran, 1991).

The use of the general term "joint custody" is also somewhat misleading in that custody awards entail both legal and physical custody. Under joint legal custody both parents have legal responsibility and authority to make decisions regarding the care and control of their child. Joint physical custody refers to either the sharing of residential care or the routinized switching of where the child lives (Folberg, 1991). In most cases, the courts prefer that a child have a primary residence and custodian, so physical custody awards still continue to favor the parent with whom the child has had the most day-to-day contact. Thus, despite changes in legal language and the imposition of a statutory presumption of joint custody, we find the perpetuation of maternal custody awards (see Cochran, 1991; *Griffin v. Griffin*, 699 P.2d 407 Colo. [1985]), even in those families where mothers are career-oriented (Heckman, Bryson & Bryson, 1977).

Why is it that regardless of efforts to make custody law more equitable between mothers and fathers, awards of physical custody are still to be made to mothers? Some research suggests that attorneys are reticent to encourage male clients to petition for physical custody due to a supposed maternal bias on the part of judges and thus, the high probability of failure (Babcock, 1989). Numerous studies on sex bias in the courtroom also indicate that physical custody of children is often awarded on grounds unrelated to the child's best interests. Yet, according to a 1986 study, when fathers contest custody in court, they win 62 to 70 percent of the time (Chesler, 1988).

Although physical custody may continue to go to the mother in the majority of cases, many fathers' rights groups perceive the move to joint legal custody as a victory for men (Mills, 1982). The idea of being "jointly" responsible for their children encourages an ongoing father-child relationship that minimizes the alienating status of "visitor" (Folberg, 1991). Some research suggests that in joint custody, or shared parenting situations fathers are more likely to continue to provide financial support (Luepnitz, 1991). It is through shared parenting that the non-custodial parent maintains a sense of involvement and control over important decisions in a child's life (Babcock, 1989; McIssaac, 1991; Wallerstein & Kelly, 1980). This is one reason why both men's and women's rights groups advocate the adoption of statutes favoring joint legal custody (Greif, 1978).

Over the past decade, language of law has become more sex-neutral, and judges are more cognizant of their limitations in making decisions regarding the best post-divorce situation for children (see *Coles v. Coles* 204 A.2d 330 D.C. [1964]). Notwithstanding these changes, the majority of custody awards continue to be maternal, and judges continue to vacillate in their applications of custody statutes. On the whole then, men remain disadvantaged in their pursuit of equality in custody law.

DIVORCE AND SPOUSAL SUPPORT

In contemporary America, we commonly refer to marriage as a partnership of equals. Unfortunately, this perception contradicts the more traditional view of marriage as the one institution best able to meet the dependency needs of women and children (Fineman, 1989). The inherent conflict between these two competing views of marriage lies at the forefront of legal (and social) debate over spouses' post-divorce economic relationship. As Llewellyn recognized in 1932, a culture's ideology of marriage lends shape to its divorce law.

In the nineteenth century, through its adoption of community property laws, California was one of the first states (along with Texas) to recognize women's independent legal identity. One consequence of this was that since women could now hold property titles, they could retain such properties upon divorce. Ownership and control, however, are two different issues. While the adoption of community property laws in the nineteenth and early twentieth centuries did provide some benefits to women, their lack of control over the day-to-day running of properties and businesses maintained the hierarchical structure of marriage well into the twentieth century (Smith, 1990).

While the incidence of divorce has been rising at a consistent rate since 1945, it increased dramatically between 1963 and 1975. This trend continued until 1981 when the annual number of divorces reached a record 1.12 million (Weitzman, 1985). Commensurate with a change in marriage patterns came a divorce reform movement. Efforts were made to bring the law in line with the reality of millions of Americans facing divorce. Few other areas of state law have changed more quickly or have had more far reaching consequences than laws regulating divorce and the disposition of property (Sugarman, 1990).

In 1970, California was a pioneer of legal reform as it ushered in the new era of no-fault divorce. Reformers heralded the new law as a step toward (1) stemming the bitterness and acrimony that often accompanied traditional fault-based divorce proceedings (Sugarman & Kay, 1990), and (2) equalizing the assets of husbands and wives as they ended their marital relationship (Weitzman, 1985). Although few states have adopted the California statute in toto (i.e., where unilateral divorce is available without delay), every state in the nation implemented some form of no-fault divorce law by 1985 (Jacobs, 1988; Sugarman, 1990).

Where traditional divorce law reinforced a gender stereotypical division of labor in which men continued to financially support the family through the payment of alimony and child support and women continued as primary caretakers of children, no-fault divorce law assumes that husbands and wives play both roles equally. Hence, while discussions of "equal partnership" routinely refer to economic equality, they also imply equal access to parental rights and responsibilities. Reflecting the dominant cultural values of the last two decades, the *partnership model* assumes that women are able to become economically self-sufficient at the time of divorce and that men are equally willing and able to personally care for their children. Unfortunately, the values defining partnership in the ideal have little to do with its legal application (Smith, 1990).

As we saw in the discussion of child custody, despite gains made by men in this area of family law, the maternal and tender years presumptions have by no means disappeared. Similarly, the contrast between the ideal and reality is substantial as related to women's assumed economic equality: where divorced men have experienced gains in terms of custody, women have experienced losses in terms of economics. As long as our society continues to value monetary contributions to the family more than it values nonmonetary ones, husbands and wives cannot be considered "equal partners" (Smith, 1990).

Despite recent trends toward equality, the economic disparities between women's and men's labor market experiences tend to perpetuate traditional family patterns. Moreover, as long as employer expectations fail to change and the demand for occupational mobility increases, these traditional patterns are likely to endure. Legislative reforms of the past twenty years have been explicit in their call for compensating wives' contributions to homemaking and child care–thus reinforcing the cultural ideal of marriage as an equal partnership–but only Colorado and California factor a homemaker's impaired *future* earning capacity into a determination of post-divorce support.

The comparison of marriage to a business partnership represents another limitation to the partnership model of marriage. Such an analogy leads to the presumption that divorcing partners have few if any continuing economic responsibilities to one another; no-fault seems to be equated with no-responsibility (Smith, 1990).

The marriage as business analogy breaks down especially in those families where dependent children are involved. To be sure, marriages are based on some sort of division of economic interests and labor. Yet they go beyond such elements to include the allocation of social rights and responsibilities that may not be considered in the formation and dissolution of business partnerships. While divorce laws have begun to confront the complexity of distributing marital assets, they also need to address the sharing of marital liabilities (Smith, 1990).

There are also few guidelines limiting judicial discretion in the area of distribution of property at the time of divorce (see *Penck v. Penck*, 32 Tex. Sup. Ct. 143 [1988]); *Vallone v. Vallone*, 644 S.W.2d 455 (Tex. [1982]). Although some states may mandate an equal division of property acquired by either spouse during the marriage (see Cal. Civ. Code sec. 4800 (West Supp. 1990); N.Y. Dom. Rel. Law sec. 236B:1:c (McKinney, 1986)), many states rely on the trial court judge to achieve "equity" on a case-by-case basis.

In sum, the partnership model "may be a realistic approach to marriage, but it is a totally unrealistic approach to divorce" (Smith, 1990, p. 733). Legislative reforms cannot be expected to change social reality (Weitzman, 1985). The legal assumption of marital partnership has not improved women's earning capacities nor led to an equal number of men and women being primary caretakers of their children. While laws may mirror transformations in social behavior, they rarely fashion them (Llewellyn, 1932).

CONCLUSIONS

Gender lies at the heart of family relations; for rights and duties of family members are inextricably linked to sex. Yet fault-based divorce laws and gender role expectations no longer match the reality of millions of men (or women) in families. Divorce reformers of the 1960s and 70s seemed to assume that, since law created the divorce problem, they only had to change the law in order to solve the problem. Experience has shown, however, that simply changing law will not ameliorate society's ills, perhaps especially as they pertain to family life. Solutions to gender inequality–particularly in terms of women's economic position relative to men's, and men's desires for custody and societal recognition of their parenting interests and skills–are not to be found in legal rhetoric, but in the culture where those laws are written.

Increased nationalization of family law in the past ten years has indeed created a more unified body of law. States are also being held accountable by the federal government for enacting and enforcing laws that are gender neutral. And yet, as Okin (1989) notes, there are clear biological differences between men and women that will necessarily mandate different treatment by the courts. To argue for a partnership view of marriage is, in her view, to deny that such substantive differences exist. The existence of such differences does not mean that we should not try to move toward a conceptualization of post-divorce responsibilities that assume and facilitate the continuation of shared parenting, as well as moving us further away from the question of "who owns the child." In addition, as long as the rest of society continues to value the characteristics and contributions of men and women unequally, a true partnership, either in or out of marriage, will never be reached.

While our laws are beginning to reflect changes in family life (albeit slowly), the shift from legal patriarchy to partnership is far from complete. And yet, such phenomena as the increasing recognition of alternative family forms, the now-widespread use of gender neutral language, and the consistent movement away from "claims" of custody and toward the "working out" of parenting arrangements, indicate that we are still moving forward. Clearly, McCant (1987) is correct: it is no longer a question of whether the culture will change, but rather, how long such change will take.

NOTE

1. California's policy was not the first. In 1957, North Carolina passed a statute clearly stating that joint custody was in the best interest of the child (see Folberg, 1991).

REFERENCES

Babcock, Ginna M. (1989). *Fathers on the Outside: Legal and Social Psychological Aspects of Post-Divorce Parenting.* Masters Thesis, Washington State University, Pullman, WA.

Bailey, Derrick Sherwin. (1975). *Homosexuality and the Western Christian Tradition.*

Barron, J. A. (1975). Notice to the unwed father and termination of parental rights: Implementing *Stanley v. Illinois. Family Law Quarterly,* 9(3), 527-546.

Bartlett, K. T. (1988). Re-expressing parenthood. *The Yale Law Journal,* 98, 293-340.

Belzer, S. & Mills, Hon. B. G. (1982). Joint custody as a parenting alternative. *Pepperdine Law Review,* 9, 853-876.

Bozett, F. W. (1988). Gay fatherhood. In *Fatherhood Today: Men's Changing Role in the Family,* edited by P. Bronstein & C.P. Cowan (pp. 214-235). New York: Wiley.

Brophy, J. (1982). Parental rights and children's welfare: Some problems of feminists' strategy in the 1920s. *International Journal of the Sociology of Law,* 10(2), 149-168.

Cherlin, Andrew (1981). *Marriage, Divorce, Remarriage.* Cambridge, MA: Harvard University Press.

Chesler, Phyllis (1988). *The Sacred Bond.* New York: Vintage Press.

Clark, H. H., Jr. (1988). *The Law of Domestic Relations in the United States,* (2nd edition). St. Paul, MN: West Publishing Co.

Clatterbaugh, K. (1990). *Contemporary Perspectives on Masculinity: Men, Women, and Politics in Modern Society.* Boulder, CO: Westview.

Cochran, R. F. (1991). Reconciling the primary caretaker preference, the joint custody preference, and the case-by-case rule. In *Joint Custody and Shared Parenting* (2nd edition), edited by J. Folberg (pp. 218-240). New York: Guilford Press.

Dizard, Ian E. & Gadlin, Howard (1990). *The Minimal Family.* Amherst, MA: University of Massachusetts Press.

Dobash, R. Emerson & Dobash, Russell (1979). *Violence Against Wives: A Case Against the Patriarchy.* New York: Free Press.

Fineman, Martha Albertson (1991). *The Illusion of Equality: The Rhetoric and Reality of Divorce Reform.* Chicago: University of Chicago.

Folberg, Jay (Ed.) (1991). Custody Overview. *Custody and Shared Parenting* (2nd edition) (pp. 3-10). NY: Guilford Press.

Foster, Henry H. & Freed, Doris Jonas (1978a). Life with father: 1978. *Family Law Quarterly,* 11(4), 321-364.

Foster, Henry H. & Freed, Doris Jonas (1978b). Divorce law in the 50 states: An overview as of August 1, 1978. *Family Law Reporter,* 4(41), 4033-4041.

Freed, Doris Jonas & Walker, Timothy B. (1990). Family law in the fifty states: An overview. *Family Law Quarterly,* 23(4), 495-608.

Freeman, Michael D. A. (1977). Le vice Anglais?–Wife-battering in English and American law. *Family Law Quarterly,* 11(3), 199-251.

Freeman, Michael D.A. (1981). If You Can't Rape Your Wife, Who Can You Rape? *Family Law Quarterly.*

Gelles, Richard J. & Straus, Murray A. (1988). *Intimate Violence.* New York: Simon & Schuster.

Glendon, Mary Ann (1981). *The New Family and the New Property.* Toronto: Butterworths.

Glendon, Mary Ann. (1989). *The Transformation of Family Law: State, Law, and Family in the United States and Western Europe.* Chicago: University of Chicago Press.

Glick, Paul C. (1984). Marriage, divorce, and living arrangements: Prospective changes. *Journal of Family Issues,* 5, 7-26.

Goldstein, J., Freud, Anna & Skolnit, A. J. (1973). *Beyond the Best Interests of the Child.* New York: Free Press.

Greif, J. B. (1979). Fathers, children, and joint custody. *American Journal of Orthopsychiatry,* 49(2), 311-319.

Grossberg, Michael (1985). *Governing the Hearth: Law and Family in Nineteenth Century America.* Chapel Hill, NC: University of North Carolina.

Hale, Sir Matthew. (1736). Historia Placitorum Coronae 636.

Hanisch, Carol. (1971). The personal is political. In *The Radical Therapist,* edited by J. Agel (pp. 152-157). New York: Ballantine.

Hanson, S. M. H. (1988). Divorced fathers with custody. In *Fatherhood Today: Men's Changing Role in the Family,* edited by P. Bronstein & C.P. Cowan (pp. 166-194). NY: Wiley.

Heckman, N. A., Bryson, R. & Bryson, J. B. (1977). Problems of professional couples: A content analysis. *Journal of Marriage and the Family,* 39, 323-330.

Jacob, Herbert (1988). Silent Revolution: *The Transformation of Divorce Law in the United States.* Chicago: University of Chicago Press.

Kay, H. H. (1990). Beyond no-fault: New directions in divorce reform. In *Divorce Reform at the Crossroads,* edited by S.D. Sugarman and H. H. Kay (pp. 6-36) New Haven, CT: Yale University Press.

Kaye, D. H. & Kanwischer, R. (1988). Admissability of genetic testing. *Family Law Quarterly,* 22(2), 109-116.

Kinsey, Alfred C., Pomeroy, W. B. & Martin, C. E. (1948). *Sexual Behavior in the Human Male.* Philadelphia: W. B. Saunders.

Krause, Harry D. (1986). *Family Law in a Nutshell,* (2nd edition). St. Paul, MN: West.

Krause, Harry D. (1971). *Illegitimacy: Law and Social Policy.* Indianapolis: Bobbs-Merrill.

Lamb, Michael E. (Ed.). (1986). The changing role of fathers. In *The Father's Role: Applied Perspectives,* (pp. 3-27). New York: Wiley.

Leashore, B. R. (1979). Human services and the unmarried father: The "Forgotten Half." *The Family Coordinator,* 28, 529-534.

Levy, Martin R. & Duncan, Elaine C. (1976). The impact of *Roe v. Wade* on paternal support statutes: A constitutional analysis. *Family Law Quarterly,* 10(3), 179-201.

Llewellyn, Karl (1932). Behind the law of divorce (part I). *Columbia Law Review,* 32, 1281-1286.

Luepnitz, D. A. (1991). A comparison of maternal, paternal, and joint custody: Understanding the varieties of post-divorce family life. In *Joint Custody and Shared Parenting* (2nd edition), edited by Jay Folberg (pp. 105-113). NY: Guilford Press.

McCant, J. W. (1987). The cultural contradiction of parents as nonparents. *Family Law Quarterly,* 21(1), 127-143.

McIsaac, H. 1991. California joint custody retrospective. In *Joint Custody and Shared Parenting* (2nd edition), edited by Jay Folberg (pp. 262-274). NY: Guilford Press.

McKnight, M. (1991). Issues and trends in the law of joint custody. In *Joint Custody and Shared Parenting* (2nd edition), edited by Jay Folberg (pp. 209-217). NY: Guilford Press.

Morgenbesser, M. & Nehls, N. (1981). *Joint Custody: An Alternative for Divorcing Families.* Chicago: Nelson-Hall.

Oakley, Mary Ann B. (1974). Test tube babies: Proposals for legal regulation of new methods of human conception and prenatal development. *Family Law Quarterly,* 8(4), 385-400.

Okin, Susan Moller (1989). *Justice, Gender, and the Family.* New York: Basic.

Orthner, Dennis & Lewis, K. (1979). Evidence of single-father competence. *Family Law Quarterly.*

Oster, A. (1965). Custody proceedings: A study of vague and indefinite standards. *Journal of Family Law,* 5, 21-38.

Quinn, S. (1976). Fathers cry for custody. *Juris Doctor* (May).

Raab, J. J. (1984). *Lehr v. Robertson:* Unwed fathers and adoption–how much process is due? *Harvard Women's Law Journal,* 7, 265-286.

Roth, A. (1977). The tender years presumption in child custody disputes. *Journal of Family Law,* 15, 423-462.

Rotundo, E. Anthony (1987). Patriarchs and participants: A historical perspective on fatherhood. In *Beyond Patriarchy: Essays by Men on Pleasure, Power, and Change,* edited by M. Kaufman (pp. 64-80). Toronto: Oxford University.

Rubin, Eva R. (1986). *The Supreme Court and the American Family.* New York: Greenwood.

Russell, Graeme (1986). Primary caretaking and role sharing fathers. In *The*

Father's Role: Applied Perspectives, edited by M. E. Lamb (pp. 29-57). New York: Wiley.

Sachs, Albie & Wilson, Joan Hoff (1978). *Sexism and the Law.* Oxford: Martin Robertson.

Salt, Robert E. (1986). The legal rights of fathers in the U.S. *Marriage & Family Review,* 9(3/4), 101-115.

Santrock, J. W. & Warshak, R. A. (1986). Development of father custody, relationships, and legal/clinical considerations in father-custody families. In *The Father's Role: Applied Perspectives,* edited by M. E. Lamb (pp. 135-163). NY: Wiley.

Smart, Carol & Sevenhuijsen, Selma (1989). *Child Custody and the Politics of Gender.* New York: Routledge.

Smith, B. A. (1990). The partnership theory of marriage: a borrowed solution fails. *Texas Law Review,* 68(4), 689-743.

Sugarman, S. D. (1990). Dividing financial interests on divorce. In *Divorce Reform at the Crossroads,* edited by S. E. Sugarman and H. H. Kay (pp. 130-165). New Haven, CT: Yale University Press.

Uhl, B. A. (1986-87). A new issue in foster parenting–gays. *Journal of Family Law,* 25, 577-597.

Wadlington, Walter (1990). *Cases and Other Materials on Domestic Relations,* (2nd edition). Westbury, NY: The Foundation Press.

Wallerstein, Judith S. & Blakeslee, S. (1989). *Second Chances: Men, Women, and Children a Decade After Divorce.* NY: Ticknor & Fields.

Walters, Lynda Henley & Chapman, Steven F. (1991). Changes in legal views of parenthood: Implications for fathers in minority cultures. In *Fatherhood and Families in Cultural Context,* edited by F. W. Bozett & S. M. H. Hanson (pp. 83-113). New York: Springer.

Weitzman, Lenore (1985). *The Divorce Revolution.* NY: Free Press.

Deconstructing Legal Rationality: The Case of Lesbian and Gay Family Relationships

Gilbert Zicklin

The most recent phase of the gay rights movement is now twenty-five years old. A continuous part of that struggle has been the effort on the part of those who identify as gay and lesbian to acquire the same privileges, rights and immunities in their partner and parenting relationships as their heterosexual counterparts are given by law and custom.[1] The chief examples of such privileges accorded to legally married couples include:

- the right to inherit from a spouse who dies without a will
- the right to consult with doctors and make crucial medical decisions in the event of a spouse's critical illness or mental incompetence
- immunity from having to testify against a spouse in a criminal proceeding
- the right of residency for a foreign spouse of a U.S. citizen
- the right to sue for emotional harm from wrongful damage sustained by one's spouse
- the right to visit one's spouse in government-run institutions, such as prisons and hospitals
- the right to Social Security survivor's benefits
- the right of an employee to include a legally married spouse on his or her health insurance coverage

Gilbert Zicklin is Professor of Sociology, Department of Sociology at Montclair State College.

[Haworth co-indexing entry note]: "Deconstructing Legal Rationality: The Case of Lesbian and Gay Family Relationships." Zicklin, Gilbert. Co-published simultaneously in *Marriage & Family Review* (The Haworth Press, Inc.) Vol. 21, No. 3/4, 1995, pp. 55-76; and: *Families and Law* (ed: Lisa J. McIntyre, and Marvin B. Sussman) The Haworth Press, Inc., 1995, pp. 55-76. Multiple copies of this article/chapter may be purchased from The Haworth Document Delivery Center [1-800-3-HAWORTH; 9:00 a.m. - 5:00 p.m. (EST)].

55

- the option to reduce the couple's tax liability by filing joint returns
- other organizational benefits such as married student housing, reduced tuition fees, and access to an organization's facilities.

As this list shows, legally married couples receive considerable material advantages. For example, savings on the cost of health insurance for a spouse who is included on his or her married partner's employment-based insurance coverage ranges in the area of several thousand dollars per year. Legally married couples may also avoid the expense of drawing up wills and affidavits of medical guardianship, both of which are necessary for same-sex couples in order to protect their right to inherit from one another and to have medical decision-making power in the event of incapacitation or mental incompetence. Couples who are legally married may also realize significant tax savings from joint filing of income taxes.

As important as the material advantages are the psychological benefits that accrue to those who may legally marry. In our culture marriage is pictured as one of the most valuable features of civilized life. The state defines, regulates, and promotes it; the religious order sanctifies it. Through the licensing process and the wedding, society bestows a sense of specialness on the heterosexual couple and their future life together. It encourages a couple to feel that by marrying they are undertaking something meaningful and elevated.

A legally married couple may not avail itself of all these forms of societal recognition and privilege. Nevertheless, the forms reflect the general esteem in which marriage is held in this society. Even where marriage may penalize a partner, as in the provision that one's debt obligates one's spouse, it does so as an extension of a moral principle, the mutual responsibility of spouses.

None of these material and psychological benefits are available to gay and lesbian couples. They are cut off from this central source of self-esteem, from the experience of the community's full respect and validation. As a result, gay and lesbian couples occupy a marginal status, their choice of a partner chronically devalued by the institutions that surround them.

Similarly, the safety and security that heterosexual parents enjoy does not exist for gay and lesbian parents in a variety of situations and ways. The legally married couple can think about having a child in the knowledge that society is fully supportive of their desire to be parents, but those couples whose sexuality is marked as deviant, by contrast, obtain little recognition of, or protection for, their desire to become or remain parents. For instance, in most jurisdictions, same-sex couples face stiff barriers if they want to adopt a child. Often, couples must hide their relationship in order to give one member of the couple a chance to adopt. This means that only one parent becomes legally related to the child, which, in turn, deprives both the child and its nonlegal parent of privileges that normally attend the parent-child bond.[2] The child is deprived of any medical or social security benefits the nonlegal parent might convey, and does not stand to automatically inherit in the event of the death of that parent. Moreover, in the event the couple breaks apart, the child's connection to the nonlegal parent can be sundered by the legal parent, and the relationship brusquely ended.

The nonlegal parent's tie to the child he or she may have loved with the same care and attention, and for the same length of time, as the legal parent, is equally insecure. The legal limbo of these "second parents" has its psychological costs. Their connection to the child is not only legally fragile; it carries with it the implication that they are not *real* parents and their relationship is not as important to the society, or, more hurtfully, to the child.[3]

Even when a parent has a biological connection to a child, entering into a same-sex relationship can jeopardize it. Divorced husbands or wives may charge a former spouse who has become involved in a same-sex relationship with endangering their child(ren)'s moral development. Ex-spouses have won such challenges before judges who consider a parent's homosexuality grounds for denying custody, or altering or ending legally agreed-upon custody and visitation agreements.[4]

The gay and lesbian movement has mounted a variety of legal challenges to the foregoing set of material and psychological privileges of the legally marriageable and married. These cases have been fought in a variety of venues. The result is a collection of uneven rulings on a host of partner- and parenting-related issues. On some issues, there are jurists ready to advance toward equality; but, overall, progress for gays and lesbians has been markedly slow. Legal defeats have set back their cause, while the victories have mainly been won in local jurisdictions, with limited legal influence.[5] Moreover, when courts recognize the rights of lesbians and gays at all, they tend to construe them narrowly. As a result, courts wind up, de facto, protecting the main privileges of marriage and marital reproduction.

One might imagine from the number of decisions that have rejected gay and lesbian claims for equal treatment and from the arguments that jurists offer in these cases, that there is some legal stumbling block in the structure of state regulation of family life which will not permit the extension of heterosexual marital and family privileges to the gay and lesbian community.[6] On the contrary, the main argument of this paper is that there is no legal stumbling block. A careful examination of relevant cases will reveal that the barrier to gay equality is, in fact, the view prevalent in our culture that the only good and proper way to form an intimate sexual relationship or have a child is in a heterosexual, reproductive arrangement, and that married-heterosexual-reproducing-couples represent the pinnacle of hier- archically-arranged, morally-approved family relationships. This family constellation exists as a sacred image that is celebrated and protected as a veritable totem of family life. That such devotion is taken for granted rather than articulated as an ideology makes gay and lesbian claims for alternative personal and family configurations seem tendentious, and ren- ders them relatively ineffective.

Unsurprisingly, judges are not immune to the powerful appeal of this totem. In parts of the society where the traditional family ideal has been least touched by new sex-family-reproduction practices, judges are more likely to respond with contempt and hostility toward gays.[7] In areas where a diversity of family forms is evident, judges are likely to be more tolerant. Some in the gay and lesbian community rest their hopes on the presence of these "tolerant" judges. But we shall argue that even tolerant judges tend to enforce the cultural code. Though they may try to interpret the law in a self-consciously unbiased manner, they are the conveyors of barely-per- ceived, societally-shared biases and sentiments about what it means to be gay or lesbian. Whether tolerant or not, judges who personally cannot accept the full equality between different- and same-sex couples will be unlikely to do so in their legal decisions.[8] We argue that an examination of cases involving gay and lesbian partner and parenting issues reveals that the decisions in these cases are as likely to reflect the moral biases and the sociopolitical beliefs of judges as the conclusions called forth by chains of legal reasoning.[9]

The most direct question posed to judges by the rise of gay and lesbian legal activism is whether gay and lesbian couples can contract a "mar- riage." There are several cases from the early 1970s in which same-sex marriage is the contested issue (Rubenstein, 1993: 418-420). Though near- ly forgotten in the contemporary debates on gay acceptability, they are an indication of the duration of the gay community's fight for recognition of their partner relationships. In *Baker v. Nelson* (1972) and *Singer v. Hara* (1974) the states of Minnesota and Washington, and the U.S. Supreme Court in *Baker*, rejected arguments that same-sex couples were unlawfully treated in being denied the right to marry. The gay and lesbian couples argued that limiting marriage to a different-sex couple involved an abridgement of equal protection and due process, and/or constituted un- lawful sex discrimination. The courts in *Baker* and *Singer* rejected these arguments.

In these cases, the court had to determine whether the state could withhold the right to marry from a same-sex couple that otherwise met all the requirements for marriage (age, consanguinity, etc.). For our purposes, let us examine two of the arguments arising in those cases, that of equal protection and sex discrimination. The courts ruled that equal protection for gays and lesbians was not abridged because the state did not unduly discriminate against them. Surely the state differentiated between same- and different-sex couples with respect to the right to marry. But the court allowed a very weak defense of this policy when it ruled that such treatment did not constitute discrimination on the face of it. If the court had accepted the appellants' claim that distinctions in law based on the sex of one's partner should be subject to the same standard as those based on race, a standard called "heightened scrutiny," it would have made it very difficult, if not impossible, for the state to justify its policy. The appellants' analogy of their own case against discriminatory marriage laws to that of *Loving v. Virginia* (1967), in which the Supreme Court struck down Virginia's anti-miscegenation law, did not convince the judges.

In *Loving,* the state of Virginia argued that there was no violation of equal protection because the statute punished white violators the same as black violators; it then purported to show a rational basis to the anti-miscegenation measure. But the court determined that the law was, in fact, racially motivated, and went on to say: "At the very least, the Equal Protection Clause demands that racial classifications . . . be subjected to the 'most rigid scrutiny' . . . and, if they are ever to be upheld, they must be shown to be necessary to the accomplishment of some permissible state objective . . ." (*Loving,* in Rubenstein, 1993: 395). The court then concluded that there was "no legitimate overriding purpose independent of invidious racial discrimination" which justified the anti-miscegenation marriage statute.

What the appellants in *Baker* and *Singer* got from the courts was very different from what they hoped to gain by citing *Loving*:

> [I]n common sense and in a Constitutional sense, there is a clear distinction between a marital restriction based merely upon race and one based upon the fundamental difference in sex. (*Baker*, in Rubenstein, 1993: 408)

> In *Loving* . . . the parties were barred from entering into the marriage relationship because of an impermissible racial classification. There is no analogous sexual classification involved in the instant case because appellants are not being denied entry into the marriage relationship because of their sex; rather . . . because of the recog-

nized definition of that relationship as one which may be entered into only by two persons who are members of the opposite sex. (*Singer*, in Rubenstein, 1993: 412-13)

In effect, the courts held that state laws limiting marriage to different-sex couples are not *prima facie* discriminatory, and only require a "reasonable" defense in order to show they are not merely arbitrary. The courts then agreed the states had a legitimate reason to exclude same-sex relationships from the marriage statutes based on their desire to advance and protect the moral status of *procreation*:

> The institution of marriage as a union of man and woman, uniquely involving the procreation and rearing of children within a family, is as old as the book of Genesis . . . This historic institution manifestly is more deeply founded than the asserted contemporary concept of marriage and societal interests for which petitioners contend. . . . (*Baker*, in Rubenstein, 1993: 407)

And, in *Singer*:

> [t]he fact remains that marriage exists as a protected legal institution primarily because of societal values associated with the propagation of the human race . . . For constitutional purposes, it is enough to recognize that marriage as now defined is deeply rooted in our society . . . [M]arriage is so clearly related to the public interest in affording a favorable environment for the growth of children that we are unable to say that there is not a rational basis upon which the state may limit the protection of its marriage laws to the legal union of one man and one woman. (*Singer*, in Rubenstein, 1993: 415)

But if this is the state's rationale for barring same-sex marriages, how could it grant licenses to different-sex couples who would not, or could not, procreate? The *Singer* court acknowledged this seeming contradiction in its thinking, but claimed that such couples are merely "exceptions" to the rule that the institution of marriage is the guarantor of continued procreation. But why not under that construction make an "exception" for same-sex couples who want to marry? Presumably they would not be harming the procreative motives of different-sex couples any more than the different-sex couples who did not intend to procreate. In fact, heterosexual couples who chose not to procreate but still wanted to marry probably constituted a greater threat to the court's notion of marriage, since they actually rejected procreation and could have set an example for other heterosexual couples. Furthermore, and most unimaginatively, the court took for granted that same-sex couples would not be interested in procreating–". . . [I]t is apparent that no same-sex couple offers the possibility of the birth of children by their union" (*Singer*, in Rubenstein, 1993: 415)–a view which, while understandable as an aspect of the then-prevailing homophobic ideology, shows little awareness of gay and lesbian parental aspirations, and whose logic could not have withstood even cursory scrutiny. To have been consistent in its regard for procreation, the court should have held out the opportunity of marriage at least to those same-sex couples who themselves desired to reproduce or become adoptive parents.[10]

Quite recently, however, the Supreme Court of Hawaii issued an advisory opinion on a case that once again raised the question of same-sex marriage. In this case, *Baehr v. Levin,* the majority found that denial of a marriage license did constitute sex discrimination and therefore violated the equal protection provision of Hawaii's constitution. In order to permit such differential treatment on the basis of sex, the state would have to show, not that there is a rational basis to the policy, but that there is a "compelling justification" for it. The case was sent back to the lower court for trial on the question of whether the state has such a "compelling justification" for its exclusion of same-sex couples from the right to marry (Leonard, 1993: 39).[11] This is an instructive case, since it reverses the findings in *Baker* and *Singer,* and does so on the same grounds which the court in the latter case had earlier rejected. Unlike the courts of the early 1970s, the court in *Baehr v. Levin* found that Hawaii's equal protection guarantee, which includes protection against sex discrimination, was violated when Baehr was refused a marriage license. While *Baker* and *Singer* rejected the analogy with *Loving,* the court in *Baehr* embraced it: "Relying heavily on *Loving v. Virginia* . . . the plurality rejected the argument that excluding same-sex couples from marriage was not sex discrimination because both men and women were equally forbidden from marrying persons of the same sex" (Leonard, June, 1993: 39). All the Hawaii court had to do was substitute the word "sex" for "race" in *Loving* to show how the state's view of what constitutes sex discrimination is "an exercise in tortured and conclusory sophistry" (*Baehr,* in Lesbian/Gay Law Notes, June 1993: 39). But this is only because the *Baehr* majority must already have been convinced that discrimination against same-sex couples is on a similar level of unacceptability as racial discrimination, for there is no greater logic in their reasoning than in *Baker.* The *Baker* court, because it was little outraged by discrimination against same-sex couples to begin with, could reject the analogy with *Loving.*

If we cannot conclude that the court's decision in *Baehr* is any more *legally astute* than that of *Baker* or *Singer,* it is certainly more sympathetic to gays and lesbians. The years between *Baker* and *Singer,* on the one hand, and *Baehr,* on the other, have seen significant changes in heterosexual practice and in the practice of gays and lesbians, including a relatively open and lively interest in becoming parents.[12] In general, gays and lesbians appear less "different" from the majority in 1993 than they did in the early 1970s in terms of their sexual/relational mores. In some circles, especially in the worlds of art and entertainment, they have even been invested with a degree of moral stature in relation to the AIDS crisis.

These changes in the image and ideas about gays, combined with the unusual level of cultural diversity present in the state of Hawaii, probably had more to do with why the Hawaii Supreme Court found in favor of the same-sex appellants than did a marked "improvement" in legal reasoning in the period between the early 1970s and the 1993 *Baehr* decision. Courts do not rule in a social vacuum; the perception of the moral standing of the appellants is as important as their arguments in the interpretation of contested laws. In 1993, in Hawaii, the moral standing of the gay and lesbian community apparently made their invidious treatment significantly less tolerable than it had been a generation ago.

Gay and lesbian legal activists in the early 1970s presumed the relatively equal moral stature of gays and nongays. When they presented their briefs for the right to marry and for associated rights, they implicitly claimed a moral equivalence between the family relationships gays and lesbians formed, and those formed in the majority culture. The appellants' arguments in *Baker* and *Singer* were rejected as ostensibly legally unconvincing. But as *Baehr* suggests, these decisions were made at a level more decisive for the outcome than that of legal reasoning alone; they stem from the rejection of the gay and lesbian claim at the moral level. Courts have interpreted existing law in favor of gay and lesbian interests before *Baehr,* though the significance of the latter, should it open the way for same-sex marriage, cannot be overestimated. At least two important decisions on same-sex family issues have been based, like *Baehr,* on favorable interpretations of existing statutes. One, *Braschi v. Stahl* (1989), concerned the question of whether the surviving member of a male couple could inherit his partner's lease to a rent-controlled apartment. Under the then-prevailing housing laws of New York City, only a resident "family member" of the leaseholder was eligible to take over the lease. The case hinged on whether the court would consider Braschi's relationship to his partner as equivalent to a legal or biological family tie.

The New York State Court of Appeals decided in favor of Braschi on the grounds that while his relationship to the deceased leaseholder was neither biological nor established by marriage, it nevertheless conformed to the underlying sense of what it *means* in this society to be a family member. The court argued that protection from eviction under rent-control rules "should not rest on fictitious legal distinctions or genetic history, but instead should find its foundation in the reality of family life" (*Braschi*, in *Rubenstein*, 1993: 451). In reaching this decision, the court laid out a set of criteria for determining whether family status exists, including:

- emotional commitment and interdependence
- interwoven social life (holding yourself out as a couple/family, thinking of yourselves as a couple/family, visiting each other's families of origin, etc.)
- financial interdependence (sharing household expenses and duties, joint arrangements such as checking or savings accounts, power of attorney, life insurance, wills, etc.)
- cohabitation
- longevity
- exclusivity.

Needless to say, the criteria listed above would not have to be met, and quite often are not met and might not even apply, in deciding whether the surviving spouse in a legal marriage could inherit the lease to an apartment; the fact of legal marriage alone would suffice. Nevertheless, *Braschi* gave to the gay community a way of arguing that gays form the functional equivalent of marriage, and that their relationships should be treated as such.

Another case recognizing the familial nature of the gay or lesbian relationship, *In Re the Adoption of Evan* (1992), was decided by a Surrogate Court Judge in New York City. The issue was whether to allow an adult partner of the same sex as the biological parent to adopt the biological parent's child. Such adoptions had taken place already in several jurisdictions around the country, but in none had a written decision accompanied the ruling.

Judge Preminger adduces two features of legitimacy in granting the adoption. She specifically equates the women's relationship to that of a married couple, the vehicle for fully legitimate child-rearing in this culture: "The petitioners are a committed, time-tested life partnership. For Evan, *they are a marital relationship* at its nurturing supportive best . . ." [italics added] (*Adoption of Evan,* in Rubenstein, 1993: 534). But she also selects as a standard for deciding such cases what is in the child's best interest. It is in Evan's financial and emotional interest to have his "other mother" become a legal parent to him. The financial interests are obvious:

better medical and educational benefits, entitlement to inheritance, the
legal right to be supported. Judge Preminger spells out the emotional
benefits, as well. Referring to the protection adoption offers a child in the
event of the dissolution of his parents' relationship, she writes that:

> Even if, as anticipated, the [two parents] remain together, there is a
> significant emotional benefit to Evan from adoption which is perhaps
> more crucial than the financial. . . . [T]he adoption brings Evan the
> additional security conferred by formal recognition in an organized
> society. As he matures, his connection with two involved, loving
> parents will not be a relationship seen as outside the law, but one
> sustained by the ongoing, legal recognition of an approved, court
> ordered adoption. (*Adoption of Evan,* in Rubenstein, 1993: 533-4)

This case, like *Braschi,* shows how a judge who wants to interpret the
spirit of the law is not daunted by its letter. The spirit of adoption law is to
do what is in the best interest of the child. Even though the law mandated
that an adoption must result in the extinction of the same-sex biological
parent's rights in the child, Judge Preminger cites a set of cases in which
judges ruled that the circumstances in the cases before them made the
following of such rules counter-productive to the child's best interests.
Preminger quotes directly from a Vermont decision rejecting a literal
application of its state's cut-off provision: "It would be unfortunate if the
court were compelled to conclude that adoptions so clearly in the best
interests of the [child] could not be granted because of a literal reading of a
statutory provision obviously not intended to apply to the situation presented . . . " (*Adoption of Evan,* in Rubenstein, 1993: 535). Here, as in
Braschi, judges have taken the liberty to reinterpret existing law in order
to take into account changed social conditions.

An entirely different area affecting same-sex relationships is involved
in *Gay Teachers Association of New York v. the New York City Board of
Education.* This case deals directly with whether same-sex couples are
entitled to the same benefits as married couples. The lawsuit has been filed
on the grounds that the Board of Education, in refusing same-sex partners
of city employees the health insurance coverage to which the spouse of a
married employee is entitled, is violating the laws of New York City.
These laws forbid discrimination on the basis of sexual orientation and/or
marital status.

The City of New York argues the plaintiff has no legitimate grievance
since the employee benefit refers only to *spouses,* which means "married
partners," and therefore cannot apply to same-sex couples. A lower court
judge denied the City's motion to dismiss the case, which, according to

Lambda Legal Defense, "marks the first time any state judge has upheld the viability of a claim for domestic partnership rights" (*The Lambda Update,* Spring 1992: 17). The plaintiffs are asking for the same reinterpretation of existing law as did Braschi and the parents of Evan in their respective cases. They, too, argue that a literal reading of the law (employment benefits policy) would invalidate what is a fair and just claim. They take the position that the same-sex relationship they have formed is the moral equivalent of legal marriage, in a time and place where same-sex marriage is not legally recognized.

But the history of such litigation bodes ill for the Gay Teachers Association. In similar cases in California and Wisconsin, judges rejected the claim that either marital discrimination or discrimination on the basis of sexual orientation had taken place. In essence, both courts argued that only married spouses and dependent children were covered by the employee's contract, and since a same-sex domestic partner is not a married spouse, no violation of law occurred when domestic partners were refused coverage. The court in *Phillips v. Wisconsin Personnel Commission* admits that in the absence of same-sex marriage, Phillips will not be able to include her partner in her coverage. But it suggests that the court is helpless to render assistance in this matter, and that the proper venue for the redress of such a state of affairs is the legislature. (This will become a familiar refrain when we consider the rights of co-parents.) The *Phillips* court is clearly unwilling to accept the precedent set by *Braschi,* that changed social situations may require changes in the interpretation of a law.[13] On the contrary, the *Phillips* court claims that even if changes in society have made it right that same-sex partners should be covered, it is beyond the court's power to "create . . . verification and registration systems" that would establish who is a domestic partner for insurance coverage purposes. But after *Braschi* this is disingenuous, since the court could indeed *suggest* guidelines. Courts do this regularly; they rule on discrimination charges and establish plans for removing the condition that is considered discriminatory, e.g., mandating busing to achieve racial balance in the schools. Courts in the past have seen it as their responsibility to assist minorities facing discrimination. If they do not act this way with gays and lesbians it is because they do not yet see this minority as deserving of help, not because "the separation of powers" doctrine forbids it.

Like *Phillips,* the case of *Alison D. v. Virginia M.* (1991) shows a court unwilling to admit that a changed social reality requires a new, rather than a literal, reading of a relevant law in order for justice to be done. This case came to the New York Court of Appeals two years after the court had decided *Braschi.* The facts in the case were that two women who were living together for two years decided to have a child. As the court states: "Together, they planned for the conception and birth of the child and agreed to share jointly all rights and responsibilities of child-rearing" (*Alison D.* [77 NY2d 655]). Virginia was artificially inseminated and bore the child but the two women shared all the birthing expenses. They were equally involved in all parenting responsibilities for two years, until the couple broke up. After that, Alison continued to support the child and to visit regularly for more than two years. When Virginia forbade further contact Alison petitioned the court for visitation rights.

Alison argued that since she and Virginia acted as a couple in planning for the birth of the child, and in caring for it afterward, she was the child's other original parent. She argued that she was as related to the child as any parent, in effect, claiming she was the equivalent of the father in a heterosexual parental arrangement, and that the child was born into an already existing family, consisting of her and Virginia.

The court majority rejected Alison's claims, saying: "We decline petitioner's invitation to read the term parent in section 70 [relevant section of domestic relations law] to include categories of nonparents who have developed a relationship with a child or who have prior relationships with a child's parents and who wish to continue visitation with the child" [77 NY2d 657]. The majority argued that since she was neither a biological nor an adoptive parent, and did not enjoy any other status that would grant her a right to sue, under the domestic relations law she had no standing to seek visitation rights. The court refused to extend its line of thinking in *Braschi,* that "family" should be defined not only as a matter of legal statuses or biological relationships but also in functional terms. They refused to accept that Alison's relationship with Virginia entitled her to the same rights and obligations that pertain to legally married spouses in the area of custody and visitation.

The lone dissenting judge in the case, Judith Kaye, did recognize the need to flexibly interpret the relevant statute. She argued that there was room in the way the law read to acknowledge Alison's parental status, that the court could refrain "from imposing upon itself an unnecessarily restrictive definition of 'parent'" (*Alison D.* [77 NY2d 660]). According to Kaye, the court could have decided to use a broadened meaning of "parent" the way it broadened the meaning of "family" in *Braschi*. Nothing in the original domestic relations legislation directed the court to interpret the word "parent" as referring only to a biological or adoptive relationship. The court was not bound by legislative intent, therefore, from going beyond the strictly biological and adoptive referents the majority held itself to. After mentioning some criteria that could be used to determine whether

Alison, or any other petitioner, stood *in loco parentis,* Judge Kaye continued: "Other factors likely should be added to constitute a test that protects all relevant interests–much as we did in *Braschi*" [77 NY2d 662]. Kaye argues that just as in *Braschi* the court did not change the definition of spouse for all laws but only for tenancy so, too, the court could have expanded the definition of "parent" for the purpose of applying the domestic relations law governing visitation without overturning the established notion of who a parent is in other areas of parent-child relations.

Even such an acknowledgedly restrictive change in the definition of parent was not acceptable to the court. It would not read the relationship between Virginia and Alison, or that between Alison and the child, as anything more than that of "biological and legal strangers." Had it recognized Alison's relationship to Virginia as tantamount to a marriage, and her relationship to the child as that of a parent, it would have notably reinforced and extended the gains made by gays and lesbians in *Braschi* and in *Adoption of Evan.* It would have once again shown that when existing laws are interpreted literally, in disregard of critical social changes in adult and adult-child relationships, a significant miscarriage of justice, with consequent harm to adults and children, results.

In trying to understand why the court rejected the precedent of *Braschi* in deciding *Alison D.,* why it read the term "family" more flexibly than it was prepared to read the term "parent," Rubenstein (1991) points out that legal precedents in the areas of housing rights and family relations may have prepared the ground for each decision. But, at bottom, the difference in decisions depended much more upon what was at stake in each case. The court stipulated very clearly in *Braschi* that the way it redefined "family" was for the single purpose of amending the law governing the inheritance of rent-controlled apartments in New York City. Even if the court had tried to carefully delimit the applicability of *Alison D.,* as Judge Kaye urged, it would still have significantly widened the avenue of social acceptance of gay and lesbian familial relationships in a way that *Braschi,* dealing as it did with a leaseholder's, as opposed to a parent's, rights, did not. That legal arguments alone were not what convinced the court is suggested by the legal strength of Judge Kaye's dissent. Rather, we may assume it was the reluctance to take a sociopolitical position in favor of Alison's rights as a parent, which would have been far more threatening to the status quo, and potentially far more in conflict with the opinions of the public at-large, than the position the court took in *Braschi.*[14] Alison was implicitly seeking legal recognition of her status as a partner of Virginia, and explicitly the right to play a role in the life of the child whose coming into being she co-instigated and whom she co-reared. Touching as it does

on the symbolic core of the larger public's resistance to the moral acceptability of homosexuality and homosexual relationships, Alison's pursuit of
legal recognition of her tie to Virginia and to the child they raised was
more than likely to provoke intense public controversy.[15] Could the majority in *Alison D.* not have been mindful of that possibility? And so soon
after *Braschi,* might they not have thought twice about whether this was
the right time for such a fateful decision?[16] Again, the point is that courts
do consider the sociopolitical consequences of rulings that have the potential to shift the social landscape significantly; their decisions in such cases
will depend on the ideologies of the judges who compose them. In suggesting that the matter raised in *Alison D.* be dealt with by the state
legislature, the court sent a signal that it had reached the limits of how far
it was willing to go politically in acknowledging the rights of a partner/
parent in a same-sex relationship.

The New York Court of Appeals is not alone in setting such limits.
Courts in other jurisdictions have rendered decisions that use the same
reasoning as in *Alison D.* Two such cases were heard by the highest courts
of California and Wisconsin, *Michele G. v. Nancy S.* (1991), and *In the
Matter of ZJH* (1991). In the first, the two women had been together even
longer than had Virginia and Alison, considering the time both before and
after the birth of the children, though this availed little to the petitioner. In
these cases, too, the courts were unwilling to grant the status of "family"
to same-sex relationships, or acknowledge a nonlegal parent's right to a
hearing on custody or visitation.[17]

But in the same way that some judges approached the limits of their
tolerance of gay and lesbian acceptability when faced with a case like
Alison D., others have moved beyond it. A judge in Maryland ruled in a
1990 case that "in the best interests of the child," a nonlegal parent should
have some visitation rights (Margolick, NYTimes, 1990). And in a very
recent decision in New Mexico *(A.C. v. C.B. 1993),* the Court of Appeals
held that the nonlegal mother seeking shared custody or visitation "does
have the right to present evidence to establish that an oral co-parenting
agreement existed between the two adults" (National Center for Lesbian
Rights Newsletter, 1992:4). Taken all together, the decisions of courts
adjudicating the rights of nonlegal parents reveal a marked degree of
arbitrarity. This, in turn, suggests that ideology rather than legal rationality
or precedent is guiding the courts' thinking on this issue.

If adoption by a nonlegal parent is one way to insure the child's best
interest, joint adoption by a same-sex couple in the case of a nonbiological
child is another. Courts in more liberal regions of the country have been
quietly countenancing this legal move since the early 80s (Ricketts and

Achtenberg, 1990). Apparently, once a court overcomes its initial hesitancy at the idea of a child having two legal parents of the same gender, it can find no reason consistent with the doctrine of "the best interests of the child" to refuse second parent and joint adoptions. But as Ricketts and Achtenberg conclude: "Despite the obvious benefits to a child of second-parent adoption, such adoptions will be a long time coming in most areas of the country. The symbolism and strength of gay family relationships recognized in law is not lost on those who make these decisions" (Ricketts and Achtenberg, 1987: 99). As Ricketts and Achtenberg suggest, it is difficult to isolate the factor of cultural prejudice from the other ingredients that go into making up legal decisions in such cases.

One further way in which the law affects lesbian and gay parental relationships is crucial to address, for it crystallizes the issue of prejudice like no other. These are the cases where homosexuality, *per se,* becomes the grounds for one parent to try to limit or terminate the custody/visitation rights of a former spouse.[18] In some states, it is accepted legal doctrine that when a parent is in a homosexual relationship it is *per se* detrimental to the child. For example, the Virginia Supreme Court found in *Roe v. Roe* (1985) that a custody decision of a lower court which permitted a gay father to visit with his child was an abuse of discretion by that court. The court held that "[t]he father's continuous exposure of the child to his immoral and illicit relationship renders him an unfit and improper custodian as a matter of law" (*Roe v. Roe,* in Rubenstein, 1993: 492).

In a similar case before the Missouri Court of Appeals, *S.E.G. v. R.A.G.* (1987), the court claimed not to be relying on the *per se* approach, yet ruled that the mother's refusal to keep her lesbian relationship secret "present[ed] an unhealthy environment for minor children." It is worth quoting at length from this decision since it exemplifies the way prejudicial thinking is entwined with a ruling supposedly based in law alone:

> Wife and lover show affection toward one another in front of the children. They sleep together in the same bed at the family home . . . When Wife and four children travel to St. Louis to see [Wife's lover], they also sleep together there. All of these factors present an unhealthy environment for minor children. Such conduct can never be kept private enough to be a neutral factor in the development of a child's values and character. We will not ignore such conduct by a parent which may have an effect on the children's moral development. (*S.E.G. v. R.A.G.*, in Rubenstein, 1993: 496)

Of course, the only reason that sleeping in the same bed and showing affection to one another is held against the mother and her lover is because they are a same-sex couple. We may conjecture that the same behavior in a heterosexual context would not have elicited such juridical concern about the threat to the moral development of the children. The decision concludes with the following:

> We are not forbidding Wife from being a homosexual, from having a lesbian relationship, or from attending gay activist or overt homosexual outings. We are restricting her from exposing these elements of her 'alternative life style' to her minor children. (*S.E.G.*, in Rubenstein, 1993: 497)[19]

Homosexuality is considered to be immoral, and a mother who "exposes" her children to the knowledge that she is in a homosexual relationship is believed, *ipso facto,* to be doing them harm. Engaging in this "immoral relationship" thus constitutes *per se* evidence of unfitness, even though the court denies it has invoked the *per se* doctrine at all. In fact, the court claims to have acknowledged the mother's plea that "there must be a nexus between harm to the child and the parent's homosexuality." The "nexus" doctrine is the alternative to the *per se* approach; it means that the court must find that actual harm is being done to the children. Yet in *S.E.G.* there is no analysis of actual harm, only an assumption of harm. The court simply assumes that because the mother lives in "a small conservative community" there will be "peer pressure, teasing and possible ostracizing" of the children. It further assumes that should such behavior occur, the children will actually be harmed by it. The court was convinced that the environment created by an uncloseted lesbian mother will both damage the children's moral development and subject them to the hurtful prejudice of others, regardless of evidence. Together these *possibilities* create sufficient risk, in the court's thinking, to warrant that contact with the mother be restricted.[20]

But what if the case had been about a white mother marrying a black man, instead of living with another (white) woman? In fact, just such a situation was litigated in *Palmore v. Sidoti* (1984), where the issue was miscegenation rather than homosexuality. When the case was before the Florida court, the father was awarded custody on the grounds that the child, if she remained with her mother and stepfather, would "suffer from the social stigmatization that is sure to come" (*Palmore*, in Rubenstein, 1993: 493). Reviewing the state court's decision, the U. S. Supreme Court wrote:

> There is a risk that a child living with a stepparent of a different race may be subject to a variety of stresses not present if the child were

living with parents of the same racial or ethnic origin . . . The question, however, is whether the reality of private biases and the possible injury they might inflict are permissible considerations for removal of an infant child from the custody of its natural mother. We have little difficulty concluding that they are not . . . Private biases may be outside the reach of the law, but the law cannot, directly or indirectly, give them effect. (*Palmore*, in Rubenstein, 1993: 494)

But the court in *S.E.G.* rejected the analogy with *Palmore*. It reasoned instead that "[h]omosexuals are not offered the constitutional protection that race, national origin, and alienage have been afforded." It seems to be saying that the imputed prejudice of local neighbors and the children's peers against homosexuals is a legitimate reason to remove the children from the mother's home, suggesting that in the case of homosexuality as opposed to race, such prejudice is permissible.

The Missouri court cites *Bowers v. Hardwick* (1986), the Supreme Court decision that upheld the right of the state of Georgia to criminalize "homosexual sodomy," in holding that the mother does not have a Constitutional right to the privacy of her sexual life. Courts that cite *Bowers* to defend the proposition that lesbian and gay fathers are dangerous to their children are more likely to be in sodomy states like Missouri, Virginia and Georgia. Such states are more likely to be religiously and politically conservative, as well. The educational level of the population will generally be lower than in other states, and people will be less geographically mobile (Klassen, Williams, and Levitt, 1989). In addition, anti-homosexual attitudes tend to be both more widely held and highly correlated with other conservative, often religiously-based attitudes on sexual issues (Klassen et al., 1989). As long as the Supreme Court accepts the argument that it is constitutional to discriminate on the basis of sexual preference, state courts in conservative regions of the country will likely be applauded for using *Bowers* to enforce and interpret laws in ways that are directly harmful to gay and lesbian partners and to their children, as in *S.E.G.* More liberal jurisdictions will ignore *Bowers*. Such arbitrariness once again highlights the extralegal nature of cases involving gay and lesbian rights.

The usual way to think about gay and lesbian rights is within the framework of increased toleration, and my argument thus far may be taken by some to indicate that I strive to expand the sphere of toleration of sexual diversity. But this does not apply here; in this area, tolerance is not enough. What the legally married, different-sex couple receives is not toleration, but approbation, praise, blessings. For gays and lesbians to ever achieve legal equality with different-sex couples, they, too, must be approved of and esteemed for their affiliative and parenting aspirations and achievements. To accord gays and lesbians the right to marry is, finally, to celebrate and esteem them in the same way that society does different-sex couples. The internal reactions of acceptance, abstention, or scornful hostility that judges have had to this proposition accounts for the collection of illogical, unconnected and partisan decisions we have reviewed here. Tolerance runs the gamut from the judges in *S.E.G.* who were not "forbidding Wife from being a homosexual, from having a lesbian relationship, or from attending gay or overt homosexual outings," only forbidding her from living this life in such a way that her children knew, to drawing the line at the recognition of a nonlegal parent's right to custody/visitation hearings. But neither kind will ever lead to equal rights for gays and lesbians.

We are left, then, with a mixed picture of the court's impact on gay relationships. In the most conservative areas of the country it is difficult to find judges who recognize any moral equivalence between gays and non-gays. In the highest courts in several liberal states, there is tolerant acceptance, such as gays achieved in *Braschi,* but retreat in the face of the more difficult decisions represented by *Alison D.* Some judges–the majority in *Baehr,* Judge Preminger of the Surrogate Court in New York City, Judge Kathleen O'Ferrall Friedman in Maryland, and the majority on the New Mexico Court of Appeals in *A.C. v. C.B.,* among others[21]–appear to accept the claim of moral equality that the gay community has put forth. They offer that community the promise of the legal recognition it has been seeking.

But everywhere the morality and the politics of sexuality enter into legal deliberations.[22] It is in the nature of the legal process for judges to reflect the community's thinking, perhaps not in every place and not all the time, but often enough for the law to be thought of more as a conservator of the political and moral status quo than as an agency of social change. For every decision that takes account of a new social reality in its reading of the law, there is a *Bowers,* an *S.E.G.,* an *Alison D.* Clearly, deciding cases dealing with the rights of gays and lesbians is not simply a question of "being smart about the law," as it is the burden of this paper to have shown. Legal decisions convey political judgments about the moral standing of social groups, and about how much society should change and how fast. Judges are no wiser about this matter than anyone else. Therefore, the task for the gay community is what it was in 1969: to convince the rest of society of the moral nature of same-sex attraction and of the human relationships that flow from it. Favorable legal decisions will follow.

NOTES

1. In this paper, use of the terms "gay" and "lesbian" is a shorthand way of referring to "people who identify themselves as gay and lesbian." The terms are social identities which people apply to themselves and others, not biological facts about them. This is analogous to another social identity, that of a "black" person. The term "black" does not designate a specifiable color but rather includes persons in a range of hues some of whom are identified by others or identify themselves by that term.

2. This term will be used to refer to the parent without a legal tie to the child, as opposed to the adult who is either the biological or adoptive parent. Other terms used to denote this relationship are "second parent" and "co-parent." See Cox, 1991: 7, note 11, for similar usage.

3. This situation also pertains to legally married couples who adopt a child, since they, too, can be made anxious about their right to parent someone else's biological offspring. See, in particular, the recent case surrounding the Schmidts and the DeBoers over who will parent little Jessica (Lewin, 1993). The impact on present and future adoptive parents of the legal victory of the Schmidts over the adoptive couple who had been the child's only parents for two and one-half years, cannot be doubted.

4. Biological parents in a same-sex couple have this much in common with heterosexual adoptive parents, single parents, stepparents: they all fall somewhat short of the privileged reproductive situation of the legally married heterosexual couple.

5. Since jurisdictions deciding these issues are local, one sees a situation where one part of a state may be radically different from that in another part of the same state, while whole states, New York and California in particular, may be better for gays and lesbians than others.

6. For the view that the problem for gays and lesbians is not the law but its interpreters, and that while it may be desirable to secure new legislation extending the family rights of gays and lesbians, no new legislation is required to extend those rights now, only a willingness to interpret existing legislation favorably, see Cox, 1991; Halley, 1989; Harvard Law Review, 1989.

7. For an egregious example, see the opinions of a Justice Henderson in *Chicoine v. Chicoine,* a 1992 South Dakota case (in Rubenstein, 1993: 485-6).

8. The term "different-sex" will be used instead of "opposite-sex," which tends to reinforce a polarized view of gender forms. For a provocative critique of the idea of "opposite sex," see Laqueur (1990). Neither opposite- nor different-sex is adequate to describe the gender makeup and sexual practices of couples. Same-sex couples are not necessarily homosexual and different-sex couples not necessarily heterosexual. Obviously, gender and sexual preference/practice are not isomorphic.

9. For the claim that judges craft their decisions with sociopolitical implications in mind, see Rubenstein, 1991: 104-5; and MacKenzie, 1993.

10. That it didn't do so is no surprise given the views on homosexuality then current (early 1970s), even in the federal judiciary. *McConnell v. Anderson*

(1971), for example, is a case dealing with whether a gay man, the partner of the appellant in *Baker,* had for that reason been passed over for promotion. The federal judge hearing the case wrote that for the court to rule in favor of the plaintiff was equivalent to "foist[ing] tacit approval of *this socially repugnant concept* [gay marriage] upon his employer" [italics added].

11. The use of the "compelling justification" standard in sex discrimination cases is based on the legal doctrine that a group which has historically been discriminated against and can neither protect itself politically from a prejudiced majority nor easily change the feature that identifies it as a group, such as gender, race or alienage, should be able to resort to the courts for relief.

12. In the contemporary ordering of sex-reproduction-family fewer heterosexuals feel that reproduction is a necessary aspect of marriage. With fairly reliable birth control techniques available, couples can share in the pleasures of married sex without having to worry about reproduction. It has become more awkward, therefore, for judges to argue that marriage is to be protected strictly because it is the reproductive engine of the society.

13. This is put very nicely in a recent decision by the Vermont Supreme Court: "When social mores change, governing statutes must be interpreted to allow for those changes in a manner that does not frustrate the purposes behind their enactment" (AP story, June 20, 1993).

14. See Rubenstein, 1991, for a fuller discussion of the possible rationale behind the court's differing decisions in *Alison D* and *Braschi,* including the role played by the AIDS crisis in New York City in moving judges to protect the housing rights of those like Braschi, bereft of their partners by AIDS.

15. With respect to parenting by gays and lesbians, public opinion polls show the majority is not favorable. See, "Gays under fire," *Newsweek,* Sept. 14, 1992: 35-40, for a report on recent survey data.

16. This raises a particularly interesting issue in the sociology of law: under what conditions will jurists stake out new grounds in socially controversial issues, moving ahead of public opinion and before legislative action. For a discussion of this question, see Bumiller, 1988, and Rosenberg, 1992.

17. These courts that rejected a nonlegal parent's request for shared custody or visitation were not necessarily opposed to the idea in principle. Like the New York court, the California and Wisconsin courts suggested that the legislatures of their respective states should clarify, and, if necessary, amend the domestic relations statutes. They also proffer adoption as a way of circumventing entirely the situation that arose in these cases. For the reasons why leaving such matters to state legislatures will not move the gay and lesbian agenda on parental rights forward, see Cox, 1991.

18. There are a number of such cases, including *Fox v. Fox* (Oklahoma); *Jacobson v. Jacobson* (North Dakota); *Johnson v. Schlotman* (North Dakota); *Blew v. Verta* (Pennsylvania); *Diehl v. Diehl* (Illinois); *Mize v. Mize* (Florida); *S.N.E. v. R.L.B.* (Alaska); *S. v. S.* (Kentucky); *Thigpen v. Carpenter* (Arkansas). For brief descriptions of each case, see *Lambda Update,* Fall 1991 and Fall 1992; *NCLR Newsletter,* Spring 1992; *Lesbian/Gay Law Notes,* January 1993: 2; and Rubenstein,

1993: 490; 502. For further case references, see Rubenstein, 1993: 492, Notes 1 and 3; 500-503.

19. There is something disingenuous in the court's statement, since a mother engaging in a lesbian relationship is now bound to fear the possibility that the children will learn of it. A single mother of young children in a state with a sodomy statute is not free to have intimate sexual relations with a same-sex person she desires. Any such freedom she would exercise in such states, like Missouri, would be on pain of the loss of a full parental relationship with her children.

20. A New Jersey court had already ruled in 1979 that such reasons were not sufficient grounds for changing a custody agreement in that state. The New Jersey case, *M.P. v. S.P.* (1979), takes a different approach to the issue of neighbor and peer prejudice and its putative effects on the well-being of children in a lesbian household. Referring to the children in this case, the judge wrote: "Neither the prejudices of the small community in which they live nor the curiosity of their peers about [their mother's] sexual nature will be abated by a change of custody. Hard facts must be faced. These are matters which the court cannot control, and there is little to gain by creating an artificial world where the children may dream that life is different than it is" (in Rubenstein, 1993: 499).

21. It has probably already been noted that of the judges who have ruled or written favorably in cases involving gay family issues, a disproportionate number have been women. Especially when adoption and custody and visitation is at stake, they seem more willing to value the adults' relationship and the child's interests and to be willing to modify the law to take these into account.

22. Clearly this position dismisses Max Weber's metaphor of justice–a "vending machine" from which emerges a rational decision based on the inserted facts and the automatic application of case law and legal principles–as irrelevant for the type of cases where personal biases and political considerations enter into decision-making.

REFERENCES

Bumiller, Kristin. (1988). *The Civil Rights Society*. Baltimore: Johns Hopkins University Press.

Cox, Barbara J. (1991). "Love Makes a Family–Nothing More, Nothing Less: How the Judicial System Has Refused to Protect Nonlegal Parents in Alternative Families." *The Journal of Law and Politics*. Vol. VIII, No. 1, Fall 1991.

Halley, Janet E. (1989). "The Politics of the Closet: Towards Equal Protection for Gay, Lesbian, and Bisexual Identity." *UCLA Law Review*. Vol. 36:915-976.

Harvard Law Review. (1989). "Custody Denials to Parents in Same-Sex Relationships: An Equal Protection Analysis." Vol. 102:617-636.

Klassen, Albert D., Colin J. Williams and Eugene E. Levitt (1989). *Sex and Morality in the U.S.* Middletown, CT: Wesleyan University Press.

Lambda Legal Defense and Education Fund. (1992). *The Lambda Update*. Spring, 1992.

Laqueur, Thomas. (1990). *Making Sex: Body and Gender from the Greeks to Freud*. Cambridge, MA: Harvard University Press.

Leonard, Arthur S. (1993). *Lesbian/Gay Law Notes*. January 1993; June 1993.

Lewin, Tamar. (1993). "The Strain on the Ties of Adoption." *The New York Times*. 8/8/93: Section 4: 1.

MacKenzie, John P. (1993). "Supreme Court Strategy: Justices Have Power to Shape Rulings." *The New York Times*. 7/20/93: A-24.

Margolick, David. (1990). "Lesbian Child-Custody Cases Test Frontiers of Family Law." *The New York Times*. 7/4/1990: A-1.

National Center for Lesbian Rights (NCLR). (1992). *NCLR Newsletter*. Spring, 1992: 4.

Newsweek. (1992). "Gays Under Fire." 9/14/92: 35-40.

Ricketts, Wendell and Roberta Achtenberg. (1987). "The Adoptive and Foster Gay and Lesbian Parent," in Frederick W. Bozett (ed.), *Gay and Lesbian Parents*. NY: Praeger.

_____(1990). "Adoption and Foster Parenting for Lesbians and Gay Men: Creating New Traditions in Family." In Frederick W. Bozett and Marvin B. Sussman (eds.), *Homosexuality and Family Relations*. NY: Harrington Park Press.

Rosenberg, Gerald. (1992). *The Hollow Hope: Can Courts Bring About Social Change?* Chicago: University of Chicago Press.

Rubenstein, William B. (1991). "We Are Family: A Reflection on the Search for Legal Recognition of Lesbian and Gay Relationships." *The Journal of Law and Politics*. Vol. VIII, No. 1.

Rubenstein, William B., ed. (1993). *Lesbians, Gay Men, and the Law*. NY: The New Press.

The African American Family and the U.S. Legal System

Willa M. Hemmons

BACKGROUND

Talcott Parsons (1966) informs sociologists that social institutions are functionally related and develop dependent and interactive dynamics. Hence, the manner in which the legal system interacts with the family system ultimately operates to preserve predominantly held values in the society. From Parsons' interpretation of the sociological perspective also, it is understood that the legal system is a manifestation of what Parsons deems to broadly identify as the "religious" institution. As such, the legal system performs the function of rationalizing and justifying the existing political order. In other words, the religious institution includes any organization which helps to promote a feeling of unity, solidarity, patriotism, altruism and brotherhood. This function is important because in encouraging such feelings, the society thereby accepts the existing social order as just. This means that the edicts of any such organization are considered right and binding upon the individual. For the purposes of this discussion, then, if a participant in the legal system goes to it for grievance redress and the result as pertains to that participant is negative, that verdict is still accepted as right. The faith in the process and product of the legal system is unshaken–as long as the values and principles being espoused are still accepted as uncontrovertible.

Willa M. Hemmons is Associate Professor, Department of Social Work, Cleveland State University, Cleveland, OH.

[Haworth co-indexing entry note]: "The African American Family and the U.S. Legal System." Hemmons, Willa M. Co-published simultaneously in *Marriage & Family Review* (The Haworth Press, Inc.) Vol. 21, No. 3/4, 1995, pp. 77-97; and: *Families and Law* (ed: Lisa J. McIntyre, and Marvin B. Sussman) The Haworth Press, Inc., 1995, pp. 77-97. Multiple copies of this article/chapter may be purchased from The Haworth Document Delivery Center [1-800-3-HAWORTH; 9:00 a.m. - 5:00 p.m. (EST)].

The legal system is part and parcel of the political institution insofar as it creates in and of itself, a group of elites who administer a form of order. The Power Elite was the term that C. Wright Mills adopted for the various sectors of the U.S. society which were directed by their respective leading rulers. Including the Military-Industrial Complex, Education, as well as the Political arena, these leaders define and control the positions, relationships and operations in those arenas. The family is ostensibly less controlled than these more formalized organizations. Still, any controversy about 'family values' is ultimately decided in the legal arena which is presided over by judges. Indeed, in most family/domestic relations/children's courts in the United States juries are not even allowed because they have been defined as courts of 'equity.' Equity courts are super legal authorities beyond the pale of the usual legal controls of peer review by a jury. During the Middle Ages, they developed as a response to an alleged lack of normal legal remedies resolvable by neighbor consensus. Family values, then, are still essentially defined and decided by a group of judicial elites who have thus far come from Eurocentric, upper middle-class backgrounds. Further, the values which they impose upon their client populations, e.g., those who use the services of the divorce court, are generally perceived to be the "unwashed masses." This is true even though divorce courts service mainly those who are generally felt to be middle-class participants. In addition, it is not unknown that the "upper" classes often impose standards not adhered to by the members of the inner circle themselves. Thus, these working middle classes often are governed by a more rigid code of behavior for family dissensions than their upper-class counterparts.

Those from the so-called "lower" classes for various reasons have not participated in the structured marital ceremony process to as great an extent as the middle classes. In the resolution of their family conflicts, then, juvenile and criminal courts are many times called into play. Hence, the development of the codes of behavior to which they are subject are many times even more unresponsive to their true needs than the ones devised in the divorce courts.

Along these lines, we note that Robert Merton (1954) has formulated propositions which maintain that social institutions generally develop mutually, reciprocal functions that serve the interests of the members of the society who are in power. This discussion considers the processes through which the 'rulers' of the legal system have been effectual in preserving the status quo as it relates to the African American family. The inequities experienced by the African American family are just as intractable and result in just as disparate social positions as when reported by

W.E.B. Dubois (1903) or Carter G. Woodson (1933) or Jessie Bernard (1966) or Robert Staples (1986) or Joyce Ladner (1972) or Harriette Pipes McAdoo (1988). Also, cf. Robert Hill (1971; 1989). In light of these documented social conditions vis-à-vis the African American family, it is rather futile to expect a European American dominated legal system to effectuate justice for African Americans (cf. Hutchinson, 1990; Haley and X (Malcolm), 1964; Cleaver, 1968; and Freire, 1990). For instance, Eldridge Cleaver related that the true issues of the legal system derived not from trigger-happy cops (see also the Rodney King situation)[1] but "a trigger happy social order" in his book, *Soul on Ice*, in the chapter entitled "Domestic Law and International Law" (p. 158). In this vein also, Molefi Kete Asante (1990) further explains in *Kemet, Afrocentricity and Knowledge*, that the fundamental principles of justice from which Eurocentric jurisprudence developed, originally came from the Kemet (Egyptian/African) Priests Imhotep and Pepi' ideals of proof as a rational way of demonstrating a valid and reliable version of reality. Before that adaptation, European Germanic tribes relied upon such methods as trial by fire and water to "deduce" the veracity of an assertion. Through the principles of the Kemet, logical persuasion formed the foundation for decision making and problem solving. Adopting these Kemetan principles into their system of justice, the Anglo-Saxons of England went on to develop a court system which was presumably based upon the persuasive abilities of two otherwise, presumptively 'equal' opponents. Thus, that same–in terms of principles–system of legal jurisprudence being used so oppressively against African Americans is a rather twisted outcome when one of the legal system's origins are taken into account and the history of law as a conceptual phenomenon is considered.

The real reason for this result, of course, is that in the United States, people of African origins were never considered equal. In fact, that unequal premise as regards Afrogeneric people was a fundamental principle itself of the newly conceived United States. This conclusion is illustrated by the U.S. Supreme Court in cases such as *Dred Scott v. Sanford* in 1857 (declared that "Negroes" were to be counted as citizens of the United States and that further, Congress was prohibited from eliminating slavery in a federal territory) and *Plessy v. Ferguson* in 1896 (maintained the separate but equal doctrine) as well as *R.A.V. v. St. Paul*, No. 90-7675 in 1992 (struck down an ordinance which prohibited crimes of hate–e.g., cross burning on an African American family's lawn). Therefore, it is evident that political, social and economic forces (Billingsley, 1968) which are predominant in U.S. society have been further developed and disseminated by the legal system with respect to African Americans and their families as predicted by Parsons and Merton.

This disparagement of the African American family by the legal system has been in turn reinforced somewhat by negativisms presented by some sociologists (e.g., Moynihan, 1965; Liebow, 1967). Even though such negative conclusions about African American family life were disputed by other sociologists and social scientists (e.g., Frazier, 1966; Billingsley, 1968; Glasgow, 1981; Hill, 1971; Ladner, 1973) social policy–and, hence legal determinations–as constructed by the Power Elite is primarily based upon the constructs of a negative view of African American family life.

It is also important to point out that the legal system in America consists not only of courts, but of legislation made by legislative bodies such as the Congress, state assemblies and city councils. Law also includes the edicts and orders which emanate from the administrative offices of the executive branch of the government at the federal, state and local levels. Thus, many of the issues regarding the legal system here center not so much around its function as a forum for feuding individual parties; but, rather, viewing it in its totality, around its capacity to provide fair and equitable policies for the enhancement of the quality of African American family life. These determinations include issues such as housing, child care, credit, health, employment and other types of social welfare concerns. These concerns must consider the African American family from a social contextual frame of reference as well as from that of the legal perspective (Blackwell, 1985). These dynamics even include the ostensibly private ones of the African American male/female relationship (Staples, 1976; Rodgers-Rose, 1980; Aldridge, 1989). For that relationship is necessarily influenced by the existence of educational, job, health, housing and even entrepreneurial opportunities. It would be an interesting study to identify how many more "men would act right" if those opportunities were reasonably and equitably available to them.

In this discussion of the manner in which the U.S. legal system impacts upon African American families, James E. Blackwell's presentation of 'Controversial Family Issues in the Black Community' is very informative. Blackwell's chapter, "The Black Family in American Society" in his 1991 book, lists four 'controversial family issues.' They are (1) divorce, (2) illegitimacy, (3) public welfare, and (4) "the black matriarchy" (p. 51). These four issues greatly inform the analysis here regarding how the U.S. society's legal structures impact African American and other disadvantaged families in their pursuit of equal opportunities and justice under the law. The legal system, operating in conjunction with the other systems, result in Black female-headed households struggling at a decided disadvantage.[2] In other words, Black women have been subjected through these systemic forces of control (e.g., the legal system) to a double jeopardy.[3] Further, because the African American female-headed household has the lowest median income ($12,537 as of 1990 according to the U.S. Bureau of the Census) of any other family type (cf. $20,867 for European American female-headed households; $24,048 for African American male-headed households; and, $32,869 for European American male-headed households); the legal situation of the Black single-parent family will be used as the illustrative model primarily during this discussion as regards the major issues of a family's legal well-being in the areas of: domestic relations, economics, employment, credit, housing and child care.

DOMESTIC RELATIONS

Because divorce necessarily means that the parties have sought sanction for their union in the 'mainstream' American society, there are segments of the African American population which do not have recourse to its "advantages" or its disadvantages. Jesse Bernard in the sixties, possibly for that reason, asserted that it was a middle and upper-class phenomenon (1966). If a woman has never been married, then she does not have access to divorce court for awarding or enforcement of any child support order. Rather, her redress lies with perhaps a juvenile court. In Cuyahoga County, Ohio (Greater Cleveland), having to go through Juvenile Court means most probably that the Child Support Award is significantly less. This is the 'reward' that society inflicts for flouting its tenets and not being *legally* married. Ending a relationship in which children have resulted, as described by Blackwell, by desertion or separation means, then, that there are less legal protections.

Unfortunately for African American women, the likelihood of their having been married in the first place is substantially less. This has been the situation since the 1940s (Bernard, 1966) and seems to be growing (National Urban League, 1992). Black female teenagers are most likely to be particularly subject to the Catch-22 status of unwed motherhood. David Swinton (p. 87, 1992) notes that the youngest Black householders–age 15-24–experience the most severe economic hardship insofar as their median income of $9,816 is only 49.9% of that of their White cohort. Needless to say, they would seem to be the ones who would require the greatest protection from the courts. Conversely, because of the greater probability of having a *non-legal* marital status, they receive the least.

There are historical rationales for this phenomenon which are rooted in slavery (Franklin, 1948; Herskovits, 1941; 1958; Elkins, 1959; Myrdal,

1944). The same legal and economic disenfranchisement which prevented slaves from forming legal unions are operative now (Akbar, 1991). Legally robbed of the opportunity to earn a legitimate income and provide adequately for their families, Black males engage in *non-traditional* activities and form *non-traditional* unions. These unions, unsanctioned by the prevailing legal system, further disenfranchise and alienate the African American family. Such alienation serves to increase the disparities in income, education and employment (Swinton, 1992) that otherwise might encourage 'legitimate' participation in the U.S. social structure. That such alienation is intentional is uncontrovertible to some African and African American scholars (Madhubuti, 1990; Fanon, 1966; Hare, 1970; Asante, 1990; Kunjufu, 1985). Sociologists such as Robert Hill (1971) maintain that despite the lack of legal recognition, other supports have come into play which have been a source of strength for the Black family. However, the absence of the support of the legal system is a handicap. African American families must garner additional resources which have become increasingly scarce.

Trends in the country in the current law and order regime are towards strengthening and further institutionalizing the principles of family legal disenfranchisement. For instance, in Ohio the General Assembly eliminated recognition of Common Law marriages alleged to have begun after October, 1991. Common Law marriages are *defacto* unions. Because of certain circumstances endemic to the relationship they are retroactively declared legal and thereby under the jurisdiction of domestic relations courts. That the forms and styles of African American family structure are not "lawful" renders them much more vulnerable to attack by the economic and political forces which sustain the legal system in the first place. So, while the wealthy can obtain retroactive protection in states such as California where 'palimony' suits (cf. the *Lee Marvin* case) are retroactively sanctioned, the poor (which disproportionately consist of ethnic and racial categories such as Hispanic and African American) are left without recourse within the legal system. And, of course, if they did have recourse the defendants against which action would be sought are disproportionately 'uncollectible'–meaning they do not have a job or source of income from which judgment could be enforced.

One resource which in the past was particularly helpful to Black single-parent families was Legal Aid. When Reagan entered office, however, he complained that federally-funded lawyers bring lawsuits:

> . . . which are in reality attempts to enforce a judicial resolution of political and public policy issues properly left to the electorate.

Nevertheless, in terms of bringing legal relief to the deserted family, the Legal Services Corporation fills a much needed gap. This is especially true because of the monopoly which lawyers have on entry into the court system. Generally, no one, for instance, can obtain an order restraining an abusive ex-spouse or former boyfriend, or procure an award of child support or regain legal custody of offspring spirited away from school by a spiteful parent, but a lawyer. Prior to the establishment of Legal Aid, the poor did not have access to these services.

In fact, it seems difficult to conceive that the Reagan-Bush plan to put greater reliance upon Child Support Enforcement for the reduction of AFDC payments would have much success without the cooperation of Legal Services. For one thing, who would obtain the necessary Child Support Award judgments to enforce? The obtaining of such a judgment through private resources is a timely and costly procedure which few African Americans, particularly female headed families, can afford.

The Uniform Reciprocal Enforcement of Child Support Act, the Uniform Child Custody Jurisdiction Act, the Parent Locator Service, all invaluable legal tools to the single-parent family, would be useless aids to such poor families without Legal Aid.

ECONOMIC

AFDC (Aid to Families with Dependent Children) and Other "Welfare" Benefits

Because of the aforementioned political and economic conditions controlling the distributions of income in the United States and enforced most directly by the nation's legal systems, a disproportionate number of Black single parent families are on what has come to be known as "AFDC." The Aid to Families with Dependent Children program began in 1935. Unbeknownst to many, the Social Security Act governs both AFDC, as well as the program more traditionally (and more widely accepted) known as "Social Security." Both are designed to fill gaps in survival opportunities for various classes of people.[4] However, the receipt of Social Security is less stigmatic than that of AFDC. Although the reason for this difference is obscure, it is felt that it has something to do with a distinguishing comparison made at administrative levels between the "deserving" and the "nondeserving" poor; or, in other terms the ascertainment of the "truly needy."

The way this translates for single parent families, for instance, is that it is probably more "deserving" to lose the support of one's spouse through death than through desertion or divorce. With the latter, AFDC would more possibly be one's lot.

At any rate, the creation of these federal public assistance categories began what is now called "welfare." In describing Social Security in those early days, President Roosevelt was careful not to use the words "welfare" and "social insurance." Likewise, unemployment compensation was seen as being a protection for the "deserving poor." In other words, one has to be more than poor to obtain government aid–one has to belong to the "deserving poor" which is to be old, young, blind, permanently disabled or temporarily separated from one's employment through "no fault of one's own."[5]

Thus, single parent families who receive Social Security are seen as somehow being more acceptable. Still, as a public assistance mechanism, Social Security is defective. First of all, it fails to reach people outside the labor force who never had any income to insure (its original charge was to insure against loss of income). And, secondly, it has developed funding problems related to its special feature of relying upon employer-employee contributions. Benefit levels increased faster than payroll taxes resulting in sporadic shortages in the fund used to pay benefits. When the postwar generation–the baby boomers–"comes of age" after 2010, the shortage will be critical, unless other funding alternatives are found. Lastly, the program contained many outdated social assumptions of the 1930s–for example, divorced women received less than did married women.[6] Concerning the last point, however, a change was made in 1979 reducing the number of years a man or woman had to be married to receive his or her spouse's Social Security benefits from 20 to 10 years. However, the Reagan-Bush administrative philosophy would have done away with benefits for dependent spouses had Congress allowed such. Social Security "beneficiaries" (as well as AFDC "recipients"), then, who head single parent families do not face a rosy future.

Another victim of the cuts in Social Security was the "adult" student. Under the Reagan-Bush plan, this "add-on" was eliminated. Previously, family heads who had lost a spouse's income through death or disability could rely upon Social Security to help support their children through college. Under this change, the single-parent family head's burden is increased to the point that college will be an impossibility for many Black children, as well as many White. This obstacle was exacerbated by the fact that college financial aid programs have been reduced to a fraction of what they were in the early seventies. This fact also poses problems for single family heads who wish to obtain additional training themselves.

And, suppose one is so incapacitated by hypertension, high blood pressure, heart disease, diabetes, sickle cell anemia, tuberculosis, AIDS, or any of the other illnesses which disproportionately affect Blacks that the ability to just get up in the morning is a day-to-day struggle. (Of the 37 million Americans in the United States who do not have health insurance 25% are Black.) Suppose also, that one is the sole caretaker for one's children. If one is under fifty, the chances of one being eligible to receive disability benefits under Social Security are becoming increasingly slim. It was revealed in 1992 by Legal Services that 50% of all claims that were denied by the Social Security Administration were reversed at the appellate court level–raising the specter that the presidential administration was trying to cut domestic spending by denying Social Security claims. For instance, as long as one is determined to be able to engage in any "substantial gainful activity"[7]–in *any* work which exists in the national economy, one may not receive Social Security. In practical terms, this has meant that if one can walk to the Social Security office, sit in a chair and fill out the disability application, one probably has enough "residual functional capacity"[8] to make one ineligible for disability.

And, if this is the prospect for survival of one alone with a family under Social Security, one may imagine how things look with regard to AFDC.

Going back, we note that generally AFDC is provided for financially eligible single caretaker-relative (single parent or other relative) families, and families with an incapacitated father. It is a federally regulated program, but is funded through a matching funds program in combination with the states with the result that benefits from state to state vary widely. Variations widened under the Reagan Administration's funds as each one "sees fit." Variations in AFDC expenditures vary widely from state to state by fiscal capacity.[9] A welfare recipient receives the lowest amount from Mississippi and the largest monthly amounts from New York and California depending upon cost-of-living standard determinations. AFDC is not intended to provide a comfortable living, either. For example, in this author's state of Ohio, AFDC provides only 47% of the state-determined need standard and in April of 1992 almost half of all of the General Assistance recipients were "purged" from the "welfare" rolls.

This situation reflects the fact that originally, AFDC was provided not only for widows, but for widows who were "morally upstanding" and who managed a "wholesome home." By 1960, however, an Eisenhower Administration study reported that AFDC provided financial assistance for "homeless, dependent, and neglected children . . . found not where a parent is dead or physically incapacitated, but also in families where there is desertion, divorce, or indeed where there was no marriage."[10]

Moralistic-type judgments still permeate the requirements for AFDC.

Although legally overruled,[11] the "Man in the House" rule still imposes itself in recipient eligibility determinations and charges of failure of disclosure or welfare fraud. Currently, there seems to be a trend towards findings of common-law marriages, step- or substitute father, when a man is present in the household. Interestingly enough, AFDC rules impute an obligation of a stepfather to support a child who is living in his home even when Domestic Relations laws do not. This brings us to another major defect in the AFDC law insofar as it encourages families to separate.[12] As President Carter's Panel on Government and the Advancement of Social Justice pointed out:

> . . . a Minnesota mother of three could receive AFDC, Medicaid, and food stamps until her income reached $8,000 a year. A Minnesota father who remained with his family and worked full-time at a low wage disqualified his family for aid, regardless of need.[13]

With the cuts inflicted by the Reagan-Bush Administration, the possibility of a man's desertion of his family resulting in increased benefits to them from AFDC is greatly diminished. Major changes in AFDC which were proposed by Reagan-Bush and adopted by many states included:

> Counting the income of a child's stepparent as a source of support in determining the child's AFDC eligibility benefits.

> Counting a family's earned income tax credit (EITC) on a current basis in determining the monthly AFDC benefit to reflect better the family's actual, current need for assistance.

> Limiting deductible child care costs and standardizing other work-related expenses (which offset earned income in determining AFDC benefits) and reforming other earned income disregards.

> Requiring states to determine a family's AFDC eligibility and benefits based on previous actual income and circumstances.

> Prohibiting AFDC payments below $10/month to simplify and reduce the costs of administration for marginal cases that may be on and off the rolls from month to month.[14]

Reagan tied these "reforms" to the Child Support Enforcement Program, which financed 75% of the state's costs of enforcing and collecting child support from liable absent parents. These Child Support Enforcement changes were:

Charging an applicant fee in non-AFDC cases to reimburse CSE costs of states and the federal Government, which have no direct stake in such cases and do not otherwise share in such collections.

Financing incentive payments out of the state, as well as the federal share of collections.

Extend CSE activities to include the collection of alimony.

Mandating that the Internal Revenue Service intercept federal income tax returns to collect child support arrearages from liable absent parents where a court judgment has already been obtained.[15]

Obviously, the greatest impact of these changes was upon the one-earner family. And, since almost half of all African American children will spend some time in a single-parent family before their eighteenth year[16]–the most severe impact was really ultimately upon them.

To make a long story short, then, these policies have resulted in the fact that the poverty rate as of 1990 for persons in Black female-headed households was 50.6%.[17] In comparison, it should be noted that the poverty rate for those in White female-headed families was 29.8%. These figures compare, in turn, with an overall poverty rate for Black and White persons in poverty in 1990 of 31.9% and 10.7%, respectively.

EMPLOYMENT

For 1991, the unemployment rates for African American females and males were almost twice as high as those for their European American counterparts.[18] In addition, African American women with children under six are considerably more likely to be in the labor market than their European American cohort. Perhaps the most devastating news in terms of the employment picture for the Black single-parent family (90% of whom are women) was the phasing out by the Reagan Administration of the Comprehensive Employment and Training Act (CETA) jobs.[19] This cutback affected 340,000 jobs nationwide that could have been provided to low-income, unemployed persons.[20] CETA,[21] passed in 1973, consolidated manpower programs and moved away from training programs toward more meaningful work experience, particularly Public Service Employment (PSE).[22] These federally funded public service jobs were intended for the unemployed, underemployed and economically disadvantaged, however, some workers had Master's and Ph.D. degrees.

Other statutes which are intended to protect the rights of workers in-

clude: The National Labor Relations Act (unionization),[23] Fair Labor
Standards Act (guarantees a minimum wage),[24] Equal Pay Act of 1963
("equal pay for equal work"),[25] Occupational Safety and Health Act (a
safe and healthy workplace),[26] Title VII of the Civil Rights Act of 1964
and the Civil Rights Restoration Act of 1991 (prohibits employment discrimination on the grounds of race, color, sex or national origin).[27] Obviously, these statutes, as well as cases which have been litigated pursuant
to them were not the ultimate solution. In spite of them, African American
female family heads are still subject to great disparity in terms of median
income, poverty rates and unemployment rates. Further, the prospects for
the agencies which administer employment protections look bleak as those
privileged enough to be "taxpayers" become more impatient with pur-
portedly "unnecessary, superfluous and/or duplicative" regulatory governmental agencies. Such agencies are seen as inhibiting the viability and
increasing the costs of free enterprise, thereby artificially sustaining society's "unfit." Recourse to the courts may not prove a very effective offset
to the retreat of the social welfare system as the ideology of "rugged
individualism" seems to be taking hold in that forum as well. And, of
course, most of the proposals advocating fewer governmental props for
the economically marginal, would have remained just that without the
cooperation of Congress in enacting corresponding legislation.

Since it looks as if, then, the Black single-parent family will probably
have less expendable income in the near future, we may assume that it will
have to depend more on credit for its survival. So, let us look at how it
fares with reference to that system.

CREDIT

The Equal Credit Opportunity Act[28] went into effect on October 28,
1975. At that time, it prohibited discrimination based on sex or marital
status. In March, 1977, it extended coverage to prohibit discrimination
based on race, color, national origin, age, receipt of public assistance, or
good faith exercise of rights under the Consumer Protection Act.[29]

The Act prohibits: (1) Discrimination with respect to any aspect of a
credit transaction on any of the prohibited bases (see former); and, (2) Discrimination because all or part of an applicant's income is derived from
public assistance.

Within thirty days of rejecting a credit application, a creditor must
notify the applicant of the action taken along with either: (1) A specific
statement as to the reason such adverse action was taken; or, (2) A statement advising the applicant that he or she has a right to receive a specific

statement of reasons for the adverse action. Although the Federal Reserve Board has promulgated regulations under ECOA, the major enforcement agency for violations under this Act is the Federal Trade Commission. Persons who believe they have been subjected to credit discrimination should file an administrative complaint, then, with the FTC. In addition, many states have their own administrative agencies which regulate credit discrimination. Also, an individual may file a private civil action within two years of the discriminatory act with the appropriate federal district court. Despite these "official" protections, many female-headed families are discriminated against in credit worthiness decisions because of their lack of knowledge of these resources. Even with extension of credit, many Black single-parent families get into financial difficulty maintaining themselves because of their very finite, limited resources and hence are subject to such nightmares as repossession, cognovit notes, judgment liens, foreclosures, bank account attachments and garnishments. Further, the way these debt collection techniques are structured, the average debtor has very little recourse against them. How many debtors who cannot pay a $200 debt can afford to pay an attorney $300 to defend them in the collection process?

Some relief has been given to the inundated debtor by recent liberalization in the bankruptcy and other federal debt resolution codes.[30] Under these reforms, a debtor can retain much more of his or her equity in such assets as a house or a car while totally (under bankruptcy) liquidating most debts except for such notables as alimony, tax obligations, government-insured student loans and a few others. Still, the stigma of having gone bankrupt or been in trusteeship is repugnant to many, and many Blacks feel that they already have enough strikes against them without adding anymore. Thus, they go through what is for most insolvents a humiliating process, never having heard of a Fair Debt Collection Practices Act and unaware of any legal remedies for which they might be eligible.

HOUSING

Besides the provision of food, shelter is perhaps the most onerous burden shouldered by the Black single-parent family head. Housing becomes increasingly problematic the more children one has. Even without escalating mortgage interest rates, more Blacks have been renters than have been homeowners. An example of this lies in the fact that only 43.46% of all Blacks have equity in a home as opposed to 66.72% of Whites who own their homes.[31] Blacks, thus, have been subject to imbalanced state laws that favor the landlord over the tenant. Although these state laws vary, they are generally universal in this feature.

At the federal level, Title VIII of the Civil Rights Act of 1968, as amended,[32] The Fair Housing Act, prohibits discrimination in the sale or rental of housing or the provision of services, including financial services, relating to housing, on the basis of race, color, religion, sex or national origin. Despite the language of this statute, housing remains one of the most segregated areas of American life. Black children being raised in a single-parent home are particularly likely to grow up in an entirely segregated environment. Among Blacks, it is especially crucial that there are two incomes in order to enable a family to "escape" to the perhaps more integrated suburbs. For relief under the Fair Housing Act, it is probably more feasible to pursue federal district court remedies because HUD (Housing and Urban Development) cannot order a respondent to cease its discriminatory practices. Nor can it award a complainant any damages.[33] A court, on the other hand, can grant any relief it deems appropriate, including temporary or permanent injunctive relief, actual damages, and punitive damages not to exceed $1,000. Furthermore, the court can award a plaintiff the costs of his or her action as well as reasonable attorney's fees.[34]

The Housing and Community Development Act of 1974[35] consolidated a number of federal categorical programs into one block grant program which decentralized planning and implementation of activities funded through Community Development monies. Its stated purposes included:

The elimination and prevention of slums and blighting conditions, primarily for persons of low and moderate income (families whose income is less than 80% of the median income of the SMSA);

The conservation and expansion of the nation's housing resources, principally for persons of low and moderate income;

The expansion of the quality and quantity of community services, principally for persons of low and moderate income;

The spatial deconcentration of income groups throughout communities.[36]

Despite these laws, and recent ameliorative housing and landlord/tenant legislation passed by some states,[37] the conditions in which many Black inner-city single-parent families live are deplorable. If taken to task in court, the tenant is lucky to have a large commercial landlord ordered to pay a fine. Courts seem to be sympathetic with the argument that a piece of property is not worth putting an "excessive" amount of money into if it is

located in an "undesirable" area where no one will live but the unmoti-
vated, the unambitious, and–again, the term–the undeserving.

If the Black single parent is a woman, her problems in obtaining adequate housing for her children are complicated, since she usually has less
income to procure decent living quarters; and, despite the federal and state
laws, it is the private public service law firms and non-profit agencies who
have taken the responsibility to react against housing discrimination on the
basis of race and/or sex through such methods as sending out "checkers,"
demanding tenants' rights, lobbying for housing code legislation and enforcement, and bringing class action suits in court.

Because of discrimination in this area, many Black single-parent families live in the public housing authorized by the aforementioned Housing
and Community Development Act, otherwise known as "subsidized housing." The Reagan Administration revamped the state of this supplement to
the income of the poor, also. It related, for instance, that:

> Under current regulations, tenants living in Section 8 subsidized
> housing, public housing, and other HUD subsidized units . . . pay not
> more than 25% of their adjusted incomes toward rent. The Federal
> Government subsidizes the difference between the actual market rent
> charged for the unit (or, in the case of public housing, the per unit
> operating cost) and the tenant's rent contribution.[38]

Due to the reason, among others, that poor people living in subsidized
housing represent only "9%" of the total number of the United States'
poor, it therefore decided that it was necessary to:

> . . . gradually increase the maximum allowable rent contribution
> paid by tenants living in federally subsidized housing from 25% to
> 30% of their adjusted incomes.[39]

Thus, the Black single-parent family living in subsidized housing has to
pay a higher proportion of its income for housing that is often in a deterio-
rating area with subhuman conditions, leaving it with even less money to
go towards other life necessities. Such second-class housing conditions,
unfortunately, will be present for a longer period of time in public housing
units than planned. This is due to Reagan-Bush cutbacks in the funds
necessary for public housing renovation, repair and new building. The
original public housing modernization program approved by Congress
was a comprehensive effort to help ensure that all public housing projects
met minimum health and safety standards, were made more energy-efficient and less costly to operate.[40] Obviously, since this plan was not

funded, it will be a long time before many public housing units meet minimum health and safety standards, are made more energy-efficient and less costly to operate. Although these reformulations made the construction industry rather unhappy, the biggest losers were those who have had to live in substandard housing.

Before we leave housing, we must make note of the fact that it was the banking and insurance establishments and their corresponding laws which helped underscore discrimination in that area. This was done most blatantly through a procedure known as *redlining*. In February, 1981, a contract for $448,000 awarded to the National Training and Information Center by the Federal Insurance Administration to study redlining was cancelled. The study was proposed to give the FIA data to present to Congress in the Fall of 1981, during hearings on renewal of the Urban Property Protection Reinsurance Act of 1968, which created the so-called FAIR plan insurance for distressed neighborhoods.[41] H. Robert Weiss, an FIA contracting officer, defended the cancellation saying, "There's no sense in having someone do a study on something you already know."[42] The point is, however, even though the problem was already "known," how will systematic data be collected which will accurately identify its nature, extent and methodology so that decision makers can develop responsive, counteractive strategies? The fact that no study was done has probably contributed greatly to the fact that more than ten years after it was cancelled, the practice of redlining is still very prevalent. For instance, *The Atlanta Journal Constitution* in Georgia carried a series which documented its persistence entitled "The Color of Money" in May of 1988. Thus, the Black single-parent family, despite housing and credit reforms to the contrary, must still live in densely populated, segregated, substandard environments.

CHILD CARE

Currently, in spite of any attention to the issue spawned by "Murphy Brown"-type mass media blitzes, there is no national program for child care. The Federal Government does give tax credits for certain amounts of child care expenses. And, some private corporations have instituted "Family Leave" volunteer initiatives, but despite the reported success of programs such as Headstart, it appears that the Federal Government has no intention of further infringing on the "right to privacy" of the family by interfering in this area. Along these lines, even tangential impacts such as school lunch programs have been decreased.

With reference to AFDC, as mentioned earlier, the Reagan Administration limited deductible child care costs which were used to help determine eligibility. Also, Title XX of the Social Security Act, implemented in 1974, provided $2.5 billion dollars to the states to provide a variety of social services, including child care, to low-income residents including those who are poor, but who do not qualify for public assistance. Under reduced allocations for such social welfare expenditures, however, most states have had to discontinue many such benefits.

CONCLUSION

With regard to the aforementioned legal system generated "welfare reforms," C.W. Joe of the University of Chicago's Center for the Study of Welfare Policy stated:

> President Reagan's proposals to reduce federal spending for . . . public assistance programs have two critical flaws: they strip low-income families of their already meager resources, while inflation continues to erode the value of their incomes, and they shift significant fiscal burdens onto states and localities whose budgets are already in the red.[43]

This held true for most of the welfare reform measures which have thus far been proposed. Thus, the major conclusion one can make from this discussion is that what is termed relief under the legal system is grossly misnomered. There were few social and legal resources for Black single-parent families in the past, and it looks like in the future there will be even fewer. In other words, due to the reciprocal societal structural interface, the legal systems continue to fail the African American family.

This is not to say that the Black female-headed family will not survive, for it has always in times of travesty and adversity–risen to the occasion. What the more concerted, blatant impositions of deprivation through the legal system point out is simply that Black people cannot put their faith in the source of their oppression.

However, when one talks of relying upon Black community resources, one has to be selective. African Americans indisputably have a rich cultural heritage–one which gives them the ability to withstand continuous onslaughts to their dignity, humanity and self-esteem. Still, when a car is being repossessed, a family evicted, a worker laid off, many times the Black community has to stand by helplessly. This helplessness is what must be attacked through economic, political, as well as cultural reawakening and mobilization.

NOTES

1. *The New York Times*, "Jury Acquits Los Angeles Policemen in Taped Beating," April 30, 1992, p. A1, A8.

2. Rose Brewer (1988). Black Women in Poverty: Some Comments on Female-Headed Families. *Signs*, 13 (2): 331-39.

3. Frances Beale (1988). Double Jeopardy: To be Black and Female. *The Black Woman: An Anthology*, Toni Cade Bambara (Ed.).

4. 42 U.S.C. Sec. 601, *et seq., as amended.*

5. *Government and the Advancement of Social Justice–Health, Welfare, Education and Civil Rights in the Eighties*, Presidents Commission (Carter's) for a National Agenda for the Eighties, Washington, 1980, p. 57-64.

6. Ibid. p. 59.

7. 20 C.F.R. Sec. 404.1572; 20 C.F.R. Sec. 416.972 (rev.).

8. 20 C.F.R. Sec. 404.1505 (1980).

9. Coleman, Henry A. (1992). Interagency and Intergovernmental Coordination: New Demands for Domestic Policy Initiatives. *State of Black America*, New York: National Urban League, pp. 249-263.

10. Op. cit. Government and the Advancement of Social Justice, p. 64.

11. *King vs. Smith.* (1968). 393 U.S. 309.

12. Op. cit. Government and the Advancement of Social Justice, p. 64.

13. Op. cit. p. 66.

14. *America's New Beginning* (1981). The White House, Office of the Press Secretary, February 18.

15. Ibid., pp. 1-13.

16. Felicity Barringer (1992). Rich-Poor Gulf Widens Among Blacks. *The New York Times* (September 25), p. A 7.

17. U.S. Dept. of Commerce (1991). Bureau of the Census, *Poverty in the United States*, September, Tables 2 and 3.

18. Bureau of Labor Statistics (1991). *Employment and Earnings*, January, Table 5; October, Table A-44.

19. Op. cit. American's New Beginning, pp. 4-26.

20. Gary R. Clark (1981). *The Plain Dealer*, March 7.

21. 29 U.S.C. Sec. 801, *et seq.*

22. *The American Economy*, President (Carter's) Commission for a National Agenda for the Eighties, Washington, 1980, p. 39.

23. 29 U.S.C., Sec. 151-69.

24. 29 U.S.C., Sec. 201-19.

25. 29 U.S.C., 206(d).

26. 29 U.S.C., 651-78.

27. 42 U.S.C., Sec. 2000(e) *et seq.*

28. *Credit: A Workshop Guide*, National Commission on the Observance of International Women's Year, 1977, Washington, D.C.

29. Title VIII of the Consumer Credit Protection Act.

30. The Bankruptcy Reform Act of 1978, Title 11, U.S.C. Ch. 1-7; Chapter 13 of the Bankruptcy Code.

31. David H. Swinton (1992). The Economic Status of African Americans: Limited Ownership and Persistent Inequality. *State of Black America*, New York: The National Urban League, pp. 61-117.
32. 42 U.S.C. 3601, *et seq.*
33. 42 U.S.C. 3610.
34. 42 U.S.C. 3612.
35. 42 U.S.C. 5301, *et seq.* as amended in 1977 and 1978.
36. Op. cit. Sourcebook, p. 23.
37. Cf. Ohio Revised Code, Section 5321, *et seq.*
38. Op. cit. America's New Beginnings, pp. 1-19.
39. Op. cit.
40. Op. cit.
41. Thomas S. Andrzejewski (1981). *The Plain Dealer*, March 7.
42. Ibid.
43. *The Cleveland Plain Dealer* (1981). March 20.

REFERENCES

Asante, Molefi Kete (1980). International/intercultural relations. In M. Asante & A. Vandi (Eds.), *Contemporary Black Thought*, (pp. 15-28) Beverly Hills: Sage.

Asante, Molefi Kete (1987). *The Afrocentric Idea*, Philadelphia: Temple University Press.

Asante, Molefi Kete (1990). *Kemet, Frocentricity and Knowledge*. New Jersey: Africa World Press.

Beale, Frances (1970). Double Jeopardy: To be Black and Female. In Toni Cade Bambara (Ed.) *The Black Woman: An Anthology*, pp. 90-100. New York: Signet.

Bell-Scott, Patricia and Beverly Guy-Sheftall (1993). *Double Stitch: Black Women Write About Mothers & Daughters*. New York, N.Y.: Harper-Perennial.

Bernard, Jessie (1966). *Marriage and Family Among Negroes*. Englewood Cliffs, N.J.: Prentice-Hall.

Billingsley, Andrew (1968). *Black Families in White America*. Englewood Cliffs, N.J.: Prentice-Hall.

Billingsley, Andrew (1992). *Climbing Jacob's Ladder: The Enduring Legacy of African-American Families*. New York, N.Y.: Simon & Schuster.

Blackwell, James E. (1975, 1985). *The Black Community: Diversity and Unity*. New York: Dodd, Mead & Company.

Bynum, Victoria (1991). *Unruly Women: The Politics of Social and Sexual Control in the Old South*, Chapel Hill, N.C.: The University of North Carolina Press.

Cleaver, Eldridge (1968). *Soul on Ice*. New York: Dell Publishing, Inc.

Davis, Angela Y. (1983). *Women, Race & Class*. New York: Vintage Books–A Division of Random House.

Diop, Cheikh Anta (1991). (trans. from the French by Yaa-Lengi Meema Ngemi,

Edited by Harold J. Salemson and Marjoliun de Jager). *Civilization or Barbarism: An Authentic Anthropology.* Brooklyn, New York: Lawrence Bill Books.

Drake, St. Clair and Horace R. Cayton (1945). *Black Metropolis Volume 2: A Study of Negro Life in a Northern City.* New York: A Harbinger Book-Harcourt, Brace & World, Inc.

Du Bois, W. E. B. (1903). *The Souls of Black Folk.* New York: Avon Discuss Series 1968.

Etzioni, Amitai (1968). *The Acitve Society: A Theory of Societal and Political Processes.* New York, N.Y.: The Free Press.

Fanon, Frantz (1963). *The Wretched of the Earth.* New York: Grove Press, Inc.

Freire, Paulo (1990–Thirty Second Printing). *Pedogogy of the Oppressed.* New York: The Continuum Publishing Company.

Harrington, Michael (1984). *The New American Poverty.* New York, N.Y.: Penguin Books.

Hill, Robert B. (1971). *The Strengths of Black Families.* New York: The National Urban League.

Hill, Robert B. (1989). *Research on the African American Family: A Holistic Perspective.* Boston: William Monroe Trotter Institute, University of Massachusetts Press.

Hill Collins, Patricia (1991). *Black Feminist Thought: Knowledge, Consciousness, and the Politics of Empowerment,* New York, N.Y.: Routledge, Chapman and Hall, Inc.

Kunjufu, Jawanza (1984). *Developing Positive Self Images and Discipline,* Chicago, Illinois: African-American Images.

Ladner, Joyce (1972). *Tomorrow's Tomorrow.* Garden City, New York: Doubleday.

Liebow, Elliot (1967). *Tally's Corner.* U.S.A.: Little Brown and Company Inc.

McAdoo, Harriette Pipes, ed. (1988). *Black Families,* 2nd ed. Newberry Park, CA: Sage Publications.

Madhubuti, Haki R. (1990). *The Black Male, Obsolete, Single, or Endangered?* Chicago: Third World Press.

Merton, Robert K. (1954). *Social Theory and Social Structure,* Glencoe, Ill.: The Free Press.

Moynihan, Daniel Patrick (1965). *The Negro Family: The Case for National Action.* Washington, D.C.: U.S. Government Printing Office.

Mills, C. W. (1959). *The Power Elite,* New York: Oxford University Press, (Paper).

Nobles, Wade W. (1980). Extended Self: Rethinking the So-Called Negro Self Concept. In R.L. Jones (Ed.), *Black Psychology* (2nd ed.) New York: Harper and Row.

Parsons, Talcott (1951). *The Social System,* New York: The Free Press, 1951.

Parsons, Talcott, *Societies: Evolutionary and Comparative Perspectives.* Englewood Cliffs, N.J.: Prentice-Hall, 1966.

Perlo, Victor (1975). *Economics of Racism U.S.A.: Roots of Black Inequality.* New York, N.Y.: International Publishers.

Pivon, Frances Scott and Cloward (1980). Poor People's Movements: Why They Succeed, How They Fail, *Rural Sociology.* Spring, Vol. 45, No. 1, pp. 171-173.

Prestage, Jewell, L. (1980). Political Behavior of American Black Women: An Overview. In LaFrances Rose (Ed.) *The Black Woman*, pp. 233-50. Beverly Hills, Calif.: Sage.

Rodgers-Rose, LaFrances (1980). *The Black Woman*, Beverly Hills, Calif.: Sage.

Ryan, William (1972). *Blaming the Victim.* New York, N.Y.: Vintage Press.

Sennett, Richard and Jonathan Cobb (1973). *The Hidden Injuries of Class.* New York, N.Y.: Vintage Books.

Shakur, Assata. (1987). *Assata: An Autobiography.* 57 Caledonian Road, London N1 9BU, UK: Zed Books Ltd.

Staples, Robert (1986). *The Black Family: Essays and Studies.* Belmont, CA: Wadsworth Publishing Company.

Thomas, W. I. (1931). *The Unadjusted Girl.* Boston, Mass.: Little, Brown.

Warfield-Coppock, Nsenga (1990). *Afrocentric Theory and Applications, Volume I: Adolescent Rites of Passage.* Washington, D.C.: Boabab Associates, Inc.

Whyte, William F. (1943). *Street Corner Society, the Social Structure of an Italian Slum.* Chicago, Ill.: University of Chicago Press.

Wilkinson, Doris Y. (1984). "Afro-American Women and Their Families." *Marriage and Family Review* 7 (3-4): 125-42.

Williams, Juan (1987). *Eyes on the Prize: America's Civil Rights Years, 1954-1965. New York: Penguin Books USA Inc.*

Wirth, Louis (1929). *The Ghetto.* Chicago: University of Chicago Press.

Woodson, Carter G. (1990 edition). *The Mis-Education of the Negro.* Trenton, New Jersey: Africa World Press, Inc. (First Published by Associated Publishers, 1933).

X, Malcolm and Alex Haley (1965). *The Autobiography of Malcolm X*, New York: Grove Press.

Divorce Law in the United States

Cheryl Buehler

SUMMARY. The purpose of this paper is to review recent changes in divorce law in the United States. Divorce grounds, distribution of property, spousal support, and child support are each discussed within the context of the following: the effects of no-fault legislation, the trend toward gender neutrality and equality, and child support reform. The paper is concluded by discussing the role of divorce law in our culture.

Demographic projections suggest that approximately 50% of our population will end their first marriage by divorce (Glick, 1984) and that 60% of American children will live in a single-parent home before they are 18 years old (Norton & Glick, 1986). Many of the children of divorce live with their mothers and also live in poverty (about 35%–U.S. Bureau of the Census, 1990). Zimring (1990) has argued convincingly that "when it occurs, divorce is a high-impact experience: its economic effects are more substantial than those of any other legal event in the life of the average citizen, and child custody matters are of surpassing importance to the adult

---

Cheryl Buehler is Professor, Department of Child and Family Studies at the University of Tennessee.

Author Note: The author would like to express her sincere appreciation to Sarah Sheppeard, Attorney at Law, and to acknowledge her consultative support on this paper. She reviewed each section and offered guidance and clarification when needed. Her assistance provided both substantive direction and professional encouragement. The author also would like to thank the anonymous reviewers for their supportive critiques and aid.

[Haworth co-indexing entry note]: "Divorce Law in the United States." Buehler, Cheryl. Co-published simultaneously in *Marriage & Family Review* (The Haworth Press, Inc.) Vol. 21, No. 3/4, 1995, pp. 99-120; and: *Families and Law* (ed: Lisa J. McIntyre, and Marvin B. Sussman) The Haworth Press, Inc., 1995, pp. 99-120. Multiple copies of this article/chapter may be purchased from The Haworth Document Delivery Center [1-800-3-HAWORTH; 9:00 a.m. - 5:00 p.m. (EST)].

litigants and their children. . . . Thus, no area of state law is more important than the rules surrounding marriage and divorce, and no area of law in the United States has changed more rapidly" (p. vii).

The purpose of this paper is to review recent changes that have occurred in divorce laws. The paper is divided into four sections. In section one, the changes in divorce grounds are discussed and the basic issues related to no-fault legislation are reviewed. In section two, the trend toward gender neutral and equal divorce law is discussed. In section three, recent legislation related to child support is reviewed. In the conclusion, the role of divorce law is discussed.

Within this framework, changes that have occurred in divorce grounds, property distribution, spousal support, and child support are discussed, with the heaviest emphasis on factors that influence postdivorce economics. Child custody and visitation/access issues are not discussed because of page limitations.

NO-FAULT LEGISLATION

Grounds for Divorce

Divorce law has changed dramatically during the past twenty years. Although the federal government is becoming increasingly involved (Garfinkel & McLanahan, 1990), most divorce law is determined at the state level as structured by the Tenth Amendment of the United States Constitution (Bahr, 1985). (Generally, the Tenth Amendment has been construed as leaving most issues of family law to the state legislatures and courts, rather than federal.) In 1969, California made legislative history by enacting unilateral no-fault grounds for divorce. This new ground replaced all other grounds based on marital fault. Following California's lead, it only took a few years for most states to adopt at least one no-fault ground (e.g., irreconcilable differences). Zimring (1990) has suggested that "from the standard of legislative acceptance, no-fault was a brilliant success" (p. vii). This rapid legislative acceptance of no-fault divorce grounds by the various states is discussed and analyzed by Jacob (1988). In his book, he outlines the processes by which no-fault legislation was enacted and discusses the minimal sources of resistance. And although the effects of no-fault laws on family economic well-being are debated currently, most scholars agree that society, families, and most individuals are better served by a no-fault philosophy than by one based on fault (Bahr, 1983; Sugarman, 1990b).

Prior to the adoption of no-fault grounds, it generally was not permissible for couples to obtain a divorce by mutual consent. Evidence had to be presented that one spouse had misconducted him/herself in the marriage and was at fault in the divorce. Cruelty and adultery were common grounds used during the fault regime. The philosophy and procedures associated with fault-based divorce were questioned seriously during the late 1960s. As a result, several influential think tanks decided that "divorce based on fault no longer represented wise social or legal policy" (Kay, 1990, p. 7). The suggested standard to replace fault was that the marital relationship was no longer viable. In his discussion of the origins of no-fault legislation, Jacob (1988) does not seem to agree that "think tanks" were the responsible source of change. Rather, he suggested that changes resulted from divorce reformers using nonconflictual, routine methods of policy making, and that this method of implementing reform resulted in the rapid adoption of no-fault divorce grounds by the state legislatures.

Philosophy and legal discourse aside, the fault-based system worked poorly in practice. Spouses were forced to conjure up fault evidence where none existed (e.g., staging adultery for a private detective), collude, lie, and perjure themselves in court (Bahr, 1983). Furthermore, fault-based divorce grounds caused an emphasis on the misconduct of the spouses, thus perpetuating the marital war. Therefore, two of the purposes of including no-fault grounds in state divorce statutes were to reduce spousal acrimony and collusion. Although most states rapidly followed California's lead by reforming legal grounds for divorce, it is very important to note that most states did not adopt unilateral no-fault grounds nor did they drop the option of using a fault ground. Currently, 12 states employ a no-fault ground as the sole basis for divorce and require no waiting period from filing to divorce. In the remaining 38 states and the District of Columbia individuals may choose either a fault or no-fault ground when they file and/or "live separate and apart" for a specified time period (Walker, 1992; Table I).

What have been the consequences of these changes in grounds for divorce? Research suggests there have been at least four. First, there is some evidence from the analysis of court records that divorce proceedings are less acrimonious and adversarial (Dixon & Weitzman, 1980). However, these findings will need to be replicated because recent research suggests that both informal negotiations and court hearings still remain fairly adversarial (Erlanger, 1987; Glass, 1984). Second, although one of the concerns generated by the adoption of no-fault grounds was that the divorce rate would increase, there is no evidence currently to suggest that this has occurred (Dixon & Weitzman, 1980; Wright & Stetson, 1978). The third consequence is that more husbands are filing for divorce since the enactment of no-fault legislation (Dixon & Weitzman, 1980; Gunter & Johnson, 1978). Finally, the fourth consequence is that no-fault divorce seems to be less expensive because fewer cases have resulted in contested trials (Bahr, 1985).

Financial Aspects of Divorce

One of the most debated issues in the area of divorce law is whether or not the adoption of no-fault statutes has financially harmed women and their children. Recent research suggests that women's financial plight postdivorce has *not* resulted from the adoption of no-fault *grounds* (Garrison, 1990; Sugarman, 1990a). However, the analysis of the relationship between no-fault legislation and women's economic well-being postdivorce has been complicated by three important considerations. First, no-fault reform has two different meanings. It can be interpreted as the reform under which the grounds for divorce changed and individuals could obtain a divorce by mutual consent. A second meaning connotes a broader point-of-view. From this broader perspective, no-fault reform includes the exclusion of fault from decisions about property distribution, spousal support, and custody. The second consideration is that no-fault reform occurred during a time in American history in which several other significant changes also were occurring, such as changes in women's employment patterns and the evaluation of the Equal Rights Amendment. Third, it is important to realize that divorce proceedings are influenced by case law, as well as by changes in state statutes (Bahr, 1985). These three considerations, the meaning of no-fault, concurrent historical changes, and the influence of case law, complicate the analysis of the effects of no-fault reform on women's economic well-being postdivorce.

In 1985, Lenore Weitzman published an insightful and influential book entitled "The Divorce Revolution." Although her discussion was broader in scope, most of her analysis was based on California law and court proceedings. One of the major points of her treatise was that no-fault divorce reforms resulted in several negative and unintended economic consequences for women and their children. These effects included reduced property settlements, as well as less frequent and shorter alimony awards. Garrison (1990) and Sugarman (1990a) disagree with Weitzman's conclusion that these problems resulted or were exacerbated by no-fault reforms, although they do not disagree that women experience serious economic problems postdivorce.

In understanding this debate, it is important to realize that the adoption of no-fault divorce grounds and removal of fault or marital misconduct from decisions regarding property and spousal support *occurred at the same time in California.* This was *not true* in most other states. Examination of the (a) effects of changes in no-fault divorce grounds, and the (b) effects of changes in criteria for property division and spousal support need to include data from a variety of states that enacted the two different set of changes separately from one another. Thus, to analyze this debate, it is important to be aware of the role of fault in determining financial allocations postdivorce. Walker (1992; Table V) reported that fault has been removed explicitly as a factor in property decisions in 18 states (although 22 states allow for the consideration of economic misconduct). In terms of alimony decisions, marital fault is not considered in 29 states (Walker, 1992; Table VII). Thus, any analysis of the role of no-fault in women's economic well-being postdivorce must consider this variability in statutory reform, and attempt to distinguish between the economic effects resulting from changes in grounds and economic effects resulting from changes in property and spousal support statutes.

Garrison (1990) has done this by asking the question of whether it is changes in grounds or changes in the financial transfer rules (e.g., property division) that have produced the unintended economic consequences. She has stated that "the principal hypothesis that has been offered to explain how no-fault divorce has yielded reduced economic outcomes for divorced wives postulates that women have less bargaining power in the no-fault era because they have lost the ability to block the divorce . . . If reduced bargaining leverage has played a major role in producing lower divorce awards to women, one would expect that women will fare best in states without unilateral divorce, second best in states that require a waiting period, and worst in states that permit unilateral divorce upon demand" (pp. 78, 80). The results of her comparison of data from several states indicated that women were more damaged economically in 1984 than they were in 1978, *but that this was true in most states regardless of the type of no-fault ground employed.*

Sugarman (1990a) responded to Weitzman's conclusions using a somewhat different strategy. Rather than examine various state ground statutes, he reexamined Weitzman's data and has come to a different set of conclusions. He concluded that women experienced serious economic deterioration postdivorce before no-fault reform was adopted and that this did not change with the advent of no-fault. It is his position that no-fault is no more unfair to women economically than was the fault system. For example, in terms of property distribution, Sugarman notes (as does Weitzman) that over 50% of the couples in Weitzman's sample had very little property to divide. Thus, it is evident that these women would do no better or worse under no-fault regime transfer rules. The majority of other couples had the family home to divide, and in Weitzman's data the award rate to wives drops from 24.5% to 21%. This was a fairly small reduction.

In terms of spousal support, Sugarman drew a similar conclusion. Alimony was infrequently awarded under the fault system. His reading of Weitzman's data was that somewhere between 2% and 6% of the women who received alimony under the fault rules would not have received an award under no-fault rules. He also disagreed with her conclusions that awards of shorter duration account for women's economic declines and that these changes affected women from longer marriages to a greater extent than women in marriages of shorter duration (Sugarman, 1990a, p. 134). Although he disagreed with Weitzman's conclusions, he states that "ironically, even though I strongly believe that getting women back to where they were financially under the fault regime is very much the wrong goal of divorce law, it is perhaps oddly good for the political future of women's interests that Weitzman found the changes she did" (p. 135). Thus, it seems that Weitzman's attention to the effects of divorce reform served to increase public awareness with regards to women's and children's economic problems postdivorce. Without her work, it is very possible that this economic injustice would have remained unexamined and ignored.

GENDER NEUTRALITY AND EQUALITY

"At about the same time no-fault legislation was being passed, the U. S. Supreme Court gave a new interpretation to the Fourteenth Amendment of the Constitution" (Bahr, 1985, p. 98). In 1971, the Court decided that a law which gave preference to males as estate executors violated the Equal Protection Clause of the Fourteenth Amendment (*Reed v. Reed,* 404 U.S. 71, 1971). Importantly, Bahr has recognized that many of the divorce laws were changed because of this new interpretation, which has had as much to do with the removal of gender from divorce laws as has the no-fault divorce reform. (This analytic distinction between the move toward gender neutrality and equality, and the reform in fault-based divorce grounds also is emphasized by Fineman, 1991). In 1972, the Equal Rights Amendment passed the U.S. Congress, although it was not added to the Constitution because it was not ratified by three-fourths of the states (Bahr, 1983). In 1979, the Supreme Court redefined alimony (from the common law notion that husbands are responsible for the economic support of their wives) by invalidating the gender-based characterization of alimony (*Orr v. Orr,* 440 U.S. 268 [1979]). It seems likely that the removal of fault and gender from divorce statutes occurred during the same time period because both were consistent with the social climate and values of the 1960s and 1970s.

"Gender neutral" often has been interpreted as "gender equal" in divorce law reform (Fineman, 1991). Gender equality has served as a guiding principle in many of the statutory reforms related to property division and spousal support postdivorce. Increasingly, the law is beginning to conceptualize marriage as an economic partnership rather than a system of economic dependencies (Fineman, 1991). The focus on marriage as a partnership recognizes that husbands and wives each make major contributions to the economic status of the family (husbands through market production primarily and household production secondarily; wives through household production primarily and market production secondarily). This productive activity by husbands and wives results in the accumulation of economic assets (property) and enhanced earning potential that often results in a future stream of income (Combs, 1979). One of the results of the shift in focus from the acknowledgement of economic dependency to the acknowledgment of a marital partnership has been to reconsider the criteria for property distribution and the award of spousal support.

Property

Before discussing the recent changes in property distribution rules, it is important to recognize that there are two different types of law relating to marital property in the United States. Seven states have adopted community property laws in which spouses share equal (50/50) ownership of marital property (California, Idaho, Louisiana, New Mexico, Texas, Washington, Wisconsin; Walker, 1992, Table IV). Three community property states have adopted equitable (fair) property division rules (Arizona, Mississippi, Nevada). The other states and the District of Columbia have adopted common law property laws which *historically* have designated individual ownership of property based on whose name is on the property title and on whose resources were used to acquire the property. However, in actuality, most states do not consider individually titled property as separate property.

Kay (1990) has suggested there have been two adaptations that have functioned to bridge the differences between common and community property laws. First, most of the common law states have authorized the courts to distribute individually titled property in a fair manner or in the form of a spousal support award. Second, the definition of property is being reexamined. Levy (1989) discussed the issue of marital property by breaking it into four sub-issues: the *identification* issue (Is it in fact property?), the *characterization* issue (Is it marital or nonmarital property?), the *valuation* issue (How much is it worth?), and the *distribution* issue (How much does each spouse get?). The definition of property is an identification issue and has centered recently on employment-related benefits, such as pensions. Most states define pensions as marital property eligible for distribution upon divorce (Kay, 1990).

In addition, the enhanced earning capacity of each spouse during marriage (labelled career assets by Weitzman [1985]) and the production of future income postdivorce have been considered in terms of each of Levy's property issues. Are they property? If so, are they marital or separate property? Which criteria should be used to arrive at an accurate valuation? Which distribution rules should be used to determine each spouse's share? Currently, none of the states define enhanced earning capacity as marital property and only 12 states have statutes requiring the consideration of professional degrees in property division determinations (Freed & Walker, 1989; Kay, 1990). Before enhanced earning capacity is defined as property, it is clear that the issues related to characterization, valuation, and distribution need to be addressed much more thoroughly.

Current status of property allocations. Findings from three studies which have examined court record data on property distributions using large samples are reviewed. Seltzer and Garfinkel (1990) examined court records from 1980 and 1984 within 22 Wisconsin counties. An analysis of representativeness indicated that the Wisconsin data were very similar to those from the Current Population Survey. Dixon and Weitzman (1980) analyzed court records in California from 1972 and 1977. Garrison (1990) examined court records from 1978 and 1984 within several counties in New York.

The findings from these studies revealed that most people have some property when they divorce, but that the value of these assets is low. In Seltzer's and Garfinkel's (1990) sample, the median value of all property was $7,800. Most people own a car and have some equity in a house. However, these two assets frequently constitute a couple's wealth. Thus, one of the problems in terms of postdivorce economic well-being is that there is very little wealth to divide.

Although the scope of this paper inhibits a detailed discussion of each point, it is important to note that there seem to be at least five important issues related to property distribution at divorce: the standards used for distribution, the impact of length of marriage upon distribution decisions, the marital home, the distribution rules used in pension allocation decisions, and the consideration of nonmonetary factors in property allocations. With regards to the issue of standards, most states (37 and the District of Columbia) have specific statutory guidelines regarding property and/or maintenance decisions (Walker, 1992). One aspect of these guidelines focuses on the standards of "equal division" or "equitable division" of property. Equal division usually means a 50/50 split, whereas equitable usually means a "fair" split between husband and wife, given other factors that are taken into consideration (e.g., where the children are living). Kay (1990) states that "a consensus seems to be developing that the equitable distribution laws have not lived up to their promise of providing a fair apportionment of assets between the parties. . . . The courts are not treating the wife as an equal partner and so her property share has been lower than thought to be fair" (p. 12). Kay's observation is supported by data that indicate wives receive about one-third of the total property postdivorce (Price & McKenry, 1988). (The data from Wisconsin indicate higher percentages; mothers received 54% of the family wealth.) Fineman (1991) argued that neither equal nor equitable distribution rules will result in fair outcomes because women (especially mothers) do not have equal or fair educational, employment, or earning opportunities.

The lack of equitable division of property is one of several explanations for wives' relative (to their husbands') economic deterioration postdivorce. However, Seltzer and Garfinkel (1990) have shown that even if women received all of the available property, women would still have lower levels of economic well-being postdivorce than men. This can be explained by the lack of accumulated family wealth, by men's higher earnings at the time of divorce, and men's advantageous position in the social and economic structure which influence future streams of earnings.

There is some evidence suggesting that length of marriage is correlated positively with the value of wives' property awards (Rowe, 1991). Seltzer and Garfinkel (1990) report that, on the average, each year of marriage is worth $268 in the property settlement.

The disposition of the marital home is an important issue in property decisions postdivorce. One of the concerns raised by Weitzman (1985) was that, in order to meet the statutory requirement of equal property division, the California courts were ordering the sale of the marital home when there were inadequate assets to accommodate the equal division rule. Also, Weitzman has argued that children have a right to a stable home and that homemakers in marriages of long duration have certain occupancy rights. Both she and Fineman (1991) have recommended that the sale of the home be delayed until minor children have grown and that homemakers from marriages of long duration be awarded the house outright, not as part of the equal division of other assets.

With regards to the marital home, the data from New York divorce records indicate that the gender-neutral distribution rules have not prompted an increased likelihood in the sale of the family home; the home was sold in about 25% of the cases both before and after statute changes

(Garrison, 1990). However, the emphasis on gender neutral and equal distribution does seem to have disproportionally affected wives ending long marriages. The percent of wives awarded the marital home decreased from 62% to 52% following statutory reform in New York (Garrison, 1990). The issue of the marital home requires additional research and debate, and probably requires additional statutory and judicial (caselaw) attention.

The fourth property issue discussed in this section is the distribution of pensions. One of the major inequities in the recent past was that retirement pensions were considered individual entitlements and were distributable only to the pension holder. This meant that many women (particularly full-time homemakers) were not entitled to any portion of the husband's pension upon divorce (Bahr, 1985). The individual entitlement characteristic of pensions was tested in the case of *McCarty v. McCarty*, in which the couple had been married for 18 years and the California court awarded the wife 45% of the military pension. However, the U.S. Supreme Court overturned this decision and found that the military retirement was not property subject to division (453 U.S. 210 [1981]). The situation was similar for private pensions. As reviewed by Bahr (1985), recent laws have changed this situation such that marriage is recognized as a marital partnership and pensions (both private and military) are considered marital property available for distribution upon divorce in most states (Freed & Walker, 1989).

The final property issue discussed in this section is the treatment of nonmonetary contributions in the determination of property settlements. This issue often focuses on the household production activities of the primary caretaker. "The majority of states (35 and the District of Columbia) recognize the contributions of a spouse as homemaker, parent, and contributor to the economic well-being of the family. The trend is toward recognition by all states" (Freed & Walker, 1989, p. 407). This recognition of household production has been advocated strongly by several scholars (Bahr, 1983; Combs, 1979; Price & McKenry, 1988; Weitzman, 1985).

Although most states currently recognize the contributions of household production, several difficulties still remain. Household production is difficult to value accurately and this difficulty often results in undervaluation (Bahr, 1985). Also, the nonmonetary contributions of each spouse are just one of several factors used to make decisions about property, and given that valuation is difficult, this factor may be ranked low in the hierarchy of relevant factors (Fineman, 1991).

Spousal Support/Maintenance

Until the 1970s, alimony was the primary vehicle by which the husband continued his legally-defined marital obligation of financial support (Kurtz, 1977). A secondary purpose of alimony was to punish a spouse for marital misconduct that caused the divorce (Oster, 1987). However, it is important to recognize that alimony as punishment also was gender-based. Before alimony was desexed, husbands who were "at fault" often were ordered to pay more alimony (than if not at fault), whereas wives who were "at fault" were not eligible for an alimony award. Husbands could not be awarded alimony.

During the 1960s and 1970s, the philosophy of alimony began to change. The Uniform Marriage and Divorce Act of 1970 (UMDA) based its alimony recommendations on the philosophy that each spouse should be able to support his/herself financially and that the primary objective of alimony should be to provide temporary support for a spouse who needs a short amount of time to become self-sufficient (Oster, 1987). (A uniform act is one that is a statement of law or policy that, after endorsement by several key national legal organizations, serves as a model for state legislatures as they draft their own laws [Jacob, 1988]). Thus, alimony (when ordered) changed from being a relatively permanent financial award (it ended when the wife remarried or either former spouse died) to a temporary, transitional financial award (Jacob, 1988). In 1979, the U.S. Supreme Court invalidated gender-based alimony in *Orr v. Orr* (440 U.S. 268 [1979]; Foster & Freed, 1979). Thus, by the end of the 1970s, alimony had been desexed and in some states renamed to either spousal support or maintenance.

As a society, we are still wrestling with the "modern" philosophy and objectives of spousal support. It is clear that, in terms of financial support postdivorce, marriage is conceived as a partnership of theoretical coequals (Fain, 1977; Fineman, 1991) and that self-sufficiency for each spouse is a major guideline. In addition, most states have adopted statutes that include need and ability to pay as two primary considerations in the award of spousal support (Freed & Foster, 1977). Duration of marriage, the presence of young children, and health status also are important factors because each helps specify need (Inker, Walsh, & Perocchi, 1978; Weitzman, 1985). There seem to be four modern objectives of spousal support: (a) to prevent a spouse from becoming dependent on the state, (b) to ease the transition from married to single status, (c) to serve as a supplement to a property settlement, and (d) to compensate a spouse for household production (goods and services) during the marriage (Fain, 1977; Garrett, 1979; Kurtz, 1977).

Research on spousal support during the 1980s has produced several important findings. First, the award rate is very low–somewhere between 10% and 20% in most states (Dixon & Weitzman, 1980; Garrison, 1990; U.S. Bureau of the Census, 1990). Second, the amount awarded also is low (e.g., in New York the average amount awarded in 1984 was $93/year for all cases and $606/year when only cases with maintenance awards were included [Garrison, 1990]). Third, the award rate is influenced strongly and positively by duration of marriage, even though the rate is still relatively low for spouses with long marriages (e.g., in New York, 34% of women married 20 years or more received a support award in 1984 [Garrison, 1990]). And fourth, the noncompliance rate is high (Kay, 1990; Price & McKenry, 1988).

These findings on spousal support have prompted some scholars to suggest that our current system of financial support postdivorce is unfair and poses serious economic dilemmas and disadvantages for women, particularly mothers (Bahr, 1985; Combs, 1979; Fineman, 1991; Kay, 1990; Price & McKenry, 1988; Rhode & Minow, 1990; Rowe, 1991; Sugarman, 1990a; Weitzman, 1985). These scholars have noted that women's economic disadvantages stem from the structure of marital roles and the social and economic structure of our society. Husbands and wives in our culture often make decisions that serve to develop the husbands' earning capacities to a greater extent than the wives'. Although wives often are employed, their earning potential often is capped by decision making that places family needs before employment. These decisions are reinforced reciprocally by a lack of social and economic support in society for family decisions that facilitate equal development of both husbands' and wives' earning capacities (e.g., inadequate child care, an inadequate parental leave system, no federal system of economic support for children). Thus, one of the concerns related to current spousal support philosophy and practice is that the laws focus on spousal equality and self-sufficiency, but the institution of marriage and societal supports do not contain equal opportunity (Fineman, 1991; Price & McKenry, 1988; Rowe, 1991; Sugarman, 1990a).

As Weitzman (1985) has indicated, most couples invest in future earning potential (human capital) rather than property. Therefore, it seems important to examine current divorce law in light of this pattern of family decision making. Does current divorce law adequately address the issue of spouse's investments in one another's earning potential and the resultant future income stream? Probably not. Kay (1990) and Sugarman (1990a) both have addressed this issue and have offered several suggestions for policy revision. Importantly, Kay (1990) argues that the issue of future income division should not be addressed under the rubric of the current maintenance system. She suggests the creation of a new hybrid form of award that incorporates the flexibility of support awards with the permanency of property awards. After reviewing several possible policy guidelines, Sugarman (1990a) argues for the adoption of one of two guidelines that focuses on duration of marriage. The basic idea behind his proposals is that the lower-earning spouse would be entitled to a share of the future income earned by the higher-earning spouse, and that this share would be determined based on the length of marriage, the spouse's ability to pay, and some sort of vestment rules. For example, under the "merger over time" model, each spouse could be entitled to a specified percentage (1.5%-2%) of the other's future income after a three-year vesting period. These various proposals address the issues of human capital investments and spouses' rights to one another's postdivorce income. Future research and policy considerations need to consider and evaluate these proposals carefully in order to address more effectively issues of fairness in economic settlements postdivorce.

CHILD SUPPORT

The issue of child support has received a lot of attention during the past 10 years. Like spousal support, child support has been desexed—both men and women can be ordered to pay child support.

Although progress has been made in terms of gender neutrality and equality, the child support system has been plagued with problems, including low award rates for never-married custodial parents, inadequate award amounts, and high rates of noncompliance. The child support award rate for never-married women was 20% as of spring 1988 as compared with the 74% award rate for ever-married women. In 1987 only one-half of the women due child support received full payment, one-quarter received partial payment, and one-quarter received no payment at all (U.S. Bureau of the Census, 1990). The average amount of child support received by divorced mothers in 1987 was $3,073 (U.S. Bureau of the Census, 1990). Income from child support accounted for 18% of the total income of divorced mothers. These problems have led some to label the lack of child support in our country as our "national disgrace" (Bahr, 1985; Brokaw, 1992).

Pre-1980

Krause (1990) has stated that 25 years ago child support was not a public concern. At that time, the average amounts for awarded support were very low and compliance enforcement was poor, particularly across state lines. Child support was almost exclusively a state matter and judges exercised a great deal of discretion in child support decisions and enforcement (Garfinkel & McLanahan, 1990). Critics began to suggest various reforms, and as noted by Garfinkel and McLanahan (1990), "the common element to virtually all of these suggestions was to replace judicial discretion with bureaucratic regulation" (p. 208).

In 1975, Congress strengthened support policies by creating the Child Support Enforcement Program (called IV-D). The state remained the primary enforcement structure, however, states were required to follow federal guidelines in order to obtain federal funding. The federal government reimbursed about 70% of the cost of establishing paternity, locating noncustodial parents, and collecting child support (Nichols-Casebolt, 1986). One of the primary objectives of this reform was to reduce federal costs associated with the AFDC program (Cassetty, 1984; Krause, 1990). Although this 1974 reform was important because it signalled the federal government's increasing commitment to child support reform, Beller and Graham (1986) reported that the Title IV-D legislation had little effect on the overall child support award rates (however, the award rate did increase for Blacks, who were more likely to be receiving AFDC funds).

The 1984 Legislation

In the summer of 1984, Congress passed the Child Support Amendments (CSA) of 1984. This legislation represented sweeping child support reform. The CSA required that states pass laws that did the following (Bahr, 1985; Glass, 1989; Kay, 1990; Price & McKenry, 1988):

1. Establish mandatory wage withholding if payments are one month late.
2. Establish numeric formulas/guidelines for the determination of child support award amounts.
3. Allow for the imposition of liens against property to collect child support arrears.
4. Withhold income tax refunds if in arrears.
5. Provide credit bureaus information on child support arrears that are over $1,000.
6. Establish more efficient and expeditious processes for awards, modifications, and collections (90% of the cases must be settled within three months).
7. Provide collection services to non-AFDC mothers (for a small charge).

These reforms were predicated on a few basic principles and values. One of the important principles was that both parents share legal responsibility for the financial support of their child/children (Krause, 1990). Other principles cited by Krause (1990) included beliefs that: (a) parents should be ordered to provide at least some support, regardless of their financial status; (b) the support policies should be gender-neutral; and (c) the policies should avoid creating disincentives for future labor force participation or remarriage.

Values espoused in these policies included uniformity, economic security for children, and equity between coparents (Rettig, Christensen, & Dahl, 1991). In addition to these principles and values, several objectives of the 1984 reforms have been identified. A first goal was to reduce the amount of variability of award amounts of any specified level of income (Cassetty, 1984; Kay, 1990; Seiling, Jackson, & Stafford, 1989). This goal reflects the values of uniformity and consistency (Rettig et al., 1991). A second goal was to ensure adequate levels of child support so as to reduce children's chances of living in poverty (Kay, 1990; Seiling et al., 1989). This goal reflects the value of economic security for children (Rettig et al., 1991). A third goal was to distribute fairly the responsibility of economic support for children between the custodial and noncustodial parent (Kay, 1990; Seiling et al., 1989). This goal reflects the value of coparental equity (Rettig et al., 1991). Finally, a fourth goal was to increase the effectiveness of enforcement, and subsequently, to reduce the noncompliance rate (Glass, 1989; Kay, 1990). This goal reflects the value of private parental responsibility (Krause, 1990).

These goals highlight the importance of the numerical child support guidelines. There were three basic approaches used to establish the state guidelines that had to be in place by October 1, 1987. The *cost sharing* approach assumes that there are relatively fixed and measurable costs for raising a child and that these costs should be apportioned between the mother and father (Cassetty, 1984). Very few states used this approach to develop their guidelines. A second approach is the *income shares* method. This approach is based on the belief that a child should benefit from each parent's attained standard of living (Cassetty, 1984; Rettig et al., 1991; Seiling et al., 1989). Using this approach, awards are determined by totalling both parents' incomes and then apportioning the support obligation between the custodial and noncustodial based on the proportion of income contributed. This approach was used by a number of states (e.g., Ohio) to develop their guidelines (Williams, 1987 cited in Seiling et al., 1989). A third approach is the *taxation method,* in which the award amount is based on a specified percentage of the noncustodial parent's net or gross income

(Rettig et al., 1991). The number of minor children is factored into the formula. This approach was used by many states. For example, in Tennessee, the child support obligation is 21% of the obligor's *net* income for 1 child, 32% for 2 children, 45% for 3 children, and 50% for 4 or more children. In Wisconsin, the obligation is 17% of the obligor's *gross* income for 1 child, 25% for 2 children, 29% for 3 children, 31% for 4 children, and 35% for 5 or more children.

In addition to understanding the bases for determining the state's child support guidelines, there are three other important points related to the 1984 CSA. First, although states were required to establish child support guidelines, use of the guidelines in any particular case was discretionary, not mandatory (Krause, 1990). Hence, judges in family courts could elect to follow or ignore the state guidelines. Second, none of the approaches to guideline development included assessments of nonmonetary services, such as child care provided by the custodial parent (Kay, 1990). And third, the 1984 provisions did not require that states address the erosion of award adequacy over time caused by inflation and the increased childrearing costs associated with children becoming older (Price & McKenry, 1988; Rowe, 1991; Seiling et al., 1989).

With these caveats in mind, several studies have been conducted to evaluate the effectiveness of the 1984 CSA. Although detailed review of these studies is not possible due to page limitations, several general conclusions can be outlined. In terms of the uniformity goal, the findings are a bit contradictory. Seiling and associates (1989) reported increased uniformity using Ohio data, whereas Rettig and associates (1991) reported uniformity *only* at the very lowest obligor income level. There was little consistency/uniformity at moderate and higher levels of obligor income.

In terms of the adequacy goal, most research indicates that the actual awards have been lower than awards suggested by the guidelines and the actual awards are inadequate to cover the costs of raising a child (Ellis, 1991; Garfinkel & McLanahan, 1990; Pearson & Thoennes, 1988; Rettig et al., 1991; Seiling et al., 1989). For example, the Ohio data suggest that the average support award covers somewhere between 39% (using Espenshade's cost figures) and 58% (using poverty level figures) of the costs of raising a child (Seiling et al., 1989). When interpreting these data, it is important to realize that this method of evaluating adequacy considers only the awarded amount and does not reflect the received amounts. The incorporation of noncompliance information would reveal even greater support inadequacy.

In terms of equity between custodial and noncustodial parents, most research suggests that proportionately custodial parents contribute a greater share of their income to child support than that contributed by noncustodial parents (Rettig et al., 1991; Seiling et al., 1989).

Finally, in terms of the enforcement goal, research has suggested that wage withholding will increase the compliance rate somewhere between 11% and 30% (Garfinkel & Klawitter, 1989 cited in Garfinkel & McLanahan, 1990). There is some evidence that improved enforcement efforts are effective. The average amount of child support received by mothers increased 16% from 1985 to 1987 (U.S. Bureau of the Census, 1990). This is important given that between 1983 and 1985 the average amount received actually *decreased* by 12.4%.

One of the controversial issues related to compliance has been whether or not noncustodial fathers are financially able to comply fully with their support obligations. Research has suggested that most fathers should be able to comply (Nichols-Casebolt, 1986; Weitzman, 1985). However, one of the major predictors of compliance is full-time, regular employment (Pearson & Thoennes, 1988; Wallerstein & Huntington, 1983). Hence, when unemployment rises, noncompliance will increase. Another important consideration is the realization that many children will still be very poor even if the nonresidential parent fully complies with the support obligation because each parent is poor (Chilman, 1991). Thus, structural factors which account for poverty also contribute to child support noncompliance.

In accordance, Glass (1989) and Krause (1990) have suggested that, in addition to adequate enforcement policies, child support reform must reflect the recognition that the financial support of children is a societal responsibility, in addition to a parental one. These scholars have argued that all children (regardless of the parent's marital status) have a basic right to economic adequacy and security, and that the government should enact policies to support parents' efforts to provide for their children (e.g., better tax benefits, social insurance, basic medical care). If needed, the government also should supplement parents' contributions (e.g., provide a minimum family wage). This point of view can best be expressed by quoting Krause (1990):

> To sum up what I see, the next issues in child support include (1) the reality that many defaulting fathers simply do not have what it takes to support their children–as enforcement becomes comprehensive, fewer defaults will be due to irresponsibility, (2) my growing (if heretical) notion that it may not be fair to ask all absent fathers to foot the entire bill, and (3) the need to understand that children have a direct claim on society at large, along with their parallel claim on their parents. (p. 176)

Thus, one of the important issues emerging from recent child support reform is the need for both private *and* public responsibility for children.

The 1988 Legislation

In 1988, Congress passed the Family Support Act. This act contained several provisions on child support that served to strengthen greatly the 1984 CSA. States were required to pass laws that included the following reforms (Garfinkel & McLanahan, 1990; Kay, 1990; Krause, 1990):

1. Child support guidelines became mandatory; deviations from the state guideline have to be recorded by the judge in writing.
2. Mandatory wage withholding of all support payments must be in place by January 1, 1994.
3. Judges can no longer dismiss arrearages.
4. Child support orders must be reviewed every three years (applies only to IV-D cases).
5. Increased financial support for interstate enforcement.

Because of the more comprehensive and presumptive characteristics of the 1988 reforms, it is more likely the 1984 goals of uniformity, adequacy, and child support compliance will be accomplished. However, several issues will need additional attention in future reforms. These include: (a) updating all child support orders to account for the deleterious effects of inflation and increased child rearing costs, (b) better attention in child support agreements to children's future medical and educational expenses, and (c) the need to monitor closely states' compliance to the requirements set forth in the 1988 reform (Chilman, 1991; Garfinkel & McLanahan, 1990; Pearson & Thoennes, 1988). Krause (1990) has suggested that the state guidelines for child support be replaced with a federal guideline that includes adjustments for regional variations in the costs of living. Finally, the role of society in ensuring that children do not live in poverty needs to be addressed in much greater substantive detail.

CONCLUSIONS

Divorce law in the United States has changed a great deal during the past two decades. In their attempts to respond to broad economic and social changes, legislators have drafted and enacted less punitive (in terms of fault) and sexually-biased legislation. Using the criteria of gender neutrality, progress has been made by divorce reform.

However, serious problems still remain. Some of these problems can be addressed through additional reforms. Specifically, the disposition of the family home and spouses' right to one another's future incomes need more debate and attention. A new type of award that combines characteristics of property and maintenance awards may need to be developed as suggested by Kay (1990) and Sugarman (1990a). Future legislation also needs to structure the regular updating of all child support orders. In addition to inflation and increased childrearing costs, orders need to be updated systematically to reflect changes in parents' incomes, particularly the obligor's.

Although these problems can be handled specifically through legislative changes in the divorce law and principled, informed judicial decision making, many of the problems discussed within the context of divorce, such as women's economic deterioration following divorce, are reflections of broader issues and concerns in our society. Structural gender and racial inequalities, unemployment, underemployment, poverty, inadequate child care, an inadequate medical system, and nonsynchronous linkages between work and family each contribute to the economic problems postdivorce. In other words, many of the divorce-related problems actually mirror structural problems within the larger society.

Given the recognition that the issues faced in current divorce reform are not isolated from general societal issues, what is the role of divorce law? Generally, I agree with the principles and goals forwarded by Kay (1990) and Rhodes and Minow (1990). At a minimum, divorce law should do no harm. At its best, the law should set forth positive, societal ideals. Kay (1990) suggests that we continue working toward a "nonpunitive, nonsexist, and nonpaternalistic framework for divorce" (p. 28). Others recommend we commit ourselves to three general principles: substantive and result-based equality between sexes, sharing principles in intimate relationships, and policies that maximize children's interests and well being (Fineman, 1991; Rhode & Minow, 1990, p. 209). These are high ideals and the development of specific legislation consistent with these ideals will require much debate and research, as well as a strong commitment to reform. However demanding, our commitment to additional reform will be rewarded by the creation of a more fair and humane society.

REFERENCES

Bahr, S. J. (1983). Marital dissolution laws: Impact of recent changes for women. *Journal of Family Issues, 4*, 455-466.

Bahr, S. J. (1985). Impact of recent changes in divorce laws for women. *Family Perspective, 20*, 95-103.

Beller, A. H., & Graham, J. W. (1986). Child support awards: Differentials and trends by race and marital status. *Demography, 23*, 231-245.

Brokaw, T. (1992, March 20). *Families in crisis.* NBC Special Report.

Cassetty, J. (1984). Child support: Emerging issues for practice. *Social Casework: The Journal of Contemporary Social Work*, February, 74-80.

Chilman, C. (1991). Working poor families: Trends, causes, effects, and suggested policies. *Family Relations, 40*, 191-198.

Combs, E. R. (1979). The human capital concept as a basis for property settlement at divorce: Theory and implementation. *Journal of Divorce, 2*(4), 329-356.

Dixon, R. B., & Weitzman, L. J. (1980). Evaluating the impact of no-fault divorce in California. *Family Relations, 29*, 297-307.

Ellis, W. L. (1991). The effects of background characteristics of attorneys and judges on decision making in domestic relations court. In C. A. Everett (Ed.), *The consequences of divorce: Economic and custodial impact on children and adults* (pp. 107-119). New York: The Haworth Press, Inc.

Erlanger, H. S. (1987). Participation and flexibility in informal processes: Cautions from the divorce context. *Law and Society Review, 21*, 585-604.

Fain, H. M. (1977). Family law–"whither now?" *Journal of Divorce, 1*, 31-42.

Fineman, M. A. (1991). The illusion of equality: The rhetoric and reality of divorce reform. Chicago: The University of Chicago Press.

Foster, H. H., & Freed, D. J. (1979). Orr vs. Orr: The decision that takes gender out of alimony. *Family Advocate, 1*, 7-9.

Freed, D. J., & Foster, H. H. (1977). Divorce in the fifty states: An outline. *Family Law Quarterly, 11*, 297-313.

Freed, D. J., & Walker, T. B. (1989). Family law in the fifty states: An overview. *Family Law Quarterly, 22*, 367-525.

Garfinkel, I., & Klawitter, M. (1989). The effects of routine income withholding on child support collections. Discussion paper #891-89. Madison, WI: Institute for Research on Poverty, University of Wisconsin-Madison.

Garfinkel, I., & McLanahan, S. (1990). The effects of the Child Support Provisions of the Family Support Act of 1988 on child well-being. *Population Research and Policy Review, 9*, 205-234.

Garrett, W. W. (1979). Alimony and child support enforcement. *Family Advocate, 1*, 18, 20, 21, 42-44.

Garrison, M. (1990). The economics of divorce: Changing rules, changing results. In S. D. Sugarman & H. H. Kay (Eds.), *Divorce reform at the crossroads* (pp. 75-101). New Haven, CT: Yale University Press.

Glass, B. L. (1984). No-fault divorce law: Impact on judge and client. *Journal of Family Issues, 5*, 47-69.

Glass, B. L. (1989). Child support enforcement as a means to reduce poverty: A critical essay. *Family Perspective, 24*, 345-356.

Glick, P. C. (1984). Marriage, divorce, and living arrangements: Prospective changes. *Journal of Family Issues, 5*, 7-26.

Gunter, B. G., & Johnson, D. P. (1978). Divorce filing as role behavior: Effect of no-fault law on divorce filing patterns. *Journal of Marriage and the Family, 40*, 571-574.

Inker, M. L., Walsh, J. H., & Perocchi, P. P. (1978). Alimony orders following short-term marriage. *Family Law Quarterly, 12*, 91-111.

Jacob, H. (1988). Silent revolution: The transformation of divorce law in the United States. Chicago: The University of Chicago Press.

Kay, H. H. (1990). Beyond no-fault: New directions in divorce reform. In S. D. Sugarman & H. H. Kay (Eds.), *Divorce reform at the crossroads* (pp. 6-36). New Haven, CT: Yale University Press.

Krause, H. D. (1990). Child support reassessed: Limits of private responsibility and the public interest. In S. D. Sugarman & H. H. Kay (Eds.), *Divorce reform at the crossroads* (pp. 166-190). New Haven, CT: Yale University Press.

Kurtz, P. M. (1977). The state Equal Rights Amendments and their impact on domestic relations law. *Family Law Quarterly, 11*, 101-150.

Levy, R. J. (1989). An introduction to divorce-property issues. *Family Law Quarterly, 23*, 147-161.

Nichols-Casebolt, A. (1986). The economic impact of child support reform on the poverty status of custodial and noncustodial families. *Journal of Marriage and the Family, 48*, 875-880.

Norton, A. J., & Glick, P. C. (1986). One parent families: A social and economic profile. *Family Relations, 35*, 9-17.

Oster, S. M. (1987). A note on the determinants of alimony. *Journal of Marriage and the Family, 49*, 81-86.

Pearson, J., & Thoennes, N. (1988). Supporting children after divorce: The influence of custody on support levels and payments. *Family Law Quarterly, 22*, 319-339.

Price, S. J., & McKenry, P. C. (1988). *Divorce.* Newbury Park, CA: Sage.

Rettig, K. D., Christensen, D. H., & Dahl, C. M. (1991). Impact of child support guidelines on the economic well-being of children. *Family Relations, 40*, 167-175.

Rhode, D. L., & Minow, M. (1990). Reforming the questions, questioning the reforms: Feminist perspectives on divorce law. In S. D. Sugarman & H. H. Kay (Eds.), *Divorce reform at the crossroads* (pp. 191-210). New Haven, CT: Yale University Press.

Rowe, B. R. (1991). Economic of divorce: Findings from seven states. In C. A. Everett (Ed.), *The consequences of divorce: Economic and custodial impact on children and adults* (pp. 5-17). New York: The Haworth Press, Inc.

Seiling, S. B., Jackson, G., & Stafford, K. (1989). Child support guidelines: What effect on women and children? *Family Perspective, 24*, 357-371.

Seltzer, J. A., & Garfinkel, I. (1990). Inequality in divorce settlements: An investigation of property settlements and child support awards. *Social Science Research, 19*, 82-111.

Sugarman, S. D. (1990a). Dividing financial interests on divorce. In S. D. Sugarman & H. H. Kay (Eds.), *Divorce reform at the crossroads* (pp. 130-165). New Haven, CT: Yale University Press.

Sugarman, S. D. (1990b). Introduction. In S. D. Sugarman & H. H. Kay (Eds.), *Divorce reform at the crossroads* (pp. 1-5). New Haven, CT: Yale University Press.

U.S. Bureau of the Census. (1990). Child support and alimony: 1987. *Current Population Reports,* Series P-23, No. 167. Washington DC: U.S. Government Printing Office.

Walker, T. B. (1992). Family law in the fifty states: An overview. *Family Law Quarterly, 25,* 417-520.

Wallerstein, J. S., & Huntington, D. S. (1983). Bread and roses: Nonfinancial issues related to fathers' economic support of their children following divorce. In J. Cassetty (Ed.), *The parental child-support obligation* (pp. 135-155). Lexington, MA: Lexington Books.

Weitzman, L. J. (1985). *The divorce revolution.* New York: Free Press.

Williams, R. (1987). Guidelines for setting levels of child support orders. *Family Law Quarterly, 21,* 281-324.

Wright, G. C., & Stetson, D. M. (1978). The impact of no-fault divorce law reform on divorce in American states. *Journal of Marriage and the Family, 40,* 575-580.

Zimring, F. E. (1990). Forward. In S. D. Sugarman & H. H. Kay (Eds.), *Divorce reform at the crossroads* (pp. vii-viii). New Haven, CT: Yale University Press.

Children's Legal Rights in the U.S.

Mark C. Stafford

The topic of children's rights entails such issues as child labor legislation, entering into contracts, making wills, voting age restrictions, educational and health needs, limitations on drinking and driving, access to pornography, corporal punishment, owning and disposing of property, freedom of expression, compulsory school attendance and dress codes, state imposed curfews, and due process guarantees. Those issues involve fundamental relationships among children, their families, and others, including educational, religious, economic, and political institutions. However, given the diversity and complexity of the issues, it is scarcely surprising that there is no single principle, or even a single set of principles, for designating children's rights (Burt, 1976, p. 225; Dodson, 1984, p. 116; Wald, 1979, pp. 258-259). As Rodham (1973, p. 487) described the situation, children's rights do not flow from a "coherent doctrine regarding the status of children as political beings," but are a "slogan in search of definition." To illustrate, the principle of paternalism can explain why most contracts of children are voidable, but it cannot account for why children usually can be held liable for their torts. Similarly, paternalism can explain why a fourteen-year-old girl may be required to obtain parental consent for marriage, but the "same principle did not persuade the Supreme Court to require her to obtain parental consent if she wishes to terminate a pregnancy by abortion" (Houlgate, 1980, pp. 3-4).

This paper delineates some of the rights that are granted to children in

Mark C. Stafford is Associate Professor of Sociology and Associate Rural Sociologist, Departments of Sociology and Rural Sociology at Washington State University, Pullman, WA.

[Haworth co-indexing entry note]: "Children's Legal Rights in the U.S." Stafford, Mark C. Co-published simultaneously in *Marriage & Family Review* (The Haworth Press, Inc.) Vol. 21, No. 3/4, 1995, pp. 121-140; and: *Families and Law* (ed: Lisa J. McIntyre, and Marvin B. Sussman) The Haworth Press, Inc., 1995, pp. 121-140. Multiple copies of this article/chapter may be purchased from The Haworth Document Delivery Center [1-800-3-HAWORTH; 9:00 a.m. - 5:00 p.m. (EST)].

the U.S. Thus, the emphasis is *not* on what rights ought to be granted to children. Moreover, the paper has to do with legal rights rather than moral or human rights. That is, the focus is on rights identifiable by "an appeal to law in a given system," and not rights "held to exist prior to, or independent of, any legal or institutional system of rules" (Houlgate, 1980, pp. 9-10). Throughout, "child" refers to any person under age 18 (the age of majority), or under 21 for some purposes.

TYPOLOGY OF RIGHTS

Before delineating children's rights in the U.S., it is necessary to consider what is meant by the term "right." Hohfeld's (1919, p. 60) classic definition is that "a right is one's affirmative claim against another." However, there are different types of claim rights. Whereas a "positive [claim] right is a right to other persons' positive actions, a negative [claim] right is a right to other persons' omissions or forbearances" (Houlgate, 1980, p. 6). Examples of positive children's rights are the rights to a proper home, education, and medical care, which impose "on others the duty to do something for the child" (Houlgate, 1980, p. 7). Examples of negative children's rights are the right not to be abused by adults and the right to an undamaged reputation.

In addition to positive and negative rights, Hohfeld's (1919, p. 60) typology includes "privileges or liberties," involving "freedom from the right or claim of another." Children are denied many liberties because of their relationship to parents (Houlgate, 1980, p. 22). For example, a parent, not the child, has the right to choose the child's name, religion, and place of residence. Moreover, the doctrine of *in loco parentis* (in the place of a parent) gives school authorities the right to regulate student conduct. So students can be subjected to dress codes, regulations about hair length for males, and prohibitions of secret societies. Children also are denied liberties outside of the family and school–for example, by curfews and by limitations on their work, driving, and drinking (Houlgate, 1980, pp. 22-26).

According to Hohfeld (1919, p. 60), "a power is one's affirmative 'control' over a given legal relation as against another; whereas an immunity is one's freedom from the legal power or 'control' of another as regards some legal relation." To say that children lack the power to marry means that they are unable to alter their relations with other people in that way (with one of those other people being a prospective spouse–Houlgate, 1980, p. 26). One of the more important immunities children possess is that they ordinarily cannot be tried as adults for violating the criminal law, but there are many others (e.g., as mentioned previously, the right to void most of their contracts–Houlgate, 1980, pp. 8, 29).

THE CENTRAL CONTROVERSY

Whereas children in the U.S. have more positive and negative rights and immunities than do adults, children have fewer liberties and power rights. Controversy over children's rights has tended to center on which types of rights should be extended. One camp believes that children lack the capacity to care for themselves or make effective independent decisions. Consequently, children require even more positive/negative rights and immunities, or what Wald (1979, p. 264) designates as "protective" rights (for accounts of the historical origins of this position in the U.S., see Platt, 1969, and Sutton, 1988). A second camp believes that protectionists' assumptions about children's incapacity are invalid and that children can decide just as well as adults what is in their best interests. Children, then, should be granted more liberties and power rights (see, e.g., Cohen, 1980; Farson, 1974; Holt, 1974), or what has been termed "liberating rights" (Purdy, 1992, p. 25).

The controversy is shaped by difficulties in granting children *both* protective and liberating rights:

> If we agree with the second group of child advocates (the liberationists), then consistency seems to demand that we not only grant children all the liberty and power rights that we now grant to adults, but we must give up our attempts to have children accorded more positive and negative claim rights than we now accord to adults: justice demands it. Alternatively, if we side with the first group (the protectionists), then in the name of consistency it appears that we must not only try to have enacted legislation that will give children more positive and negative claim rights than we give to adults, but we must restrict their liberty whenever we feel that it is in their "best interests" to do so: beneficence demands it. (Houlgate, 1980, p. 16)

The controversy is illustrated by a recent disagreement over children's rights in the American Civil Liberties Union (Rosenbaum, 1989). A brief drafted by the A.C.L.U. for the U.S. Supreme Court appeal of a fifteen-year-old killer (*Thompson v. Oklahoma*, 487 U.S. 815 [1988]) claimed that teenagers are ineligible for the death penalty because they lack the capacity to make rational decisions about committing capital offenses. However, another group in the A.C.L.U. was arguing at the same time in abortion rights cases before the Court that teenage girls do have the capacity to make rational decisions to have abortions. The controversy rested on whether to advocate a protective right (in particular, an immunity) or a liberating right (a liberty) for teenagers; and after failing to reconcile the two positions, the A.C.L.U. settled the issue by declining to file a brief in the death penalty case.

Difficulties in granting children both protective and liberating rights will be seen throughout the following commentary. However, children in Western societies, including the U.S., had few legal rights of any type until fairly recently.

CHILDREN'S RIGHTS IN HISTORICAL PERSPECTIVE

According to ancient Roman law, a father had the power of life and death over his children, the principle being that "he who gave [life] had also the power of taking [it] away" (Blackstone, *I*, 1769, p. 440). Such absolute power eventually was rescinded as Blackstone (*I*, 1769, p. 440) told of the banishment of a Roman father for killing his son. However, paternal power remained substantial. For example, "a son could not acquire any property of his own during the life of his father; . . . all his acquisitions belonged to the father" (Blackstone, *I*, 1769, p. 440).

The power of the father in 19th-century English common law was "more moderate" than in Roman law, but "still sufficient to keep the child in order and obedience" (Blackstone, *I*, 1769, p. 440). A father could correct his children to properly socialize them, and paternal consent was required for marriage (Blackstone, *I*, 1769, p. 441). Nonetheless, there were limits to a father's power (mothers had no legal power over their children, either in ancient Roman law or English common law). Although a father served as guardian of his son's estate, the father had to account for the profits when the son reached 21, the age of majority. The "empire of the father" even could continue after his death "for he may by his will appoint a guardian to his children" (Blackstone, *I*, 1769, p. 441). The father could also delegate a portion of his power during his life to a tutor or schoolmaster, who could act *in loco parentis.*

Although children had few rights in English common law, Blackstone (*I*, 1769, pp. 434-440) wrote that parents of legitimate children had three duties: the maintenance, protection, and education of their children ("the duty of parents to their bastard children . . . [was] principally that of maintenance"–Blackstone, *I*, 1769, p. 446). Legitimate children, then, had several positive rights; but even these were more moral than legal.

EARLY AMERICAN CHILDREN'S RIGHTS

Early American law mirrored English common law by supporting strong parental control over children and by granting children few rights. For example, the Massachusetts Bay stubborn child law in 1646 made it a capital offense for children to disobey their parents (Sutton, 1988, chapter 1).

With the 19th-century, however, came extensions in protective (both positive and negative) rights for children. Many social reformers in the U.S. feared that with increasing industrialization, immigration, and urbanization, any child "not carefully and diligently trained to cope with the open, free-wheeling, and disordered life of the community would fall victim to vice and crime" (Rothman, 1971, p. 210). These fears were especially pronounced for orphaned, poor, and vagrant children, whose families were unable or unfit to protect against the perceived moral decline in American communities. If families were not up to the task, child-saving institutions would intervene. Houses of refuge and, later, reformatories were created for destitute, abandoned, vagrant, and disobedient youth (Rothman, 1971, pp. 207-209).

Reformers demonstrated little concern that they might be infringing on the liberating rights of children as they believed that "a good dose of institutionalization could only work to the child's benefit" (Rothman, 1971, p. 209). State courts affirmed that belief by dismissing parental objections to houses of refuge and reformatories. The seminal decision was issued in the 1838 case of *Ex parte Crouse* (4 Whart. [Pa.] 9 [1838]), which supported a state's *parens patriae* (parent of the country) power to protect children (Horowitz, 1984, p. 3). On her mother's complaint that she was incorrigible, Mary Ann Crouse was committed to the Philadelphia House of Refuge by a justice of the peace. However, her father sought a writ of *habeas corpus* on the grounds that her institutionalization without a jury trial was unconstitutional. The Pennsylvania Supreme Court denied the writ, arguing that a house of refuge was more a school than a prison and, consequently, that she did not need the constitutional rights accorded adults in a criminal trial. Asserting the government's power to remove children from family situations that might lead to criminal behavior, the court asked:

> May not the natural parents, when unequal to the task of education, or unworthy of it, be superseded by the *parens patriae* . . . ? . . . That parents are ordinarily entrusted with it [the business of education], is because it can seldom be put into better hands; but where they are incompetent or corrupt, what is there to prevent the public from with-

drawing their faculties . . . ? The right of parental control is a natural, but not an unalienable one. (in Bremner, *I,* 1970, pp. 692-693)

In addition to asserting a state's power to act in the best interests of children by removing them, if necessary, from undesirable families, the *Crouse* case also bore on the role of public schools in educating children (Schlossman, 1977, p. 10). Many of the leaders of the public school movement in Philadelphia also served as managers of the house of refuge. This was an early point in the public school movement, and an adverse ruling on the constitutionality of houses of refuge could "have tarnished the reformers' larger educational mission and the benevolent assumptions which underlay it" (Schlossman, 1977, p. 10). Hence, the judges in the *Crouse* case were asked to place both houses of refuge and public schools under the *parens patriae* doctrine and establish the state's duty to educate children. The judges complied and stated that the "public has a paramount interest in the virtue and knowledge of its members and that, of strict right, the business of education belongs to it" (in Bremner, *I,* 1970, pp. 692-693). Compulsory school attendance laws followed; and, as will be explained later, those laws eventually conferred a children's positive right to attend school.

At the same time that 19th-century reformers recognized the importance of public education in an increasingly industrial society, they acknowledged the dangers of oppressive child labor. By the 1830s, child labor was common in a variety of industries, such as cotton textile manufacturing; and the work often involved long hours, low wages, and unsafe conditions (Bremner, *I,* 1970, pp. 595-612). Early state efforts to regulate child labor were linked to compulsory education. For example, an 1836 Massachusetts compulsory school attendance law "declared that children under fifteen could be employed in manufacturing only if they had received three months of schooling in the year preceding their employment" (Bremner, *I,* 1970, p. 559). Other states patterned their laws after that of Massachusetts; and although those laws granted protective rights to working children (and conversely restricted their liberties), they were often "so poorly enforced or so unenforceable that their . . . effect in protecting child laborers was negligible" (Bremner, *I,* 1970, p. 559).

A WATERSHED IN CHILDREN'S RIGHTS

Despite extending protective rights for children in the 19th century, there was no special legal machinery for enforcing those rights or for handling children charged with crimes. It was not until 1899 that Illinois created the first statewide juvenile court system to handle such problems as child abuse, neglect, dependency, and juvenile delinquency. To sustain the state's *parens patriae* power, the juvenile court was "designated a . . . non-criminal court . . . which . . . assumed that disposition of juvenile cases would be in the best interests of the child and need not be overly concerned with the child's legal [liberating] rights" (Bremner, *II*, 1970, p. 440). Court sessions were to be informal; and the law that created the court was to "be liberally construed, to the end that . . . the care, custody and discipline of a child shall approximate . . . that which should be given by its parents" (*Revised Statutes of the State of Illinois*, 1899, Sec. 21, in Bremner, *II*, 1970, p. 511).

By mid-20th century, all states had established juvenile courts (Caldwell, 1961, p. 496), and there were few challenges to the *parens patriae* doctrine. "Protection and rehabilitation remained the keystone, giving judges almost unlimited discretion. Mere suggestions of due process, [or] adversarial settings . . . were anathema" (Horowitz, 1984, p. 4). However, the situation changed substantially in the mid-1960s with two watershed cases, *Kent* and *Gault,* that the U.S. Supreme Court used to limit the power of the juvenile court. The Court argued that children have most of the due process rights accorded adults in criminal trials, thus introducing a new era of children's rights.

SUPREME COURT DECISIONS ON CHILDREN'S RIGHTS

Supreme Court decisions are one means for identifying children's rights. Because the Supreme Court is the final arbiter of the Constitution, it is important to review some of its decisions relating to children's rights. Those decisions mainly have involved children's liberties rather than their positive and negative rights and immunities or their power rights; and the decisions have been limited primarily to the areas of education, child welfare, privacy, and juvenile court procedures. The Court has eschewed a principle that all rights constitutionally guaranteed adults can be granted to children. Instead, the Court has balanced children's rights against the rights of the state and parents.

Compulsory School Attendance and Child Labor

One of the earliest Supreme Court cases involving children's rights was *Pierce v. Society of Sisters* (268 U.S. 510 [1925]). The issue was whether Oregon could require parents to send their children to public schools. The respondents contended that the requirement interfered with "the right of parents to choose schools . . . , the right of the child to influence the parents' choice of school, [and] the right of schools and teachers therein to engage in a useful business or profession" (p. 534). The Court did not question "the power of the state . . . to require that all children of proper age attend some school" (p. 534). However, it ruled that a requirement of *public* school attendance interfered with parents' right to direct their children's education.

The Court heard another compulsory school attendance case many years later. In *Wisconsin v. Yoder* (406 U.S. 205 [1972]), several Amish parents had been convicted of violating a law requiring them to send their children to school, either public or private, until age 16. The parents claimed that the law violated their religious beliefs and jeopardized the survival of their communities. In ruling for the parents, the Court asserted that the state's interest in educating citizens "is not totally free from a balancing process when it impinges on fundamental rights and interests, such as those specifically protected by the . . . First Amendment, and the traditional interest of parents with respect to the religious upbringing of their children" (p. 214).

The *Yoder* decision may appear to have contradicted an earlier case, *Prince v. Massachusetts* (321 U.S. 158 [1944]), that also involved a claim of religious freedom. *Prince* had to do with the constitutionality of child-labor statutes prohibiting children from selling newspapers, magazines, periodicals, etc., in public places. The statutes also prohibited anyone from furnishing those materials to a child for sale in a public place. The aunt and guardian of a nine-year-old girl was convicted of giving her religious pamphlets, "knowing she was to sell them unlawfully" (p. 160). The conviction was appealed on the grounds that the statutes violated (1) the aunt's freedom of religion under the First Amendment and (2) her parental rights as guaranteed by the due process clause of the Fourteenth Amendment (p. 164).

Unlike *Yoder,* the Court ruled against the aunt: "And neither rights of religion nor rights of parenthood are beyond limitation. Acting to guard the general interest in youth's well being, the state as *parens patriae* may restrict the parent's control by . . . regulating or prohibiting the child's labor and in many other ways" (p. 166). The Court further ruled that states may regulate children's behavior more than the behavior of adults, especially in "public activities and in matters of employment" (p. 168). The Court identified several possible ways that children may be "harmed" by "street preaching," including "emotional excitement and psychological or physical injury" (pp. 168-170). The issue of possible harm distinguished *Prince* from *Yoder.* Whereas the health or safety of the child was believed to be at risk in *Prince,* the Court maintained that this was not so in *Yoder* (p. 230).

Free Expression in School

Although *Pierce* and *Yoder* had implications for children's right to choose the school to attend or whether to attend school at all, the Court's focus in those cases was more on parents' right to make choices for children (because it cannot be assumed necessarily that children's wishes correspond to the wishes of their parents–see Mr. Justice Douglas' dissent in *Yoder,* pp. 241-249). In contrast, *Tinker v. Des Moines Independent Community School District* (393 U.S. 503 [1969]) was a "pure" children's rights case that considered the right (liberty) to free expression in school (Davis & Schwartz, 1987, pp. 56-58).

In violation of school district policy, several students came to school wearing black arm bands to protest the war in Vietnam. They were suspended and sent home as a result. However, the Court held that "students in school as well as out of school are 'persons' under our Constitution" (p. 511) and that the students' actions constituted speech protected by the First Amendment in that the actions "neither interrupted school activities nor sought to intrude in the school affairs or the lives of others" (p. 514).

This does not mean that there are no restrictions on students' right to free expression. In *Hazelwood School District v. Kuhlmeier* (484 U.S. 260 [1988]), the Court distinguished between "educators' ability to silence a student's personal expression that happens to occur on the school premises" (the issue addressed in *Tinker*) and "educators' authority over school-sponsored publications . . . and other expressive activities that . . . [people] might reasonably perceive to bear the imprimatur of the school" (p. 271). Arguing that the publication of student newspapers involves the latter issue, the Court held that "educators do not offend the First Amendment by exercising editorial control over the style and content of student speech in school-sponsored expressive activities so long as their actions are reasonably related to legitimate pedagogical concerns" (p. 273).

Procedural Due Process in School

A student accused of violating a school rule is entitled under the Fourteenth Amendment to procedural due process, meaning that the student must be provided notice of the charges and a hearing. This right was elucidated in *Goss v. Lopez* (419 U.S. 565 [1975]), which had to do with the suspension of nine high school students for periods up to 10 days. The students brought suit against school officials to have the Ohio statute permitting their suspensions declared unconstitutional. A federal district court previously had ruled that the students were denied due process because they had been suspended without a hearing, but the state appealed.

The Supreme Court first considered the state's claim that the Due Process Clause does not protect against school suspensions because there is no constitutional right to an education. The Court observed that the Fourteenth Amendment protects people against deprivation of life, liberty, and property without due process of law but that property interests are normally created by state laws rather than the Constitution. In Ohio, lawmakers had created a positive right to public education by providing a "free education to all residents between five and 21 years of age, and [establishing] a compulsory-attendance law" (p. 573). Hence, "having chosen to extend the right to an education to people . . . generally, Ohio may not withdraw that right . . . , absent fundamentally fair procedures" (p. 574).

But what are "fundamentally fair procedures"? The Court stopped short of requiring that students be given the opportunity to secure counsel, confront unfavorable witnesses, and present favorable witnesses (p. 583). With short suspensions, oral or written notice of the charges must be given to the student; and, if the student denies the charges, he or she must be given "an explanation of the evidence the authorities have and an opportunity to present his side of the story" (p. 581). In most instances, the notice and hearing must precede the suspension (p. 582).

Children's Abortion Rights

In the last several decades, the most controversial children's rights cases have involved abortion. In *Planned Parenthood of Central Missouri v. Danforth* (428 U.S. 52 [1976]), the Court held that both children and adults have a privacy right (a liberty) that extends to the abortion decision. In particular, a state cannot give a third party, including parents, a veto over the decision of a girl and her physician to terminate a pregnancy (p. 74). The Court did not deny that children had protective rights–that "certain decisions are . . . outside the scope of a minor's ability to act in his [her] own best interest or in the interest of the public . . . , [for example] the sale of firearms and deadly weapons to minors without parental consent" (p. 72). However, the Court declared that "constitutional [liberating] rights do not mature and come into being magically only when one attains the state-defined age of majority. Minors . . . possess constitutional rights" (p. 74).

A few years later in *Bellotti v. Baird* (443 U.S. 622 [1979]) the Court considered a Massachusetts statute requiring an unmarried minor to obtain parental consent for an abortion. If one or both parents withheld consent, the minor could petition a court to overrule the parents' (or parent's) decision; but the parents were to be notified of the court proceedings (p. 630). Even if "the minor is capable of making, and has made, an informed and reasonable decision to have an abortion," the judge could withhold consent if the "best interests of the minor will not be served by an abortion" (p. 630).

Four justices in the Stevens opinion considered the statute unconstitutional because, contrary to *Danforth,* the "minor's decision to secure an abortion is subject to an absolute third-party veto" (p. 654). Moreover, the statute was excessively burdensome by requiring a pregnant minor to initiate the court proceedings (p. 655).

Four other justices, in what has become the more influential, Powell opinion (Dodson, 1984, p. 140), found the statute unconstitutional because it did not provide an alternative court proceeding in which a minor could show either: "(1) that she is mature enough and well enough informed to make her abortion decision, . . . independently of her parents' wishes; or (2) that even if she is not able to make this decision independently, the desired abortion would be in her best interests" (pp. 643-644). The alternative court proceeding must be conducted expeditiously and confidentially (i.e., the parents need not be notified). If found to be sufficiently "mature," the minor must be permitted to make her own abortion decision.

In *H.L. v. Matheson* (450 U.S. 398 [1981]), the Court upheld the constitutionality of a Utah requirement that, if possible, a physician notify the parents of an "immature, dependent minor" before an abortion is performed (pp. 407-410). According to the Court, parents cannot veto their immature daughter's decision, but they can counsel her and provide her physician with a medical history (pp. 411-413).

Due Process Rights

Houlgate (1980, pp. 8-9) indicates that the right to due process is actually a mixture of several types of rights. For example, the right to confront opposing witnesses is a liberty, the right to avoid double jeopardy an immunity, and the right to a speedy trial a positive right. However typified, many due process rights have been granted to children.

In *Kent v. United States* (383 U.S. 541 [1966]), the justices of the Court observed that, while there can be no doubt about

> the original laudable purpose of juvenile courts, studies and critiques in recent years raise serious questions as to whether actual performance measures well enough against theoretical purpose to make tolerable the immunity of the process from the reach of constitution-

al guaranties applicable to adults. . . . There is evidence, in fact, that there may be grounds for concern that the child receives the worst of both worlds: that he gets neither the protections accorded to adults nor the solicitous care and regenerative treatment postulated for children. (pp. 555-556)

The *Kent* decision specified the necessary procedures to transfer a child from juvenile to criminal court. Morris A. Kent, Jr. was 16 and on probation when he was charged with several serious offenses, including rape. Kent's mother retained an attorney who filed a motion for a hearing on whether to waive jurisdiction to juvenile court (p. 545). The attorney also filed a motion for access to the juvenile court's probation records.

The juvenile court judge did not rule on the motions. He held no hearing and did not confer with Kent, Kent's mother, or Kent's attorney. The judge simply ordered the case to be transferred to criminal court, entering no reason for the transfer. At criminal trial, Kent was found guilty on several charges and sentenced to a lengthy prison term.

After noting that the potential consequences of transfer to criminal court make the transfer decision an important stage in a juvenile court proceeding, the Supreme Court asserted that "there is no place in our system of law for reaching a result of such tremendous consequences without ceremony" (p. 554). At the very least, Kent should have been provided a hearing; he was entitled to an attorney at that hearing; his attorney should have been granted access to the records considered by the juvenile court; and the judge should have stated the reasons for his decision.

The case of *In re Gault* (387 U.S. 1 [1967]) further clarified children's due process rights. Gerald Gault was 15 when charged with making a lewd telephone call to a neighbor. After several juvenile court hearings, he was committed to a state industrial school where he could have been held until age 21. If he had been an adult, the maximum punishment would have been a fine of $50 or a jail sentence of two months (p. 29).

Gault had been arrested and held in detention without notifying his parents. No formal notice of the charges was served to him or his parents. The complainant was never called before the juvenile court as a sworn witness. There was no transcript or recording of the juvenile court proceedings, and Gault was not represented by counsel. He allegedly confessed to making the lewd telephone call, but his confession was never "reduced to writing"; and it was obtained "out of the presence of Gerald's parents, without counsel and without advising him of his right to silence" (p. 56).

Delivering the opinion of the Court, Mr. Justice Fortas wrote:

> Under our constitution, the condition of being a boy does not justify
> a kangaroo court. The traditional ideas of Juvenile Court procedure
> . . . contemplated that time would be available and care would be used
> to establish precisely what the juvenile did and why he did it. . . .
> Under traditional notions, one would assume that in a case like that
> of Gerald Gault, . . . the Juvenile Judge would have made a careful
> inquiry and judgment as to the possibility that the boy could be
> disciplined and dealt with at home. . . . The essential difference
> between Gerald's case and a normal criminal case is that safeguards
> available to adults were discarded in Gerald's case. The summary
> procedure as well as the long commitment was possible because
> Gerald was 15 years of age instead of over 18. (pp. 28-29)

The *Gault* decision represented a marked departure from the reasoning
used in the (Pennsylvania Supreme Court's) 1838 *Crouse* case by limiting
a state's *parens patriae* power. Mr. Justice Fortas declared that although a
juvenile court hearing involving the possibility of institutionalization need
not have all the protections of a criminal trial, it does require "the essentials of due process and fair treatment" (30–quoting from *Kent,* p. 562).
Those "essentials" are notice of charges, right to counsel, the right to
confront and cross-examine witnesses, and the right against self-incrimi-
nation.

The Court reaffirmed those same principles in the *In re Winship* case
(397 U.S. 358 [1970]). It also added to the list of "essentials of due
process and fair treatment" a requirement that for an "act which would
constitute a crime if committed by an adult" (p. 359), guilt be established
by proof beyond a reasonable doubt rather than by the less stringent
standard of a preponderance of evidence (the standard used in civil
courts). Proof beyond a reasonable doubt had long been required in criminal court, and "the same considerations that demand extreme caution in
factfinding to protect the innocent adult apply as well to the innocent
child" (p. 365).

Contrary to the direction the Court seemed to be moving in granting
children the same due process rights as adults, it held in *McKeiver v.
Pennsylvania* (403 U.S. 528 [1971]) that the right to a trial by jury does
not extend to adjudication hearings in juvenile courts. States were not
prohibited from authorizing jury trials for children, but that "is the state's
privilege and not its obligation" (p. 547).

More consistent with the direction of prior cases, the Court held in
Breed v. Jones (421 U.S. 519 [1975]) that a juvenile court could not

adjudicate a child for an offense and then transfer the case to adult criminal court for the same offense because that would constitute double jeopardy.

In 1984 in *Schall v. Martin* (467 U.S. 253 [1984]), the Court upheld the constitutionality of the New York Family Act that authorized "pretrial detention of an accused juvenile delinquent based on a finding that there is a 'serious risk' that the child 'may before the return date commit an [criminal] act'" (p. 255). The Court (1) rejected a contention that pretrial detention is a form of punishment (p. 271) and (2) eschewed any liberty right that children might possess, since "juveniles, unlike adults, are always in some form of custody" (p. 265). Seemingly returning to the logic in the *Crouse* decision, Mr. Justice Rehnquist indicated that "children, by definition, are not assumed to have the capacity to take care of themselves. They are assumed to be subject to the control of their parents, and if parental control falters, the State must play its part as *parens patriae*" (p. 265).

TORT, CONTRACT, AND PROPERTY LAW

Like due process, several types of children's rights are combined in tort, contract, and property law. For example, children have the power right to make certain contracts. However, most children's contracts are voidable; that is, a child has an immunity from most contracts and a liberty or power right in many situations to void a contract if he or she chooses (Houlgate, 1980, p. 27). Also, like due process as well as other rights previously delineated, children have some of the same rights as adults when it comes to torts, contracts, and property; but they do not have equal rights with adults. As in other areas of law, there are difficulties in granting children both protective and liberating rights for torts, contracts, and property; and there is no single principle for designating those rights.

Torts

Children ordinarily can be held liable for their torts where they have injured others or damaged property (Keeton, Dobbs, Keeton, & Owen, 1984, p. 179). However, there are exceptions in that children have certain immunities. For example, "when children are sued on intentional tort grounds such as battery, slander, trespass, or deceit, they may be deemed too young to have formed the necessary intent" (Horowitz & Hunter, 1984, p. 81). Children also may have an immunity from negligence because they cannot understand the risks of which an adult should be aware. Whereas the negligence of an adult is measured against a *reasonable person* standard, or an assessment of whether he or she exercised the care expected of a "person of ordinary prudence" (Keeton et al., 1984, p. 174), the negligence of a child is judged by a more subjective standard, which recognizes that there is enormous *variation* among children in maturity and experience (Keeton et al., 1984, p. 179). Hence, the standard for children is individualized; a child's negligence is assessed against what reasonably can be expected of a child of similar "age, intelligence, and experience" (Keeton et al., 1984, p. 179). An exception is when a child engages in an adult activity, such as operating an automobile, airplane, or boat. In those situations, the child can be held to the reasonable person (adult) standard (Davis & Schwartz, 1987, p. 27; Horowitz & Hunter, 1984, p. 83; Keeton et al., 1984, p. 181).

At common law, parent and child were not barred from suing each other. However, in 1891 in *Hewellette v. George* (68 Miss. 703, 9 So. 885 [1891]), the Mississippi Supreme Court announced the parent/child immunity doctrine "refusing to allow actions between parent and minor child for personal torts, whether . . . intentional or negligent" (Keeton et al., 1984, p. 904). The principal argument for the immunity doctrine has been that it promotes family harmony. However, it is doubtful that uncompensated torts achieve that end (Keeton et al., 1984, p. 905). For example, the immunity doctrine was used to disallow a suit by a fifteen-year-old victim of incestuous rape (*Roller v. Roller* (37 Wash. 242, 79 P. 788 [1905]), summarized in Horowitz and Hunter, 1984, p. 84, and in Noel and Phillips, 1980, p. 165). Probably in response to such cases, over half of the states now have revoked the immunity doctrine, either by court decisions or by legislation (Keeton et al., 1984, p. 907). However, a major exception remains–suits for inadequate parenting still are barred by immunity (Davis & Schwartz, 1987, pp. 27-28).

Sometimes parents are held responsible for the torts of their children. Although children may be liable for their own torts, they are not "financially responsible" and, thus, are usually judgment proof (Keeton et al., 1984, p. 913). Unless the parents can be held vicariously accountable, the injured party will be uncompensated; and, consequently, virtually all states have enacted parental responsibility, or parental liability, laws (Geis & Binder, 1991, p. 310; Horowitz & Hunter, 1984, p. 101; Keeton et al., 1984, p. 913). Those laws vary considerably, but most "are limited to wilful or wanton torts of the child" (Keeton et al., 1984, p. 913). Moreover, most states place limits on the maximum amount recoverable, ranging from $250 in Vermont to $15,000 in Texas, with the average being about $2,500 (Geis & Binder, 1991, p. 311).

Apart from parental responsibility laws, a parent may be held responsible for a child's torts if the parent is "independently negligent in failing to supervise the child properly" (Davis & Schwartz, 1987, p. 27). For example, a parent may be liable if he/she has directed or encouraged the child's tortious behavior. Or the parent may be liable if the child's tort occurred while conducting business for the parent. Or the parents may be liable if they entrust a dangerous weapon, such as a gun, to their child and injury results from the child's misuse of it (Keeton et al., 1984, pp. 914-915).

Contracts

Unlike torts, children usually are not liable for their contracts. Reflecting the view that children need protection, their contracts typically are voidable by the doctrine of disaffirmance, or avoidance (Davis & Schwartz, 1987, p. 28; Murray, 1983, p. 245). To illustrate, suppose a child and an adult enter into a contract, with the child agreeing to buy and the adult agreeing to sell an automobile. The child makes a down payment and agrees to pay the balance over time. But after a few months, the child returns the automobile and demands that the seller return all of the money previously paid. In such a situation, "the law is of the view that the minor has the absolute power to disaffirm his contract; therefore, he is entitled to return of his money and release from any further obligation" (Davis & Schwartz, 1987, p. 28). Disaffirmance is "one-way"–the adult cannot void the contract if the child wishes to enforce it (Horowitz & Hunter, 1984, p. 103).

For adults who contract with children in good faith and who fulfill their contractual obligations, disaffirmance creates unfair hardships. Consequently, certain exceptions to the disaffirmance doctrine have been recognized. One such exception (a denial of immunity) is that children cannot disaffirm contracts for "necessaries" (e.g., food, clothing, shelter, and medical care). Murray (1983, p. 245) indicates that the child is "liable for the *reasonable value* of such necessaries in quasi contract, i.e. restitution." Educational opportunities may also be considered "necessaries," although "the exact ingredients of this as with all other necessities remain a question of fact" (Horowitz & Hunter, 1984, p. 103).

Another limitation on a child's right to disaffirm contracts is that most states have legislated that minors above age 18 have the same contractual obligations as adults (Davis & Schwartz, 1987, p. 29; Horowitz & Hunter, 1984, p. 104). Moreover, many states limit children's disaffirmance rights if they are professional athletes or entertainers. For example, in *Shields v. Gross* (58 N.Y. 2d 338, 448 N.E. 2d 108, 461 N.Y.S. 2d 254 [1983]), Brooke Shields attempted to prevent publication of nude photographs of her, taken when she was a ten-year-old model. "Section 51 of New York's Civil Rights Law creates a civil cause of action for use of a living person's name, portrait, or picture for advertising purposes, or if the person is a child, his or her parent or guardian" (Davis & Schwartz, 1987, pp. 31-32). Shields sued the photographer to disaffirm the consent given by her mother. However, the New York Court of Appeals ruled against her. Conceding that common law grants children a disaffirmance right, the court held that in this instance the New York legislature had revoked that right by permitting parental consent on the child's behalf. So Shields was bound by the contract (Davis & Schwartz, 1987, p. 30).

Still other limitations on disaffirmance pertain to the consequences of such actions. If a child "disaffirms the contract but still possesses the goods, he has an obligation to return them" (Murray, 1983, p. 246). But what if the goods are damaged, destroyed, or lost? The child need only return the goods in his or her possession, whatever their condition. Because lost goods cannot be returned, a child has no further contractual obligation and may even seek to recover what has been paid previously (Davis & Schwartz, 1987, p. 30). Because of the possible hardships to an adult who enters into a contract with a child, some courts have limited a child's "recovery of prior payments by permitting the defendant to offset either the depreciation of the goods or the value of their use" (Murray, 1983, p. 246). Other courts have adopted the *benefit* (or New Hampshire) rule, allowing children to disaffirm contracts, but requiring restitution for any benefit received from the goods, whether the goods are necessaries or non-necessaries (Horowitz & Hunter, 1984, p. 106; Murray, 1983, p. 246).

Property

All Americans, including children, "have the legal right to acquire and hold property" (Altschuler & Sgroi, 1992, p. 147), and this holds for both real property (real estate) and personal property (all property other than real estate, including stocks and bonds). Nonetheless, children are considered incapable of managing their property (Horowitz, Bullock, & Hunter, 1984, p. 47). Guardians of property traditionally have been appointed to serve this function, although "increasingly management of the property of minors is being accomplished through the use of trusts and gifts given under the Uniform Gifts to Minor Act" (Horowitz et al., 1984, p. 47). The only exception is money; children are considered to be capable of managing any money they legally possess. For example, they have the liberty/ power right to deposit money in a bank; and they may reclaim it at any time, subject to the rules that apply to adults (Horowitz et al., 1984, p. 49).

Children can inherit property from others, but there are age restrictions for testamentary disposition of it (Davis & Schwartz, 1987, p. 34). At common law, a male had to be at least 14 and a female 12 to legally dispose of personal property by a will. Disposition of real property by a will was allowed only at age 21 or older. In virtually all states today, the age requirement is the same for testamentary disposition of both real and personal property. Moreover, all but three states specify that anyone 18 or older can make a valid will (Davis & Schwartz, 1987, p. 34).

CONCLUSIONS

The law in the U.S. does not take a unitary stance toward children's rights. In some areas the law is paternalistic, granting children positive and negative rights and immunities, or protective rights. In other areas, children are granted liberties and power rights, or liberating rights. For example, the law is generally protective of children in the area of contracts, tending to grant them immunity from their contractual obligations; but children have been accorded a liberty right with regard to abortion. According to Davis and Schwartz (1987, p. 201), the designation of children's rights in the U.S. reflects "an inherent conflict . . . –a kind of schizophrenia–between the desire to accord children a greater degree of control over their lives and freedom of choice and the need . . . to protect them."

Children in the U.S. have more protective rights than do adults, but fewer liberating rights. To be sure, several Supreme Court decisions since the mid-1960s have extended children's liberating rights regarding free expression in school, abortion, and due process. However, even in those areas, children have fewer rights than adults.

An important question that largely has been ignored in discussions of children's rights is: what are the consequences of granting children different types of rights? Both those who believe that children require more protective rights and those who believe that children should be granted more liberating rights need to demonstrate the actual benefits. For example, it needs to be shown how much protective rights enhance the physical, social, and psychological well-being of children and their families. Similarly, it needs to be shown that liberating rights for children produce more responsible citizens and ultimately a better state.

CASES

Bellotti v. Baird, 443 U.S. 622 (1979)
Breed v. Jones, 421 U.S. 519 (1975)
Ex parte Crouse, 4 Whart (Pa.) 9 (1838)
Goss v. Lopez, 419 U.S. 565 (1975)
Hazelwood School District v. Kuhlmeier, 484 U.S. 260 (1988)
Hewellette v. George, 68 Miss. 703, 9 So. 885 (1891)

H.L. v. Matheson, 450 U.S. 398 (1981)
In re Gault, 387 U.S. 1 (1967)
In re Winship, 397 U.S. 358 (1970)
Kent v. United States, 383 U.S. 541 (1966)
McKeiver v. Pennsylvania, 403 U.S. 528 (1971)
Pierce v. Society of Sisters, 268 U.S. 510 (1925)
Planned Parenthood of Central Missouri v. Danforth, 428 U.S. 52 (1976)
Prince v. Massachusetts, 321 U.S. 158 (1944)
Roller v. Roller, 37 Wash. 242, 79 P. 788 (1905)
Schall v. Martin, 467 U.S. 253 (1984)
Shields v. Gross, 58 N.Y. 2d 338, 448 N.E. 2d 108, 461 N.Y.S. 2d 254 (1983)
Thompson v. Oklahoma, 487 U.S. 815 (1988)
Tinker v. Des Moines Independent Community School District, 393 U.S. 503 (1969)
Wisconsin v. Yoder, 406 U.S. 205 (1972)

REFERENCES

Altschuler, B.E. & Sgroi, C.A. (1992). *Understanding Law in a Changing Society.* Englewood Cliffs, NJ: Prentice Hall.
Blackstone, W. (1769/1979). *Commentaries on the Laws of England.* Four volumes. Chicago: The University of Chicago Press.
Bremner, R.H. (1970). *Children and Youth in America: A Documentary History.* Three volumes. Cambridge, MA: Harvard University Press.
Burt, R.A. (1976). Developing constitutional rights of, in, and for children. In M.K. Rosenheim (Ed.), *Pursuing Justice for the Child* (225-245), Chicago: The University of Chicago Press.
Cohen, H. (1980). *Equal Rights for Children.* Totowa, NJ: Rowman & Littlefield.
Davis, S.M. & Schwartz, M.D. (1987). *Children's Rights and the Law.* Lexington, MA: Lexington Books.
Dodson, G.D. (1984). Legal rights of adolescents: Restrictions on liberty, emancipation, and status offenses. In R.M. Horowitz & H.M. Davidson (Eds.), *Legal Rights of Children* (114-176), New York: McGraw-Hill.
Farson, R. (1974). *Birthrights.* New York: Macmillan.
Geis, G. & Binder, A. (1991). Sins of their children: Parental responsibility for juvenile delinquency. *Notre Dame Journal of Law, Ethics & Public Policy, 5,* 303-322.
Hohfeld, W.N. (1919). *Fundamental Legal Conceptions.* New Haven, CT: Yale University Press.
Holt, J. (1974). *Escape from Childhood.* New York: Dutton.
Horowitz, R.M. (1984). Children's rights: A look backward and a glance ahead. In R.M. Horowitz & H.M. Davidson (Eds.), *Legal Rights of Children* (1-9), New York: McGraw-Hill.

Horowitz, R.M. & Hunter, B.G. (1984). The child litigant. In R.M. Horowitz & H.M. Davidson (Eds.), *Legal Rights of Children* (72-113), New York: McGraw-Hill.

Horowitz, R.M., Bullock, A.G. & Hunter, B.G. (1984). Economic interests of children. In R.M. Horowitz & H.M. Davidson (Eds.), *Legal Rights of Children* (10-71), New York: McGraw-Hill.

Houlgate, L.D. (1980). *The Child & the State: A Normative Theory of Juvenile Rights*. Baltimore: The Johns Hopkins University Press.

Keeton, W.P., Dobbs, D.B., Keeton, R.E. & Owen, D.G. (1984). *Prosser and Keeton on the Law of Torts, 5th Edition*. St. Paul, MN: West.

Murray, J.E. (1983). *Cases and Materials on Contracts, 3rd Edition*. Charlottesville, VA: The Michie Company.

Noel, D.W. & Phillips, J.J. (1980). *Cases and Materials on Torts and Related Law*. Indianapolis: Bobbs-Merrill.

Platt, A. (1969). *The Child Savers: The Invention of Delinquency*. Chicago: The University of Chicago Press.

Purdy, L.M. (1992). *In Their Best Interest? The Case against Equal Rights for Children*. Ithaca, NY: Cornell University Press.

Rodham, H. (1973). Children under the law. *Harvard Educational Review, 43*, 487-514.

Rosenbaum, R. (1989). A tangled web for the supreme court. *The New York Times Magazine*, March 12, 60.

Rothman, D.J. (1971). *The Discovery of the Asylum*. Boston: Little, Brown.

Schlossman, S.L. (1977). *Love and the American Delinquent: The Theory and Practice of "Progressive" Juvenile Justice, 1825-1920*. Chicago: The University of Chicago Press.

Sutton, J.R. (1988). *Stubborn Children: Controlling Delinquency in the United States, 1640-1981*. Berkeley, CA: University of California Press.

Wald, M.S. (1979). Children's rights: A framework for analysis. *University of California, Davis, Law Review, 12*, 255-282.

Cohabitation and the Law

Monica A. Seff

SUMMARY. In the eyes of the law, cohabitation is not the legal equivalent of marriage or common-law marriage. This review examines the extent of heterosexual cohabitation in the United States and judicial responses to issues raised by couples who have chosen nonmarital cohabitation. Issues examined include the effect of nonmarital cohabitation on the institution of marriage, contemporary legal considerations in cohabitation, the use of cohabitation contracts, and key legal differences between cohabitation and marriage. Since state laws have not established cohabitation as a legal relationship, the rights of cohabitors have been established through court decisions. Consequently, cohabitors are likely to find themselves in a position of uncertainty with respect to their legal rights. Three legal approaches to cohabitation are discussed and several issues that still need to be addressed by the law are reviewed.

INTRODUCTION

Our society's high regard for the marital relation is demonstrated in a number of legal respects: special rules of inheritance, property ownership, financial support rights, to name just a few, manifest society's concern for the integrity of marriage at the same time as they acknowledge the critical social significance of marriage.

Yet, as many have noted, few recent changes relating to marriage and

---

Monica A. Seff is Assistant Professor, Department of Sociology, University of Texas at Arlington.

[Haworth co-indexing entry note]: "Cohabitation and the Law." Seff, Monica A. Co-published simultaneously in *Marriage & Family Review* (The Haworth Press, Inc.) Vol. 21, No. 3/4, 1995, pp. 141-168; and: *Families and Law* (ed: Lisa J. McIntyre, and Marvin B. Sussman) The Haworth Press, Inc., 1995, pp. 141-168. Multiple copies of this article/chapter may be purchased from The Haworth Document Delivery Center [1-800-3-HAWORTH; 9:00 a.m. - 5:00 p.m. (EST)].

family life have been as dramatic as the increase in the number of unmarried couples cohabiting. Has legal practice and policy kept up with the increase in nonmarital cohabitation? What are the social and legal implications of cohabitation as opposed to marriage? In what respects is living together the equivalent of marriage? To understand the contemporary positions of the law with respect to cohabiting couples, a brief survey of the history of marriage law is useful; especially, it is important to distinguish between three types of relationships: formal marriage, common law marriage and cohabitation.

As noted elsewhere in this volume (McIntyre 1995), the beginnings of American family law can be traced back to the laws of England. When the first English colonists arrived on these shores they brought with them a legal tradition that allowed for two principal forms of marriage: formal marriage (that is, ceremonial marriage created according to ecclesiastical or church doctrines) and informal marriage–also known as common law marriage. Common law marriage required no ceremony; a marriage could be effected by a man and woman declaring an intention to marry one another in words of the present tense (*sponsalia per verba de praesenti*).

Although Lord Harwick's Marriage Act of 1753 ended the legality of common law marriage in England (Freeman and Lyon 1983, p. 8; Lucas 1990), many new world jurisdictions retained the option. One underlying theory of the common law tradition is that principles of law are determined by the community's social needs and are adapted to new conditions as society changes (Abraham 1986; Lucas 1990; Murphy and Pritchett 1986; Parker 1990; Parry 1981). Common law marriages were necessary in many parts of the new country. Communities were isolated, and travel was made difficult by poor road conditions (Duff and Truitt 1991; Glendon 1989; Parker 1990). Especially on the frontier, many couples had only limited access to public officials who could formalize and record marriages. The need for such officials was lessened by the availability of common law marriage for this conferred the same legal status, obligations and rights on the parties as formal marriages.

In the nineteenth and twentieth century, state governments began to enact more laws regulating marriage and the family. Because of the possibility of fraudulent claims to property and inheritance, the states needed proof of the parties' marital status. This led many states to change their views on the legality of common law marriage which was viewed as undermining the stability and sanctity of the marriage institution. Ultimately, most states took the position that only state-sanctioned ceremonial marriages should be promoted and protected by the laws. Presently, in the United States, common law marriages are allowed only in the District of

Columbia and thirteen states (Alabama, Colorado, Georgia, Idaho, Iowa, Kansas, Montana, Ohio, Oklahoma, Pennsylvania, Rhode Island, South Carolina and Texas) (Duff and Truitt 1991).[1] Such marriages are created at the moment when a man and woman agree to marry and then begin to hold themselves out to the community as husband and wife. In all respects, in the jurisdictions which recognize these unions, common law marriages are the legal equivalents of formal ceremonial marriages and a divorce is required to legally terminate the relationship (Duff and Truitt 1991, p. 48).

As opposed to common law marriage, cohabitation generally refers to living together in a sexual relationship when not legally married (either formally or according to common law tradition). It must be stressed that "cohabitation" is different from common law marriage. Indeed, some jurisdictions (e.g., Idaho) that recognize the validity of common law marriage have enacted statutes prohibiting cohabitation.[2]

The remainder of this review will focus on heterosexual cohabitation and will examine judicial responses to issues raised by couples who have chosen to cohabit. The review begins with an analysis of the sociological data on the growing incidence of cohabitation among unmarried heterosexual adults and the effect of nonmarital cohabitation on the marriage institution. Next, several precedent-setting cases that illustrate the relationship between the law and cohabiting couples, both during an ongoing relationship and at the point of dissolution, are examined. The review ends with a discussion of the use of nonmarital contracts and legal differences between marriage and cohabitation.

THE EXTENT OF COHABITATION

It is difficult to estimate the extent of nonmarital cohabitation in the United States from surveys because there is no agreed upon definition of cohabitation. Definitions tend to differ in terms of whether the focus is on (1) common living facilities; (2) economic functions; (3) sexual relations; and/or (4) childbearing and rearing (Freeman and Lyon 1983). Distinctions can also be drawn between short-term and long-term cohabitation, between a casual affair and a stable relationship (Parry 1981, p. 3), and between cohabitation that is a precursor to marriage or an alternative to being single (Rindfuss and VandenHeuvel 1990). Some researchers define cohabitation simply as a nonmarital living-together relationship with a member of the opposite sex. Other researchers include a time element; for example, sharing a residence and/or a bedroom with someone of the opposite sex to whom one is not married for several consecutive months (e.g., Macklin 1972; Tanfer 1987). In much of the recent literature, the researchers have left it up to the respondents themselves to decide what constitutes cohabitation, and whether their relationship can be classified as such. For example, the National Survey of Families and Households 1987-1988, which is used in many studies of cohabiting couples, uses the following question: "Nowadays, many unmarried couples live together. Sometimes they eventually get married and sometimes they don't. Did you and your (first) (husband/wife) live together before you were married?" (e.g., Bumpass and Sweet 1989; DeMaris and Rao 1992).

According to Census Bureau data, the number of unmarried adults living together tripled between 1970 and 1980. In 1970 it was estimated that 523,000 unmarried couples–households occupied by two unrelated adults of the opposite sex–lived together (U.S. Census Bureau 1971). By 1980 the number of unmarried cohabiting couples had increased to 1,560,000 (U.S. Census Bureau 1981). In 1990 the number of cohabitors was estimated to be 2.9 million couples (U.S. Census Bureau 1991). This represents an 80 percent increase in the number of cohabiting couples from 1980 to 1990.

One problem with the Census Bureau's data, however, is that we do not know whether these unmarried cohabitors are sexual partners. The data may overstate the extent of cohabitation if a significant number of these couples are platonic roommates.[3] On the other hand, Weitzman (1981) suggests that census data may understate the extent of cohabitation because individuals receiving AFDC, or other government transfer payments, or those concerned about losing child custody may be reluctant to admit that they are cohabiting. Moreover, there may be an underreporting of cohabiting couples among those in short-lived relationships, among those who are concerned about what others may think about their cohabiting (i.e., social desirability bias), as well as among groups that are commonly undercounted in the census including minority group members and illegal aliens. In fact, various sources have concluded that the number of unmarried cohabitors is so understated by the census that the true figure is between three and eight million couples (e.g., Duff and Truitt 1991; Weitzman 1981).

Other survey estimates, however, confirm the conclusions drawn from the census data regarding future trends: cohabitation is on the rise, and it crosses age, marital status, race, class, and parenthood boundaries. In fact, nonmarital cohabitation is rapidly becoming part of the normative culture. Spanier (1983) and Macklin (1983) both attribute the increases in the number and proportion of cohabiting couples to its greater acceptance among the general public. This acceptance is due, in part, to the general increase in sexual experience among unmarried persons (Bumpass 1990,

p. 486; McLaughlin et al. 1988; Modell 1989). Changes in American norms regarding premarital sexuality have been occurring for some time. McLaughlin et al. (1988) and Modell (1989) both suggest that since the 1900s there has been a gradual increase in premarital sexual experience, and that the rate of increase accelerated during the 1960s and 1970s. In fact, cohabitation is viewed by some researchers as a life course experience of the younger generations (e.g., Rindfuss and VandenHeuvel 1990, p. 703; Thornton 1988). Thornton's (1988, p. 501) data suggest that the greatest growth in cohabitation occurred during the middle 1970s. The growth in the popularity of premarital cohabitation between the 1970s and the 1980s is dramatically demonstrated by Gwartney-Gibbs' (1986) finding that over half of all couples applying for a marriage license in Lane County, Oregon in 1980 were cohabiting premaritally, compared to only 13 percent in 1970.

Among Americans aged 19 and older, four percent were currently cohabiting in 1988, 17 percent had cohabited before first marriage, and about 15 percent cohabited at some other time[4] (Bumpass and Sweet 1989, p. 518). Although cohabitation is more frequent among younger people (e.g., under age 35), about six percent of people aged 60 and older have cohabited at some time (Bumpass and Sweet 1989). In fact, the range of benefits of cohabitation among older adults may outweigh the benefits perceived by younger adults. These benefits include greater retirement monies, fewer inheritance complications, and simplified estate planning (Hughston and Hughston 1989, p. 164).

Among people aged 25-29 (the age range within which most Americans marry), 16 percent of the never-married and 28 percent of previously married persons are cohabiting currently (Bumpass and Sweet 1989, p. 618). Moreover, 36 percent of people in this age group cohabited before their first marriage, and more than 40 percent of those still single had cohabited at some point. Cohabitation is even more frequent among people who have been married before. Nearly 70 percent of previously married people under age 35 have cohabited (Bumpass and Sweet 1989, p. 618). And 60 percent of people marrying recently for the second time reported cohabiting, either with their spouse or someone else, before their second marriage (p. 619). This suggests that people who have been married before are opting for cohabitation prior to remarriage. In regard to socioeconomic factors, Bumpass and Sweet (1989) found that cohabitors were less educated than noncohabitors. Tanfer (1987) found that female cohabitors were more likely to be white, to have lower income and educational levels, and were two and a half times more likely to be unwed mothers than women who have never cohabited. About 40 percent of all cohabiting couples have children living with them (Bumpass, Sweet, and Cherlin 1991). Bachrach (1987) reports that among never-married women who cohabit, few children result from the relationship.

THE EFFECT OF NONMARITAL COHABITATION ON MARRIAGE

The increase in nonmarital cohabitation may explain some recent demographic trends with respect to marriage including the leveling off of the divorce rate, the increase in the average age of first marriage, and the decline in the U.S. marriage rate (Bachrach 1987; Bumpass 1990; Bumpass, Sweet, and Cherlin 1991; Tanfer 1987; Thornton 1988). In regard to the stabilization of the divorce rate, nonmarital unions that break up before couples marry are not included in the divorce statistics (Castro Martin and Bumpass 1989). Tanfer (1987) reports, however, that most cohabitors view marriage as desirable. Similarly, Wiersma (1983), in her cross-national study, states that compared to cohabiting couples in the Netherlands, Americans who cohabit are not repudiating marriage, but are trying to prevent the possibility of divorce. It is not surprising, then, that the proportion of persons who lived with a partner before their first marriage has quadrupled from 11 percent for marriages occurring during the period 1965-1974 to 44 percent for marriages occurring during the period 1980-1984 (Bumpass and Sweet 1989, p. 619), thus, resulting in an increase in the average age of first marriage.

The rising prevalence of cohabitation offsets declines in the U.S. marriage rate. Bumpass and Sweet (1989, p. 619) report that 82 percent of women born during the years 1940-1944 were married before age 25. Only 61 percent of women born in the early 1960s were married at that age. While the marriage rate decreased for women under the age of 25, the cohabitation rate increased. Only 3 percent of women born in the early 1940s were cohabiting before age 25, compared with 37 percent of women born in the years 1960-1964.

Contrary to popular belief, couples who cohabit before they marry are more likely to divorce. Margaret Mead (1966) and others (e.g., Rapoport 1965) had argued that cohabitation should lead to better and stronger marriages because it affords couples the opportunity to become better acquainted and to try out conjugal roles. Such opportunities, however, may not lead to more stable marriages. Bumpass and Sweet (1989, p. 620) found that 57 percent of first marriages that start with cohabitation end in divorce within ten years, compared with 30 percent of those where the partners did not live together before the marriage. Teachman and Polonko

(1990) also found that premarital cohabitation increases the risk of divorce. They suggest that the higher divorce rate is due to the cohabitors having spent more time living together compared to the noncohabitors.[5] Bennett et al. (1989), surveying 5,000 women in Sweden (Sweden's social trends tend to foreshadow American trends by about 15 years), found that people who cohabit premaritally are less committed to the institution of marriage, and are more inclined to divorce than couples that do not live together before marriage.

Booth and Johnson (1988), in a national survey, also found higher levels of divorce among those who cohabited before marriage compared to couples who did not. Booth and Johnson suggest that divorce rates may be high for couples who cohabited before marriage because of non-traditional attitudes including a disregard for traditional marriage norms. Similarly, other researchers also report that cohabitors compared with noncohabitors hold less traditional sex roles, are less likely to desire children, and are more likely to value personal freedom (Bachrach 1987; Clayton and Voss 1977; Denmark, Shaw, and Ciali 1985; Newcomb and Bentler 1980; Tanfer 1987; Thomson and Colella 1992). Booth and Johnson report that cohabitation itself may negatively influence subsequent marriage. Even among couples who remain married, those who cohabited report "lower levels of marital interaction, higher levels of marital disagreement and marital instability" (Booth and Johnson 1988, p. 261). Watson (1983; Watson and DeMeo 1987) found poorer marital adjustment during the first year of marriage among couples who cohabited than among couples who did not cohabit. Likewise, DeMaris and Leslie (1984) report that among recently married couples, those who had cohabited reported lower marital satisfaction for both spouses compared with couples who had not cohabited. In sum, these findings do not support the popular belief that cohabiting before marriage leads to a more stable and satisfying marriage.[6]

Nonmarital cohabitation generally does not last for long; couples either break up or they marry. Bumpass and Sweet (1989, p. 620) found that only 59 percent of cohabiting couples continue to live together without marrying after one year; 33 percent remain after two years, and only 9 percent last for five or more years. If marriage is going to occur, the couple generally marries quickly: 25 percent of first-time cohabitors marry within the first year, and half marry within three years. But Bumpass and Sweet (1989) report that almost 30 percent break up within the first two years of marriage.

CONTEMPORARY LEGAL CONSIDERATIONS
IN COHABITATION

The longer a cohabiting relationship lasts, the greater the chance that legal problems will arise. The legal problems for cohabiting couples generally start not when they move in together, but when the relationship is terminated. There are legal implications when one of the partners believes an agreement exists, even an oral or implicit agreement, that gives each partner rights to the other's property as well as to property they acquire together. The law does not get involved when couples who are terminating a relationship agree on how to divide their assets and liabilities. But when unmarried cohabitors disagree, one or the other partner may invoke the courts to resolve the dispute. The division of property, combined with the protection of individuals' rights and obligations, means that the court system may become involved to bring justice and fairness to the dissolution of a non-marital relationship. This section describes some of the legal considerations involved in nonmarital cohabitation.

Macklin (1983) points out in her classification of cohabitation relationships that a primary motive underlying the popularity of cohabitation is the belief that there will be no strings attached if a couple merely lives together instead of marrying. In fact, cohabitation is often viewed as courtship in the 1980s and 1990s (e.g., Macklin 1987; McLaughlin et al. 1988; Modell 1989). Schnaiberg and Goldenberg (1989, p. 260) observe: "One of the great appeals of cohabitation to young adults in recent years is that it has, superficially, all the benefits of marriage without the apparent costs of divorce." Still, most individuals who cohabit want to marry and to marry successfully. Wiersma (1983, p. 89), contrasting the U.S. with the Netherlands, finds that U.S. couples who cohabit regard marriage as solidifying their love. Additionally, for many individuals, cohabitation is thought to establish more egalitarian domestic relationships[7] free from the jurisdiction of marriage law (Denmark, Shaw, and Ciali 1985; Kingdom 1990; Smart 1984, p. xii; Weitzman 1981). Whereas marriage implies non-egalitarian conjugal relations,[8] commitment, and legal obligations, nonmarital cohabitation, it is thought, allows the freedom to leave the partner when it is determined that the relationship is no longer satisfying without the problems of a legal divorce. But is this view reflected in legal practice and policy? Moreover, in the spirit of common-law principles, has the law changed to adapt to the prevalence of nonmarital cohabitation?

State laws have not adapted to the recent increases in nonmarital cohabitation even though, as Spanier (1983) and Macklin (1983) point out, cohabitation is now part of the normative culture. Moreover, there is little consistency from state to state regarding the rights and duties of couples who cohabit. While much is said about the lack of coherence–state to state–in family law, the situation is much more confusing with respect to cohabitors. There is as yet no body of legislation, state or federal, that deals systematically with cohabitation. The one point of consistence is that no state recognizes cohabitation as a legal relationship creating the same rights and privileges as does marriage (Jorgensen 1986). In fact, the California State Supreme Court has ruled that to grant unmarried cohabitors the same rights as married persons would seriously damage the state's support for the institution of marriage (*Marvin v. Marvin,* 18 Cal. 3d 660, 134 Cal. Rptr. 815, 557 P.2d 106 [1976]). One of the premises of marriage in all states is that the marriage contract assures both partners certain rights to property acquired during the marriage. If a divorce occurs, the distribution of property acquired during the marriage is decided upon by a divorce court judge in compliance with the statutes of the state.[9] In contrast, since no state statutes have been enacted to establish cohabitation as a legal relationship, rights, privileges, and/or obligations concerning the couples' property have been established through court decisions. Change occurs state by state; thus, change occurs slowly and in piecemeal fashion. Consequently, couples who cohabit rather than marry are likely to find themselves in a position of uncertainty with respect to their legal rights (Kingdom 1990, p. 288; Myricks 1980; Weitzman 1981). This, however, does not mean that cohabitation is a "no strings attached" relationship. It suggests that there is much ambiguity and the lack of guidelines leaves unmarried cohabitors in a position of legal insecurity. A review of several precedent-setting cases will illustrate the effect of cohabitation on the legal system with respect to property.

Prior to the mid 1970s, where the law did not prohibit cohabitation, it took one of two approaches to these types of relationships. The traditional approach was for the courts to deny any rights at all to "meretricious" couples (Wagner 1988; Weitzman 1981). This means that agreements between nonmarital cohabiting partners were held not binding to the extent that they were based on meretricious sexual services (i.e., prostitution), which are illegal or contrary to public policy. Additionally, because cohabitation, until recently, was illegal in many states, there was little judicial recognition of economic claims by one cohabitor against another after the dissolution of a relationship. Courts have denied claims on the ground that parties to an illegal relationship do not have rights based on that relationship (Wagner 1988).

The denial of economic claims based on an illegal relationship is illustrated in *Hewitt v. Hewitt* (77 Ill. 2d 49, 394 N.E.2d 1204 [1979]). In *Hewitt* a woman sought half of the property accumulated over a fifteen-year period (1960-1975) of cohabitation. The woman alleged that the man had promised to share his life and his property with her, that she assisted him with domestic services and as a mother to their three children, helped him in his career as a dentist, as well as financially assisting him while he was in dental school. The Illinois Supreme Court reasoned that the plaintiff's claim contravened the public policy of encouraging marriage (Wagner 1988). The Supreme Court of Illinois said:

> ... of substantial greater importance than the rights of the immediate parties is the impact of such recognition upon our society and the institution of marriage. Recognition of mutual property rights between unmarried cohabitants would ... violate the policy of our recently enacted Illinois Marriage and Dissolution of Marriage Act ... the act gives the state a strong continuing interest in the institution of marriage and prevents the marriage relation from becoming in effect a private contract terminable at will. This seems to us another indication that public policy disfavors private contractual alternatives to marriage. (*Hewitt v. Hewitt* 1979)

In effect the *Hewitt* court expressed concern that recognizing property rights for unmarried cohabitors would resurrect common-law marriage, which would violate state policy. Furthermore, the court held that the desirability of common-law marriage was a question for the state legislature and not the court system.

McCall v. Frampton (90 Misc. 2d 159, 415 N.Y.S.2d 752 [1979]) was another case that illustrates the denial of economic claims because the claims were based on an illegal relationship. In *McCall v. Frampton* the New York State Supreme Court refused to enforce an oral contract because the court believed the contract was contrary to the common good of society (Myricks 1980). A famous rock star, Peter Frampton, was sued by his former cohabiting partner, Penny McCall, who was seeking one half of his earnings between 1973-1978, one-half interest in a 53-acre estate in Westchester, and a share of his future earnings. McCall alleged that Frampton asked her to quit her job and to leave her husband, Frampton's business manager. McCall further claimed that Frampton promised to live with her and to provide financial support. McCall indicated that she left "her husband in reliance on such representations and began to live with Frampton, and used for their benefit all her resources and efforts which left her without funds" (Myricks 1980, p. 213). The New York State Supreme Court ruled that the alleged oral contract was contrary to the public good because in its performance, adultery, which was illegal, had been committed. McCall had left her husband, but did not divorce, to live with Frampton. The court ruled that such a contract would be a renouncement of McCall's existing marriage and, therefore, was illegal (Myricks 1980). In effect, the court was trying to discourage implied contracts that it considered contrary to the common good of society, and the performance of this contract resulted in the commission of adultery which is against the common good.

In some cases, courts resolved the obvious inequities that resulted from refusing to recognize cohabiting couples by treating this sort of relationship as if it *were* a marriage, or something akin to marriage. Several scholars have construed this judicial approach to cohabitation to mean that the differences between cohabitation and legal marriage are diminishing. Glendon (1989) argues, for example, that recent changes in the law in the U.S. and Europe reflect a "withering away" of traditional marriage. She argues that governments are gradually withdrawing from their regulation of the institution of marriage. As a result, cohabitation has emerged as a new legal institution that imitates marriage.

Perhaps more important than the "withering away" of traditional marriage is the absence of legal clarity with respect to cohabitation. Cohabitors could be treated as married by default rather than design and their legal obligations constructed by analogy with those of married persons simply because there are no laws regulating nonmarital cohabitation. An illustrative case is *McCullon v. McCullon* (96 Misc. 2d 962, 410 N.Y.S.2d 226 Sup. Ct. [1978]). In McCullon the New York State Supreme Court heard a case in which a woman, who had lived with a man for 28 years, was suing for alimony and child support for their 18-year-old daughter. Although New York does not recognize common-law marriage, the woman was represented by the man to be his wife through their joint tax returns, bank accounts, and property title for their home. The court held that the woman had made an implied promise to be a homemaker and to not work because of the man's implied promise to live with her and to financially support her, and thus was entitled to support (Myricks 1980).

Illustrative of a third more contemporary, legal approach to cohabitation is the case of *Marvin v. Marvin* (18 Cal. 3d 660, 134 Cal. Rptr. 815, 557 P.2d 106 [1976]). In 1976, the Supreme Court of California tried to establish the rights of two people who lived together. The court acknowledged that cohabitation is not marriage, but that equitable principles could be applied to prevent hardship and injustice (Duff and Truitt 1991, p. 46). The concept of equitable principles, incorporated in the American legal system, provides for remedies for individuals in unjust situations.

The case was brought by Michelle Triola Marvin, a singer, against the actor Lee Marvin, with whom she had lived for almost seven years in California. During that time Lee Marvin acquired property in his own name worth more than one million dollars. When they broke up, Lee Marvin agreed to pay Michelle $850 a month for the next five years providing she did not discuss any aspects of Lee Marvin's personal life with the press. After eighteen months he refused to make any further payments, and Michelle Triola Marvin sued him for $1 million for breach of contract. The case was taken to the California Supreme Court, which ruled in 1976 that their cohabitation did involve an implicit contract similar to marriage and that Michelle Triola Marvin was entitled to half of the property. Eventually, the case was returned to a lower court for further hearing of the facts. The lower court held that community property law did not apply, and should not be extended by analogy, to nonmarital cohabitors (Glendon 1989, p. 287); however, the court awarded Michelle $104,000 in rehabilitative alimony ($2,000 per week for two years).[10]

Consistent with the concept of equitable principles, which provides remedies for individuals in unjust situations, the court decided that although community property rights, in this case, did not apply, Michelle was entitled to rehabilitative alimony to be used to retrain her to participate in the labor force. The court did not use the term palimony. The news media referred to the financial award as palimony–alimony awarded to a cohabitation partner after the relationship was terminated (Myricks 1980). In effect, the court was adopting a sociological rather than a legal definition of marriage by focusing on the exclusive relationship and joint household economy and de-emphasizing the legal marriage document (Weitzman 1981). The California Supreme Court stated that "the mores of the society have indeed changed so radically in regard to cohabitation that we cannot impose a standard based on alleged moral considerations that have apparently been so widely abandoned by so many." The court's actions signaled recognition and acceptance of new social mores with regard to intimate relationships.

Essentially, the California Supreme Court's decision was that nonmarital cohabitors had the right to have their express agreements, even oral agreements, enforced unless the agreements depended solely on unlawful meretricious relations. The court stated:

> Adults who voluntarily live together and engage in sexual relations are nonetheless as competent as any other persons to contract respecting their earnings and property rights. Of course, they cannot lawfully contract to pay for the performance of sexual services, for such a contract is, in essence, an agreement for prostitution, and is unlawful for that reason. But they can agree to pool their earnings and to hold all property acquired during the relationship in accord with the law governing community property. (*Marvin v. Marvin* 1976)

Are all cohabitors now liable for the same divorce procedures and property claims as married couples? Before drawing definitive conclusions on the implications for cohabitation and marriage, it should be kept in mind that the *Marvin* ruling was based on particular circumstances that limit its application to other cases. The California Supreme Court relied on three legal theories by which it could require a division of assets in the dissolution of a nonmarital relationship: (1) as a result of an express contract between nonmarital partners, as long as the contract is not explicitly founded on the consideration of meretricious sexual services; (2) through an implied contract, an agreement of partnership or joint venture, or some other tacit understanding between the parties, entitling a cohabitor to property acquired together; and (3) as a result of the doctrine of quantum meruit which permits courts to use equitable remedies such as constructive trusts when the facts of the case warrant such an action (Liss 1987, p. 789; Stenger 1988, p. 437).[11] Michelle Triola Marvin claimed that Lee Marvin had made an explicit oral contract to support her, in return for giving up her singing career to live with him. She treated this relationship as a marriage, and even legally changed her name from Michelle Triola to Michelle Marvin. Legally binding contracts may be verbal as well as written, although verbal contracts are harder to prove. In this case, the judge believed that a verbal contract existed. In the absence of such contracts or promises, a cohabiting couple does not incur such liabilities.

Although reserving the notion that agreements between nonmarital partners are not binding to the extent that they are based only on meretricious sexual services, the *Marvin* decision recognized the capacity of unmarried couples to contract between themselves, and that the courts had the power to determine a division of the property of cohabitors who decide to terminate their relationship (Duff and Truitt 1991, p. 51). Additionally, because courts may use equitable remedies such as constructive trusts when the facts of a case warrant such action, a cohabitor may be entitled to property acquired together. One problematic aspect of the *Marvin* decision is the court's opinion that the parties' intentions can be determined by the court inquiring into the nature of the relationship. Such searching inquiries can turn cohabitation lawsuits into soap opera-like spectacles involving all the worst aspects of fault divorce including allegations and counter allegations of unjust financial gains, illicit love affairs, one-night stands, and substance abuse. Incidentally, this kind of public mudslinging occurred in the *Marvin* case. Glendon (1989, p. 292) suggests that we've gone around full circle: "Thus, the implied–in fact contract theory, as elaborated in *Marvin,* seems to have revived something very like the old heart-balm actions (alienation of affection, breach of contract to marry) which had been abolished in most states largely because they lent themselves to blackmail and other forms of abuses." Ironically, cohabitation lawsuits, potentially, can be worse than divorces. The public mudslinging of fault divorce, invasion of privacy and court-imposed separations are precisely the aspects of marriage and divorce that cohabitors are often trying to avoid (Glendon 1989; Sonenblick 1981).

In sum, there are three approaches that a court might take with respect to cohabitation lawsuits: (1) to treat the relationship as meretricious; (2) to treat the relationship as a marriage; or (3) to acknowledge the rights of cohabitors. This means that cohabitors are likely to find themselves in a position of uncertainty with respect to their legal rights because there is no assurance that a court will choose one judicial approach over another. However, because of the *Marvin* decision, it cannot be assumed that living together is a "no-strings attached" relationship. The *Marvin* decision essentially permits judges to treat their interpretation of an unmarried couple's behavior with respect to the relationship as an enforceable contract (Sonnenblick 1981, p. 103). Such a contract may not be what the partners had in mind. Consequently, if nonmarried cohabitors want a "no-strings attached" relationship, they need to put this into a written cohabitation contract.

COHABITATION CONTRACTS

Although courts have not consistently conferred all the rights and benefits of marriage to nonmarital cohabitors, the argument in favor of doing so is the same as the argument against (Duff and Truitt 1991; Kingdom 1990; Weitzman 1981). Many argue that in the promotion of marriage and the family by the state, coupled with the concern for social stability, it seems society's best interest might be served by recognizing a stable, marriage-like relationship. Similarly, the desires of cohabitors who do not want to be viewed as married should also be respected. Certainly, past efforts to discourage cohabitation have not led to a decrease in its popularity, nor a return to traditional family structures. Several legal and feminist scholars suggest that until the laws begin to offer more legal protection, cohabiting couples need to make provisions for each other in the event of death or dissolution of their relationship. Cohabitation contracts[12] may be an important step toward the clarification of the legal position of cohabiting couples (Kingdom 1990; Rouse 1990; Weitzman 1981). Cohabitation contracts are agreements between cohabitors which are intended to be legally binding.

In general, the courts treat property accumulated by unmarried cohabitors as the property of the individual who holds the legal title (Weitzman 1981, p. 382). An exception, however, will be made in the event that an unmarried cohabiting couple has an explicit contract that details the disposition of jointly accumulated property. Cohabitation contracts specify what property belongs to each partner, and who will be reimbursed for what should the couple split up. However, it is still uncertain whether the standards of contract law or family law will be used to adjudicate claims associated with cohabitation (Weitzman 1981, p. 411). In more recent years, it appears that nonmarital relationships tend to be governed by contract law, and disputes are adjudicated in civil rather than family court. If contract law is used, then the intent of the parties is at issue. If family law is used, then the parties' current circumstances and needs are the key issues. Cohabitation lawsuits, however, are expensive. Roha (1990, p. 74) states that it may cost upwards of $15,000 to take a cohabitation dispute to court. Cohabitation contracts may help to resolve disputes, or at least make their resolution less costly.

Weitzman (1981) suggests that to clarify rights and obligations the following points need to be addressed in cohabitation agreements: (1) whether either partner has rights to the property and income of the other; (2) which assets each partner owns; (3) whose debts are whose; (4) titles to assets acquired together and; (5) the quid pro quo for the agreement (i.e., to be enforceable, it is necessary that one party give something to the other expecting something in return). Like any contract, a nonmarital cohabitation agreement requires something of value on each side. This can involve the sharing of services, responsibilities, or money. Services may include homemaking. The only things that must not be included are meretricious services, which the courts consider prostitution. The following additional points should also be addressed in cohabitation agreements: how assets will be divided, including a home, if the couple separates; whether assets acquired together are owned individually, as joint tenants with the right of survivorship (property owned as joint tenants with the right of survivorship goes to the surviving joint owner), or tenants in common; arrangements for the emotional and financial care of children from this or other relationships; and circumstances (e.g., death of a partner, or marriage either to each other or to someone else) that would indicate the termination of the cohabitation agreement (Duff and Truitt 1991; Roha 1990; Rouse 1990).

If a couple lives where common-law marriages are recognized and the couple does not want to be considered married, this can also be documented in a cohabitation contract. For example, in Texas where common-law marriage is recognized, a nonmarital cohabitation agreement might state that the couple does not intend to marry either ceremonially or informally in the foreseeable future, and they do not intend their nonmarital relationship to be governed by family law (Rouse 1990, p. 47). (See Appendix A for a sample cohabitation agreement.) On the other hand, couples who consider themselves married under common law do not need a cohabitation agreement because the same marriage laws apply to them as would any other formally married couple.

More than half the states in the U. S. have expressly stated that they will recognize and enforce cohabitation contracts. Only three states have expressly stated that they will not recognize such contracts: Georgia, Illinois, and Louisiana (Duff and Truitt 1991, p. 61). How does a couple know when they need a cohabitation contract? Young couples with few assets do not necessarily need a cohabitation contract (Duff and Truitt 1991; Roha 1990). Cohabitation contracts may be advantageous for individuals who believe their relationship to be long-term; who plan to purchase major assets, including real estate; and when one of the partners makes a major lifestyle change including moving or giving up a job. Additionally, if one of the partners contributes money while the other contributes services such as housekeeping and childcare, a written cohabitation agreement may help to ward off potential disputes (Duff and Truitt 1991; Roha 1990). The primary negative consequence of not having a written cohabitation agreement is that if there is a lawsuit a court may refuse to infer an oral agreement from the actions of the partners because the existence of such agreements is difficult to prove.

KEY LEGAL DIFFERENCES BETWEEN COHABITATION AND MARRIAGE

In an earlier section, we saw how under certain conditions (i.e., if there is an implied contract) cohabitation has received judicial recognition when it comes to property rights. However, there are some key differences between the status of spouse and the status of cohabitor.

Formally legitimatizing a relationship through marriage provides some distinct economic advantages. Of primary importance, cohabitors are denied the conjugal rights of the marital relationship. A spouse's role may be that of wage-earner, homemaker, companion, and lover. When a third party interferes with the ability of one spouse to perform these roles, the other spouse is deprived of the "consortium" of his/her partner. A court action for loss of consortium depends on proof of marriage; as such, cohabitors cannot file an action for loss of consortium (Duff and Truitt 1991; Weitzman 1981). Moreover, marriage confers the right to gain access to the spouse's pension, Social Security benefits, disability benefits, Workman's

Compensation, and some insurance policies, but cohabitation in most cases does not (Duff and Truitt 1991). Married persons may also find it easier to secure mortgages, loans, credit, homes, apartments and may pay lower insurance premiums because they are defined as better risks by the business community. Some companies sell life insurance to one unmarried partner on the life of the other. Most will not (Wojcik 1991). As an alternative, it is suggested that an individual buy a policy on his/her own life and make the partner the beneficiary (Vreeland 1989; Wojcik 1991). Additionally, while common-law marriage partners are considered married by the Internal Revenue Service, unmarried couples cannot file their federal income tax returns as a married couple filing jointly.

Most rental leases do not prohibit an unmarried couple from living together. However, unless there are laws prohibiting discrimination based on marital status, a cohabiting couple may be refused a rental (Duff and Truitt 1991). In some areas, local covenants and homeowners association rules may prohibit cohabitation. In 1974, the United States Supreme Court upheld the constitutionality of such laws (*Belle Terre v. Boraas,* 416 U.S. 1).

While historically common-law marriage has had legal validity for the purposes of property and inheritance settlements, this is not necessarily the case for cohabitation (Thayer 1982). If a person should die intestate (without a will), state laws will recognize family members rather than cohabiting partners as the legally binding recipient of a deceased person's property and possessions. However, assuming the person is of sound mind, she/he may execute a legally valid will that bequeaths her/his possessions to the cohabiting partner. Similarly, with proof of parentage, children born during the relationship would have inheritance rights. Homeowners' and renters' insurance are offered at the same rates as married couples. Similarly, some auto insurance companies will sell one auto policy to cohabiting couples if the car is owned jointly.

Health insurance through an employer rarely covers unmarried partners. A few cities such as Seattle, Berkeley, Santa Cruz, and West Hollywood have passed local legislation that allows unmarried partners to register as "domestic partners," but these cities are the exception. Such registration, however, does not impart the same conjugal rights as marriage; consequently, domestic partner registration may simply be symbolic.

Some city employees can include domestic or live-in partners as "family" for health insurance purposes and can use their sick leave to care for their partners (Fritz 1989; Gilbert 1991a; 1991b; Taravella 1986). One of the problems live-in or domestic partnerships pose for municipalities and employers is that there are few standards concerning who qualifies as a domestic partner. This, in fact, is the same problem discussed earlier with respect to the issue of how best to define cohabitation. How long does a couple have to live together before they exhibit adequate commitment to be domestic partners? Is sharing finances a sufficient criterion? To date, different companies and communities have answered this question differently, leading to differences in eligibility standards. For example, in Washington, D.C., the city's new family-leave law defines "family" as anyone with whom an employee is sharing a residence and has a committed relationship. However as Macklin notes (1983) there are varying degrees of commitment among cohabitors. Eventually, the law will have to address these differences in commitment.

In regard to child custody, Bumpass, Sweet, and Cherlin (1991) report that 40 percent of cohabiting couples have children living with them. Many of these children are from previous relationships (Bachrach 1987). Can cohabitation affect child custody decisions? In general, court decisions regarding child custody are determined by the best interests of the child. The child's age, sex, physical and emotional health and the child's preference, are all taken into consideration. The court is also concerned with the physical and emotional environment of the custodial parent's home. Consequently, courts have addressed whether living with a parent who is cohabiting is in the best interest of the child. In *Foss v. Leifer* (1976, p. 1309), the Montana Court ruled that a lower trial court, which transferred child custody from the mother to the father because the mother was cohabiting, had erred. The Montana court held that the trial court was not able to show that the mother's cohabiting with her partner negatively affected either the physical or the emotional health of the child. This suggests, however, that if there was evidence of detrimental effects, and if it could be demonstrated that living with a parent who's cohabiting with a partner is not in the best interests of the child, child custody can be transferred to the noncustodial parent.

CONCLUSIONS

Over the last two decades, the number of cohabiting couples has grown dramatically. In several European countries, including Denmark and Sweden, cohabitors have the same legal rights as married couples. In the United States, the rights of cohabiting couples are less clear, and there is quite a bit of state and local variation.

It is clear, however, that cohabitation is not the legal equivalent of marriage, or common-law marriage. Marriage is a civil contract between a man, a woman, and the state. Traditionally, informal marriage referred to an agreement between a man and a woman to be married followed by their living together; such common-law marriages are recognized in thirteen states and the District of Columbia as legally binding. These two sorts of unions are legally equivalent in that conjugal rights are conferred and a divorce is required to legally terminate them. In contrast, cohabitation generally refers to living together in a sexual relationship when not legally married.

In recent years, nonmarital cohabitation has gained greater acceptance among the general public, although in some states it is still illegal. Increases in cohabitation have affected the divorce rate, the average age of first marriage, and rates of marriage and remarriage. But contrary to widespread belief, cohabiting before marriage may not lead to more stable and satisfying marriages. Most cohabiting relationships do not last long because couples either break up or they marry. In fact, fewer than ten percent of cohabitors continue to live together for five or more years.

The longer a cohabiting relationship lasts, however, the greater the chance that legal problems can arise. There are legal implications when one partner believes he or she has rights to the other's property as well as property acquired together.

Unfortunately for cohabitors, state laws have not kept up with the recent increases in nonmarital cohabitation, although cohabitation is part of the normative culture. Since no state statutes exist establishing cohabitation as a legally permitted relationship, the rights of cohabitors have been established through court decisions. Because of the changes in the mores of society regarding cohabitation, nonmarital relationships that have many of the characteristics of marriage, in particular, are receiving increased judicial recognition. In the absence of a written cohabitation agreement, the distribution of property acquired during a nonmarital relationship is subject to judicial decision. The courts may take one of three approaches: (1) to treat the relationship as meretricious; (2) to treat the relationship as a marriage; or (3) to acknowledge the rights of cohabitors including the right to contract between themselves. The consequences of each of these approaches can be quite different for the cohabitors. Written cohabitation contracts may be an important step toward the clarification of the legal position of cohabiting couples.

What aspects of cohabitation still need to be addressed by the law? In the future, the courts will have to deal with several issues including the following: (1) Can contract rights, implied or written, exist in the states in which cohabitation is illegal? (2) Will cohabitation contracts which are legally recognized in one state be recognized in another state that usually considers such contracts invalid? (3) How long must a couple live together before the court can infer implied contractual rights? (4) Is each party legally obligated to disclose all of his or her assets in order to validate a cohabitation agreement? And (5) Will the bankruptcy or credit problems of one cohabitor affect the credit of the other? Lastly, while researchers have examined the social implications of the increase in cohabitation, what, however, are the social implications of the anticipated increase in cohabitation *contracts?* Will haggling over cohabitation contracts destroy the relationships they are supposed to protect, especially the "no-strings attached" relationships?

Society, as viewed by the courts, is based on the institution of marriage and the family. As such, the law encourages and protects marriage as opposed to cohabitation. There are practical difficulties for cohabitors ranging from traditional legal sanctions against cohabiting to unforeseen responsibilities created by the new judicial acceptance of their rights and obligations. Yet, the law also reflects society's views, and as cohabitation becomes increasingly socially acceptable, the law is beginning to recognize such relationships.

NOTES

1. An additional nineteen states, while not allowing common law marriages to be contracted within their own boundaries, do recognize common law marriages validly contracted in other states: Arizona, California, Delaware, Florida (if entered into before 1968), Kentucky, Maine, Maryland, Missouri, Nebraska, Nevada, New Jersey, New Mexico, North Carolina, Oregon, Utah, Virginia, Washington, West Virginia, and Wyoming (Duff and Truitt 1991).

2. Besides Idaho, Florida, Illinois, Michigan, Mississippi, New Mexico, North Carolina, North Dakota, Virginia and West Virginia have statutes criminalizing nonmarital cohabitation.

3. Sweet and Bumpass (1987, p. 376), for example, report that the number of cohabiting households was overstated in 1960 and 1970 because of an erroneous classification of boarders as cohabitors.

4. Because many cohabiting relationships are of short duration, "currently cohabiting" rates are much smaller than "ever cohabited before" rates (Macklin 1980, p. 907).

5. DeMaris and Rao (1992), however, were unable to replicate Teachman and Polonko's findings, possibly because the latter researchers did not include high school dropouts, a segment of the population with one of the highest rates of cohabitation. DeMaris and Rao (1992, p. 189) find "that the association of cohabitation with increased odds of dissolution persists even after accounting for the extra time that cohabitors have been together."

6. Indeed, some researchers report that cohabiting couples are more physically violent with each other compared with married couples. Controlling for a variety of background variables, cohabiting women are almost five times as likely to suffer from severe physical violence compared with married women (Stets 1991; Stets and Straus 1990). Stets and Straus (1990, p. 242) suggest that perhaps "some

enter cohabitation, rather than marriage, to keep more of their own independence, only to find that there are frequent arguments over rights, duties and obligations which may lead to violence."

7. In reality, cohabitation does not generally result in less traditional gender role performance than does marriage. Studies show that while cohabitors say they believe in gender role equality, their behavior reflects traditional gender roles (Denmark, Shaw, and Ciali 1985). For example, men who cohabit are not likely to do more housework than husbands (Cunningham, Braiker, and Kelley 1982). Interestingly, one gender role reversal evident among cohabitors is that cohabiting women are more likely than married women to financially support male partners (Kotkin 1983; Denmark, Shaw, and Ciali 1985).

8. Weitzman (1981, p. 2) points out that the traditional marriage contract embodies four nonegalitarian provisions: (1) the husband is head of the household; (2) the husband is responsible for supporting the wife; (3) the wife is responsible for domestic services; and (4) the wife is responsible for child care, and the husband for child support.

9. The fifty states are divided into community property and separate property states. The idea of marital community property comes from the Napoleonic Code (Duff and Truitt 1991; Weitzman 1981). The premise of community property is that all assets accumulated during a marriage belong to both spouses equally. Similarly, all debts and financial obligations also belong to both spouses equally. In the community property states (Arizona, California, Idaho, Louisiana, Mississippi, Nevada, New Mexico, Texas, Washington, Wisconsin and Puerto Rico), upon divorce or death of a spouse one half of all property acquired during the marriage belongs to the dependent or surviving spouse (Walker 1992). The remaining forty-two states and the District of Columbia apply the English common law theory of separate property to marital property ownership. This means that "all income or property acquired before or during the marriage belongs to the acquiring spouse" (Sonenblick 1981, p. 83).

10. In a 1981 decision, the California Court of Appeals reversed and rejected the $104,000 award. The California Court of Appeals ruled that the Los Angeles Superior Court was in error when it awarded Michelle Triola Marvin $104,000. The rehabilitative alimony award was denied by the California Supreme Court because Lee Marvin had no obligation to support Michelle Triola Marvin, who had benefitted from the relationship; moreover, Lee Marvin had not received unjust enrichment (*Marvin v. Marvin*, 122 Cal. App 3d 871, 176 Cal. Rptr. 555 [1981]). The fact that Michelle Marvin lost her case in trial does not alter the implications of the California Supreme Court's decision.

11. A constructive trust is defined as "a relationship with respect to property subjecting the person by whom the title to the property is held to an equitable duty to convey it to another on the ground that his acquisition or retention of the property is wrongful and that he would be unjustly enriched if he were permitted to retain the property" (Black 1983).

12. Terms which are equivalent to cohabitation contracts include interpersonal contracts, intimate contracts, and living together contracts (Kingdom 1990, p. 201).

REFERENCES

Abraham, H. J. (1986). *The Judicial Process.* NY: Oxford University Press.

Bachrach, C. A. (1987). Cohabitation and Reproductive Behavior in the U. S. *Demography*, 24, 623-637.

Bennett, N. G., Blanc, A. K. & Bloom, D. E. (1988). Commitment and the Modern Union: Assessing the Link Between Premarital Cohabitation and Subsequent Marital Stability. *American Sociological Review*, 53, 127-138.

Black, H. C. (1983). *Black's Law Dictionary.* St. Paul, MN: West Publishing.

Booth, A. & Johnson, D. (1988). Premarital Cohabitation and Marital Success. *Journal of Family Issues*, 9, 261-270.

Bumpass, L. L. (1990). What's Happening to the Family? Interactions Between Demographic and Institutional Change. *Demography*, 27, 483-498.

Bumpass, L. L. & Sweet, J. A. (1989). National Estimates of Cohabitation. *Demography*, 26, 615-625.

Bumpass, L. L., Sweet, J. A. & Cherlin, A. (1991). The Role of Cohabitation in Declining Rates of Marriage. *Journal of Marriage and the Family*, 53(4): 913-926.

Castro Martin, T. & Bumpass, L. L. (1989). Recent Trends in Marital Disruption. *Demography.*

Clark, H. H., Jr. (1980). *Cases and Problems in Domestic Relations.* Third Edition. St. Paul, MN: West.

Clayton, R. & Voss, E. (1977). Shacking Up: Cohabitation in the 1970s. *Journal of Marriage and the Family*, 39, 273-283.

Cunningham, J. D., Braiker, H. & Kelley, H. H. (1982). Marital-Status and Sex Differences in Problems Reported by Married and Cohabiting Couples. *Psychology of Women Quarterly*, Summer, 415-427.

DeMaris, A. & Leslie, G. R. (1984). Cohabitation with the Future Spouse: Its Influence upon Marital Satisfaction and Communication. *Journal of Marriage and the Family*, 46, 77-83.

DeMaris, A. & Rao, K. V. (1992). Premarital Cohabitation and Marital Stability. *Journal of Marriage and the Family*, 54, 178-190.

Denmark, F. L., Shaw, J. S. & Ciali, S. D. (1985). The Relationship Among Sex Roles, Living Arrangements, and the Division of Household Responsibilities. *Sex Roles*, 12, 617-625.

Duff, J. & Truitt, G. G. (1991). *The Spousal Equivalent Handbook.* Houston, TX: Sunny Beach Publications.

Freeman, M. D. A. & Lyon, C. M. (1983). *Cohabitation Without Marriage: An Essay in Law and Social Policy.* Aldershot, England: Gower House.

Fritz, N. R. (1989). New York Is for Lovers. *Personnel*, 66(4), 4.

Gilbert, E. (1991a). Major N.Y. Hospital Offers Domestic Partners Benefits. *National Underwriters*, 95 (April 15) 8.

Gilbert, E. (1991b). New Homeowners Policy Will Accept All Domestic Partners. *National Underwriters*, 95 (January 21), 15-16.

Glendon, M. A. (1989). *The Transformation of Family Law.* Chicago: University of Chicago Press.

Glick, P. C. & Spanier, G. B. (1980). Married and Unmarried Cohabitation in the United States. *Journal of Marriage and the Family*, 42, 19-30.

Gwartney-Gibbs, P. A. (1986). The Institutionalization of Pre-Marital Cohabitation: Estimates from Marriage License Applications, 1970 and 1980. *Journal of Marriage and the Family*, 48, 423-434.

Hewitt v. Hewitt, 394 N.E. 2d 1204 (1979).

Hughston, D. S. & Hughston, G. A. (1989). Legal Ramifications of Elderly Cohabitation: Necessity for Recognition of Its Implications by Family Psychotherapists. *Journal of Psychotherapy and the Family*, 5, 163-172.

Jorgensen, S. R. (1986). *Marriage and the Family: Development and Change.* NY: Macmillan.

Kingdom, E. (1990). Cohabitation Contracts and Equality. *International Journal of the Sociology of Law*, 18, 287-298.

Kotkin, M. (1985). To Marry or Live Together? *Lifestyles: A Journal of Changing Patterns*, 7(3), 156-170.

Liss, L. (1987). Families and the Law. In M. B. Sussman and S. K. Steinmetz (Eds.), pp. 767-793, *Handbook on Marriage and the Family*. NY: Plenum Press.

Lucas, P. (1990). Common Law Marriage. *Cambridge Law Journal*, 49, 117-134.

Macklin, E. D. (1972). Heterosexual Cohabitation Among Unmarried College Students. *Family Coordinator*, 21, 463-472.

Macklin, E. D. (1980). Nontraditional Family Forms: A Decade of Research. *Journal of Marriage and the Family*, November, 905-922.

Macklin, E. D. (1983). Cohabitation in the United States. In J. Gipson Wells (Ed.), pp. 65-66, *Current Issues in Marriage and the Family*. NY: Macmillan.

Macklin, E. D. (1987). Nontraditional Family Forms. In M. B. Sussman and S. K. Steinmetz (Eds.), pp. 317-353, *Handbook on Marriage and the Family*. NY: Plenum Press.

Marvin v. Marvin, 18 Cal. 3d660, 134 Cal. Reptr. 815, 557 P. 2d 106 (1976).

Marvin v. Marvin. Family Law Reporter (1979) 5, 3077.

Marvin v. Marvin, Family Law Reporter (1981) 7, 2661.

McCall v. Frampton. Family Law Reporter (1979) 5, 3109.

McCullon v. McCullon, 410 *New York Supp.* 226 (1978).

McIntyre, L. J. (1995). Law and the Family in Historical Perspective: Issues and Antecedents. *Marriage and Family Review, 21 (3/4).*

McLaughlin, S. D. et al. (1988). *The Changing Lives of American Women*. Chapel Hill: 27 University of North Carolina Press.

Mead, M. (1966). Marriage in Two Steps. *Redbook*, 127, 48-49, 85-86.

Modell, J. (1989). *Into One's Own*. Berkeley: University of California Press.

Murphy, W. F. & Pritchett, C. H. (1986). *Courts, Judges, and Politics: An Introduction to the Judicial Process*. NY: Random House.

Myricks, N. (1980). Palimony: The Impact of Marvin v. Marvin. *Family Relations*, 29, 210-215.

Newcomb, M. & Bentler, P. (1980). Cohabitation Before Marriage: A Comparison of Married Couples Who Did and Did Not Cohabit. *Alternative Lifestyles*, 3, 65-83.

O'Donnell, W. J. & Jones, D. A. (1982). *The Law of Marriage and Marital Alternatives*. Lexington, MA: D. C. Heath.

Parker, S. (1990). *Informal Marriage, Cohabitation, and the Law, 1790-1989*. NY: St. Martin.

Parry, M. L. (1981). *Cohabitation*. London, England: Sweet and Maxwell.

Rapoport, R. (1965). The Transition From Engagement to Marriage. *Acta Sociological*, 8, 36-55.

Rindfuss, R. R. & VandenHeuvel, A. (1990). Cohabitation: A Precursor to Marriage or an Alternative to Being Single? *Population and Development Review*, 16, 703-726.

Roha, R.A. (1990). Legal Side of Living Together. *Changing Times*, October, 73-76.

Rouse, L. P. *Marital and Sexual Lifestyles Workbook*. (1990). Arlington, TX: Center for Social Research.

Schnaiberg, A. & Goldenberg, S. (1989). From Empty Nest to Crowded Nest: The Dynamics of Incompletely Launched Young Adults. *Social Problems*, 36(3), 251-269.

Smart, C. (1984). *The Ties That Bind*. NY: Routledge.

Sonenblick, J. (1981). *The Legality of Love*. NY: Jove.

Spanier, G. B. (1983). Married and Unmarried Cohabitation in the United States: 1980. *Journal of Marriage and the Family*, 45, 277-288.

Stenger, R. L. (1988). Cohabitants and Constructive Trusts–Comparative Approaches. *Journal of Family Law*, 27, 373-452.

Stets, J. E. (1991). Cohabiting and Marital Aggression: The Role of Social Isolation. *Journal of Marriage and the Family*, 53, 669-680.

Stets, J. E. & Straus, M. A. (1990). The Marriage License as a Hitting License: A Comparison of Assaults in Dating, Cohabiting, and Married Couples. In M. A. Strauss and R. Gelles (Eds.), pp. 227-244, *Physical Violence in American Families*.

Sweet, J. A. & Bumpass, L. (1987). *American Families and Households*. NY: Russell Sage Foundation.

Tanfer, K. (1987). Patterns of Premarital Cohabitation Among Never-Married Women in the United States. *Journal of Marriage and the Family*, 49, 483-497.

Teachman, J. D. & Polonko, K. A. (1990). Cohabitation and Marital Stability in the United States. *Social Forces*, 69, 207-220.

Thayer, N. S. T. (1982). We Need to Recognize Pluralism in Our Adult Relationships. In R. T. Francoeur (Ed.) *Taking Sides: Clashing Views on Controversial Issues in Human Sexuality*, pp. 242-249, Guilford, CT: Dushkin.

Thomson, E. & Colella, U. (1992). Cohabitation and Marital Stability: Quality or Commitment? *Journal of Marriage and the Family*, 54, 259-267.

Thornton, A. (1988). Cohabitation and Marriage in the 1980s. *Demography*, 25, 501-506.

U. S. Bureau of the Census. (1991). *Current Population Reports, Series P-20*.

No. 450. Marital Status and Living Arrangements: March 1990. Washington, DC: U. S. Government Printing Office.

U. S. Bureau of the Census. (1981). *Current Population Reports, Series P-20. No. 365. Marital Status and Living Arrangements: March 1980.* Washington, DC: U. S. Government Printing Office.

U. S. Bureau of the Census. (1971). *Current Population Reports, Series P-20. No. 218. Household and Family Characteristics: March 1970.* Washington, DC: U. S. Government Printing Office.

Vreeland, L. N. (1989). The Delicate Balances of Living Together. *Money,* 18, 88-90.

Wagner, L. (1988). Recognizing Contract and Property Rights of Unmarried Cohabitants in Wisconsin: Watts v. Watts. *Wisconsin Law Review,* 6, 1093-1121.

Walker, T. (1992). Family Law in the Fifty States: An Overview. *Family Law Quarterly,* 25(4), 417-520.

Watson, R. E. L. (1983). Premarital Cohabitation vs. Traditional Courtship: Their Effects on Subsequent Marital Adjustment. *Family Relations,* 32, 139-147.

Watson, R. E. L. & DeMeo, P. W. (1987). Premarital Cohabitation vs. Traditional Courtship: A Replication and Follow-Up. *Family Relations,* 36, 193-197.

Weitzman, L. J. (1981). *The Marriage Contract: Spouses, Lovers, and the Law.* NY: Free Press.

Wiersma, G. E. (1983). *Cohabitation. An Alternative to Marriage?: A Cross-National Study.* Boston, MA: Kluwer.

Wojcik, J. (1991). Few Offer Benefits to Unwed Couples. *Business Insurance,* 25 (March 11), 1.

APPENDIX A

THE STATE OF TEXAS
COUNTY OF TARRANT

S A M P L E ONLY
FOR EDUCATIONAL
PURPOSE NOT TO
BE DUPLICATED

NON-MARITAL COHABITATION AGREEMENT

This agreement was made by and between JOHN DOE, of Arlington, Tarrant County, Texas, hereinafter referred to as "DOE" and JANE SMITH, hereinafter referred to as "SMITH," and hereinafter collectively referred to as "the Parties."

RECITALS

WHEREAS, the parties to this agreement are a man and a woman who desire to without the benefit of matrimony, to divide only their homemaking expenses and ties, and to keep as their respective separately owned property, their individual income, and separately acquired property; and

WHEREAS, the parties do not intend to marry either ceremonially or informally in the foreseeable future, and they do not intend their non-marital relationship to be governed by the Texas Family Code;

IT IS THEREFORE AGREED;

I.

The following described property and property acquired therewith shall remain the separately owned property of DOE, to-wit: (list)

II.

The following described property and property acquired therewith shall remain the separately owned property of SMITH, to-wit: (list)

III.

All property acquired by gift, bequest, devise, descent, with the rents, issues, and profits thereof shall be the separately owned property of the party who acquires it.

IV.

All earnings, income, salaries, and commissions generated by each of the parties, and all property acquired therewith, shall remain the separately owned property of the party who generated it.

V.

This agreement shall terminate upon the earliest occurrence of either the ceremonial marriage of the parties performed pursuant to a valid marriage license issued by one of the fifty (50) United States, or upon thirty (30) days written notice personally delivered by one party to the other.

VI.

This agreement is made in consideration of the mutual promises of the parties to each other contained herein.

VII.

If any legal action is brought by either of the parties to enforce any provision of this agreement, the parties agree that the prevailing party shall be entitled to recover reasonable attorney fees and costs from the other party.

VIII.

Each party to this agreement warrants that he or she has made a full and complete disclosure to the other party of the nature, extent, and probable value of all his or her property, estate, and expectancy. However, each party to this agreement acknowledges that the mutual promises and covenants contained herein are not dependent upon such full disclosure, and that failure to disclose the nature, extent, and probable value of any other property owned by either party shall not be the basis for this agreement nor making it unenforceable.

IX.

Each party to this agreement acknowledges that he or she has consulted an attorney of his or her choice, or has had an opportunity to consult an attorney of his or her choice. Moreover, each party to this agreement acknowledges that he or she has read the agreement, and is executing this agreement knowingly, voluntarily, and without any reservation.

X.

This agreement supersedes any and all other agreements, either oral or written, between the parties relating to their rights and liabilities arising out of a non-marital relationship. This agreement contains the entire agreement of the parties.

XI.

If any provision of this agreement is held by a court to be invalid, void, unenforceable, the remaining portions shall, nevertheless, continue in full force and effect without being impaired or invalidated in any way.

APPENDIX A (continued)

XII.

This agreement may be amended or modified only by a written instrument signed by both parties.

XIII.

This agreement shall be governed by, and construed in accordance with the laws of the State of Texas.

SIGNED on this   day of   , year.

_____
JOHN DOE

_____
JANE SMITH

THE STATE OF TEXAS
COUNTY OF TARRANT

This agreement was acknowledged before me on the _____ day of ____ , year, by JOHN DOE.

_____
NOTARY PUBLIC, STATE OF TEXAS

This agreement was acknowledged before me on the ____ day of ____ , year, by JANE SMITH.

_____
NOTARY PUBLIC, STATE OF TEXAS

Law and Stepfamilies

Candan Duran-Aydintug
Marilyn Ihinger-Tallman

INTRODUCTION

"When a man marries a woman with minor children to whom she has certain obligations, what are the relative rights and obligations of all parties involved? The children? Stepchildren? The new married partners? The children of the new marriage? The non-custodial parent of the children of remarriage?" Marie Kargman raised these questions in 1969 (p. 174) but provided no answers. Twenty-four years later there are still few answers and a great deal of confusion over the issues of stepfamily member rights and obligations.

It is the purpose of this article to explicate the current situation regarding the legal rights and obligations of stepfamily members. We do this by discussing legal aspects of remarriage, the concept of *in loco parentis,* the current state of the law vis-à-vis stepparents, and reviewing the law as it pertains to benefits to stepchildren (e.g., worker's compensation, wrongful death, etc.). We conclude with a summary of recommendations and a discussion of needs that still need to be addressed.

To what extent are the law and the legal system relevant to family life? Consider the following profile. According to current estimates, about 62%

Candan Duran-Aydintug is Assistant Professor, Department of Sociology, University of Colorado at Denver. Marilyn Ihinger-Tallman is Professor, Department of Sociology, Washington State University.

The authors wish to thank Lisa McIntyre and Emily and John Visher for their helpful comment on an earlier draft of this paper.

[Haworth co-indexing entry note]: "Law and Stepfamilies." Duran-Aydintug, Candan, and Marilyn Ihinger-Tallman. Co-published simultaneously in *Marriage & Family Review* (The Haworth Press, Inc.) Vol. 21, No. 3/4, 1995, pp. 169-192; and: *Families and Law* (ed: Lisa J. McIntyre, and Marvin B. Sussman) The Haworth Press, Inc., 1995, pp. 169-192. Multiple copies of this article/chapter may be purchased from The Haworth Document Delivery Center [1-800-3-HAWORTH; 9:00 a.m. - 5:00 p.m. (EST)].

of all first marriages will end in divorce (Martin & Bumpass, 1989; Bumpass, Martin, & Sweet, 1991). It is known that the divorce rate among couples where at least one spouse has had a prior marriage is about equal to that of first marriages–62% (Glick, 1984, 1989). Trend data show that nearly half of all marriages in the United States are now remarriages (White & Riedmann, 1992). Since about 60% of couples who divorce have children, a high proportion of remarriages are stepfamilies–defined as a family that includes offspring of one partner whose spouse is not the child(ren)'s biological parent. At the present time, about 35% of children born in the early 1980s are expected to live with a stepparent before they reach the age of 18 (Glick, 1989). This figure does not include thousands of children who live in single parent households but whose absent parents have remarried and may or may not include them as members of the household (Ihinger-Tallman & Pasley, 1987).

The several family transitions–marriage, divorce, remarriage, redivorce–that men, women, and children experience are increasingly discussed and studied by social scientists, those in the helping professions (e.g., clinicians, social workers) and recently by lawyers. The challenges associated with stepfamily living are clearly identified: boundary ambiguity, normlessness, loyalty conflicts, etc. As a result of these challenges, remarriage and the stepfamily have been defined as an incomplete institution. Andrew Cherlin (1978) first articulated the concept of remarriage as an incomplete institution, emphasizing remarriages with children. He attributed part of this incompleteness to the position of the law with regard to stepparents. Stepparents have no legal right to "parent" their stepchildren. That is, they cannot legally discipline a stepchild, sign school report cards or other administrative school forms, or approve emergency medical treatment (Chambers, 1990). Cherlin indicated that the lack of attention to stepfamilies' family law leads to conflict and confusion. Stepparents' lack of legal standing–combined with norm ambiguity, complexity of kinship structure, and lack of consensus regarding behavioral expectations that are inherent in this family structure–helps foster instability in stepfamilies. Stepparents not only suffer from role ambiguity in their newly assumed positions, but, having no legally recognized status in relation to their stepchildren, they are left to find their own solutions with few places to go for legal protection or advice (Cherlin, 1978; Goetting, 1982). Elsewhere in this volume the history and sources of family law are described in detail. Suffice it to say that there is wide variation among the 50 states regarding the role of courts vis-à-vis the family. Even within a single jurisdiction family law is not always clear (Kruse, 1986).

Remarriage is complicated by the presence of children (White and

Booth, 1985). This is because children in a remarriage increase the probability that there will be third parties who hold a vested interest in the lives and behavior of remarried family members, e.g., grandparents, ex-spouses, and after divorce, ex-stepparents. Visitation, custody, and support involving third parties are areas of dispute the courts must address. Some hypothetical examples which illustrate the potential conflict are provided below:

> Sam married Diane, who, two months later gave birth to a daughter, Susan, fathered by James. Sam acted as stepparent to Susan, rearing her as his own for five years. Sam and Diane then divorced. When Diane went to court the judge found no legal basis to require Sam to pay child support.

> George went to court to sue for the right to continue seeing his six-year-old stepson, Terry. George's ex-wife Bette (Terry's mother) had agreed to let George and Terry visit each other regularly after the divorce. However, Bette had recently remarried and felt that George and Terry's relationship was interfering with her newly established family, especially the relationship between Terry and her new husband. George's request for visitation rights was refused.

> Mary willingly relinquished custody of Elizabeth, age two, after her divorce from Tim, Elizabeth's father. Tim met and married Nancy when Elizabeth was three, and she continued to be reared by her father and stepmother. Mary rarely visited Elizabeth but she had kept her one month during the summer when Elizabeth turned six. When Elizabeth was ten her father died. Mary and Nancy both sought custody of Elizabeth. Custody was awarded to Mary.

While these three cases are hypothetical, in similar suits the decisions reported above reflect actual decisions of the judges hearing the cases. In each of these cases the stepparent had lived with (taken the child into his or her home) and treated the child as his or her own. That is, the stepparent acted *in loco parentis* (in the place of parent). This is the concept relied upon most often when resolving disputes surrounding support, visitation and custody after divorce in stepfamilies. This concept is discussed next.

IN LOCO PARENTIS

Under common law, marriage does not obligate the stepparent to support a stepchild.[1] In other words, when there is no statute that requires stepparents to take on parental responsibilities, the legal rights and duties that arise out of steprelationships are based only on voluntary assumption (Berkowitz, 1970). This voluntary assumption under which a stepparent (or any other person) assumes the liability to maintain, rear, and educate a child or "receives the child into his family" where there is presumption that she or he assumes such liability without legally adopting the child, is called an *in loco parentis* relationship (Berkowitz, 1970). In other words, the stepparent relationship alone does not create an *in loco parentis* relationship. But when a stepparent intentionally assumes parental responsibilities an *in loco parentis* relationship can occur (Ramsey and Masson, 1985). This doctrine represents a self-imposed relationship (Cheifetz, 1985). A more current term for *in loco parentis* is a "psychological parent" or "one who has assumed the status and obligations of a parent without formal adoption of the child" (Buser, 1990, p. 5).

If the intention to parent the stepchild is evidenced, then the courts consider a stepparent to be a parent. The types of evidence the courts take into account to determine financial responsibility include the performance of household services for the child, counseling by the stepparent, and payment of the child's expenses (Mahoney, 1984). Again, common law requires no obligations or duties from the stepparent other than those voluntarily assumed. The adoption of the stepparent's last name or the absence or presence of the other natural parent does not affect the courts' decision (Mahoney, 1984). Furthermore, courts determine whether an *in loco parentis* relationship exists on a case by case basis.

Under common law, the stepparent (or the stepchild) may end the voluntary *in loco parentis* relationship and its corresponding financial responsibility at will, at any time, even though there might have been promises to provide future support (Mahoney, 1984). Thus, the *in loco parentis* doctrine is a useful tool to categorize past behavior but not future behavior (Ramsey, 1992).

The fact that a stepparent stands *in loco parentis* to a stepchild does not necessarily mean that the child may assume the status of a natural child in all circumstances. The only legal obligations, without a statute, are the duty of support, the right to have services rendered, and the right to participate in suits involving third parties (Berkowitz, 1970). In other areas, such as workmen's compensation, wrongful death, insurance, or descent and distributions certain statutes make stepchildren exempt from any legal rights (Berkowitz, 1970). An *in loco parentis* relationship is typically terminated as a result of divorce or separation between the biological parent and the stepparent since the stepparent would no longer be living with the child. This is true except in cases when a statute imposes an absolute liability regardless of an *in loco parentis* relationship (Berkowitz, 1970).

In the past, courts have presumed that the death of one spouse (where no child of the present marriage had been born) terminates any relationship by affinity (or marriage). Recently, there has been a tendency to avoid applying this principle if a case involves a step relationship. In other words, once the stepchild-stepparent relationship is created, it is not generally regarded as terminated by the death of one of the parties of the marriage. Therefore, if the stepparent voluntarily continues to support the stepchild, "the incidents arising out of relationship shall also continue" (Berkowitz, 1970, p. 227). As of 1989, 15 states (Alaska, Arizona, California, Connecticut, Delaware, Hawaii, Kansas, Kentucky, Maine, New Jersey, Oregon, Tennessee, Utah, Virginia, and Washington) have specifically established a "broad range of custody, visitation, and support rights for stepparents either through legislative enactments or appellate case decisions" (Victor, 1989, p. 45). All 50 states have either case law or legislative statutes in some form that pertain to custody, visitation, and support regarding stepparents, grandparents, and stepchildren. These rights are discussed below.

STEPCHILD SUPPORT (DURING MARRIAGE AND AFTER ITS TERMINATION)

A few state statutes and the common law doctrine of *in loco parentis* oblige stepparents to support their stepchildren. Fourteen states (Delaware, Hawaii, Kentucky, Missouri, Nebraska, Nevada, New Hampshire, New York, North Dakota, Oregon, South Dakota, Utah, Vermont, and Washington) have statutes requiring stepparents to support stepchildren. However, the stepparents' obligation is much more limited than a biological parent's obligation to support (Ramsey and Masson, 1985). Seven state statutes (Delaware, Hawaii, Missouri, North Dakota, South Dakota, Oregon, and Utah) specify that the biological parent remain primarily responsible for support of a child (Ramsey and Masson, 1985). State statutes which do not hold the biological parent responsible do not specifically apportion liability between natural and stepparents.

There is also variation among state statutes with regard to whether stepchildren must be living in the same household as the stepparent before any duty to support arises. In six states (Delaware, Hawaii, Missouri, North Dakota, Oregon, and Washington) statutes indicate that only when the stepchild is living with the stepparent is the stepparent obligated to support the stepchild (Ramsey and Masson, 1985). In the remaining states statutes are silent on the subject of residence.

There is less variation in state statutes with regard to continuation or termination of the obligation to support after marital dissolution between the stepparent and the biological parent. In a few states, such as Delaware, Washington, and Utah, statutes explicitly state that the termination of such a marriage causes an end to the obligation to support (Ramsey and Masson, 1985). Statutes have been interpreted along the same line in several other states. Only North Dakota provides for continuation of the support obligation after the termination of the marriage as long as the stepchild "has been received into the stepparents' family and the stepchild continues to reside in the stepparent's family" (Ramsey, 1992, p. 22; Victor, Robbins, Bassett, 1991). There are some states where statutes indicate a continuation of the support obligation when the biological parent and stepparent are separated.

Aside from a direct obligation to support imposed by statute or by an *in loco parentis* relationship, if a court considers the stepparent's income to be a resource for the biological parent, then the stepparent may have an indirect duty to support the stepchild. According to the common law of property, the court is not supposed to take the stepparent's income into account when making a child support award. However, in some states the stepparent's income is considered when the court determines a biological parent's ability to pay support, even though the stepparent's income could not be drawn upon directly without a statutory requirement (Ramsey and Masson, 1985). In these states, the stepparent is indirectly required to bear part of the child support obligation. In some cases, noncustodial parents in these states have sought to rely upon stepparent support as the basis for reducing their own child support obligations. Other states are less clear regarding the issue of stepparent's income.

The great majority of children whose parents are divorced receive either no financial support, or far less support than they are entitled to by law, from their noncustodial parent (Weitzman, 1985). Consequently, many children live at even lower standards of living than they would if the support award was upheld. Some scholars (Mahoney, 1987; Weitzman, 1981) have argued that during marriage a stepparent should be required by law to share the financial obligations of the custodial parent. Opponents of involuntary stepparent support have argued that such requirements might discourage the marriage of parents with minor children. However, others argue that the trend in some states of requiring stepparents to support stepchildren during marriage encourages marriage as it increases the pressure put on women to remarry (Mahoney, 1987).

Courts and legislatures that consider stepparent support to be terminated after marital dissolution seemed to have overlooked the effect of this on dependent children. In the eyes of most lawmakers the stepparent-stepchild relationship is based on a derivative model; that is, it is considered to exist as long as the marriage lasts. This model ignores the various and complicated relationships, expectations, and emotions occurring in stepfamily settings. A law which extends support in appropriate cases beyond marital dissolution would recognize and protect these interests.

VISITATION

Visitation (meaning rights of physical access) excludes decision making and childrearing responsibilities of legal custody. As with custody decisions, in most cases ambiguous statutes provide little guidance to courts deciding visitation cases. The 1970 Uniform Marriage and Divorce Act deals only with the rights of biological parents. However, some courts have stretched the statutory language in order to consider stepparent visitation awards (Mahoney, 1987). According to some legal scholars, in order to serve the child's interest in the best possible way after marital dissolution the continuity and integrity of the primary custodial relationship should be protected (Goldstein, Freud, and Solnit, 1973). Therefore, visitations to adults other than the biological parents should not be allowed without the consent of the primary custodian. In actuality, the laws concerning visitation rights reject this view. In some circumstances, it is possible to override the "traditional" autonomy of the biological parent if the stepparent has stood *in loco parentis*. If such a situation exists, a hearing is required to determine the future relationship between stepparent and stepchild. The court also has to decide whether a continuing relationship would negatively affect the primary custodial relationship (Mahoney, 1987). In determining stepparent visitation rights courts consider the closeness of the stepparent-stepchild relationship, the number of persons asserting competing parental claims, support to the child by the stepparent during the marriage and after the divorce, and whether or not the child needs the stepparent for his or her well being (Ramsey, 1992). In cases where the non-custodial biological parent has visitation rights, the courts must determine the effect of granting stepparent's visitation rights on the relationship between the child and this parent. Stepparents stand a higher chance of obtaining visitation rights after the death of a spouse, however, they still face the barrier of overcoming a preference for the biological parent (Mahoney, 1987). As of 1991 all states grant some third party visitation, and California, Kansas, Tennessee, Virginia, and Wisconsin specifically recognize stepparents (Victor, Robbins, and Bassett, 1991).

STEPPARENT CUSTODY

On rare occasions, when a stepparent seeks to obtain custody of a stepchild a change of custody happens without any expression of hostility. For example, after the death of a custodial parent all family members may agree that the child's interests will be best served if the stepparent becomes the custodial parent (Chambers, 1990). However, courts usually are called on to consider a stepparent's request for the custody of a stepchild over the objection of a biological parent when there is a divorce between the stepparent and the custodial parent. In cases where judges must choose between stepparents and biological parents, custody decisions are not simply based on the best interests of the child. Stepparents have to overcome obstacles that are designed to protect the biological parent from interference with his or her parental rights (Ramsey, 1992). The court decisions in these types of custody cases show wide variation. In some states courts limit the categories of persons who are allowed to ask to obtain custody or they use very stringent standards when reviewing stepparents' requests (Ramsey, 1992).

The varying nature of court decisions also reflects "our society's conflicting and unresolved attitudes about stepparents, even when loving, and about biological parents, even when indifferent" (Chambers, 1990, p. 122). In only one state (Oregon) has legislation been adopted that treats stepparents by name as potential custodians, and only in a few other states are courts authorized to consider petitions for custody by long-term caretakers.

If there is a basis for jurisdiction, then the courts have to decide whether the biological parent and the residential stepparent can be treated as equals. When these decisions are made they usually reflect a negative bias against stepparents. Many courts hold stepparents to tougher standards in order to protect the right of the biological parent. Some states require evidence that extraordinary circumstances are present and/or that the biological parent is unfit (Ramsey, 1992). Even though the current picture favors biological parents, some change is occurring. Many courts are considering orders for visitation for stepparents, and one court ordered joint legal custody between a stepmother and the biological mother after the custodial father died (Bartlett, 1984).

ADOPTION

Adoption entails the termination of parental rights and obligations of one or both biological parents and the assumption of those rights and obligations by a new adult (Chambers, 1990). In a typical stepparent adoption, the explicit consent or acquiescence of the biological parent must be obtained (Rowe, 1968). However, in some places adoption laws were expanded so that courts can approve adoptions by stepparents in a wider range of cases even over strong objections from the noncustodial biological parent (Chambers, 1990). This can happen when there has been abuse by the biological parent, parental neglect, parental incarceration, mental or physical illness of the parent, or there is a strong psychological bond between the stepchild and stepparent and the biological parent provides only token amounts of support and contact (Clark, 1987).

Adoption statutes vary widely among the states. In some states the Uniform Adoption Act is in use. This act permits adoption by a stepparent without the consent of the noncustodial biological parent if that parent failed to communicate with the child or to provide for the child's support without a justifiable cause for a period of at least a year. In some states (California and Michigan), some period of time has to pass during which the parent both failed to communicate with and support the child for the stepparent to be allowed to adopt the child. In states that permit a court to allow stepparent adoption without the consent of the biological parent when there has been both failure to communicate and to support, a biological parent can prevent the stepparent adoption by making occasional child support payments, even though there is no communication with the child (Chambers, 1990). In a few other states if courts determine that consent is being unreasonably withheld contrary to the child's best interest, adoption by a stepparent is authorized (Chambers, 1990).

Very little is known about the factors that stepparents and custodial parents consider when deciding to seek adoption, or what noncustodial parents' concerns are when deciding to consent (Wolf and Mast, 1987). A study of British families in which the stepparent was petitioning to adopt his or her stepchild found the principle reason for adoption was ". . . to make the family like a proper family" (Masson, 1984: 230). A "proper" family meant all members having the same surname, all children in the family having the same status, eliminating interference by the non-custodial parent, or not having to explain the stepfamily composition and history to representatives of social agencies (schools, hospitals, etc.) (Masson, 1984). While information about why stepparents seek to adopt is scarce, we know even less about why noncustodial parents agree to let their children be adopted.

To this point we have discussed issues that concern stepparents. In the next section attention is turned to stepchildren and the benefits that may or may not accrue to them.

THE RIGHTS OF STEPCHILDREN TO LEGAL BENEFITS

According to law, biological children receive priority over stepchildren (Redman, 1991). Law notwithstanding, in practice, research findings indicate that child support to biological children generally decreases when a divorced father remarries, especially when his new spouse has children. This happens regardless of the parents' ability to pay (Redman, 1991). In addition to support, there are several other types of benefits for which stepchildren are eligible. These are summarized below.

Worker's Compensation

Worker's compensation laws include provisions for children of injured workers. In general, under these statutes, the term children has been held to include stepchildren both by statutory expression and judicial interpretation (Berkowitz, 1970). Massachusetts is the only state in which all step relationships are excluded from worker's compensation law. In situations when compensation was denied to stepchildren in the other 49 states, rulings were based on very different grounds. For example, in some cases if the stepchild was not actually dependent on the stepparent (there was no *in loco parentis* relationship), or if the child was illegitimate, compensation was denied (Berkowitz, 1970). Some courts dealt with illegitimacy by granting compensation if there was evidence shown of some dependency upon the stepparent. However, there have been cases where stepchildren were denied compensation even though the stepparent provided the majority of the support because the biological parent still had a legal duty to support (Berkowitz, 1970). In other cases, absolute liability within the worker's compensation act was imposed by virtue of the step relationship alone without requiring parents to stand *in loco parentis*.

Wrongful Death

Biological children have rights under wrongful death statutes to recover damages for the death of their parents when the Worker's Compensation law is not applicable. Stepchildren, on the other hand, generally have no rights in this area unless the act specifically provides for them (Berkowitz, 1970). This has given rise to various types of suits, including suits by the stepchild against a stepparent for the negligent or intentional death of the child's natural parent; suits by the stepchild against a third party for the wrongful death of his or her stepparent, and suits for the wrongful death of the biological parent. These suits raise the question of the stepparent-spouse's priority over the stepchild to bring suit (Berkowitz, 1970).

Insurance

In cases involving insurance, the courts usually look for the presence of an insurable interest. Insurance law generally includes stepchildren and stepparents as dependents when it comes to benefit insurance societies. Generally the law recognizes that a steprelationship creates an insurable interest between stepparent and child (Berkowitz, 1970). In these cases an *in loco parentis* relationship is most often the determining factor in obtaining benefits. In other words, in the case of steprelations, if evidence can be provided about any dependency, expectation of aid, or benefit when needed, then the stepchild may have an insurable interest in the life of a stepparent or person *in loco parentis* (Berkowitz, 1970).

Inheritance

Stepchildren are neglected in the law of inheritance. While the status of adopted and illegitimate children has been dealt with, the status of stepchildren is generally ignored. The term children has been understood as excluding stepchildren under the testate law. In these cases the courts generally do not concern themselves with the existence of an *in loco parentis* relationship. What is considered is the intent of the testator reflected in the use of particular words at the time of the will. If the court does find an ambiguity in the will then the relationship between the testator and his stepchildren may be a factor in reaching a decision (Berkowitz, 1970).

The Social Security OASDI Program

The Old-Age, Survivors, and Disability Insurance Program (OASDI) under the Social Security Act provides benefits to dependent family members who suffer economic loss due to the lost earning capacity of an insured wage earner (Booth, 1973). In 1939, Congress added the child's insurance component to the OASDI Program to extend benefits to the dependent children of insured workers. Even though the child's insurance provision expressly included stepchildren, ambiguity surrounded the definition of stepchildren (Social Security Act as amended, 1939). According to the Social Security Act, the eligibility requirements for the child's insurance benefits under the OASDI Program specify that the child must be unmarried, dependent on the insured worker at a relevant time set out in the statute, and under age eighteen, a student, or under a disability at the time of application for benefits. This provision defines a child to include "a stepchild who has been such stepchild for not less than one year immediately preceding the day on which application for child's insurance benefit is filed or, if the insured individual is deceased, no less than nine months immediately preceding the day on which the individual died" (Mahoney, 1987). The date of the insured individual's marriage to the child's parent is used to measure the steprelationship.

The dependency requirement was intended to limit eligibility to those family members who suffer actual economic loss due to lost earning capacity of the insured. The dependency requirement has been defined by Congress more strictly for stepchildren than for biological or adopted children of the insured worker (Mahoney, 1987). In the case of these latter children, dependency exists by virtue of the parent-child relationship. Questions of dependency are raised for such children only in cases where the child is neither the legitimate nor the adopted child of the insured individual, or when the child has been adopted by some other individual. When it comes to stepchildren, however, the dependency requirement can only be met upon showing that "the child was living with or was receiving at least one-half of his support from the insured stepparent" (Mahoney, 1987). The test of dependency (living together or support) has to be proved in every case involving a stepchild.

As Congress has set a maximum amount of benefits payable based on the account of a single worker, eligible stepchildren may cause a reduction in the amount of benefits to other qualified family members, such as the insured individual's biological children from a prior marriage. According to the current program these benefits are distributed equally among all children (biological, adopted, and step). It has been argued that greater equity would be obtained by a rule which distributes the fixed funds according to the relative need for financial dependence upon the insured in cases involving the claims of multiple families (Mahoney, 1987).

As stated above, under the OASDI Program the stepchild eligibility requires age, marital status and dependency (cohabitation or support) criteria be met. The Social Security Administration pronounced an additional requirement for stepchild eligibility in 1979 (Mahoney, 1987). According to this rule a child can only be eligible for the benefits as an insured stepchild if, after the child's birth, the child's parent married the insured. This regulation, for the first time, excluded those children born during the marriage who are children of one spouse only. However, as this limitation set forth in 1979 is inconsistent with the congressional purpose of providing family members with benefits who are likely to suffer economic loss due to the insured's loss of earning, it does not deserve judicial deference, and thus it is not binding on the courts (Mahoney, 1987).

In spite of the 1979 regulatory requirement, the definition of stepchild under the Social Security Act is still ambiguous on the question of whether children born during rather than prior to the remarriage are stepchildren within the Act. Still, the requirement of a valid marriage between the biological parent and the insured is clear. The OASDI Program specifies that the marriage between the insured and the natural parent must be a valid marriage under state law for stepchildren eligibility. As marriage laws of states vary, the actual limitations on stepchild eligibility depend upon where the insured person resides.

Immigration Law

Even though the dependency provision of the Social Security Act clearly requires de facto family status by limiting stepchild eligibility to cases where the child receives one half of his/her support from, or resides with, the insured spouse of the child's biological parent, the absence of a corresponding limiting provision in the Immigration Act has created problems for stepchildren in the immigration law (Mahoney, 1987). Under the Immigration Act, to enter the United States legally, every immigrant alien must obtain an immigrant visa (Gordon and Rosenfield, 1985). There are limitations in the number of visas issued each year. However, this restriction is relaxed for the category of aliens who are the immediate relatives of a United States citizen (Gordon and Rosenfield, 1985). The ambiguity surrounding stepfamily status in the immigration law relates to the qualification of stepchildren as "immediate relatives" of a citizen stepparent.

Prior to 1952, the definition of the term "child" in the immediate relative provision of the Immigration Act did not include stepchildren. Congress added stepchildren in 1952 to the definition of "child" in this act; the stepfamily was then recognized for this federal law purpose (Auerbach, 1955).

The immediate relative provision of the Immigration Act specifies the basic requirements for qualification as a nonquota stepchild. In order to qualify for immediate relative status, children must be unmarried and under the age of twenty-one at the time of visa application and when they enter the United States. In the case of stepchildren the provision explicitly requires a marriage between the child's biological parent and the citizen stepparent (Mahoney, 1987). To qualify for nonquota status, a stepchild must be under the age of eighteen at the time of this marriage. The validity of a marriage under the Immigration Act is determined as a general rule by reference to the marriage law of the state or foreign country where the marriage occurred or the parties resided; the sham marriage doctrine denies recognition in cases where the ceremonial marriage took place for the sole purpose of establishing eligibility for special immigration status.

Other than age and marital status, there are no other additional requirements for eligibility as a nonquota stepchild. However, administrative hearing officers and judges have been asked to determine whether any other additional restrictions were intended by the Congress in the absence of statutory ad regulatory guidance. As the stepparent-stepchild relationship is one of affinity, created through the marriage of the stepparent and the child's biological parent, the question of whether this relationship is derivative and thus dependent on the continuation of the marriage has arisen in a number of contexts. It is argued that the question of a continuing legal stepparent-stepchild status following dissolution of the marriage is best resolved on a case-by-case basis, and that the legal rights that arise during the marriage should be preserved only if the relationship has continuing importance for the parties involved after the termination of the marriage (Mahoney, 1987). In fact, on the basis of three cases and decisions of the Board of Immigration Appeals, a rule has emerged which has broadened the standard for stepchild eligibility: today, proof of an actual continuing relationship between the parties is the only nonstatutory requirement.

Aid to Families with Dependent Children and Stepfamilies

Aid to Families with Dependent Children (AFDC) is one of four assistance programs established under the Social Security Act. This program, which has now become the largest and most expansive of the assistance programs, was established in 1935. Even though states have autonomy in setting benefit levels, they must follow federal eligibility requirements and must provide aid to all eligible individuals. According to federal law, a needy child is eligible for assistance if the child is deprived of parental support or care because of death, continued absence from home, or the parent is mentally and physically incapable of supporting the child. An adult has to qualify as a "parent" to have a legal obligation to support the child. Because the Social Security Act fails to define the term "parent," states have often applied a broad definition to reduce the category of eligible AFDC recipients (Goldsmith, 1978). A person qualifies as a parent if the person is the child's natural or adoptive parent, or a stepparent who is ceremonially married to the child's natural or adoptive parent and is legally responsible for supporting the child under a state law of general applicability which requires stepparents to support stepchildren to the same extent that natural or adoptive parents are required to support their children. As only seven states (Nebraska, New Hampshire, Oregon, South

Dakota, Utah, Vermont, and Washington) are considered by the Department of Health and Human Services to have laws of general applicability, most stepparents do not qualify as "parents." In those states that do not have laws of "general applicability" a stepparent's income has to be considered in determining eligibility and benefit amounts (Goldsmith, 1978). Under the amendments to the AFDC program contained in the Omnibus Budget Reconciliation Act (OBRA) the stepparent's income has to exceed a certain dollar amount. The income to be considered is that which exceeds (a) the sum of the first $75 of the total of such stepparents' earned income for such month, (b) the state's standard of need for the family group, (c) the amount paid by the stepparent to individuals not living in such households and claimed by him or her as dependents for tax purposes (e.g., payments by a stepparent in the form of alimony and child support to individuals not living in such household). If all these obligations are met and the stepparent's income still exceeds the requisite amount, then the state presumes that the stepparent's income is available to support the stepchild (Ramsey and Masson, 1985).

The new OBRA amendments actually allow what the prior policy was designed to prevent: a reduction in welfare benefits without any guarantee of support. These amendments not only make needy children dependent upon the charity of their stepparents but, in a majority of states, they put a burden on the stepparents of needy children as well.

In these states, because of income considerations, stepparents can give priority to support for their own biological children. However, if the stepchild's noncustodial parent is either unwilling or unable to support the child, the stepparent can be held indirectly responsible. There is no consideration of what might be a fair contribution by the stepparent with the state paying the balance of the absent or deceased parent's share. Only stepparents who live with custodial parents are taken into account for the indirect obligation. The states are not required to consider noncustodial stepparents' income when determining the amount of support to be paid. Additionally, only a stepparent who is legally married to the custodial parent can be held responsible. In the case of a divorce between the stepparent and the custodial parent, the stepparent's income cannot be presumed available, even if they continue to live together (Ramsey and Masson, 1985).

RECOMMENDATIONS FOR LEGAL REFORM

Kargman (1969) and Cherlin (1978) were among the first social scientists to call attention to the ways that the law failed to take into account the growing number of stepfamilies and their need for direction in arbitrating or resolving the problems that accompany this family structure. This need for direction is compounded by the diversity and complexity of stepfamilies. Family relationships that form when couples with children divorce and remarry introduce a host of new, sometimes problematic situations as illustrated in the earlier sections of this paper. With few exceptions, states have not enacted laws directly addressing the problems and disputes that arise in stepfamilies. For the most part, when cases brought by stepfamily members are brought to court they are decided by existing law designed for first-married spouses who are the biological or adoptive parents of their children. Third party custody law must be stretched to include stepparents, while case law relevant to post-divorce biological parent visiting and custody must be applied to post-divorce stepparents. Disputes generally are settled on a case-by-case basis, often using creative and innovative interpretations of existing law (Redman, 1991).

Several recommendations for law reform have been offered. Before we summarize these recommendations let us list again the problems that need to be addressed. First, stepparents have no legal authority to act in behalf of their stepchildren. The law does not legitimate the roles and functions, rights and obligations of stepparents vis-à-vis their stepchildren. Following from this, stepparents have no standing that accords them the responsibility to love, support, discipline or socialize (i.e., to parent) their stepchild, or to have continued contact with them in the event of divorce. Finally, there is no power attributed to the stepparent status. A stepparent has none of the traditional powers assigned to a parent (e.g., to sign for an adolescent stepchild's driver's license application) and no standing to request custody in the event of the death of the child's custodial parent, even when he or she has been the primary caregiver for many years.

Would reform of the current law help settle stepfamily disputes when they arise? Or, more importantly, would position and standing in law help to legitimate the roles and functions stepparents generally assume when they marry a spouse who has children from a previous union–and hence forestall disputes? Several legal scholars have indicated that it would. This positive view stems in part from the legislative reform of family law that occurred in Great Britain in 1989. This legislation was called the Children Act. While it is still too early to know concretely how effective this Act is in helping to resolve the legal problems faced by stepfamily members, it is significant to the extent that it specifically addresses the problems identified in this paper.

According to Masson (1991), the Children Act "clarifies and unifies both the public and private law relating to children and is intended to bring about major changes in the legal position of parents, particularly after marriage breakdown" (p. 4). According to this Act, a stepparent can apply for a Residence Order that gives him or her almost the same authority as the parent. The Act refers to the "child of the family" and does not use the term "stepparent." A person who is in a marriage in which the child is a child of the family can apply for an Order. In addition, anyone else (e.g., the cohabiting partner of an unmarried custodial parent) with whom the child has lived for a period of at least three years can apply for a Residence Order. Parental responsibilities on the part of others are not relinquished with the granting of a Residence Order. Rather this Act increases the number of persons with these responsibilities. Yet there are limits to the power a stepparent holds. "A stepparent's rights under a residence order are not entirely co-extensive with a parent's. A stepparent with parental responsibilities cannot appoint a testamentary guardian, agree to the child's adoption, or consent to an order freeing the child for adoption" (Ramsey, forthcoming, p. 413). The Children Act expands the concept of what parent-child relations can be.

Specific Recommendations for Change

Several experts have made specific recommendations for modifying the United States family law to make it more compatible with the changing American family. Some of these recommendations are presented below.

Sarah Ramsey, a member of the law faculty at Syracuse University, has written several articles on the law as it relates to stepfamilies (see Ramsey 1984, 1985, 1986, forthcoming). She specified several possible goals of legal reform. These goals: (a) promote the child's welfare; (b) support the custodial parent-child dyad; (c) protect the rights and interests of the noncustodial parent; (d) support the new marriage; (e) reward and protect the stepparent. She also urges (f) that new, non-nuclear family norms for stepfamilies be established; and (g) that diversity of family structures be recognized. On the other hand, she feels (h) that legal administration could be simplified and state expenditures on children be decreased (Ramsey, forthcoming, p. 412). Ramsey acknowledges that legal scholars are moving away from the idea that the nuclear family is the only family model. Flexible and varied family structure and roles are slowly being acknowledged. She perceives that the law has been affected by changes in the family. However, in response to this change, legal changes have been piecemeal and have occurred in an unpredictable fashion. As one mode of initiating positive change, Ramsey suggests adopting some of the features of the Children Act of Great Britain. Specifically, she suggests that stepparents be able to apply for a court order similar to the Residence Order specified in the Children Act. This would give stepparents the parental responsibility they are currently denied (e.g., access to school records, consent to medical care). The court order also might include inheritance rights and any support obligations the stepparent might have for the child. Such a court order would not diminish the rights of the biological parent, but it would be supportive of the new stepfamily. "It would establish a new non-nuclear model in law for stepfamilies" (p. 420). In case of divorce the court order could remain in effect so that the "stepparent's legally recognized status would continue" (p. 421). In cases of dispute, which can occur among any of the potentially interested parties (e.g., the custodial parent, non-custodial parent, ex-stepparent, or new spouse/stepparent of the custodial parent), "the law could contain a presumption that the custodial parent's choice would control, absent extraordinary circumstances. However, if a stepparent had a primary caretaker role, the stepparent might be more likely to want to continue to have the child live primarily with him or at least to continue to have frequent contact. These cases might support a presumption in favor of the primary caretaker" (p. 422).

In the event of the death of a custodial parent, Ramsey suggests some guiding presumptions be derived through legislation rather then rely strictly on the basis of the best interests of the child. She made no specific recommendations except to suggest that stepparents may be in a better position to establish a claim to continuing custody if the biological parent has had little contact with the child. In an instance such as this, she recommends that continuity prevail over biology–with the specific outcome being no change in the child's home, school, and friends while he or she also was dealing with the loss of a parent. Regarding reform, Ramsey advises, "We should move cautiously and with as much information as possible because of the diversity of stepfamilies, the coercive power of the law, and the indeterminacy of the best interests standard" (p. 423).

Emily Visher, a clinical psychologist and leading authority on stepfamily issues, also recommends that stepparents be permitted legal standing vis-à-vis their stepchildren. However, Visher recommends waiting several years (she recommends five years, which puts the stepfamily past the most vulnerable period of family formation and gives it an opportunity to stabilize) after which the stepparent could apply for some type of legal status. This status would (a) permit a stepparent to sign all types of permission forms for the stepchild, (b) remove the "disinterested party" status from the stepparent-stepchild relationship, (c) legally include the stepparent as a member of "the parenting coalition" (which would permit the stepparent to be legally evaluated along with the parent when deciding custody change), and (d) provide legal weight to the stepparent's request for visitation or custody in event of divorce or death (Visher, 1992).

Visher also recommends that parents and stepparents move slowly when adoption is being considered. She and colleague/spouse, John Visher, warn that there may be undesirable side effects for children when adoption is seen as a way to create a close-knit family after remarriage (Visher and Visher, 1981). Their concern is for the child who may suffer from the loss of contact with the non-custodial parent. The Vishers' work has impressed upon them that even when children have little contact with an absent parent, emotional bonds may nevertheless be strong. Legally ending the relationship may have a serious emotional impact on children. They write (p. 36):

> To relinquish an important relationship with a biological parent in order to gain or consolidate a relationship with a stepparent can produce tension, conflict, sadness and anger. It may foster an attitude of rebelliousness rather than an acceptance of a new parenting person in their lives. Therefore, the stepchild should never feel the adoption decision hinges on surrendering the relationship with the biological parent. It is important that the child not view the issue as a loss for a gain or a substitution of one parenting figure for another . . . "Common sense advice" from friends or relatives sometimes dictates that the biological parent no longer serves a useful function and should be eased out of the picture, especially when there is a new stepparent on the scene. Much evidence is contrary to this conclusion. Divorce and custody arrangements which make the non-custodial parent feel unimportant or helpless have the effect of causing broken relationships between a parent and child which can be very harmful.

Visher is particularly concerned about two issues. First, she perceives that there are both overt and covert biases against stepfamilies that operate to put counter-pressure on the "opening door" of awareness and recognition of the stepfamily as a viable family form. This reactionary tendency may be well-intended, attempting only to foster the family of our ideals. However, its consequence may be detrimental to many stepfamilies who struggle to meet the many challenges they face in creating a family identity. Second, Visher is concerned that the movement to give more responsibilities to stepparents will not be accompanied by concomitant rights. The consequence of this imbalance is anger; less cooperation and care, not more.

David Chambers, a Professor of Law at the University of Michigan, offered recommendations for legal reform very reluctantly (Chambers, 1990). The great diversity found in stepfamilies discourages standardization. Chambers believes that it is easier to prescribe new rules about adoption and child custody than rules concerning child support. He favors "maintaining ties for children with persons who have been important in their daily lives" (p. 126). He supports the voluntary obligation of support by stepparents that accompanies adoption but is less sure about an adoption policy that puts an end to a child's relationship with an absent biological parent. After divorce he recommends that children be permitted to have continued contact with stepparents "who have lived with them for substantial periods" (p. 127). When disagreements occur over post-divorce custody he recommends placement with the parent or stepparent who has been the primary caretaker, and after divorce, recommends generous visiting time. Chambers qualifies these recommendations by stressing that these rules should be applied only in cases where the stepparent desires a continuing relationship with a child and they not be imposed on "the residential stepparent who never develops a close relationship with a stepchild and has no desire for continuing contact" (p. 127). Chambers recommends that the remarriage of either custodial or noncustodial parent not be a factor in recomputing child support awards. However, if a parent seeks to alter the amount of child support paid because of inflation or the increase of earnings of the parent paying support, then he would favor taking into account the "actual current standard of living of both family units" (p. 128). Finally, Chambers does not feel comfortable making any recommendations to change the law regarding stepparent support of stepchildren after divorce. He believes this would not be culturally or legislatively acceptable: "there are limits on the extent to which our culture perceives stepparents as responsible for children" (p. 113).

This is opposite the view held by R. Michael Redman, a Magistrate Judge in the Fifth District of Idaho. Redman's reform suggestion is that after remarriage "the replacement parent becomes financially responsible for the children, unless and until the natural parent with the children remarries someone else" (Redman, 1991, p. 89). We mentioned earlier the arguments that have been proposed against this idea (see especially Riley, 1984; the Washington Supreme Court, 1984; Bruch, 1982). Redman acknowledges that there are many cases in which this arrangement would not work. However, he believes that reform is overdue and the "legal community and its political cousins must open their eyes, clear their heads of ancient cobwebs, and move carefully but decisively to create a new and responsible system of family law" (p. 94).

So, what actually has been done towards reforming family law in the

United States? Have the experts been heard? Have there been forums for the expression of new ideas? In 1987 the American Bar Association Family Law Section acknowledged the need to respond to the issues involving the legal rights and responsibilities of stepparents (Tenenbam, 1991). An ad hoc committee to study stepfamily legal issues was created and this committee developed a preliminary Model Act which was meant to reflect the concerns of children, natural parents, and stepparents. In 1990 a revision of the Model Act was presented to the Council of the Family Law Section. It was debated intensely at a conference in 1991, where family law scholars, clinicians, and researchers gathered. As a consequence of this discussion the Act was tabled for further revision. As of February 1993, no reform has occurred.

DISCUSSION

Several problems unique to stepfamilies must be considered when attempting to write law that applies to this type of family. This is because there are several factors working against the success and stability of stepfamilies from their conception. The first of these is that not all family members are in the family voluntarily. Children have very little to say about when and who their parent marries. Stepfamilies may be formed when resentment, jealousy, or fear of loss may be the underlying emotions felt by the children in the family. Family solidarity and cohesion are difficult to attain when some members of the family are pulling in the opposite direction. Second, while the roles, functions, and behavior enacted by parents are not universally scripted and acted upon in the United States, there is even less agreement about the normative expectations and behaviors associated with being a stepparent (Ihinger-Tallman and Pasley, 1987). While the parent-child relationship normatively begins with strong bonds of affection and rests on pretty clear notions of parental duties and responsibilities, there are a variety of ways that a stepparent is attached to and relates to a stepchild (and vice versa). These lie along a continuum, with antipathy on one end and genuine love on the other. The age of the child, the differing needs of stepchild and stepparent, and the different wishes and desire for a relationship between stepchild and stepparent are variables predicting the nature of the stepparent-stepchild relationship. The ways of behaving–as a stranger, acquaintance, friend, or parent–follow from the starting place on this continuum. These differences accentuate the diversity of stepfamilies.

This diversity should not be an impediment to the formation of legislation to help guide stepfamily behavior. Rather, diversity can be handled with law that specifies conditional safeguards that permit a variety of outcomes. How might this be done? First, following from Visher and

Ramsey's recommendations, a resident order should be made available for those stepfamilies who wish to legitimate the stepparent position with the rights, duties, and responsibilities of parenthood. Visher's suggestion that this order not be attainable until after the fifth year of the remarriage is a good one, since by that time the family will likely have achieved stability and survived the most divorce-prone years. Second, with or without a resident order, a stepparent's request for visitation after divorce should be permitted and heard, conditional upon the length, nature and significance of the parental relationship with the child. Third, under conditions that can be specified, a stepparent should be held responsible for financially supporting the child post-divorce as long as concomitant rights accompany this responsibility throughout the marriage. Fourth, under conditions that can be specified, a stepparent's request for custody should be permitted and heard. If rules concerning parental rights, visitation, support and custody were clearly stated, with conditional circumstances specified, stepfamilies would be recognized in law, adults who assume the position of stepparent would have standing in the law, and they would have clearer guidelines for behavior which encourages institutionalization. Finally, legal standing would promote the authenticity of this family type and stepfamily members would feel less pressure to hide or camouflage their stepfamily identity. They WOULD be perceived to be a "real" family. Policy that is developed by lawmakers can benefit from the use of social science and clinical literature. The reality of stepfamily life is clarified by the studies of psychologists, sociologists, family life educators, family therapists, family counselors, etc. (Fine, 1989). The coming together of legal professionals and family scholars will go a long way toward making stepfamilies an integral part of the family institution.

NOTE

1. Statutory law, or laws enacted by legislators, take precedence in our legal system. However, where no statute exists, the common law rules.

REFERENCES

Auerbach, F.L. (1955). *Immigration Laws of the United States.* Indianapolis: The Bobbs-Merrill Company, Inc.

Bartlett, K.T. (1984). Rethinking parenthood as an exclusive status: The need for legal alternatives when the premise of the nuclear family has failed. *Virginia Law Review,* 70, 879-963.

Berkowitz, B.J. (1970). Legal incidents of today's "step" relationship: Cinderella revisited. *Family Law Quarterly,* 4, 209-229.

Bohannan, P. (1970). The six stations of divorce. In P. Bohannan (ed.), *Divorce and After.* New York: Doubleday and Co., Inc.

Booth, P. (1973). Social Security in America. Ann Arbor: The University of Michigan Press.

Bruch, C. (1982). Developing standards for child support payment: A critique of current practice 16. *University of California–Davis Law Review,* 49, 60.

Bumpass, L.L., Martin, T.C., & Sweet, J.A. (1991). The impact of family background and early marital factors on marital disruption. *Journal of Family Issues,* 12, 22-42.

Buser, P.J. (1991). The first generation of stepchildren. *Family Law Quarterly,* 25, 1-17.

Chambers, D.L. (1990). Stepparents, biologic parents, and the law's perception of "family" after divorce. In Stephen D. Sugarman & Herma Hill Kay (eds.), *Divorce Reform at the Crossroads.* New Haven: Yale University Press.

Cherlin, A. (1978). Remarriage as an incomplete institution. *American Journal of Sociology,* 84, 634-650.

Clark, H.H. (1987). Involuntary termination of parental rights–grounds, pp. 631-647. *The Law of Domestic Relations in the United States.* Second Edition. St. Paul, MN: West Pub. Co.

Fine, M. (1989). A social science perspective on stepfamily law: suggestions for legal reform. *Family Relations,* 38, 53-58.

Furstenberg, F.F., Jr. (1979). Recycling the family. *Marriage & Family Review,* 2, 12-22.

Glick, P.C. (1984). Marriage, divorce, and living arrangements: Prospective changes. *Journal of Family Issues,* 5, 7-26.

Glick, P.C. (1989). Remarried families, stepfamilies, and stepchildren: a brief demographic profile. *Family Relations,* 38, 24-27.

Goetting, A. (1982). The six stations of remarriage: developmental tasks of remarriage after divorce. *Family Relations,* 31, 213-222.

Goldsmith, M.A. (1978). AFDC eligibility and the federal stepparent regulation. *Texas Law Review,* 57, 79-100.

Goldstein, J., Freud, A., & Solnit, A. (1973). *Beyond the best interest of the child.* NY: The Free Press.

Gordon, C. & Rosenfield, H.N. (1985). *Immigration Law and Procedure.* New York: Banks and Company.

Griffith, M.A. (1990). *State Differences in the Provision of AFDC: Concept Definition and Causal Structure.* Unpublished Dissertation. The University of Alabama.

Ihinger-Tallman, M. & Pasley, K. (1987). *Remarriage.* Beverley Hills, CA: Sage Publications.

Kargman, M.W. (1969). Legal obligations of remarriage: What is and what ought to be. *The Family Coordinator,* 18, 174-178.

Kruse, H.D. (1986). *Family Law.* St. Paul, MN: West Publishing Co.

Mahoney, M.M. (1987). Stepfamilies in the Federal Law. *University of Pittsburgh Law Review,* 48, 491-537.

Mahoney, M.M. (1984). Support and custody aspects of the stepparent-child relationship. *Cornell Law Review,* 70, 38-79.

Martin, T. & Bumpass, L. (1989). Recent trends in marital disruption. *Demography*, 26, 37-52.

Masson, J. (1991). Stepping into the nineties: a summary of the legal implications of the Children Act 1989 for stepfamilies. In A *Step in the Right Direction*, National Stepfamily Association.

Pasley, K. & Ihinger-Tallman, M., eds. (Forthcoming). *Stepfamilies: Issues in Research, Theory, and Practice*. New York: Greenwood Press.

Ramsey, S.H. (Forthcoming). Stepparents and the law: A nebulous status and the need for reform. In K. Pasley & M. Ihinger-Tallman (eds.), *Stepfamilies: Issues in Research, Theory, and Practice*. Westport, CT: Greenwood Publishing Co.

Ramsey, S.H. (1986). Stepparent support of stepchildren: The changing legal context and the need for empirical policy research. *Family Relations*, 35, 363-369.

Ramsey, S.H. & Masson, J.M. (1985). Stepparent support of stepchildren: A comparative analysis of policies and problems in the American and English experience. *Syracuse Law Review*, 36, 659-714.

Redman, R.M. (1991). The support of children in blended families: A call for change. *Family Law Quarterly*, 25, 83-94.

Riley, J.M. (1984). Stepparents' responsibility of support, 44. *Los Angeles Law Review*, 1753 at 1776.

Rowe, J. (1968). *Parents, Children and Adoption*. London: Routledge and Kegan Paul.

Social Security Act as amended. (1939). New York: Commerce Clearing House, Inc.

Tenenbam, J. (1991). Legislation for stepfamilies: The Family Law section standing committee report. *Family Law Quarterly*, 25, 137-141.

Uniform Marriage and Divorce Act of 1970. (1987). In Uniform Laws Annotated. *Matrimonial, Family and Health Laws*, 9A, 147-692. West Publishing Co.

Victor, F.S. (1989). When third parties come first. *Family Advocate*, 12, 2, 8-9, 45.

Victor, R.S., Robbins, M.A., & Bassett, S. (1991). Statutory Review of Third-Party Rights Regarding Custody, Visitation, and Support, 25, Family L.Q. 19.

Visher, E. (1992). Personal Communication to Dee Samuels, esq.

Visher, E.B. & Visher, J.S. (1981). Legal Action is no substitute for genuine relationships. *Family Advocate*, 4, 35-38.

Wald, E. (1981). *The Remarried Family: Challenge and Promise*. New York: Family Service Association of America.

Washington State Supreme Court (1981). Van Dyke V. Thompson, 95 Wash. 2d 726, 630P 2d 420, 423.

Weitzman, L.J. (1985). *The Divorce Revolution*. New York: The Free Press.

Weitzman, L.J. (1981). *The Marriage Contract*. New York: The Free Press.

White, L.K. & Booth, A. (1985). The quality and stability of remarriages: The role of stepchildren. *American Sociological Review*, 50, 689-698.

White, L.K. & Riedmann, A. (1992). When the Brady Bunch grows up: Step/half- and full-sibling relationships in adulthood. *Journal of Marriage and the Family*, 54, 197-208.

Wolf, P.A. & Mast, E. (1987). Counseling issues in adoptions by stepparents. *Social Work*, 32, 69-74.

Bankruptcy and the Family

Teresa A. Sullivan
Elizabeth Warren
Jay Lawrence Westbrook

In 1992, 811,206 non-business bankruptcy cases were filed in the United States. In the fiscal year that ended June 30, 1992, there was one bankruptcy filing for every 96 households, compared with one case per 258 households in fiscal year 1984 (Flynn, 1992). Bankruptcy, often considered an economic problem of major import principally to corporations and businesses, has become a significant event for millions of American families, involving the possible unraveling of debts, restructuring of payments, and forfeiture of collateral and assets. This rapid growth and widespread prevalence of individual bankruptcies raises the question of the relationship of bankruptcy law to the family.

Bankruptcy is a legal remedy that can be invoked voluntarily by the debtor. A number of studies have investigated in detail the finances and consumer behavior that characterize families with major indebtedness (e.g., Ford, 1988; Caplovitz, 1979, 1974) and their legal problems (Jacob, 1969). The majority of the families with major indebtedness problems do not use the bankruptcy remedy, but this review focuses principally on families who do. We exclude any extensive review of the family finance literature.

One difficulty in sketching out the relationship between family and

Teresa A. Sullivan is Professor of Sociology, Department of Sociology, University of Texas, Austin. Elizabeth Warren is Professor, School of Law, University of Pennsylvania. Jay Lawrence Westbrook is Professor of Law, School of Law, University of Texas, Austin.

[Haworth co-indexing entry note]: "Bankruptcy and the Family." Sullivan, Teresa A., Elizabeth Warren, and Jay Lawrence Westbrook. Co-published simultaneously in *Marriage & Family Review* (The Haworth Press, Inc.) Vol. 21, No. 3/4, 1995, pp. 193-215; and: *Families and Law* (ed: Lisa J. McIntyre, and Marvin B. Sussman) The Haworth Press, Inc., 1995, pp. 193-215. Multiple copies of this article/chapter may be purchased from The Haworth Document Delivery Center [1-800-3-HAWORTH; 9:00 a.m. - 5:00 p.m. (EST)].

bankruptcy law is that bankruptcy stems from multiple causes, and bankruptcy potentially has multiple effects. In the sections following, we review the methods used to study bankruptcy, the general issue of families and indebtedness, the types of bankruptcy, the problematic inclusion of the family in bankruptcy, profiles of families in bankruptcy, and the relationship of marital instability to bankruptcy.

APPROACHES TO STUDYING BANKRUPTCY

The study of bankruptcy has sporadically engaged the attention of a wide variety of researchers, including legal scholars, economists, statisticians, and sociologists. The long-term rise in the number of filings has sparked inquiries to explain the trends in the aggregate data (e.g., see Apilado, Dauten, and Smith, 1978; GAO, 1983: 90-96; Shepard, 1984). Correctly specifying the reasons for the trend, however, is technically difficult because of the number of macro-level covariates. The Bankruptcy Act of 1978 is often used as a watershed for "before-and-after" studies of bankruptcy, but specifying the statutory change as the reason for the increase is suspect because a number of other changes happened in the same period. For example, the Supreme Court overturned the ban on lawyer advertising at about the same time, and bankruptcy is now a widely advertised legal service.

A number of other changes were also affecting the country at the same time. The decade of the 1970s was a period of widespread divorce reform, and as we shall see, divorce and bankruptcy appear to be related. Furthermore, the late 1970s and the early 1980s were a period of deregulation of banking and relaxation of state usury laws. Credit cards, a profitable industry, were widely marketed, and new credit instruments became available to a larger proportion of the population. By the end of the 1980s, the failures of banks and of savings and loan associations were more widespread than at any time since the Great Depression of the 1930s. Finally, the 1980s were marked by regional recessions resulting in layoffs, restructuring of industries, and economic dislocation. To identify any of these phenomena as the single or even the most important cause of the bankruptcy trend is difficult without measuring the effect of the others.

Our purpose here is different: to review the individual-level or micro-level studies that investigate the characteristics of individual debtors and their families. As Hanushek and Jackson (1977: 180) remind us, "Individual level data are usually richer than aggregate data, permit estimation of more elaborate models, and thus are to be preferred when available." Compared with other topics of interest to family researchers (e.g., child abuse or adjustment to divorce), micro-level bankruptcy studies are relatively scarce and represent a number of different disciplinary perspectives. By their episodic nature, these studies are probably not useful for explaining the trends in bankruptcy.

As a group the micro-level studies are non-cumulative, partly because the state of the art varies widely among the studies. Meta-analysis has not so far been possible because of variations among the research universes, the concepts used, and the statistics reported (Sullivan, Warren, and Westbrook, 1987). Some studies use defective sampling techniques or provide too little information about the sample. Many are limited to a single judicial district, so that generalizing from them is often difficult (e.g., Brunner, 1965; Herrmann, 1965; Subrin and Rugheimer, 1976a, 1976b; Yeager, 1972). Even in multi-district studies, however, the data may be reported only with measures of central tendency or univariate distributions (Shuchman, 1985, 1983; Shuchman and Rhorer, 1984). Comparisons using routine two-sample tests require standard deviations or at least a measure of variance. In general, the studies vary in the sophistication of their use of statistical controls and their treatment of missing data.

The passage of time also affects the comparability of micro-level studies, just as it affects the macro-level studies. For example, inflation and changes in interest rates affect the meaningful comparison of dollar values across studies. Even relative figures, such as the debt-income ratio or the percentage of median income, are not comparable if not calculated in the same way. Some of the apparently discrepant findings in the literature often have a time-bound explanation. An example of such a finding is the apparent change in the socioeconomic status of debtors. A number of studies indicated that the average bankrupt was a blue-collar worker (see reviews by Heck, 1980; U.S. Congress, 1973), but GAO (1983: 22) and Sullivan, Warren, and Westbrook (1989) find increased representation of white-collar workers. The labor force as a whole, in the meantime, has become more white-collar with the growth of professional, technical, and clerical occupations (Blau and Duncan, 1967; U.S. Census, 1992: 392-394). Thus, the more recent findings may simply reflect changes in the larger society.

Another important source of differences among the studies reviewed here is the use of different data-collection techniques. Some use data from individual court petitions, for which response error is presumably minimized because debtors file these documents under penalty of perjury. On the other hand, the bankruptcy petition does not contain many of the basic data researchers would like (e.g., age, educational attainment, marital history).

Some studies use data from interviews with debtors. Although these studies have the advantage of providing the information the researcher needs, they often encounter low response rates and potential non-response bias. Stanley and Girth (1971) in their landmark study achieved a response rate of 54%, but only 125 of their 400 interviews were also with respondents from their original petition sample of 1675. Ryan (forthcoming) offers useful detail about the difficulties of conducting interviews with bankrupt debtors. He began with a 62% sampling of 242 Australian bankrupts drawn from a published list of bankruptcies. He interviewed only 76 (32% response rate); another 75 (31%) refused the interview. Another 74 (30%) could not be traced, and 15 (6%) were found to be business bankruptcies and outside his universe. Similar results had previously been found in the United States in a methodological study that used samples drawn from court files. The researchers had difficulties in locating about 30% of the respondents (Bradburn and Sudman, 1979: 7). Of those located and agreeing to an interview, 32% of respondents personally interviewed and 29% of respondents interviewed by telephone denied involvement in a bankruptcy proceeding (Bradburn and Sudman, 1979: 81). Further problems related to response rates are reviewed in Sullivan, Warren, and Westbrook (1983: 1104-1108).

These issues underscore a problem that bankruptcy researchers share with researchers who study other stigmatizing behavior. Preston (1969) provides unusual insight into these problems with his detailed notes on interviews with bankrupt debtors. Some interviewees were terse: "when the interviewer would attempt to probe deeper about an answer, the petitioner would reply, 'next question.' When he became aware the questions on the guide had been completed, he immediately came over to where the interviewer was sitting, shook hands . . . and led him to the door" (Preston, 1969: 140). In another interview, the petitioner's sister entered the room during the interview. "[W]hen his sister, who appeared to be of college age, entered the room, he asked her to leave and informed the writer that she was not aware of [the bankruptcy]. He did not want her to know" (Preston, 1969: 133).

Financial affairs are to many families an intensely personal matter, not for discussion outside the family circle. Debt problems violate the privacy of the family financial space. Bankruptcy, because of its public nature, is the most serious violation of the family's privacy. In many cities, the names of bankrupt debtors are published in the newspapers, circulated in credit newsletters, and distributed to retailers. The fact of a bankruptcy may be carried on a credit record for ten years. The Bankruptcy Act of 1978 prohibited certain forms of discrimination against bankrupt debtors, but the institution of the protection suggested in itself the stigma that bankrupt debtors still feel. Debtors who are not obliged to talk to researchers about their bankruptcies often choose not to do so, with the result that the results may be biased by selecting only those who will talk.

DEBT AND THE FAMILY

Family economic problems, of which serious indebtedness and bankruptcy are two common types, have wide-ranging impacts on family members and family structure. In common conversation, the term "bankrupt" is often used loosely as a synonym for "being in serious debt trouble." Bankruptcy and indebtedness are not the same, and the analytic distinction is critical to this article. High levels of indebtedness are one type of economic problem, and bankruptcy is one solution to problems of indebtedness. In this section, we briefly review findings on family debt problems, we describe possible solutions to debt problems, and then we turn to the particular solution of bankruptcy.

Patterns of expenditures, credit use, and indebtedness are closely linked to family structure and family life cycle. Seventy percent of Americans live in married-couple households, and married-couple families comprise 56 percent of all U.S. households but 70 percent of consumer spending (U.S. Census, 1992: Table 56; Ambry, 1993). The biggest spenders are the married couples with children under 18–just 27 percent of all households, but major consumers (Ambry, 1993). Housing expenditures, in particular, increase during these early stages of the family life cycle. In the transition from being a childless couple to being a new parent, total annual expenditures rise 0.3%, but expenditures rise about 11% in the transition to "prime-time" families (school-age children) and another 8.8% in the transition to mature families (oldest child at home beyond age 18). For the empty-nest families, expenditures drop by nearly 30% (Ambry, 1993: 32).

Families experiencing financial pressures and rising expenditures have a number of possible responses. In the nearly 2,000 families in four cities studied by Caplovitz (1979: 116-117), financially stressed families were more likely to rely on increasing income and decreasing expenditures than on increased use of credit as strategies for dealing with inflation or recession. But about 8% of the families studied relied on credit to handle inflationary pressures (Caplovitz, 1979: 114).

Credit use increases through the early stages of the family life-cycle. Caplovitz (1974: 19) in comparing a sample of defaulting debtors with a national sample of current credit users and non-users, found both higher proportions of credit users and of defaulting debtors who were young, relative to the general population. For example, among non-farm family heads in 1966, 25 percent were under 35 years of age; among credit users, 38 percent were under 35 years of age, and among those in default, those under 35 total 45 percent. A similar but less pronounced pattern is found in the 35- to 44-year age group. By contrast, 35 percent of the general population was 55 years of age or older, compared with 21 percent of the credit users and only 9 percent of the default-debtors. According to this study, debtors are disproportionately recruited from the younger segments of the population, and for at least some families the use of credit is a way to finance the increased expenditures.

Debt problems, however, do not stem only or even principally from the use of credit. Among Caplovitz's sample of defaulters (1974: 53-54), 21% reported that a problem with the creditor was the first reason for the bankruptcy, including cases of fraud, deception, and payment misunderstandings. For example, there were "debtors who returned defective merchandise to the dealer and mistakenly thought that the deal was terminated . . ." (Caplovitz, 1974: 52). Loss of income was the major reason for debt default, and usually the income was lost because of a job interruption (Caplovitz, 1974: 58). Other important reasons for default included debtor's third parties (e.g., cosigners) and marital instability.

Not all financially distressed families file bankruptcy. Debtors have a number of potential remedies at their disposal, including general belt-tightening, consolidation loans, consumer credit counseling, surrender of collateral, or simply moving away. Bankruptcy is only one remedy for a family with overwhelming indebtedness, so that bankruptcy filing rates underestimate the numbers of distressed families. Caplovitz (1974: 274) found that only 7 percent of his sample of defaulting debtors filed for bankruptcy although the proportions varied from 2% in Philadelphia to 12% in Chicago. He believed that lawyers were more likely to advertise their services in Chicago, although his study predated Supreme Court approval of lawyer advertising. Jacob (1969) found that debtors who already knew someone who had filed bankruptcy were more likely themselves to consider bankruptcy. The combination of these two filings suggests that as lawyers advertise, and as bankruptcy itself becomes more common, the propensity of financially distressed families to declare bankruptcy may increase.

Among debtors who do declare bankruptcy, the attribution for their financial difficulties is similar to that of all defaulting debtors. Although some families file bankruptcy because of troubles that stem from mismanagement, lifestyle, and consumption patterns, many other families blame economic conditions or unpredictable misfortunes. Important reasons for entering bankruptcy are the failure of one's own business or of an employer; unexpected or uninsured medical expenses; and layoffs or unemployment (Sullivan, Warren, and Westbrook, 1992a; 1992b). One-fifth of the individuals in bankruptcy are failed entrepreneurs, whose bankruptcy is attributable to the failure of a business (Sullivan, Warren, and Westbrook, 1989).

Technically, bankruptcy is a remedy available to both debtors and creditors, but very few creditors file an involuntary proceeding against debtors. (Fewer than 2,000 involuntary petitions are filed annually (U.S. Census, 1992), and it is believed that most of them are business bankruptcies.) An individual creditor has a number of remedies for collecting debts, including (depending on state law) repossession, foreclosure, legal judgments, and garnishment of wages. An aggressive creditor may gain the lion's share of a debtor's resources by being the first or the most aggressive to use such techniques. Bankruptcy differs from these other remedies because it is a single forum for bringing together all the creditors of a debtor, because it is usually voluntary on the part of the debtor, and because the debtor enjoys the protection of the bankruptcy court during the proceedings. One of the most important consequences of filing bankruptcy is the "automatic stay," a court order that forbids further efforts by creditors to collect. Commentators differ in their opinions of the extent to which debtors seek the protection of the bankruptcy court to evade creditor actions such as garnishment. Some have believed garnishment to be an important factor (e.g., Brunn, 1965; Stanley and Girth, 1971); others have found it to be less significant (Caplovitz, 1974: 275; Sullivan, Warren, and Westbrook, 1993).

For either role, bankruptcy is an event with many different possible consequences. For some debtor families, bankruptcy represents a fresh start and the climb back from terrible economic times. Some families will stay together because bankruptcy has put an end to creditors' phone calls and marital disputes over debts or credit use. For other debtor families, bankruptcy is the final financial resolution to a previous marital dissolution; still other families are planning their bankruptcy so that their subsequent divorce will be smoother.

Some bankrupt families lose their homes and others save their homes. Some families keep substantial amounts of household furnishings, while others retain little more than the shirts on their backs. Some families are immediately deemed creditworthy while others will be denied credit for ten years, the period of time during which a previous bankruptcy may legally be noted on a credit record. Results for the creditors may also vary. Even within the same bankruptcy, some creditors might be repaid one hundred cents on the dollar; while other creditors receive depreciated collateral or nothing at all. The variations in outcome depend fundamentally on the choices debtors make among their bankruptcy options.

TYPES OF BANKRUPTCY

Nearly every advanced industrial nation has some form of bankruptcy, but the forms vary widely from country to country. In the United States, the federal system of bankruptcy coexists with state law governing debtor-creditor relations. Bankruptcy is administered by federal courts and the available forms of bankruptcy are codified in Title 11 of the U.S. Code. Although a debtor need not be insolvent in the balance-sheet use of the concept, most non-business debtors are deeply in debt. One study showed that at the mean, debtors owed 3.2 times their annual income to their creditors; even if house mortgages are excluded from the total, the debtors owed 2 times their annual income to creditors (Sullivan, Warren, and Westbrook, 1989: 74-75). Similar results have been reported earlier; for example, Lane (1969) showed that the debt-income ratio for 250 petitioners in Los Angeles County was 2.68. Low income is not the only reason for high debt-income ratios. Only 12% of Caplovitz's low-income subjects, who were in financial trouble but not in bankruptcy, had debt-income ratios of 0.2 or higher, although he noted that some of them owed as much as one year's income (Caplovitz, 1963: 113).

The fundamental issue in bankruptcy is dividing the property of the debtors among multiple creditors. The average bankrupt family lists eighteen creditors in a bankruptcy. Unlike the bankruptcy laws of some times and places, American bankruptcy law has also recognized the need to leave the debtor sufficient property to make a "fresh start" economically. The taxonomy of bankruptcy revolves about three issues: who receives current assets or property, how much and what kinds of debt are paid or discharged, and whether future income will be encumbered to repay debts.

The three major forms of bankruptcy available to individuals are Chapter 7, Chapter 13, and Chapter 11. Chapter 7, sometimes called a straight bankruptcy or a liquidation, discharges most debts in return for which a trustee sells all non-exempt assets. Chapter 13, once called a "wage-earner's plan," requires a source of expected steady income and a plan to repay creditors from future income, typically for three to five years. The debtor keeps all property. A Chapter 13 plan must yield to the unsecured creditors a greater dividend than they would have received under a Chapter 7 distribution. About 30% of non-business bankruptcies are now filed in Chapter 13. Chapter 11, usually limited to businesses or to individuals with many assets, is similar to Chapter 13 and is sometimes referred to as a reorganization or restructuring of debt; Chapter 11 also requires a plan, with the additional requirements that creditors vote on the acceptability of the plan. Chapter 12, a relatively new option, provides for restructuring of the debts of a family farm, and it was a response to the fiscal farm crisis of the 1980s (see Smith, 1987).

Two critical issues for the family's post-bankruptcy situation are what debts may not be discharged, and what assets are exempt. Taxes and federally-financed or underwritten college loans are generally nondischargeable. Alimony and child support are nondischargeable. Creditors have the right to challenge the discharge of debts, and debts incurred fraudulently may be grounds for denying a discharge.

The level of exempt assets varies by state. Every state has debtor-creditor laws governing issues such as wage garnishment and home foreclosure, and these laws also specify what property cannot be taken from debtors. Although bankruptcy is reserved by the Constitution to the federal government, Congress was very deferential to the states' existing exemption laws. There is also a federal exemption level, but each state legislature is free to "opt out" from that relatively generous exemption level and reinstate its own level. Thirty-nine states have now opted out from the federal exemption laws, leaving their citizens with no option except for the state exemptions. Variation among the states reflects historical influences in debtor-creditor law as well as philosophical differences on what should be left to the debtor as part of a "fresh start."

The state exemption laws might be considered a proxy for what property legislators believe to be necessary for a family. A sociologist might categorize exempt property as producer goods, consumer goods, and sentimental goods. Many states exempt categories of property, such as tools of the trade or schoolbooks, that are analogous to *producer goods* because they help rebuild the debtors' economic life after the debt crisis. For example, exemption laws written when states were predominantly rural often specify the acreage, livestock, and farm implements that were considered minimal for farming. More recently written laws exempt minimal *consumption* essentials for an urban household, such as household goods or a car. Most creditors do not really want used bedsheets or towels, but most debtors would find replacing such goods to be a major expense. A final category of exempt property might be called "*sentimental goods*," property such as family pictures and family Bibles that are valuable only to the family. The exemption laws can be brutally pragmatic; some statutes exempt burial plots, presumably to reunite the family's next decedents in the same plot as the previous decedents. Although wedding rings are not exempt, in our study of 1547 cases we rarely saw wedding rings listed as

property, either exempt or non-exempt, and never saw any creditor efforts
to seize wedding jewelry. It is possible that both creditors and debtors have
stretched the category of sentimental goods beyond the strict requirements
of the law.

Historical and political factors underlie the state variations in exemption levels. States can be classified in terms of whether they are generally
"pro-debtor" (and high exemption) or pro-creditor (and low exemption).
California, Florida, and Texas would be characterized as generous to debtors, a fact that is sometimes attributed to their heritage of Spanish law and
sometimes to the historical facts of their settlement. The "fresh start" in
Texas leaves intact the homestead, transportation (once buggies, now two
cars), livestock, tools of the trade, and other one-time frontier necessities
such as firearms. Texas and several of the prairie states emphasized exemption of farmers' producer goods. When these statutes are applied to a
modern urban society, they may result in substantial exemption of consumer goods. The judicial reinterpretation of buggies and farm wagons to
vans and pickup trucks is a telling example. In these relatively generous
states, many families will be "judgment-proof"—that is, they will own
practically no assets except for those that are exempt. Nevertheless, debtors in these states will not necessarily seek a Chapter 7 to discharge their
debts, because many of their assets are collateral for secured debts.
Homes, cars, major furniture and other consumer durables with mortgages
or consumer financing could be lost in a Chapter 7.

Many Northeastern, Southern, and Midwestern states have low levels
of state exemptions that leave the debtors with few assets. As part of the
Puritan heritage, the Eastern states rarely provide any homestead exemption, although they might have a partial interest in a home and some
household goods (Giles, 1992: 25). In these low-exemption states, even
the poor may find that they have much to lose in bankruptcy. Low-exemption states tend to emphasize sentimental goods more than producer goods.

The change of American residence from largely rural to largely urban
posed a challenge to legislators in specifying exempt assets. A contemporary challenge is the development of new types of assets, most not anticipated in the statutes. Some examples of assets whose handling is now
problematic include retirement accounts and insurance policies. Disposition of such assets is often decided initially through litigation.

Debtors currently have broad, but not unlimited discretion to choose
between Chapter 7 or Chapter 13. Attorneys, judges, and trustees help
influence the decision (Sullivan, Warren, and Westbrook, 1993, 1988;
Chubb and Holley, 1992). The most important source of advice for many
families is probably the attorneys, many of whom have strong opinions

about the merits of the two types of bankruptcy. A 1984 amendment requires attorneys to notify their clients of the existence of both types of bankruptcy.

Judges may also influence the debtors at least by setting the tone for the district in terms of when a Chapter 13 or a Chapter 7 might be appropriate (Sullivan, Warren, and Westbrook, 1993). There is no means test to enter Chapter 7, although judges on their own motion may declare that a case represents a "substantial abuse" of the bankruptcy statutes (Wells, Kurtz, and Calhoun, 1991). The judge must also approve a Chapter 13 plan, a process called confirmation, and the court is supposed to determine that all disposable income over and above living expenses has been dedicated to the Chapter 13 plan. Trustees are appointed by the court and play a variety of functions. For any given case, there may be one or several trustees who play a role. Trustees conduct the meeting with creditors (called the Section 341 meeting), a meeting at which debtors must appear to answer questions put by their creditors. A Chapter 7 trustee sells any non-exempt property, if there is any. The Chapter 13 plan payments are made on a monthly basis to a Chapter 13 trustee, who is often a standing trustee. Some trustees also offer families advice and counseling on family budgeting; some will help petitioners to rehabilitate their credit if the Chapter 13 plan has been successfully completed. The trustees may also make motions to the court to dismiss cases, to allow a temporary moratorium on plan payments, or to institute other actions in the case.

Although the Administrative Office of the U.S. Courts has conventionally published statistics in terms of "business" and "non-business" bankruptcies, the distinction may be irrelevant for small entrepreneurs. A large proportion of the individual debtors file bankruptcy because of a failure of their own businesses. One recent study put the proportion of current or former entrepreneurs at 20% of bankrupt debtors, and they accounted for 45% of the scheduled debt of the sample (Sullivan, Warren, and Westbrook, 1989: 118). Earlier studies had reported that business-related reasons were cited 15% of a sample of Chapter 7 debtors (CRC, v. II: 35) and in another sample of debtors 13% cited business reasons (Shuchman and Rhorer, 1985).

FAMILIES AND DEBTORS: AN IMPERFECT FIT

Bankruptcy differs from other debtor-creditor proceedings because it involves all of the petitioner's creditors at once; the fundamental problems of bankruptcy are those of balancing the legitimate claims of the creditors against the welfare of the debtor and the debtor's family. It is ultimately a zero-sum game. Every dollar that is preserved for the family's welfare is a dollar not available to the creditors; every dollar that is given to creditors becomes unavailable for food, clothing, and shelter of the children. The public also has a strong interest in the outcome, both because they may have to provide for the bankrupt families through the welfare system and because they may ultimately face higher taxes to support the bankruptcy court system and higher interest rates and prices.

Families may play both roles in the bankruptcy, both as debtors and as creditors. Families sometimes discover through their mail that they are creditors of a business that is suddenly defunct, perhaps still owing them wages, accounts receivable, or a deposit. A retailer may go bankrupt holding a family's Christmas gifts in layaway. A family member injured in an automobile accident may receive a cash judgment from a court, only to see the defendant declare bankruptcy. Wage earners may become the creditors of employers who declare bankruptcy. Divorce often creates debtor/creditor relationships within what was once a nuclear family. One generation or subfamily may find itself in the debtor role with its creditors in a different generation or subfamily. Or family members who co-signed a loan may find their own assets in jeopardy, and seek bankruptcy as a solution for themselves.

In one recent study, nearly $77,000 of $23 million in scheduled unsecured debt was owed to family members, of which $63,474 was owed to ex-spouses or children (Sullivan, Warren, and Westbrook, 1989: 275, 295). Among Caplovitz's defaulting debtors, 8% cited "third-party" reasons, often their co-signing of a relative's credit instrument (Caplovitz, 1974: 53). Caplovitz (1974: 52) describes this as a problem of "misplaced trust in a friend or relative." Given the frequent financial aid that families often exchange, especially when part of a family is in serious financial difficulty, it is not surprising that many bankrupt debtors have borrowed from other family members. Some family debts, such as alimony and child support, are not legally dischargeable within bankruptcy, although the bankruptcy may make it possible for the ex-spouses and parents to concentrate their remaining resources on their family debts.

A married adult may file bankruptcy singly, or in a joint petition with a spouse. Although all of the creditors are involved in the bankruptcy, not all of the family members need be parties. Creditors would be just as satisfied if their claims were paid by a family member as by the original debtor. Creditor associations sometimes speak of debt payment as a moral responsibility shared by at least the debtors' close relatives. More practically, legal devices such as joint accounts, joint tenancy, and cosignatories make multiple family members liable. But in bankruptcy, the issues are highlighted because limited resources are being judicially allocated. Issues of family liability recur with great frequency: to what extent are the parents responsible for the debts of their college-age child? To what extent are adult children responsible for the medical expenses of their elderly relatives? May hospitals bill near relatives of their patients for medical expenses or, alternatively, refuse to admit the patient?

Not all family resources, however, are necessarily available to creditors, even when a married-couple family is involved in a joint filing. Households are not the same as families, and even the married couple is usually a subset of a larger household.

These issues are clouded further because the American family must be viewed in the bankruptcy context both as the unit of future production and as the unit of current and future consumption. Just as income is often earned by only a few household members for the benefit of the entire household, so debts may be incurred by only one member to the detriment of the entire family. Especially in Chapter 13, the issue of how much future income may be retained for consumption is critical. To what extent should wives and children suffer for the misfortune, mismanagement, or the venality of the husbands and fathers? These issues are especially pressing in bankruptcy because of the need to balance the welfare of the family against the legitimate demands of the creditors. This asymmetry between the financial actor–the borrower–and the affected family unit shows up in a number of ways.

First, bankruptcy law focuses on the individual debtors, but both judges and the statutes try to take account of the family context, even though the family or household is neither the proper unit financially (e.g., for borrowing) nor legally (e.g., for bankruptcy). Equity and welfare issues become inextricably tangled as soon as the family context is considered. The "bankruptcy family" is not legally defined, and its composition is complicated; the bankruptcy family is not even necessarily the same as the "tax family." For example, dependent children or other family dependents may live in other households. Some debts in a bankruptcy may be jointly incurred, while others are the individual debts of one or both spouses. Both Chapter 7 and Chapter 13, the most frequent consumer choices in bankruptcy, require the debtor–even if filing as an individual–to provide a budget of household income and necessary household expenses. The debtor may include in the bankruptcy budget the support of dependents who are outside the household, and the expenses of family members who are in the household but not in the bankruptcy. As we shall see later, these representations to the court may soon be obsolete, because the bankruptcy family is often in the process of recombining.

It is in Chapter 13, however, that these issues are most pronounced, principally because the Chapter 13 plan lasts for 36 to 60 months, during which the debtor is under the supervision of the court. All "disposable" income must be made available to the creditors through the Chapter 13 plan, but this does not imply that the income of all household members be turned over to creditors. For example, the teenager's babysitting money is not available to the creditors. What would happen to the householder's pay raise or worker's compensation claim or overtime payment is another story.

Indeed, some have speculated that judges might become more activist about manipulating the financial affairs of bankrupt families, either by encouraging them to increase their income or to reduce their consumption, for the benefit of creditors. For example, bankrupt families are less likely than all families to have two spouses working (Sullivan, Warren, and Westbrook, 1989: 151-157). Could a judge legitimately require that a married couple send both members into the labor force? By the same token, could the court require a worker to take a better-paid job on the night shift, or to accept a relocation transfer to another city, or even to bid on a better-paid job in the same workplace?

Especially in a Chapter 13, the court may become involved in the issue of what expenses are necessary, potentially micromanaging the household affairs of thousands of families. The law recognizes that a family's needs are greater than those of an individual. For example, many states permit higher exemptions for families than for individuals. How much greater family needs are is a cause for considerable debate. Courts have recently grappled with the issues of whether college tuition or orthodontia constitute justifiable expenses. (In state courts, parallel battles are fought over whether such expenses may legitimately be added to the child support responsibility of the non-custodial parent.) There might even be legal debate over whether the Chapter 13 household could, in the course of its plan, legitimately take on the care of a frail elderly relative or of an orphaned nephew. While most judges would far prefer not to be involved in the micro-level decision making of the Chapter 13 household after its plan has been approved, activist creditors might legitimately challenge a couple's decision to bear another child, to send a child to private school, or even to contribute money to a church or other charity.

The problems of economic sustenance within the bankruptcy family parallel those in the welfare family. Because a government benefit is being conferred in both cases–protection from creditors and perhaps debt discharge in the former, the outright provision of goods and services in the latter–the government also claims legitimacy to its efforts to oversee the economic life of the family. In both cases, there is a pervasive fear of the abuse of the system, with the unworthy or the careless contrasted with the merely unfortunate, the ill, or the victimized. With the secular increase in bankruptcies has come much greater concern over the level of abuse of bankruptcy, with increased calls for monitoring and controlling the debtors and limiting their choices in bankruptcy. The parallels are incomplete, however. Bankruptcy judges do not yet require the debtors to be working or looking for work (although a steady income source is a prerequisite for Chapter 13).

PROFILES OF THE FAMILY IN BANKRUPTCY

As already noted above, expenditures, credit use, and debt default appear to be age-linked phenomena. A number of studies have found that the bankruptcy petitioners are also relatively young. Several reviews of bankruptcy studies have indicated that the typical bankrupt debtor was in the late 20's or early 30's (Heck, 1980; U.S. Congress, 1973). Dolphin (1965) described bankruptcy as ". . . an ailment of the young man." More recent studies suggest that this conclusion may need revision, both as to age and gender.

A study conducted with 1991 data indicated that nearly 60% of a sample of bankruptcy filers are Baby Boomers, born between 1946 and 1964 (Sullivan, Warren, and Westbrook, 1992a). The corresponding proportion of the adult population is 44%. The Baby Boomers were by this time aged 27-45, and the peak bankruptcy filing rates occurred at ages 40-44, considerably older than the peak ages reported in earlier studies. It is impossible yet to determine whether the 1991 data represent a true change in an age effect, a cohort effect (i.e., the Baby Boomers are more bankruptcy-prone), or a period effect (i.e., an historical effect connected to economic or social conditions of the time period).

Previous reviews (Heck, 1980; U.S. Congress, 1973) have indicated that the typical bankrupt debtor is male. This appears to be changing, however. In 1981, only 17% of the cases were women (Sullivan, Warren, and Westbrook, 1989: 149-150), with another 56% of the sample made up of joint filings by husbands and wives. By 1991, a preliminary analysis showed that nearly 29% of the filings were by women, with 36% of them joint filings (Sullivan, Warren, and Westbrook, 1992a). The proportion of joint filings varied significantly by district. The rise in women filing bankruptcy by themselves appears to be related to their marital status, because 39% of them were divorced and another 27% have never been married.

Several early studies showed that the bankrupt debtors had less than a high school education (Stanley and Girth, 1971; Dolphin, 1965). Most earlier studies had also concluded that the bankrupt population had less education than the general population (Heck, 1980; U.S. Congress, 1973). Since these studies have been done, the average education level of the general population has risen. The relatively well-educated Baby Boomers, given their disproportionate representation in bankruptcy in the 1990s, would tend to raise the education level of the bankrupt debtors as well. A preliminary analysis of 1991 filers indicated that the bankrupt debtor sample was twice as likely as the general population to have completed "some college" but only two-thirds as likely to have completed a degree (Sullivan, Warren, and Westbrook, 1992a; see also GAO, 1983: 15). Indeed, "some college" was the modal response for the bankrupt debtors, versus "high school" for the general public. It is too early to know whether this is a one-time finding, or indicates a trend for the bankrupt population to be better educated.

A conclusion that does still appear to be correct is that the filers are at a stage in the family life-cycle at which dependency ratios are likely to be high, and information on household size and composition bears out this inference. Previous research indicates that the average household in bankruptcy is slightly larger than the average household (Sullivan, Warren, and Westbrook, 1989: 65-66). Heck (1980: 15), after citing Dolphin's (1965) study, notes: "A variety of other studies found the typical family size to be between 4 and 6 members." Whether a single adult or a married couple files, the household often includes minor children. Lane (1969) had found that petitioners in Los Angeles were significantly more likely to have children and to have more children. Other studies have also reported that bankrupt families are more likely than non-bankrupt families to have children.

In general, bankrupt debtors also appear to be more likely than the general population to be divorced (Lane, 1969). Not every study has reached this conclusion; for example, Preston (1969: 68) found that only two of 32 interviewees were divorced, although earlier divorces were mentioned as causal factors in the bankruptcy. Since these studies were conducted, both the divorce rate and the bankruptcy filing rate experienced an upward secular trend, but the proportions may have risen more in bankruptcy than in the general population. The 1991 study showed 22% of the bankruptcy sample to be currently divorced, compared with only 8.1% in the general population (Sullivan, Warren, and Westbrook, 1992a, 1992b).

MARITAL INSTABILITY AND BANKRUPTCY

The awkwardness of meshing debtor families into the assumptions of bankruptcy practice is greatly aggravated in the presence of marital instability, and yet virtually everyone agrees that bankruptcy is closely tied to marital instability. A number of studies have demonstrated an association between divorce rates and bankruptcy filing rates. Several of these are ecological studies based on aggregated data, but the studies tend to show a positive relationship between the divorce rate and the filing rate even though they represent several different time periods and different geographic areas (GAO, 1983; Heck, 1981; Shepard, 1984). Virtually all of these studies use rates (incidence per thousands or ten thousands of population), so that a simplistic size-of-place explanation can be eliminated. On the other hand, the issue of causality cannot be addressed.

In some cases, family problems lead to the debt problems. Among Caplovitz's (1974) debtors, 109 of nearly 2000 families blamed some sort of family problem for their debt default. Of them, 71 cited broken marriages, 30 cited marital tensions, and the remainder cited other family problems. In inflationary or recessionary times, 14% of families reported that their marriage was worse, and 19% more reported mixed results. Inflation contributed to the subjective sense of marital strain (Caplovitz, 1979: 156).

The causality also happens the other way, with financial problems making the marriage more unstable. About 34% of the families studied by Caplovitz reported increased quarrels. Quarrels tended to increase more when the job or income was threatened. At the time of the default, 74% of his sample were married, and 9 percent of them were subsequently divorced or separated because of their debt problems. In addition, a national sample survey conducted by the National Opinions Research Center reported that 23% of the respondents knew someone whose marriage had broken up over debt (Caplovitz, 1974: 284).

When micro-data are examined, there is again evidence for the relationship of divorce to bankruptcy. What is cause and what is effect are far from clear, however. In our studies, we have identified five types of cases that illustrate some of the permutations: the planned pre-divorce bankruptcy; the bankruptcy that becomes the precipitating incident for a divorce; the post-divorce bankruptcy; the custodial parent bankruptcy, which is a special case of the post-divorce bankruptcy; and the remarriage bankruptcy. While it is not yet possible to assign relative numbers to the incidence of these types, they illustrate some of the many ways in which divorce and bankruptcy may be entangled.

Planned Pre-Divorce Bankruptcy

In this bankruptcy, both parties anticipate that there will be a divorce; there is often a separation in process. The filing might be a joint filing, and it becomes a way to rationalize the couple's financial affairs with their creditors before the marriage is dissolved. Some couples appear to stay together just for this last legal act (Sullivan, Warren, and Westbrook, 1989: 160 n. 8). Another scenario is possible:

> Besides losing his job, Anthony was in the middle of a divorce. . . . The separation suggests another possible reason for the credit card charges: His soon-to-be-former wife may have incurred the charges, and Anthony may have been ordered to pay them as part of his divorce settlement. (Sullivan, Warren, and Westbrook, 1989: 182)

Bankruptcy Precipitating Divorce

Bankruptcy researchers would normally be unable to document this possibility unless they were following a sample of debtors for a period of time. The same financial troubles that lead to the bankruptcy may also help to destabilize the marriage. A parallel case comes from the literature on indebtedness. Caplovitz (1974: 284) describes a sequence of debt troubles leading to marital troubles in quoting a Detroit steel worker:

> I got in bad shape with the bills. I wasn't making enough money. I didn't have any money in the clear to buy clothes for the kids. We started fighting and separated.

Caplovitz (1974: 284) also quoted a Chicago waitress:

> I've had debt problems with him ever since I married him. He never wanted to pay his bills. We fought like cats and dogs, day and night.

Post-Divorce Bankruptcy

Caplovitz (1974: 53) indicates that marital instability was cited by 6% of his sample of debt defaulters as the first reason for default and by another 9% as the second or third reasons. In the 1991 sample of bankrupt debtors, 13.4% of the sample reported that they had experienced a marital change within two years of the bankruptcy. Only 9% of the currently married reported that they had had a marital change in the last two years.

But among the divorced, 45% reported that they had recently had a marital change, suggesting that the bankruptcy came within 24 months of the divorce (Sullivan, Warren, and Westbrook, 1992b). Some debtors expressed their reason for bankruptcy in their own words [verbatim transcription]:

> After separation of my marriage ex-husband incurred several bills in which my name was still linked. I am slow in real estate and my work has been *very* slow–in fact no income at all for a period of time. [emphasis in the original]

> I have had to file a bankruptcy because my ex-husband (name) divorced final 12 Oct 90, left the state of CA (address unknown) with all debts left for me to pay, all by myself. It was impossible to pay them all.

As these accounts indicate, a post-divorce problem for many petitioners is paying their debts. The amount of debt stays the same or even grows larger through accumulating interest, while the available income decreases. In the second case above, the ex-spouse had fled the jurisdiction, leaving all the debts for the bankruptcy petitioner to pay.

Custodial Parent Bankruptcy

The custodial parent is a special case of the post-divorce bankruptcy (Welch, 1992). Alimony and child support are not dischargeable by the bankrupt debtor. But the ex-spouse who becomes a creditor–the recipient of alimony and child support–nevertheless has debts to honor even if the payments do not arrive. If these debts become overwhelming, the single parent may file bankruptcy. As two petitioners poignantly put it:

> Single parent–no child support used credit cards to help support, etc.–everything just gets away from you before you realize you're far far in debt.

> Due to having become recently divorced after 7 years of shared incomes and now gaining full responsibility of maintaining a household for myself as well as for my 2-year-old child with minimum child support, I have been forced into this bankruptcy for lack of being able to make monthly consistent payments to the various accounts that I have. I would like to conclude by stating that this was the only and last resort that I had in accepting my responsibilities, which I regret has come to this point. I'd rather have taken this action

instead of just allowing the accounts to remain continuously delinquent.

In some cases, it was medical expenses incurred for the dependent child
that pushed the custodial parent into bankruptcy, occasionally because the
ex-spouse had not provided the health insurance promised in the divorce
agreement. One issue under consideration is the extent to which the Trustee might consider alimony or child support to be "accounts receivable"
owed to the bankruptcy estate, and seek to cooperate with other state or
federal agencies who try to enforce support decrees.

Remarriage Bankruptcy

The remarriage bankruptcy marks the effort by a remarried husband or
wife to rearrange the financial affairs left over from an earlier marriage by
one of them. Preston (1969: 126) describes such a case, complicated by a
job change and lower subsequent income.

> . . . [The] man had been an "over-the-road" truck driver who got
> home not over two or three times a week. This absence did not
> "make the heart grow fonder" and a divorce ensued. Child support
> of $250 per month and all the family bills to pay was the court
> award. He remarried, quit trucking, and secured a manufacturing
> plant job which paid less than half of what he had been accustomed
> to. With both him and his new wife working, they were unable to
> keep up with their obligations.

CONCLUSION

Debt in general, and bankruptcy in particular, have the potential to
affect family welfare in many ways. Although family relationships are not
merely economic relationships, the exchange of economic support remains
an important function of the family, and bankruptcy constitutes a major
disruption in the family's economic system. We do not yet understand all
of these effects, but as the number of bankruptcies in the nation increases
so does the need for further research. How much and for how long bankruptcy affects the family remain important lacunae in the literature. One
type of study that is so far missing is a longitudinal or panel study of the
impact of bankruptcy on a family during a 36-month Chapter 13 plan or
during the three to five years following a Chapter 7 discharge.

By providing an outline of some of the major findings concerning bankruptcy and the family, we have sought to guide future researchers into salient and unresolved issues. Although bankruptcy is a pathology of the credit system, its systematic study may help us understand the credit system better. In the same way, although extreme indebtedness or bankruptcy do not affect all families, understanding their effects for some families will help us to understand the nature of the family economy for a much larger set of effectively functioning families.

REFERENCES

Ambry, Margaret K. (1993). Receipts from a Marriage. *American Demographics* 15(2), 30-37.

Apilado, V.P., J.J. Dauten, and D.E. Smith. (1978). Personal Bankruptcies. *Journal of Legal Studies* 7, pp. 371-392.

Blau, Peter M. and Otis Dudley Duncan. (1967). *The American Occupational Structure.* New York: Wiley.

Bradburn, Norman and Seymour Sudman. (1979). *Improving Interview Method and Questionnaire Design.* San Francisco: Jossey-Bass.

Brimmer, Andrew F. (1981). Economic Implications of Personal Bankruptcy. *Personal Finance Quarterly Report* 35, p. 187.

Brunn, George. (1965). "Wage Garnishment in California: A Study and Recommendation." *California Law Review* 53: 1214.

Brunner, G.A. (1969). *Personal Bankruptcies in Ohio.* Unpublished Ph.D. dissertation. Columbus: Ohio State University.

Caplovitz, David. (1963). *The Poor Pay More.* New York: Free Press.

Caplovitz, David. (1974). *Consumers in Trouble: A Study of Debtors in Default.* New York: Free Press.

Caplovitz, David. (1979). *Making Ends Meet: How Families Cope with Inflation and Recession.* Beverly Hills: Sage Publications.

Chubb, Janet L. and Richard F. Holley. (1992). "Decoding the Code: A Guide to the Rules and Statutes Governing Bankruptcy." *Family Advocate* 14(3), 29-62.

Commission on Bankruptcy Laws of the United States. (1973). *Report.* Washington, DC: Government Printing Office.

Credit Research Center. (1982). *Consumer Bankruptcy Study.* 2 vols. West Lafayette, IN: Purdue University.

Dolphin, Robert, Jr. (1965). *An Analysis of Economic and Personal Factors Leading to Consumer Bankruptcy.* Bureau of Business and Economic Research. Occasional Paper No. 15. East Lansing: Michigan State University.

Flynn, Ed. (1992). Filings Per Household Increase. *ABI Journal*, November, 11.

Ford, Janet. (1988). *The Indebted Society: Credit and Default in the 1980s.* London: Routledge.

Giles, W. Jefferson. (1992). Till Debt Do Us Part. *Family Advocate* 14(3), 23-27.

Hanushek, Eric A. and John E. Jackson. (1977). *Statistical Methods for Social Scientists.* New York: Academic.

Heck, Ramona K.Z. (1981). An Econometric Analysis of Interstate Differences in Nonbusiness Bankruptcy and Chapter Thirteen Rates. *Journal of Consumer Affairs* 13-31.

Heck, Ramona K.Z. (1980). Identifying Insolvent Households. *Journal of Home Economics* 72(4), 14-17.

Herrmann, R.O. (1965). Causal Factors in Consumer Bankruptcy: A Case Study. Institute of Governmental Affairs, Occasional Paper No. 6. Davis: University of California.

Jacob, Herbert. (1969). *Debtors in Court*. Chicago: Rand-McNally.

Lane, Sylvia. (1969). Petitioners Under Chapter XIII of the Bankruptcy Act. *The Journal of Consumer Affairs* 3(1), 26-40.

Luckett, Charles. (1988). Personal Bankruptcies. *Federal Reserve Bulletin* 74(9), 591-603.

Preston, William J. (1969). *A Comparison of the Rationale and Socio-Economic Characteristics of Straight Bankruptcy and Chapter XIII Petitioners in the Denver, Colorado, Area*. Unpublished doctoral dissertation, Colorado State College.

Ryan, Martin. (forthcoming). Consumer Bankrupts in Melbourne. *Australian Journal of Social Issues*.

Shepard, L. (1984). Personal Failures and the Bankruptcy Reform Act of 1978. *Journal of Law and Economics* 27, 419.

Shuchman, Philip. (1985). New Jersey Debtors 1982-1983: An Empirical Study. *Seton Hall Law Review* 15, 541.

Shuchman, Philip. (1983). The Average Bankrupt: A Description and Analysis of 753 Personal Bankruptcy Filings in Nine States. *Commercial Law Journal* 1983, 288.

Shuchman, Philip and Thomas L. Rhorer. (1982). Personal Bankruptcy Data for Opt-Out Hearings and Other Purposes. *American Bankruptcy Law Journal* 56, p. 1.

Smith, J.P. (1987). The Social and Economic Correlates of Bankruptcy During the Farm Fiscal Crisis, 1970-1987. *Mid-American Journal of Sociology* 12, 35-53.

Stanley, D.T. and M. Girth. (1971). *Bankruptcy: Problems, Process, Reform*. Washington, DC: The Brookings Institution.

Subrin, Stephen N. and John Rugheimer. (1976a). A Statistical Study of Bankruptcy in Massachusetts, with Emphasis on the Bankruptcy Bar and an Examination of the Proposed Bankruptcy Acts. *American Bankruptcy Law Journal* 50, 137 (parts I and II).

Subrin, Stephen N. and John Rugheimer. (1976b). A Statistical Study of Bankruptcy in Massachusetts, with Emphasis on the Bankruptcy Bar and an Examination of the Proposed Bankruptcy Acts. *American Bankruptcy Law Journal* 50, 221 (parts III and IV).

Sullivan, Teresa A., Elizabeth Warren, Jay Lawrence Westbrook. (1993). Local Legal Culture. Unpublished manuscript.

Sullivan, Teresa A., Elizabeth Warren, Jay Lawrence Westbrook. (1992a). Bankruptcy and the Demographic "Curse of Job." Paper read at the Population Association of America annual meeting, Denver, CO, 1 May 1992.

Sullivan, Teresa A., Elizabeth Warren, Jay Lawrence Westbrook. (1992b). If Bankruptcy Is the Answer, What Was the Question? Paper read at the Law and Society Association annual meeting, Philadelphia, PA, 31 May 1992.

Sullivan, Teresa A., Elizabeth Warren, Jay Lawrence Westbrook. (1989). *As We Forgive Our Debtors: Bankruptcy and Consumer Credit in America*. New York: Oxford.

Sullivan, Teresa A., Elizabeth Warren, Jay Lawrence Westbrook. (1988). Laws, Models, and Real People: Choice of Chapter in Bankruptcy. *Law and Social Inquiry* 13(4), 661-706.

Sullivan, Teresa A., Elizabeth Warren, Jay Lawrence Westbrook. (1987). Uses of Empirical Data in Formulating National Bankruptcy Policy. *Law and Contemporary Problems* 50, 195-235.

Sullivan, Teresa A., Elizabeth Warren, Jay Lawrence Westbrook. (1986). Folklore and Facts: A Preliminary Report from the Consumer Bankruptcy Project. *American Bankruptcy Law Journal* 60, 293-338.

Sullivan, Teresa A., Elizabeth Warren, Jay Lawrence Westbrook. (1983). Limiting Access to Bankruptcy Discharge: An Analysis of the Creditors' Data. *Wisconsin Law Review* 1983, 1091-1146.

United States Bureau of the Census. (1992). *Statistical Abstract of the United States, 1992*. 112 ed. Washington, DC: Government Printing Office.

United States Congress. (1973). Report of the Commission on the Bankruptcy Laws of the United States. H.R. Doc. No. 137, 93rd Cong., 1st sess., pt I.

United States General Accounting Office. (1983). Bankruptcy Reform Act of 1978–A Before and After Look. GAO/GGD-83-54. Washington, DC: GAO.

Welch, Robert M., Jr. (1992). Protect the Rights of the Creditor Spouse. *Family Advocate* 14(3), 36-41.

Wells, Wayne R., Janell M. Kurtz, Robert J. Calhoun. (1991). The Implementation of Bankruptcy Code Section 707(b): The Law and the Reality. *Cleveland State Law Review* 39, 15-48.

Yeager, Frederick. (1972). *Personal Bankruptcy in the United States with Special Reference to Northern West Virginia*. Unpublished Ph.D. Dissertation. Morgantown: West Virginia University.

Yeager, Frederick. (1978). Personal Bankruptcy and Economic Stability. *Southern Journal of Economics* 41, p. 96.

The Effect of Welfare Laws on the Family

Cynthia J. Price

INTRODUCTION

It seems the American public can hardly remember a time when welfare, and its tangential issues, were not at the center of some political debate. Scarcely a week goes by when we are not reminded of the increasing number of individuals, particularly women and children, who live in poverty, and the companion issue of the skyrocketing cost of welfare.[1] As we crept through the 1991-1992 recession this problem became increasingly evident: ten percent of American families were receiving welfare, 35-40 million were without health care, food stamp use was on the increase, and assistance levels were being challenged in light of unbalanced state budgets. Welfare and welfare law and policy are part of the American fabric. Its threads have been woven in such a way that it has become interdependent with numerous social and economic policies, because legislators have little latitude to reduce budgets without inflicting some damage to the welfare system.

Although the existence of formal welfare legislation is relatively new to the United States, its roots are well grounded in American history. While federal welfare legislation, as we know it, was not enacted until 1935, social policies aimed particularly at the care of widows and their children had their foundations in the 1800s. Furthermore, the notion of a welfare state came to America from England, via the English Poor Laws (Feagin, 1975). The goal in formulating welfare policy throughout history has been

Cynthia J. Price is Assistant Professor, Department of Sociology, Seattle Pacific University, Seattle, WA.

[Haworth co-indexing entry note]: "The Effect of Welfare Laws on the Family." Price, Cynthia J. Co-published simultaneously in *Marriage & Family Review* (The Haworth Press, Inc.) Vol. 21, No. 3/4, 1995, pp. 217-237; and: *Families and Law* (ed: Lisa J. McIntyre, and Marvin B. Sussman) The Haworth Press, Inc., 1995, pp. 217-237. Multiple copies of this article/chapter may be purchased from The Haworth Document Delivery Center [1-800-3-HAWORTH; 9:00 a.m. - 5:00 p.m. (EST)].

to balance the needs and desires of the state with the local community and the individual in need. Shedding light on this balance is my goal in this paper.

Welfare research generally takes on one of two faces: (1) a statistical analysis of the occurrences, propensity and length of welfare use, and (2) the "effectiveness" of welfare policy. Such approaches, however, often ignore the relationship between welfare and the influence of the culture's values, beliefs and attitudes. Yet, welfare legislation cannot be fully understood without comprehending the context in which it was designed and formulated. The intent of this paper, then, is three-fold: (1) to synthesize the existing literature in order to present an historical picture of the development of welfare legislation; (2) to contribute to the discussion on the sociocultural underpinnings of welfare legislation in this country, and (3) to examine current policy and theories—and the likelihood of their success in light of the current social and political trends.

WELFARE IN RETROSPECT

Before welfare, families depended on themselves and their relations to maintain their economic existence. During the late nineteenth and early eighteenth centuries all members of the family, women and children included, participated in the labor force to support the family (Scott and Tilly, 1978). This was particularly true of European immigrants who worked as domestics and doing handwork in the United States. "The poor, the illiterate, the economically and politically powerless people in the past operated according to the values which fully justified the employment of women outside the home" (Scott and Tilly, 1978: 151). During the agrarian society of the 1800s mothers worked together with other family members to produce goods and services for the community. But the Industrial Revolution caused a rethinking of the woman's role. As families flocked to the industrial centers, often leaving family support systems behind, questions of domestic responsibility were raised.

In 1909, the White House Conference on the Care of Dependent Children considered Mothers' Pensions as necessary to preventing "the break-up or disruption of families solely because of poverty" (quoted in Dear, 1989: 7). This followed from the participants' ideal that "Home life is the highest and finest product of civilization. It is the great molding force of mind and character" (quoted in Garfinkel and McLanahan, 1986: 97). Inherent in these statements, as Grace Abbott noted in 1934, is the introduction of the notion of adequacy (Dear, 1989); the desire to establish some minimal level of need to support a family in order to make the home a place of safety and security where optimal development can occur. This struggle continues today.

During the early part of the 20th century, the idea arose that women should remain at home. This was particularly true for widowed women with children. By 1935, nearly all states provided some type of assistance to mothers in need of financial aid due to the death of a spouse, an effort begun in 1911 (Dear, 1989; Amenta, E. and B. Carruthers, 1988). Known officially as the Mothers' Aid Law (Mason, 1985), this program also came to be known as Mothers' Pension, Mothers' Aid, Mothers' Assistance or the Widows' Pension. Centered in local communities with ties to state legislatures, this loosely knit assistance program provided cash grants and in-kind services to homes lacking a male breadwinner (Dear, 1989). The most important focus of such legislation was the welfare of children (Mason, 1985). The Mothers' Pension, like English Poor Law, was designed to provide services for those considered destitute (Garfinkel and McLanahan, 1986). However, it differed from poor law in that aid was given outside of the poor house; a direction that would be followed by subsequent relief programs.

The aim of the Mothers' Pension was to enable mothers to remain at home to care for their children when the male breadwinner was absent (Dear, 1989). Because of the absence of formal support systems,[2] if mothers could not remain at home children were likely to be institutionalized (Mason, 1985). The provision of pensions to allow women to remain in the home, as opposed to being in the labor force, sent a message to the American public: the mother, who remained at home, was an American ideal. This notion, a new concept for women, was supported by both community values and politicians (Garfinkel and McLanahan, 1986). The Mothers' Pension impacted the family by placing the focus of family life on the role of the mother–that of being a homemaker. While mothers may have remained at home in previous generations, public policy now made this lifestyle a cultural expectation, if not a cultural norm.

The Mothers' Pension program, for the most part, accommodated those who were white and resided in the urban areas (Dear, 1987). In addition, the original program focussed primarily on providing benefits to widows, a holdover from the colonial era. These were the so called "worthy poor." As Garfinkel and McLanahan (1986) noted, two interrelated factors influenced the distribution of these benefits. First, widowhood was an involuntary state, thus there would be no intentional increase in the numbers who needed assistance. Second, was that of race and class. In 1932, 82 percent of the recipients were widowed, and 95 percent were white (Dear, 1987). "Widows who were treated the best were those whose husbands had contributed most obviously to the community good (that is, men who had died in the service of their country)" (p. 92). In other words, "widowhood was a respectable status" (Garfinkel and McLanahan, 1986: 92). As a result, women of color, those having a lower socioeconomic status and residing in rural areas, and those who were once again single for reasons other than being widowed, were often neglected. Furthermore, support levels were relatively meager during the Progressive era. While the desire was to provide an adequate environment in which children could be raised, benefits were kept low to encourage women to work (Mason, 1985). These early welfare laws sent mixed messages to poor families. Were mothers to remain at home and receive meager financial assistance? Or, were they to be in the labor force working long hours for hopes of adequate pay? The intent behind these early policies has changed little into the present day. The American public considers it a moral responsibility of the parent, in this case a single mother, to both adequately raise her children and participate in the labor force while providing little business or governmental support to do either.

Women continued to be a presence in the labor force during the Great Depression; as men were unable to find employment women often became employed through often meager jobs in order to provide at least a subsistence income. Those hardest hit by the financial downturn were of the urban and rural lower classes. The middle class felt the effects of the Depression in terms of status or reputation loss, but generally did not experience true poverty in the sense that they found themselves in need of basic necessities (Elder, 1974). Still, while many middle-class people did not experience extreme poverty they did experience some degree of deprivation. As Elder (1974) notes:

> An enduring theme of the Depression experience is its alien nature in American life and psychology, despite recurring hard times and the millions of Americans who have known only poverty. It was alien to the social character and institutions shaped by an economy geared to abundance, with its image of unlimited resources, continuing growth and vitality, and equality of opportunity; to the prosperous flush times of the 20's or New Era which "made the crack up" especially painful. (pp. 283-284)

This new-felt awareness of life under conditions of economic deprivation brought attention to the needs of poor people, particularly by those who had never experienced poverty. As unemployment rose to 18 percent those experiencing deprivation for the first time (the middle-class people who could not find employment) began to realize that becoming poor was easier than they had previously believed (Garfinkel and McLanahan, 1986).

Unemployment became so severe that within the first one-hundred days of his election, President Franklin D. Roosevelt introduced, and Congress passed, the Federal Emergency Relief Act (FERA). This was the first federal cash relief program in U.S. history. Because Roosevelt, and many of those who followed, preferred work relief to cash relief the FERA was soon replaced by the Works Projects Administration (WPA) and the Civil Works Administration (CWA) (Garfinkel and McLanahan, 1986). These programs were the beginning of the "New Deal."

In 1935, Congress passed the landmark Social Security Act, the center-piece of the New Deal, a politically appealing program whose intention was to remain small (Szanton, 1991). This legislation whose goal was to provide financial assistance–but not a full income–to those who otherwise would have "fallen through the cracks," created five federal income support programs. Of these five, two were social insurance programs, Old Age Insurance and Unemployment Insurance, while three were welfare programs, Aid to the Blind, Old Age Assistance and Aid to Dependent Children (ADC). While the two social programs were federally financed, the welfare programs were jointly financed by federal and state governments, and administered by state and local offices (Garfinkel and McLanahan, 1986).

Of central importance to the New Deal was the ADC program. The intended impact of this program was "designed to release from the wage earning role the person whose natural function is to give her children the physical and affectionate guardianship necessary, not alone to keep them from falling into social misfortune, but more affirmatively to rear them into citizens capable of contributing to society" (National Conference on Social Welfare, 1985: 34). The obvious focus was on the well-being of the child and the mother's role in that experience. Furthermore, as with the Mothers' Pension program, the emphasis was to maintain a "home" in which capable citizens could be reared. Of particular interest in this statement is the idea that a woman's "natural function" is to be a mother, to remain at home, and to rear her children. In other words, it seems the legislation created an imperative that it was the responsibility of the mother to the nation to raise competent children. Furthermore, in these words we see resolution to earlier ambiguities as to where a mother's place was–in the home.

However, it took a while to decide specifically who would receive benefits. Political and social advocates and some legislators wanted all children to receive aid, regardless of the family situation, while others wanted only those who were the children of widows to be eligible (Szanton, 1991). Although, the legislation that was finally passed considered a dependent child to be one living in a divorced, separated, never-married or widowed family, this was a hard won battle. Many legislators had argued that mothers who were single due to divorce, separation or out-of-wedlock births in some way were deserving of their status, and undeserving of financial support. Thus, the only group not covered by ADC were poor children of two-parent families (Bell, 1965). Because one parent in the household was likely to be capable of securing employment, legislators believed benefits for two-parent homes were unnecessary. The purpose of ADC, as agreed upon by Congress, was not to prevent poverty but to relieve it (Garfinkel and McLanahan, 1986).

As the Depression, and eventually World War II ended, the nation found itself in times of greater prosperity. During this era little attention was given to the needs of the poor. As a result, during the post-war years a growing debate was centered around the worthiness of women receiving welfare (Mason et al., 1985). This debate was spurred on by increasing caseloads as more women moved from rural areas and the number of minorities, primarily African-Americans, increased. In addition, the qualifications for receiving benefits were broadened as non-widows became eligible. To counteract this tide, eligibility requirements became more stringent especially for non-whites and mothers of illegitimate children (Mason et al., 1985; Szanton, 1991), significantly impacting the well-being of these families. Furthermore, during the mid-1950s, there was considerable variation in the distribution of ADC benefits as local communities had a greater role in this process. In communities where the preservation of particular ideals was a goal, stricter benefit rules prevailed.

In constant dollars benefits for ADC increased during the post-war era, contradicting the original intent of its designers to relieve but not prevent poverty. The purpose of these increases was to allow single mothers to remain at home to care for their children, as was increasingly the social norm (Garfinkel and McLanahan, 1986). This ideal was short-lived for the poor, as it eventually would be for many, when, in the 1960s, President Kennedy reiterated the need to reduce welfare dependency by "rehabilitating" single mothers into the labor force (Garfinkel and McLanahan, 1986). These changes made evident contradicting community values: that mothers should remain at home to care for children, as was their "natural function," while at the same time all adults should be "rehabilitated" to full employment. The foundation for a clash in value systems was being well laid. In addition, the 1962 amendment to the Social Security Act changed the name of the program from ADC to AFDC (Aid to Families with Dependent Children)[3] to emphasize the importance of children as the receivers of benefits.

Carrying forward Kennedy's conception of welfare reform was continued by President Johnson. In March 1964, President Johnson declared his "War on Poverty." The intent was to (1) significantly reduce poverty by providing training and education and, (2) increase benefits to a level which would enable people to "get back on their feet." Several of the programs Johnson instituted, such as Head Start and Work Study, are still in effect today; other programs, such as Job Corp, were cut by later administrations.

In accordance with the second part of Johnson's plan, benefits (in constant dollars) increased enormously. This was the beginning of nearly two decades of high welfare spending. During Johnson's tenure welfare expenditures for single mothers alone increased 61 percent. In addition to increased AFDC payments, the Johnson Administration also introduced Medicare (health care for the aged) and Medicaid (health care for the poor). By 1980, the majority of all Medicaid benefits went to female headed households (Garfinkel and McLanahan, 1986). In addition to medical assistance, the Johnson administration also expanded housing assistance and food stamp benefits.

The emphasis throughout the 1970s and 1980s was on providing work training in order to prepare the welfare mother to reenter (or enter for the first time) the labor force. As a result, job training became an increasingly important component of welfare. In fact, for some, welfare benefits were contingent on the recipient undergoing job training. However, once again, concern existed over the issue of whether mothers should be child care providers or laborers. In the late 1960s and early 1970s there arose what is now known as the National Welfare Rights movement. The aim of this movement was to eliminate discriminatory practices which had previously excluded some women from receiving welfare benefits. These activists argued that there should be a guaranteed income that allowed single mothers to remain at home to care for their children. Because the care of children is a valuable component of the nation's productivity, they argued, women should be paid wages to care for their children. Others argued, however, that such a proposal would discourage women from entering the labor force and encourage the intergenerational transmission of poverty (Mason et al., 1985).

The proportion of families on welfare has continually increased since the inception of programs such as AFDC. Between 1970 and 1979, 15% of all families were receiving AFDC, although only 2.2% had received assistance for over 8 years. The median length of time on welfare for a family is 4 years (Duncan and Hoffman, 1988). Compared to the 1980s, the 1970s were relatively more prosperous for poor families. During the 1980s welfare dependency decreased, but not necessarily because the poor were better off. Rank (1986) reports that program cuts during the tenure of the Reagan Administration increased the probability that those receiving welfare grants would exit the program, not because of greater success in programs, but because of more stringent rules for welfare qualifications. As a result of these changes, more families lived in a "no-man's-land"– earning too much to qualify for welfare, and too little to fully support the household. Thus, the decrease in the number of people receiving public assistance was not indicative of a declining population in need of assistance; rather, it represented a different standard for judging such need.

By the mid-1980s, what we refer to as "welfare" consisted of approximately 60 programs at a (1985) cost of $130 billion. In reality, there was no unified welfare system, but instead there was a "hodgepodge" of programs addressing a variety of needs (Haskins, 1991). Furthermore, welfare policy was no longer decided by Congress and the President alone, rather such legislation was influenced by party philosophy, interest groups, public opinion and the media (Haskins, 1991). The welfare system seemed unmanageable. In addition to the burgeoning bureaucracy the welfare system created, the notion that mothers should care for their children at home was also disappearing as a strong movement to have mothers work as opposed to provide in-home child care predominated.

In 1984, Charles Murray, through his influential book, *Losing Ground: American Social Policy, 1950-1980* became the conservative's voice on welfare reform. His central thesis was two-fold. First, overspending on welfare programs ultimately serves to make matters worse for its recipients, hindering their ability to exit poverty. Second, Murray argued that on a macro scale, public assistance has virtually no effect in diminishing the number of people who are poor. Murray's work voiced the concern that the outcome of welfare was not rehabilitation but dependency, arguing that welfare goes against the "work ethic" mentality. He believed that by revealing such "truths" he could effectively enrage "hard working Americans" (Haskins, 1991). Liberals, however, effectively argued to the contrary that the belief that welfare users were completely dependent on the system was unfounded (see Wilson, 1987). They emphasized the degree to which Murray and others of conservative ilk had neglected the non-economic factors that play into the poverty experience. Moreover, Murray gives superficial, if any, attention to the role of social phenomena and psychological factors, such as self-esteem and depression, in the welfare experience (Price, 1990).

The groundwork for the argument over welfare dependency was well laid in the early 1980s. As the debate escalated the battle lines were drawn on party lines. Simply put, the Republicans wanted to increase work requirements, while the Democrats wanted to increase public assistance benefits (Haskins, 1991). The welfare debate was one fought over political ideologies, as opposed to the needs of those utilizing welfare benefits. In fact, Haskins (1991) suggests that members of Congress have predetermined values which are relatively impervious to fact. Haskins further notes, facts seem to be "only mildly relevant to the fundamental questions of welfare policy" (p. 630). Even though legislators had access to a tremendous amount of data, welfare reform, perhaps not surprisingly, was formulated in terms of a political agenda.

In 1988, the debate culminated in a major overhaul of the United States welfare system, the first of its kind since the passage of the Social Security Act of 1935. Incorporating the notion of "rehabilitation" of mothers into the labor force, the Family Support Act (FSA), signed into legislation by President Reagan, emphasized the notion of workfare–requiring job training and/or education with the receipt of benefits, with the goal of making families self-sufficient and not in need of welfare. This legislation pleased the conservative contingency. In addition to these requirements, however, the legislation provided financial allowances which were considered more "family friendly," a plan which found more favor with liberals. In contrast to previous financial limitations these allowances included transitional child care and medical benefits for up to one year after employment and job training, with the expectation that all mothers be in the labor force to receive benefits, except when children under three are in the home. In addition, in hopes of encouraging struggling families to "get back on their feet," limited funds for education, child support enforcement, and welfare benefits for two-parent families are also provided (Wiesman, 1991; Dear, 1989). While the bill appeared beneficial, it also disappointed many. Republicans believed that work requirements had become too watered down. Democrats, on the other hand, regarded work requirements to be "slave fare" (Szanton, 1991).

The FSA is currently being implemented throughout the United States. While it has its detractors and its problems, some successes are being noted. Several states, prior to the implementation of the reform, instituted similar programs to provide a "test run." Washington state's Family Independence Program identifies crucial links between employment, job training and transitional child care and medical benefits. While suffering some significant cost overruns due to underfunding and the program's popularity, the program provided some positive insights into the possibilities of the Family Support Act (see Price, 1990; Weeks et al., 1990).

There is little doubt that further research is needed to understand the potential effectiveness of such programs. As the next sections of this paper will note, however, the links between the society's values and attitudes towards welfare and effective research need to be identified and understood.

WELFARE AND THE SOCIAL FABRIC

It is hard for the head of a family, male or female, black or white, who cannot support the family, to rear children to conform to cultural expectations *and* to contribute constructively to society. (Schorr, 1989: 20; emphasis added)

Poverty has long been accepted as part of the fabric of the American culture. Though there have been attempts to alleviate or eradicate its existence, it is generally accepted that poverty and poor people will always be part of this society. Those who depend upon welfare are often portrayed as "freeloaders," lazy and having no desire to work, or as promiscuous and as people who find it "cheaper to be on welfare than to get a job."

Self-sufficiency as a normative expectation of American society dates back to the Calvinistic work ethic tradition, introduced in Europe in the 17th century (Feagin, 1975). "With the emphasis on the ideology of individualism, a development which paralleled further growth of capitalism, came not only the positive view of the successful as virtuous but also the negative or critical view of poverty as punishment for those who were not virtuous" (Feagin, 1975: 92). In practical terms, the ideology of the work ethic has meant:

1. That each individual should work hard and strive to succeed in competition with others;
2. That those who work hard should be rewarded with success (seen as wealth, property, prestige and power);
3. That because of widespread and equal opportunity those who work will in fact be rewarded with success;
4. That economic failure is an individual's own fault and reveals lack of effort and other character defects. (Feagin, 1975)

These ideals were paramount during Roosevelt's structuring of the New Deal, and subsequently the Social Security Act. While the first New Deal legislation passed was for immediate cash relief (the FERA) the architects of this program continuously emphasized their belief that the answer to economic insecurity was to work. To that end, "[t]he dramatic improvement in the economic status of vulnerable groups achieved by the Social Security Act should not obscure the fact that the basic design of the act reinforced both the central role of work in American society and the commitment to self-reliance (Garfinkel and McLanahan, 1986). The work ethic, perpetrated and maintained by the middle class, has continued to the present day as each successive presidential administration has looked for new ways to train, educate, and employ those receiving public assistance.

Economic recovery from the Depression began with World War II. As employment rates increased people shared in the country's economic prosperity. The prosperity of the late 1940s and 1950s brought new hope to working Americans. However, this was a particularly difficult time for those receiving welfare benefits, as the American dream of home ownership, two happy children, a father employed outside of the home, and a mother entrenched in domestic bliss, saw its full impact. Those receiving welfare became further isolated from the mainstream of society.

This desire for self-sufficiency and individualism had been apparent since the early 1900s. Women were particularly affected by these changes. As families moved from the farms to the cities domesticity often became the woman's sole domain, as the man's role became that of the provider (Bernard, 1981). Moreover, there was a belief that the worlds of work and family life were separate (Voydanoff, 1984), further limiting women to the world of unpaid labor. The quest for this version of the American dream, however, was interrupted by the Industrial Revolution, World War I, the Great Depression, and World War II–events which all, to some degree or another, required many women to work outside of the home either to provide subsistence for the family, or to assist in a national effort. While the desire was to have women at home, it took several decades for the dream to become reality. The dream's reality, however, was short-lived. Researchers have pegged this era as an anomaly in family history (Cherlin, 1988) as no family system prior to, or since has been able to maintain this composition.

The 1960s experienced significant fluctuation in the provision of welfare benefits. These differences reflected the values and biases of the administrations. President Kennedy saw it as imperative that people needed to be held accountable for their actions, and thus should be required to work. President Johnson, on the other hand, began the war on poverty–whose goal was to eradicate the experience of being poor. The difference was obviously not one of political parties, but, instead, one of the perceptions of what it meant to be poor. The Kennedy administration perceived being poor and the use of welfare as at worst a character defect, and at best

a life situation which an individual with dogged determination could resolve. The Johnson administration, while noting the need for women to
work, also introduced the notion that other obstacles within society, such as
housing, and access to medical and child care services, inhibited people
from exiting poverty and ultimately leaving the welfare rolls. In short, the
approach of this administration was to institute broad reaching financial
benefits and programmatic changes directed at helping people out of poverty.

With the conservative swing of the late 1970s through the present,
presidential administrations and the country-at-large have returned to the
notion that being poor and being on welfare is a condition of which any
able-bodied American could cure him/herself; all that is needed is the
fortitude and the desire to leave welfare. Recent views of welfare use have
linked the poverty experience to the decimation of the American family.
President Reagan stated that "misguided welfare programs" led to a "national tragedy involving family breakdown, teenage illegitimacy and
worsening poverty" (Weintraub, 1986 as quoted in Zimmerman, 1989:
674). Furthermore, a Reagan task force examining family issues asserted
that "two liberal decades have frayed the fabric of family life bringing in
their wake increased crime, illegitimate births, teen pregnancy, divorce,
sexually transmitted disease and poverty. . . . Welfare contributes to the
failure to form the family in the first place and that its easy availability in
all of its forms has become a powerful force for the destruction of family
life through the perpetuation of the welfare culture" (Weintraub, 1986 as
quoted in Zimmerman, 1989: 674). Moreover, the experiences of the
1980s powerfully influenced the thinking about wealth and poverty. The
strong economy contributed to a notion that materialism and self-sufficiency were easily attainable, and those who were poor must have been
even more deserving of their status since they were surrounded by opportunity.

The message of self-sufficiency continues to be strong during the
1990s, despite the proliferation of research on the topic. In April, 1992, the
state of Wisconsin proposed new measures to reduce welfare expenditures. In order to reduce expenses, the governor, with the support of
President Bush, suggested that benefits be reduced for teenage mothers
who have numerous children. When asked about the availability of evidence on this topic, Governor Thompson said: "No, there isn't [any re-
search]. There really isn't, but there is no evidence to the contrary either"
(The Seattle Times, April 11, 1992). While the goal is to penalize women
for having three or more children in reality it penalizes the children, as if
they are less deserving because they are from larger families. The decision
to make such cuts, and Governor Thompson's rationale indicate a disre-

gard for the realities of both the availability of research and also of life on welfare. Furthermore, supporters believe that such a move will encourage women to enter the workforce and to marry, a particularly poor way to leave welfare. In addition, by reducing the cash grant to these mothers it will be young, developing children who will be the most significantly affected.

Research is available to guide such decisions, yet it is often dismissed because it does not reflect society's attitudes on the issue. Additionally, such attitudes reflect the prominent theme in society that welfare is the cause of family breakdown, when in reality it is symptomatic of the experiences of particular problems such as domestic violence, unemployment and under-education. The importance of the issues of family continuity, welfare and self-sufficiency to the American public became a rallying cry in the 1992 Presidential election as each side attempted to define and formulate a definition of "family values."

With the work ethic embedded in the fabric of society the low status of those receiving welfare is constantly being reinforced. Yet (re)integration into the middle class is a difficult task, not only because of the obstacles found in the social structure, but also because psychological and cultural factors tend to inhibit cross-class mobility (see Wilson, 1987). It is not a matter of simply believing people can pull themselves up by the bootstraps, instead, it is examining the dynamics of what it means to be poor and providing policy which reflects that knowledge.

WELFARE RESEARCH AND LEGISLATION TODAY

Criteria for Entering and Exiting Welfare

During the 1980s, a concerted effort has been made to understand the nature of welfare use. It can be difficult, however, to dispel the myths of welfare users in the minds of both the American public and their legislators, and replace it with solid statistical evidence. A critical question is what conditions affect how individuals enter into, and more importantly, exit from welfare dependency? A popular perspective on welfare and poverty is the idea of "spells of poverty" (Bane and Ellwood, 1983b). A spell of poverty is defined as "continuous periods during which income falls below the poverty line"[4] (Bane and Ellwood, 1983b: 9). Research indicates that the average recipient spends, at any given time, less than 4 years on public assistance (Duncan, Hill and Hoffman, 1988; Duncan and Hoffman, 1988; O'Neill, Bassi and Wolf, 1987), with many recipients only spending 1 to 3 years in the system for any given spell (O'Neill, Bassi and Wolf, 1987; Rank, 1986; Bane and Ellwood, 1983b). Only a minority of recipients remain on the welfare rolls longer than four years. It is these individuals who account, however, for the majority of welfare expenditures at any point in time because of the large amount of financial resources they used over the length of time they receive benefits. The length of time one spends receiving welfare is determined by a number of factors, but in general, the longer an individual uses public assistance, the smaller the probability of the person getting off the welfare roles (Bane and Ellwood, 1983b; Rank, 1986). In addition, the closer one lives to the poverty line, the more likely one will "weave" in and out of poverty and welfare use (Rank, 1986).

Those most likely to receive assistance for more than 8 years tend to share several characteristics: they are under the age of twenty-five, black, never-married, and their youngest child is under the age of three (Ellwood, 1986). In addition, women who come from single-parent homes themselves, had an out-of-wedlock child, are in ill health, have had more than one child, less work experience and lower wages also have longer spells of welfare use (O'Neill, Bassi and Wolf, 1987). Fifty-three percent of those who are non-whites and high school dropouts will be on welfare for longer than six years (Bane and Ellwood, 1983a). Even after controlling for age and education, Bane and Ellwood (1983a) found that welfare use was proportionally higher for blacks than non-blacks.

The group that is most severely disadvantaged is children. Of all children, 30 percent will spend part of their lives in poverty, with the probability of escaping poverty highest in the first year of life, and lowest in the 12th year (Duncan and Rodgers, 1988). Those most adversely affected are black children who will spend on average 10.7 years in poverty, more than half of their childhood years (Bane and Ellwood, 1983b; Duncan and Hoffman, 1988; Duncan and Rodgers, 1988).

Spells of Welfare Use

It is important to differentiate between a single spell of welfare use and the total time an individual spends receiving public assistance.[5] Though Bane and Ellwood's perspective on spells of poverty provides some insight into the welfare cycle, it is unable to explain the total time of welfare use. Research by Bane, Ellwood and Murray (1986) indicates that poverty-prone individuals are likely to experience multiple spells of poverty in their lifetime. Bane and Ellwood (1983b) estimate that one-third of all welfare spells are followed by subsequent spells of welfare use. As the number of spells increases, the total time on welfare (inclusive of all spells) likewise accumulates. Overall, 30% of recipients will spend a total of 1 to 2 years receiving assistance, 40% will spend 3 to 7 years, while 30% of all recipients will spend more than 8 years receiving welfare (Ellwood, 1986).

Welfare and Household Structure

In their extensive analysis of the PSID (Panel Study of Income Dynamics) Bane and Ellwood (1983b) conclude that the welfare population is extraordinarily heterogeneous and welfare dependency cannot be attributed to one single factor. They propose five categories of events that precipitate welfare use: (1) changes in earnings of the head of household, (2) a change in earnings of secondary family earners, (3) changes in family structure, (4) birth, and, (5) the movement of a young person away from his/her parent's home.

Whereas 55% of Bane and Ellwood's sample entered welfare due to a decrease in the earnings of a household member, only 37% entered welfare due to a decrease in the earnings of the household head. Differences exist depending on whether the household head is male or female. For male heads, nearly 60% entered into welfare because of a decrease in wages, while 14% of female households were on welfare due to this factor.

Changes in household structure contribute significantly to the beginning of a spell of welfare use, particularly for women. Eleven percent of all welfare use begins with the transition to a female-headed household. For families with children, 65% enter welfare as a result of the transition to a female-headed household: 45% are a result of marital break-ups, 20% are attributed to unmarried motherhood, often young women who choose to live independent of their parents after the birth of their child, and 6% from a change in their needs standard.[6] Persons who are born into an impoverished home account for 20% of all spell beginnings (Bane and Ellwood, 1983a). If a child is living in a welfare household for more than one year, which most do (Bane and Ellwood, 1983a; Duncan and Rodgers, 1988), the probability of exiting from welfare decreases with the length of time they remain in the disadvantaged situation (Bane and Ellwood, 1983a).

Intergenerational Welfare Use

The question of whether there is an intergenerational component to public assistance has long been debated. The available research indicates a small positive relationship between welfare dependence of parents and future welfare use by their children (Duncan and Hoffman, 1988; Wilson, 1987).

The degree of welfare use of the parent appears to be the determining factor. If there was little or no use by parents there will be little or no use by children, and, likewise, if there is high use among parents there is a greater likelihood there will be use among their children (Duncan, Hill and Hoffman, 1988). Nevertheless, among parents who are heavily dependent on welfare only 1 out of 5 of their daughters will be heavily dependent, while 64% of their daughters will never be dependent (Duncan, Hill and Hoffman, 1988).[7] When race was considered, only 26% of white women and 19% of black women who grew up in heavily dependent homes would ever be heavily dependent on welfare themselves (Duncan and Hoffman, 1988). Using a worst-case scenario, the chances of someone who is black, lives in a low-income environment and comes from a welfare-dependent home becoming welfare dependent herself was about 30 percent (Wilson, 1987; Levy, 1980).

Leaving Welfare

The events leading to an exit from welfare vary as much as entry events. While a decrease in wages of any household member accounts for 55% of the beginning of welfare spells, an increase in wages within a household accounts for 80% of those who exit welfare (Bane and Ellwood, 1983b). Fifty-seven percent of all households end their spell of welfare use with an increase in wages of the head of household. Sixty-nine percent of two-parent male-headed households and 34% of single-headed female households end a spell of poverty with an increase in wages. An increase in the earnings of secondary household earners accounted for 23% of families moving out of a spell in a two-parent household, while in female-headed households, 22% can attribute exiting a spell to the increase in wages of another adult.

These statistics and trends provide good insight into the effect of welfare law on the family. Traditionally, it has been women who have received welfare assistance because they are likely to be the primary caretaker for the children, thus creating what has come to be known as the traditional welfare family. Most researchers report that both the presence and the number of children are positively related to periods of welfare use (Rank, 1986; Bane and Ellwood, 1983a; Plotnick, 1983; Weiseman, 1977; Saks, 1975). Rank (1986), however, found this to be only statistically significant for families where the head of household was single and female. Only under limited circumstances has welfare allowed a family to remain intact: if a father is present in the household the family may only receive assistance if one parent is unable to work. Fathers who have caretaking responsibilities for their children, though their numbers are few, are less likely to receive AFDC benefits because they are more likely to qualify for higher salaries than women, and therefore they are more likely to be above the cut-off of receiving benefits. As a result, for women, marriage plays a significant role in exiting welfare. Twenty-seven percent of female household heads with children exited a welfare spell through marriage. It is important to note, however, that finding a job was a more significant factor than marriage in accounting for families moving off of welfare (Bane and Ellwood, 1983a). As is evident, welfare policy continues to play a significant role in the structure of family life for America's poor.

As these findings suggest, the chances of exiting welfare vary with the type of family structure. Rank (1986) found that over a 36-month period married couples experienced a 74% exit rate, averaging 1.2 years on welfare, while female heads with children experienced only a 53% exit rate while remaining on welfare for an average of 2.8 years. Thus, single parent households had the greater difficulty exiting welfare. Rank (1986) attributes this to the limited flexibility of the single-female parent to function in the economic world. Not only do two-parent families have greater economic resources, they also have an additional adult to assist with child care and household management. Women who head their own family not only have the major expense of child care, but also are limited in their income by the "segmentation and discrimination" of the workplace (Rank, 1986).

The path one takes when entering welfare affects the spell duration. Those beginning a spell due to out-of-wedlock births spend more time on public assistance than those starting with a divorce or separation (Bane and Ellwood, 1983b). Spells of welfare beginning with an out-of-wedlock birth are often longer because these mothers are not supported by a spouse and do not have the advantage of a second income in the household, experiences which delay the use of welfare.

CONCLUSION: THE ROAD TO SELF-SUFFICIENCY

Admittedly the relationship between welfare independence and employment is apparent. It is not surprising, therefore, that as wages increase for household heads and/or secondary earners the probability of exiting public assistance also increases (Bane and Ellwood, 1983b). Ironically, however, the factors that contribute to welfare dependence are often the greatest obstacles to securing and maintaining employment. Conventional wisdom assumes that if welfare recipients would "just get a job" both the problems of welfare and of the society at large would be ameliorated. Such a conclusion ignores the complexities accompanying employment for low-income individuals. Those factors which contribute most to hindering efforts to find employment are inadequate education and training, household composition, marital status and psychological and physical well-being.

There is a growing body of data which demonstrates and supports the belief that work is far more successful than transfer payment in keeping families out of poverty (Kamerman and Kahn, 1988). It follows that job training is a potentially productive way of assisting recipients to not only leave the welfare rolls, but, more importantly to remove the conditions of poverty. A potentially effective program is "one that [is] able to channel different women as they become ready for the job market, based on their needs for skills or education, or preparation other than job skills" (Kamerman and Kahn, 1988: 167). In order for education and training to be successful for the welfare mother, Kamerman and Kahn identify three components necessary to any program:

1. Support for educational endeavors for the mother which include child care, stipends, and investing in mechanisms which develop self-support for the woman.
2. Strong counseling, job search, vocational guidance, mutual support (such as job clubs), and job placement services.
3. Flexible federal rules permitting AFDC funds to be utilized for the above-listed programs, in addition to partially subsidized or supplemented private industry, non-profit and public job placement.

The flexible combination of these components will facilitate a program in meeting the needs of the variety of women currently receiving public assistance. To *enable* mothers to work is of crucial importance to the welfare of their children.

The notion of self-sufficiency for welfare recipients has been central to the efforts of many political administrations. In addition, Americans see self-sufficiency as fundamental to the way we as a culture live and work. The failing of many has been to assume that a country's work ethic alone is motivation enough to move people out of poverty and welfare. As a result, while many see only the direct relationship between welfare independence and employment, many miss the mark when it comes to understanding how the experience of being poor inhibits the ability to be employed.

The influence of welfare laws on the family has been tremendous. Not only have families been limited in terms of the financial resources provided through welfare, but people who must depend to some degree on public assistance are at the whim of a political decision-making process which is often reflective of the misconceptions of welfare use. In the future, public policy must be acutely aware of the complexities of the

555555555555555

issue. It is unrealistic to believe, let alone produce policy around the notion that asking people to pick themselves up by the bootstraps will move people off of welfare. Instead, understanding the relationship between welfare law, employment, family structure and cultural values will provide the only successful mechanism for reducing welfare use.

NOTES

1. While the terms "poverty" and "welfare" are often used interchangeably, for the purpose of this paper they will retain separate meanings. Being poor generally means that one's income falls below the federal poverty level as established annually by the U.S. Department of Agriculture. While people who receive welfare are poor, not all people who are poor receive welfare.

2. Formal support systems could include welfare services, as we know them, organized public relief services, or charitable organizations.

3. AFDC is the acronym for Aid to Families with Dependent Children, the most popular of welfare programs. AFDC is a program for children. Welfare grants are based on the size of the family, including the adult, but when the children no longer reside with the parent the payments cease. Qualification for the program may vary from state to state. In all states there must be a single parent with dependent children, under the age of 18. In some states a two-parent family may receive AFDC if one parent is incapacitated and unable to work.

Qualifying for AFDC is the "ticket" to other programs such as Food Stamps and Medical Assistance. These programs provide vouchers in exchange for goods and services. There are other programs, which are a part of the Social Security Act, such as Supplemental Security Income (SSI) and General Assistance (GA), but these focus on the needs of the single person, disabled and the elderly, and are not of primary importance to this paper.

4. Though Bane and Ellwood define a spell of poverty in this manner, they operationalize the concept by examining spells of welfare use.

5. Bane and Ellwood use the word "poverty" and "spells of poverty" to indicate length of time spent being welfare dependent.

6. A change in the need standard occurs when a new person enters a household, indicating the need for additional financial resources. The standard of need decreases when an individual leaves a household.

7. The emphasis on daughters for welfare use is predominant because few sons have primary care for children, and as such do not apply for AFDC benefits.

REFERENCES

Amenta, E. and B.G. Carruthers. (1988). "The Formative Years of U.S. Social Spending Policies: Theories of the welfare state and the American states during the Great Depression." *American Sociological Review.* 53: 661-678.
Bane, M. and D. Ellwood. (1983a). *The Dynamics of Dependence and the Routes*

of Self-Sufficiency. Final report to the U.S. Department of Health and Human Services, Urban Systems Research and Engineering, Cambridge, MA.

_____. (1983b). *Slipping Into and Out of Poverty: The Dynamics of spells.* Working paper no. 1199. National Bureau of Economic Research, Cambridge, MA.

Bane, M., D. Ellwood, C. Murray. (1986). "According to Age: Longitudinal Profiles of AFDC Recipients and the Poor by Age Group." Paper presented for the Working Seminar on the Family and American Welfare Policy, American Enterprise Institute, Washington, DC, September, 1986.

Bell, W. (1965). *Aid to Dependent Children.* New York: Columbia University.

Bernard, J. (1981). "The Good Provider Role: Its Rise and Fall." *American Psychologist.* 36: 1-12.

Cherlin, A. (1988). "The Changing American Family and Public Policy." In A. Cherlin (ed) *The Changing American Family and Public Policy.* Washington, DC: The Urban Institute.

Dear, R.B. (1989). "What's Right With Welfare? The other face of AFDC." *Journal of Sociology and Social Welfare.* 16: 5-43.

Duncan, G., M. Hill, and S. Hoffman. (1988). "Welfare dependence within and across generations." *Science.* 29 January 1988.

Duncan, G. and S. Hoffman. (1988). "The use and effects of welfare: A survey of recent evidence." *Social Service Review.* June: 239-257.

Duncan, G. and W. Rodgers. (1988). "Longitudinal aspects of childhood poverty." *Journal of Marriage and the Family.* 50: 1007-1021.

Elder, G. H., Jr. (1974). *Children of the Great Depression.* Chicago: University of Chicago Press.

Ellwood, D. (1986). "Targeting would-be long term recipients of AFDC." In *Matematica Policy Research.* Princeton, NJ.

Feagin, J.R. (1975). *Subordinating the Poor: Welfare and American Beliefs.* Englewood Cliffs, NJ: Prentice Hall, Inc.

Garfinkel, I. and S. McLanahan. (1986). *Single Mothers and Their Children: A New American Dilemma.* Washington, DC: The Urban Institute.

Haskins, R. (1991). "Congress Writes and Law: Research and Welfare Reform." *Journal of Policy Analysis and Management.* 10: 616-632.

Kamerman, S. and A. Kahn. (1988). *Mothers Alone: Strategies for a Time of Changes.* Dover, MA: Auburn House Publishing Co.

Levy, F. (1980). *The Intergenerational Transfer of Poverty.* Working paper 1231-02. Washington, DC: The Urban Institute.

Mason, J., J.S. Wodarski, and T. M. J. Parham. (1985). "Work and Welfare: A Reevaluation of Welfare." *Social Work.* 30: 197-203.

Murray, C. (1984). *Losing Ground: American Social Policy 1950-1980.* New York: Basic Books, Inc.

National Conference on Social Welfare. (1985). The Report of the Committee on Economic Security of 1935, 50th Anniversary Edition.

O'Neill, J. A., L.J. Bassi, and D.A. Wolf. (1987). "The duration of welfare spells." *The Review of Economics and Statistics.* pgs. 241-248.

Plotnick, R. (1983). "Turnovers in the AFDC population: An event history analysis." *Journal of Human Resources.* 18: 65-81.

Price, C. (1990). *Structural, Cultural and Psychological Factors Affecting the Choice of Child Care Among Low-income Women.* Unpublished dissertation.

Rank, M. (1986). "Family structure and the process of exiting from welfare." *Journal of Marriage and the Family.* 49: 607-618.

Saks, D. (1975). *Public Assistance for Mothers in an Urban Labor Market.* Princeton, NJ: Industrial Relations Section, Princeton University.

Schorr, L.B. (1989). *Within Our Reach: Breaking the cycle of disadvantage.* New York: Doubleday.

Scott, J. and L. Tilley. (1978). Women's Work and the Family in Nineteenth Century Europe. In C.E. Rosenberg (ed) *The Family in History.* Pittsburgh, PA: The University of Pennsylvania Press.

Szanton, P. (1991). "The Remarkable 'Quango': Knowledge, politics and welfare reform." *Journal of Policy Analysis and Management.* 10: 590-602.

Voydanoff, P. (1984). *Work and Family: Changing Roles of Men and Women.* Palo Alto, CA: Mayfield Publishing Co.

Weeks, G., V. Gecas, R.M. Lidman, M. Seff, E.W. Stromsdorfer, J. Tarnai. (1990). *Washington State's Family Income Study: Results from the first year.* Olympia, WA: Washington State Institute for Public Policy.

Weintraub, B. (1986). "Reagan's message appeals for unity to curb spending." *New York Times.* January 5, pg. 1.

Weiseman, M. (1977). *Changes and Turnover in a Welfare Population.* Institute of Business and Economic Research, University of California, Berkeley.

Wilson, W. (1987). *The Truly Disadvantaged: The Inner City, The Underclass and Public Policy.* Chicago: The University of Chicago Press.

Wiseman, M. (1991). "Research and Policy: A symposium on the Family Support Act of 1988." *Journal of Policy Analysis and Management.* 10: 588-589.

Zimmerman, S.L. (1989). "Myths about public welfare: Poverty, family instability, and teen illegitimacy." *Policy Studies Review.* 8: 674-688.

The Limits of Care:
A Case Study of Legal and Ethical Issues in Filial Responsibility

Roma Stovall Hanks

SUMMARY. In 1985, Roswell Gilbert was convicted of murder in the shooting death of his wife Emily who suffered from Alzheimer's disease and osteoporosis. Although Emily had asked to die in the presence of witnesses, the Florida jury was pressed toward its harsh treatment of Roswell by his choice of weapon, staunch refusal to repudiate his decision, and Emily's relatively high functional level at the time of her death. Nearly a decade later, issues of the limits of family responsibility in caregiving remain prominent in the literatures of gerontology and applied ethics. This paper revisits the Gilbert case with insights from Joseph A. Varon, Chief Counsel at the trial of Roswell Gilbert and Martha Gilbert Moran, Roswell and Emily's only daughter. The paper integrates applied ethical and sociological theories about the family into a discussion of family decision making around caregiving and its termination.

Specifically, the paper uses symbolic interaction theory with Noddings' theory of caring and exchange theory with Blustein's discus-

Roma Stovall Hanks is Assistant Professor, Department of Sociology and Anthropology, University of South Alabama, Mobile, AL.

Joseph A. Varon, Esq., Defense Counsel for Roswell Gilbert, provided assistance in interpretation of legal issues directly related to the Gilbert case and commented on early conceptual material on which this paper is based. The author appreciates Mr. Varon's interest and assistance in this research.

[Haworth co-indexing entry note]: "The Limits of Care: A Case Study of Legal and Ethical Issues in Filial Responsibility." Hanks, Roma Stovall. Co-published simultaneously in *Marriage & Family Review* (The Haworth Press, Inc.) Vol. 21, No. 3/4, 1995, pp. 239-257; and: *Families and Law* (ed: Lisa J. McIntyre, and Marvin B. Sussman) The Haworth Press, Inc., 1995, pp. 239-257. Multiple copies of this article/chapter may be purchased from The Haworth Document Delivery Center [1-800-3-HA-WORTH; 9:00 a.m. - 5:00 p.m. (EST)].

239

sion of duty and autonomy to address two questions: (1) Who owns
the decision about the termination of care? and (2) What are the
grounds for state intervention into family decision making on behalf
of an individual who has expressed, verbally or through a written
will, a desire to die? It is suggested that social scientists need to refine research methods in order to document the development of family belief systems that support life-and-death decision making. Further research is indicated on spousal and intergenerational relationships as the social context for decisions families make about care and
its termination. The approach of the paper is to integrate family sociological theory with perspectives from legal and applied ethical
analyses.

INTRODUCTION

The Gilbert Case

Emily Gilbert suffered from Alzheimer's disease and osteoporosis.
Neighbors and friends reported having heard her plead with her husband
to "please let me die" (Givens, Agrest, & Prout, 1985). On March 4, 1985,
Roswell Gilbert, a retired electronics engineer, gave his wife of 51 years a
sedative, then fired a shot from his 9mm Luger into her temple. When he
checked her pulse and found that she was still living, he returned to his
workshop, reloaded the gun, and came back into the living room to fire
another shot.

On May 9, 1985, a Broward County, Florida jury returned a verdict
against Roswell: Guilty of Murder. Subsequently, he was sentenced to 25
years in prison. Friends, family members, and even the prosecuting attorney launched a legal and media campaign that eventually led to Roswell's
release from prison on August 3, 1990.

This paper integrates sociological with ethical and legal perspectives in
a discussion of two questions about the Gilbert case: (1) Who owns the
decision about termination of care? and (2) What are the grounds for state
intervention into family decision making on behalf of an individual who
has expressed, verbally or through a written will, a desire to die? It is
suggested that social scientists need to refine research methods to document the development of family belief systems that support life-and-death
decision making. Research should be continued on spousal and intergenerational relationships as the social context for decisions families make
about care and its termination.

WHO OWNS THE DECISION TO TERMINATE CARE?

The Legal Perspective

Legally, the decision to terminate care belongs "unequivocally to the victim, or the terminally ill patient" or the person to whom authority has been delegated by a living will (Varon, 1992). This interpretation has been established in cases involving the right to die and the decision-making rights of next of kin (In the matter of Karen Quinlan, Supreme Court of New Jersey, March 31, 1976). Emily Gilbert had no living will. Further, she had no written record of her desire to die or of any statement requesting her spouse's assistance in ending her life. I communicated with Joseph A. Varon, Roswell Gilbert's defense attorney in the preparation of this paper. Mr. Varon acknowledged the legal limitations on family participation in the decision to terminate life. He recognized his defense case for Roswell Gilbert as problematic since many of the elements associated with defensible passive euthanasia were missing.

> The legal limits of family decision-making power give rise to irreconcilable controversy that may require arbitration or litigation in State courts once again. I must assume the hypothesis that there is no living will, just a patient's request for surcease. Initially, there must be a unanimity of opinion that euthanasia is indicated. The decision of necessity must be fortified by the attending doctor's view that the patient is terminal. This will obviate the possibility that the family members making the decision are not premature in their demand for termination. The family is legally limited to a realistic diagnosis based on medical certainty that the patient is terminal in order to avoid "active euthanasia" which may have criminal overtones, as opposed to "passive euthanasia" which I call a "tongue-in-cheek" charade.
>
> –Varon, 1992

In the case of Karen Ann Quinlan, a young New Jersey woman whose father petitioned the courts to permit him to decide to have her taken off life supports, evidence was presented from medical, religious, and legal sources in support of the father's right to make the decision and of the hopeless condition of the victim. Neither Karen Quinlan nor Emily Gilbert had left written expressions of their desires concerning treatment at the end of their lives (In the Matter of Karen Quinlan, Supreme Court of New Jersey, March 31, 1976).

Karen Quinlan's condition was clearly worse than Emily Gilbert's.

Evidence was presented at the Gilbert trial and in subsequent appeals that Emily's condition was not advanced enough to warrant the extreme action her husband took. For example, a photograph of Emily wearing eye make-up was presented as evidence that she was still capable of personal grooming near the time of her death (Roswell Gilbert, Court of Appeal of Florida, January 31, 1990). Certainly, Mr. Varon admits that building the defense on the grounds of euthanasia involved some legal risks:

> Frankly, the Florida courts as well as the judicial systems nationally do not recognize Euthanasia as a defense to a "mercy" homicide and Roswell Gilbert was impaled upon public and legislative lack of realistic perception . . . In Gilbert, I embarked upon uncharted waters to formulate a defense of Euthanasia and vainly attempted to "educate" the jury that Emily had the *sole* right to make the critical decision.
>
> —Varon, 1992

The difference between legal and moral argument in this case turns on the ability to accommodate more than one individual into a decision-making unit. The idea of corporate agency is further removed from legal than from moral rhetoric. Legal responsibility in U.S. courts is a concept linked to the individual. Group liability is so problematic that it is avoided by various legal means. For example, when a corporation is formed the group of individuals responsible for directing the business endeavor cease to be individually responsible and the newly-created legal individual, e.g., the corporation, becomes liable. Moral responsibility, some ethicists have argued, continues to reside in the individuals who comprise the group of decision makers in upper management (DeGeorge, 1983).

In families there is usually not the creation of a new legal individual to relieve partners of individual responsibility. There may be an informal recognition by family members of a unity of purpose and mutual liability within relationships. Emily and Roswell may have rationally chosen to be a decision-making unit, recognizing that benefit to one enhanced benefit to the other. Such choices are made routinely, although usually with far less dramatic consequences than those of the Gilbert case, when spouses independently make financial decisions and write checks on joint bank accounts.

The Ethical Perspective

Rationality. Morally, the decision to terminate care belongs to the terminally ill patient as long as rational decision making is possible. Kant links personhood with rationality; the person exists only as long as rational thought exists (Bayles & Henley, 1983; Beauchamp, 1982). Thus he is able to separate the rational self from other aspects of self. Decision making in this perspective is concerned with the integrity of the moral agent as a rational being. Emily's rationality in participating in the decision to end her life becomes important. If at the time of her death Emily could not rationally make a decision, Kant would argue that Emily's personhood had ceased: Emily was dead. Roswell made physical what had already occurred to the moral agent.

Further, if Emily had earlier realized that her disease would cause progressive deterioration of her ability to make decisions, she may have rationally decided at that earlier time to give Roswell increased decision-making power. Although a Kantian perspective does not allow moral justification of suicide, it does allow the individual to choose a role for herself if that choice is made rationally. Emily chose her dependent role while still a rational agent. The argument can then be made that Emily's choice to give Roswell decision-making power implies consent to any decisions he made for her at any time after she made her choice known.

Autonomy. The question of Emily's autonomy in this process is complex. If completely autonomous, Emily should have been self-governing and therefore able to decide for herself whether or not she would act on her expressed wish to die. Why did she not choose suicide rather than to ask Roswell to kill her? Knowing of her illness, she may have voluntarily surrendered her autonomy. In this case, she would expect and even desire that her husband act for her. Neo-Kantian argument, based on autonomy in choice, allows that "it is permissible for a competent person to exercise his autonomy to choose death, it is also permissible for another to kill him if he rationally and voluntarily chooses it" (Bayles & Henley, 1983, pp. 150-151).

It is useful to examine the broader philosophical literature of family relationships to gain insights into the meaning of duty and autonomy in a spousal caregiving arrangement. My discussion of these concepts is based on Blustein's treatise on *Parents and Children* (1982). Drawing theoretical constructs from the framework of a parent/child relationship is not intended to suggest that older people are either childlike or authoritarian. But Blustein's discussion focusses on dependency of children in relation to their parents, a concept which I believe is appropriately applied to this case of caregiver/care receiver interaction.

My discussions with the Gilberts' daughter and Roswell Gilbert's attorney as well as Roswell's testimony at the trial have convinced me that the couple were traditional in their beliefs and behaviors regarding male/female marital roles. Although Martha Moran describes her mother as sometimes manipulative, Emily seems to have usually deferred to Roswell's final judgment in decision making. Her willingness to follow the geographic mobility demands of his corporate career is one indicator of the traditional nature of the marriage (Moran, 1985).

Becker and Hill described the traditional marriage relationship in which both loss of individuality and differentiation of roles were essential to obtain and maintain a couple identity:

> . . . solidarity, based first upon sexual attraction, becomes in time overlaid with concrete expression of likeness in behavior so that there is built up a constellation of experiences which symbolize a further conviction of oneness . . . the very essence of marriage is loss of a considerable degree of individuality if the couple achieves any high degree of adjustment or unity . . . differentiation of marital roles contributes to marital stability in producing the interdependence between husband and wife, both emotional and physical. (1948: p. 348)

The symbiotic nature of the relationship of Roswell and Emily is relevant to this discussion and to further analysis of the ethics of caregiving as understood by Roswell Gilbert. The trend over the latter part of the twentieth century has been to maintain individuality within a marital partnership (Jeter & Sussman, 1985). However, indications are that the Gilbert marriage held to traditional beliefs concerning marital unity.

The Relationship of Duty and Autonomy. Blustein (1982) tries to reconcile autonomy of the child and the parent with duty to provide for, care for, and nurture. The point of departure from most philosophical discussions of autonomy and duty is his recognition of the family as a unit. "The family is not merely a collection of separate individuals, but a community in which the satisfaction of one kind of interest entails the satisfaction of the other" (p. 6). He concludes that "the achievement of autonomy is a developmental process" (p. 10). The implication is that social and psychological developmental stages are associated with the degree of autonomy accorded to children and to parents.

Blustein's analysis focuses on the parent/child relationship. The development of a child is toward autonomy; the development of a caregiving relationship flows with the positive or negative turns of the condition that makes care necessary. Both caregiver and care receiver are caught in a cycle of responses to the illness or disability. While some degree of interdependency of members characterizes solidarity in family life (Treas & Bengtson, 1987), those families attending to chronic illness frequently find themselves "ruled by the sickest member" (Sussman, 1983).

In the dependency relationship created by chronic illness, the care receiver's autonomy decreases through developmental stages as dependency increases; ". . . the ethical problem for home care becomes one of gauging the interplay of agents . . ." (Collopy et al., 1990: p. 9). Emily's illness increased her dependency on her spouse. In situations involving psychological impairment, the *caregiver's* autonomy is at risk as well. The heavy burden to give care and a decreased liberty to act in roles other than caregiver are evidence of changing autonomy of the caregiver. The body of literature on caregiver burden supports the notion that psychological impairment decreases independence of both caregiver and care receiver (Pratt et al., 1987; Cicirelli, 1992).

One way to successfully relieve the burden on the caregiver is to find sources of help to provide aspects of care: to call on friends and extended family or to use formal support systems in the community. The literature shows that spouse caregivers tend to sustain the burdensome role longer than other family caregivers. For various reasons spouses seem more reluctant than other caregivers to relinquish their caregiving roles (Colerick & George, 1986). The relationship of this phenomenon to tolerance for decreased autonomy has not been established. In his lengthy testimony, Roswell described the limitations the caregiving relationship imposed in the context of the marital relationship:

> But looking back on it, we were certainly very attached to each other, very much in love to put it that way and which is normal with people and love gets mellow in later years and everything is fine. But this damned Alzheimer's thing, it developed into her inner psychotic attachment for me. She got so dependent on me that I began to think that this was a mistake that we made in our lives. You know, she should have been more independent . . . Well, she was so dependent upon me. As I said, if I was out of the apartment for 15 minutes she'd get a fright complex and come looking for me. . . . (Gilbert, May, 1985)

Roswell testified further that Emily's increasing dependency resulted in his giving up his consulting business, limiting his social interaction with neighbors and friends, and making himself almost constantly available to assist Emily with activities of daily living. A symbiotic relationship turned to a trajectory toward Emily's total dependency and Roswell's loss of self to the caregiving role.

The duty of the caregiver is to provide for the needs of the care receiver. The dependency of the care receiver is reflected in changes in established patterns of exchange in the relationship. However, a lengthy relationship may equip the care receiver and caregiver to conceptualize current exchanges symbolically, in the context of their history together. Malinowski

(1922) and Mauss (1954) developed the symbolic interpretation of exchange theory, a useful dimension in examining exchanges in relationships in which there are diverse functional levels. Although dependent and scarcely able to contribute to the relationship in the utilitarian sense, the care receiver becomes a symbol of previous contributions. In addition, the exchanges between care receiver and caregiver become symbolic of moral codes of the society.

In the Gilbert case, Roswell and Emily represent what spouses do for each other and what families do for the health care system in America. Their choices are limited by the alternatives they recognize. Roswell's testimony concerning the final moments of Emily's life emphasizes the perceived isolation of caregivers and the impact of the long-term marriage relationship on decision making about care and its termination:

> She was all propped up on pillows. She kind of looked beautiful to me. I guess she wasn't at the time. But so then she said, "Please help me. Please, somebody help me." Who's that somebody but me, you know, and there she was in pain and all this confusion and I guess if I got cold as icewater that's what had happened. I thought to myself, I've got to do it, it's got to be mine, I've got to end her suffering, this can't go on . . . I can't go to the medical people. They have no cure for Alzheimer's. The osteoporosis was getting worse slowly in time. Everything looked like it was converging to a climax . . . So I put her in a nursing home and they won't let me stay there and she's separated from me. It would be a horrible death for her . . . I can't confide in my friends without getting them involved . . . I couldn't go to the doctor. He is a professional. He is duly bound to report it to the authorities and they would pull me out of the picture . . . the only solution to me was to terminate her suffering. That's all . . . I didn't consider what would happen to me at all. The only important thing was to terminate her suffering. I could take care of whatever happens to me and it's happening right now and that was of no consequence to me . . . there seems to be things more important than the law, at least to me in my private tragedy. (Gilbert, May, 1985)

WHAT ARE THE GROUNDS FOR STATE INTERVENTION INTO FAMILY DECISION MAKING ABOUT EUTHANASIA?

The Legal Perspective

The State has an interest in its residents. That interest is legally grounded in the powers implicit in the Public, Health, and Welfare provisions of the Constitution. The ability of the State to act on the interest of citizens "is limited in its operation to existing factual situations or exigencies" (Varon, 1992). In euthanasia cases, any differences between patient or her family and attending physician are subject to settlement in a State court, resorted to by the patient or next of kin.

State intervention is more likely to occur to assist carrying out written wishes of a patient than to establish a course of action within the bounds of family decision making. Joseph Varon (1992) gives the following opinion about State intervention in euthanasia cases:

> [An] example of State intervention is where there is an impasse between the "oral" request of a patient to be terminated and the statutory requirement of a written living will. Although we now find the State courts by their judicial decisions encouraging doctors and hospital staff members to respect and honor decisions by competent patients, the incipient dread [of malpractice lawsuits] remains and resort must be made to the local State courts for a Declaratory Decree or Mandatory Injunction authorizing euthanasia. Where a minor child is involved and the parents are dead . . . the courts can appoint a Guardian ad Litem to stand in loco parentis and make the request for euthanasia. I can only see State intervention to assist in carrying out the wishes of the patient, but under no foreseeable circumstances can I envision the State intervening in the family decisional process.

The State intervened, post mortem, in the case of Emily Gilbert. Reports indicate that Emily had verbally requested assistance in dying. Throughout his trial and subsequent appeals, Roswell had the support of his and Emily's family members. The traditional decision-making style of the couple was recognized and accepted by the family. The decision for euthanasia was consistent with previous family decisions. On at least two other occasions, members of the Gilberts' extended family had decided not to use extraordinary means to prolong the lives of suffering relatives (Moran, 1985). The family belief system seems to involve a shared definition of quality of life and its relation to the desire to live.

The Florida Court of Appeals focused on the absence of a written living will and the condition of the victim at the time of death in denying Gilbert's appeal. Emily had left no written instructions concerning her wish to die. In the opinion denying Roswell Gilbert's appeal of his conviction, the court concluded that to accept Emily's statement, "I'm so sick, I want to die," as the legal equivalent of a written living will would "sanction open season on people who, although sick, are also chronic complainers." In the same ruling, the court concluded that in the absence of a written living will Roswell's "good faith" act on his perception of his wife's wishes had no legal basis. " 'Good faith' is not a legal defense to first degree murder" (Roswell Gilbert, Court of Appeal of Florida, January 31, 1990).

Emily's condition was not as advanced as that of the patient in the case Varon used to establish precedent in Florida court decisions around euthanasia (John F. Kennedy Memorial Hospital, Inc. v. Bludworth). Her doctor testified that she could have lived another five to ten years, she was never bedridden, and she continued to carry out activities of daily living until her death (Roswell Gilbert, Court of Appeal of Florida, January 31, 1990). In the Gilbert case, Joseph Varon attempted to establish euthanasia as a defense for murder. He was unsuccessful. Florida Court of Appeals upheld the lower court's decision to disallow instruction to the jury concerning the definition of euthanasia because no statutes exist to support euthanasia as a defense for first degree murder in Florida (Roswell Gilbert, Court of Appeal of Florida, January 31, 1990).

Almost certainly, State intervention in Roswell and Emily's decision making could have been avoided, or at least restricted, if written evidence could have been produced to establish that Emily had participated in the decision-making process and had shared her family's belief system about euthanasia. But retrospective analysis of the development of shared belief systems in families is difficult because of the private nature of family interaction. "Interpersonal relationships in American society are rarely formalized to the extent that any written definition of mutually held tenets is recorded at the onset or over the developmental course of the relationship" (Hanks & Settles, 1990). The need for systematic reconstruction of the development of family belief systems suggests an area where family research can facilitate judicial process.

The case of Angela Carder, as reported by George Annas (1991), shows the extremes of willingness by the legal system to disregard family decision making in favor of protecting an individual family member. Ms. Carder was 26 years old and about six months pregnant when lung cancer created a medical emergency and she was admitted to the hospital. Doctors agreed that she would die within 48 hours and began discussions about the fate of the fetus. Her husband, mother, and personal physician agreed that Angela's comfort was highest priority and that her wishes regarding the unborn child should be honored. Ms. Carder stated that she did not want a Cesarean section. Medical staff assessed the chances of survival of the fetus at 50-60% with 20% chance of serious handicap. A District of Columbia Superior Court Judge ordered the surgery without talking with Ms. Carder, who was conscious. Three judges heard and denied a request for a stay of the order and the surgery was performed. The fetus died two hours after surgery and the mother died two days later. This case is extreme in the apparent total disregard by the legal system for the decision making processes and preferences of the family.

Family members often act as surrogate decision makers in cases of treatment of terminal illness and the preferences of victims and their family members usually carry weight in legal decisions. The preponderance of legal and ethical discussion is around cases where the victim is unable to make decisions due to extreme disability. Since Emily was not comatose at the time the decision was made by her spouse to end her suffering by killing her, it is difficult to establish his legal position as substitute decision maker by referring to previous cases in which the condition of the victim was further deteriorated. The doctrine of "substitute judgement" in laws governing mental health does permit close family members to substitute their judgement for what they believe would have been the will of a terminally ill person. However, in order to act to end the life of that impaired relative, the decision maker must be court-appointed guardian of the victim and must obtain a court order to act to terminate the use of life support (Roswell Gilbert, Court of Appeal of Florida, January 31, 1990).

The position of family members as decision makers for relatives who are chronically ill, mentally impaired, but not in comatose or extremely painful and immediately life threatening conditions has not been established. In the denial of Roswell Gilbert's appeal, the court addressed the limitations of the legal system in dealing with murder committed by well-intentioned family members:

> Whether such sentences should somehow be moderated so as to allow a modicum of discretion and whether they should allow distinctions to be made in sentencing between different kinds of wrongdoers, for instance between a hired gangster killer and one, however misguided, who kills for love or mercy, are all questions which, under our system, must be decided by the legislature and not by the judicial branch. We leave it there. (Roswell Gilbert, Court of Appeal of Florida, January 31, 1990)

Judge Glickstein's concurring opinion stated further concerns about imposing standards on family relationships different from those guiding other social interaction. His opinion is indicative of the willingness of the legal system to intervene in family decisions to protect individual members from harm at the hand of relatives.

> My thoughts lie with the victim, who was silenced forever by the appellant's criminal act. She would be no more dead if a hired

gangland killer had pulled the trigger. Can it be that we feel more comfortable about imposing severe punishment on persons we perceive to belong to a separate tribe, whom we label as criminals, than on those we see as members of our own tribe? In fact, we are all members of a common humanity. (Roswell Gilbert, Court of Appeal of Florida, January 31, 1990)

The notion of surrogate decision making in matters of life and death by members of a family wider than blood or adoptive kin is suggested by Judge Glickstein's remarks about "a separate tribe." Where are the boundaries of family in such decision making? The wider family concept has been discussed in family literature as an alternative definition of family relevant to current lifestyles (Marciano, 1988; Marciano & Sussman, 1991). The wider family is constructed of individuals united by affectional or intellectual bonds. Examples range from the interdependent members of a yacht club (Aversa, 1991) to members of religious orders and cults (Marciano, 1991). The concept has not been explored for its legal and ethical implications for family decision making.

Brother Fox had for 66 years been a member of the Society of Mary, a Catholic religious order. He suffered cardiac arrest resulting in substantial brain damage during hernia surgery and was placed on a respirator. Father Philip Eichner, fellow member of the order, was appointed guardian and petitioned the court to have life support removed based on the expressed wishes of Brother Fox prior to his disability. Although Brother Fox died awaiting resolution of the case, the decision to remove life support and Father Eichner's "substitute judgement" were upheld (In the Matter of Philip K. Eichner . . ., March 31, 1981). The wider family in the order was affirmed, although this was not the intent of the case. While it is beyond the scope of this paper to discuss similarities in dependency relationships among various family forms, further research is suggested toward such explorations.

The District Attorney in the Fox case argued that although common law gives a person the right to refuse treatment, that right resides only with the person whose life is at risk and cannot be transferred to a guardian appointed after the victim becomes incompetent (In the Matter of Philip K. Eichner . . ., March 31, 1981). I have maintained that evidence exists that Emily Gilbert transferred her decision making rights to Roswell prior to her disability and continued to affirm her desire that he decide and act on her behalf until her death.

The Ethical Perspective

The State's Duty to Protect Dependent Groups. Blustein's discussion of parent/child autonomy gives insights into the rights of the State to intervene on behalf of a dependent family member. He argues that the State should protect children from exploitation of the inherent inequality in intergenerational relationships. This duty of the State is not so much to the individual child as to children as a group in the society. The examples he offers include State intervention in children's educational opportunities, e.g., desegregation of schools and initiation of student loans. Parental autonomy suggests that children from different socioeconomic statuses will have different educational opportunities, but the State can and should work to equalize opportunities for children across families.

A similar argument was proposed in the Gilbert prosecution along the lines that there are a lot of older people in Florida who must be protected from potential harm by their caregivers. A harsh verdict in the Gilbert case would serve as an example of the State's intention to protect dependent elders. While the legal arguments of this perspective are reflected in the earlier discussion of Judge Glickstein's remarks, the ethical basis for the perspective is less supportive. The Kantian tradition suggests that using a person as means to accomplish an end is morally wrong. A situation in which a person is punished in order to deter other persons from committing similar acts, while there is no evidence that the person being punished or the society will benefit from harsh punishment of that perpetrator, approaches disregard for the personhood of the perpetrator and puts the courts in the position of using the perpetrator as means to an end that is at best uncertain.

Attribution of Motive to the Caregiver. The jury found Roswell Gilbert cold and unrepentant for his actions in the death of his wife. He was described paradoxically as a "cold, calculating scientist who killed his ailing wife because she embarrassed and inconvenienced him, not from any feeling of mercy or compassion" and as "a private, selfless person who was completely devoted to his wife–so much that, in the end, he gave her the gift of euthanasia that she wanted" (Plummer & Marx, 1985).

Gilbert's choice of a gun as a weapon was detrimental to his defense. In his trial testimony, Gilbert stated that he chose a gun because as a collector he was familiar with the consequences of a gunshot wound. Unlike poisoning which he considered to be uncertain and possibly painful, the close-range gunshot would cause immediate and relatively painless death. It is ironic that the second gunshot became the basis of Mr. Gilbert's conviction on premeditated murder since it was inflicted, according to Gilbert, to make certain that Emily's pain would not continue. He was determined to end his wife's suffering and when he felt a pulse after the first shot, he shot her again to be sure she was dead and would not have to endure vegetative existence (Gilbert, May, 1985). The final shot can be seen as evidence of premeditation or as confirmation of misguided mercy.

The attribution of motive to the perpetrator is important. The calculating scientist would have examined the contract between caregiver and care recipient. At one point in his testimony, Roswell described his caregiving role as "my job," implying role expectations for spouses as care providers. Perhaps he had analyzed the reciprocity of his and Emily's long-term marital relationship in which she had apparently subordinated her individual freedom to his career demands. Gratitude for years of marital fidelity and companionship could have spurred him to comply with Emily's wishes.

Symbolic Loss of Personhood. Alternatively, the compassionate Roswell may have perceived Emily's personhood as lost to the illness she suffered and acted to finish his task as her guardian–to end the artificial maintenance of her life before she lost all dignity. Under this scenario, the couple had developed skill over the years in dressing each other for the stage (Goffman, 1963), interpreting private pain and supporting each other's public presentation. The ultimate reciprocity for Emily's years of dutifully following his corporate career, appearing on his arm at cocktail parties and playing bridge with wives of business contacts, was a symbolic exchange–Roswell's assistance in helping Emily to die before she became unable to maintain her physical beauty and social poise.

Caring and Family Roles. Nell Noddings (1984) based her analysis of caring on a differentiation between logical and natural response to human needs. She argued that people live moral lives without entering into formal decision-making processes about morality. The essential nature of caring is the "displacement of interest in my own reality to the reality of the other" (p. 14). The caring Roswell could have been morally correct in killing Emily. Her reality became his own–no moral logic here, simply gut level reaction to emotional and physical pain. As Noddings (1984, 1988) reminds her readers, parents do not assess the correctness of soiling a diaper in deciding whether or not to change a crying baby.

Caring in the context of family or family-like relationships demonstrates the "special" nature of interactions between people who hold each other in regard, treasure, cherish, and value each other. Within these relationships, moral action is based on the "differential pull" binding emotionally-linked individuals (Hanks, 1991; Jecker, 1989; Post, 1988). Central to the ethic of caring is its orientation toward relationships rather than individuals.

One account of the case described Roswell's act as giving his wife the "gift of euthanasia that she wanted" (Plummer & Marx, 1985). Marcel

Mauss's (1954) model of symbolic exchange suggests that gifts take on meanings within relationships. Integrating Mauss's perspective on the gift with Nodding's notions about caring, the "gift" of euthanasia, given for the good of the person cared for, meant the symbolic restoration of autonomy to caregiver and care receiver. Roswell, actor for the decision-making unit, validated Emily's autonomy by granting her desire. In so doing, he reclaimed his autonomy to choose roles other than the one which confined him for the last decade. The gift was not *calculated*; it was *given*.

CONCLUSION

The Caregiving Unit

My position is that Roswell and Emily Gilbert were a decision-making unit–a corporate moral agent. Their symbiotic relationships developed over 51 years of marriage. It was validated by their daughter's perception. For example, Martha is keeping Emily's ashes until Roswell's death, when the couple's ashes will be scattered together over the waters off the Florida coast. "They have always been together," Martha reflects, "And I know they would want to remain so" (Moran, 1985). While the notion of becoming so interdependent as a member of a couple that one loses the desire to make one's own decisions may cause today's domestic partners to grimace, the Gilbert relationship is not surprising given their time and social position.

There may even be moral justification for extreme interdependency. Locke allows that the formation of a community, in this case a couple in its familial context, implies the formation of one body, empowered to act as one body, presumably with the consent of the majority. Although Locke would disallow suicide or euthanasia on the grounds that people cannot possess or transfer the power to destroy life, he would allow the decision-making power to remain within the family unit.

New Paradigms for Examining Family Caregiving

There is little indication that caregiving will become less a family matter in the near future. With this reality, legal and ethical systems need to look toward new paradigms that accommodate the difficult decisions that family caregivers must make. An early step in this process is to reconceptualize the decision-making agent in legal and moral systems when the family has done so. This new paradigm of *family as agent* will not fit all families, but it will accommodate those who have rationally chosen to move toward collective decision making and action. This paper has presented arguments that families, e.g., couples and other partners, can agree to become a decision-making unit–a moral agent–and that individuals in that unit can autonomously yield individual decision-making power to each other under conditions that do not impede rational choice.

In contrast to the individualistic paradigm that has so strongly influenced modern ethical and legal thought, this new paradigm suggests that decisions and actions of an individual can represent the interests of the collective when the members of the collective have rationally chosen to define their personhood as a member of the collective rather than as an individual actor. Under these conditions, evaluation by agents outside the unit of acts performed by the unit fall under guidelines similar to those commonly applied to individuals in the society. For example, if society permits suicide, society will permit killing within the collective under the new paradigm, but only in cases where it is clearly established that the collective has been formed and continues to exist by rational choice of its members. The moral acceptability of acts by this collective agent rests on: (1) individuals rationally and autonomously choosing to create the unit and (2) participants in the unit caring for each other. If either condition is violated, participants in the unit are at risk for exploitation. Mechanisms should exist for members to review periodically their position within the unit and renegotiate the relationship if necessary.

Methodological Difficulties. Explicating this new paradigm of family as agent within ethical and legal systems rests in the discovery of methodologies to measure and document processes that occur within the history and privacy of family life. Constructs such as symbiosis, caring, and autonomous choice are difficult to define and their measurement, particularly in a family developmental context, is limited by tremendous demands on resources and social sanctions against interference in the private, value-laden realm of family (Larzelere & Klein, 1987). The tragedy of Roswell and Emily Gilbert points not only to the failure of our caregiving system but also to the infancy of our systems of beliefs and methods of social inquiry to answer the complex problems of being human.

Ideological Barriers. We must examine myths about family relationships. Documentation is necessary to understand the process by which social ideologies such as gender equality and individualism are accepted into family belief systems around caregiving and quality of life. Ironically, laws generally favor intervention into the family on behalf of the individual while research on internal family processes is often blocked by concerns about family privacy. There are also theoretical and methodological struggles with the concept of collective agency and the family as a unit of analysis.

Suggestions in the literature that families formalize interactions through contracts have met with some resistance (Hanks & Sussman, 1991; Weitzman, 1981; Jeter & Sussman, 1985). The myths are still strong that family life is largely outside the legal realm and that formalizing family interaction violates the emotional quality of intimate relationships. These mythic structures impede the development of research and theory while maintaining laws and social programs that are inadequate to meet the challenges of family caregiving in the face of increasing life expectancy and chronic illness. Joseph Campbell (1988: p. 16) alerts us that, "The moral order has to catch up with the moral necessities of actual life in time, here and now. And that is what we are not doing." Meanwhile, the Gilberts and other families play out their private tragedies.

REFERENCES

Annas, G.J. (1991). Birth, death, and the criminal law: The New politics of privacy. In B.S. Kogan (Ed.), *A Time to be Born and a Time to Die* (pp. 35-56). New York: Aldine de Gruyter.

Aversa, A., Jr. (1991). Neptune yacht club: A Family wider than kin. In T.D. Marciano & M.B. Sussman (Eds.), *Wider Families: New Traditional Family Forms* (pp. 45-62). New York: The Haworth Press, Inc.

Bayles, M.D. & Henley, K. (Eds.). (1983). *Right Conduct*. New York: Random House.

Beauchamp, T.L. (1982). *Philosophical Ethics*. New York: McGraw Hill.

Becker, H. & Hill, R. (Eds.). (1948). *Family, Marriage, and Parenthood*. Boston: D.C. Heath.

Blustein, J. (1982). *Parents and Children*. New York: Oxford University Press.

Campbell, J. (with Bill Moyers). (1988). *The Power of the Myth*. New York: Anchor Books.

Cicirelli, V.G. (1992). *Family Caregiving: Autonomous and Paternalistic Decision Making*. Newbury Park, CA: Sage.

Colerick, E.J. & George, L.K. (1986). Predictors of institutionalization among caregivers of patients with Alzheimer's Disease. *Journal of the American Geriatrics Society*, 34, 493-498.

Collopy, B.; Dubler, N.; & Zuckerman, C. (1990). The ethics of home care: Autonomy and accommodation. *Hastings Center Report*, 20(2), special supplement, 1-16.

DeGeorge, R. (1983). Can corporations have moral responsibility? In T.L. Beauchamp & N.E. Bowie (Eds.), *Ethical Theory and Business* (pp. 57-67). Englewood Cliffs, NJ: Prentice-Hall.

Gilbert, R. (1985, May). Testimony given before the Broward County Court, Florida.

Givens, R.; Agrest, S.; & Prout, L. (1985, September 9). Mercy or murder? *Newsweek*, p. 25.

Goffman, E. (1959). *The Presentation of Self in Everyday Life*. Garden City, NJ: Doubleday.

Hanks, R.S. (1991). An intergenerational perspective on family ethical dilemmas. *Marriage & Family Review*, 16(1-4), 161-174.

Hanks, R.S. & Settles, B.H. (1990). Theoretical questions and ethical issues in a family caregiving relationship. In D.E. Biegel & A. Blum (Eds.), *Aging and Caregiving: Theory, Research, & Policy* (pp. 98-120). Newbury Park, CA: Sage.

Hanks, R.S. & Sussman, M.B. (1991). Inheritance contracting: Implications for theory and policy. Paper presented at the 21st Annual Theory Construction and Research Methodology Workshop, National Council on Family Relations, November 16, Denver, CO.

In the Matter of Philip K. Eichner, On Behalf of Joseph C. Fox, Respondent, v. Denis Dillon, as District Attorney of Nassau County, Appellent, March 31, 1981.

In the Matter of Karen Quinlan, an Alleged Incompetent, Supreme Court of New Jersey, March 31, 1976.

Jecker, N.S. (1989). Are filial duties unfounded? *American Philosophical Quarterly*, 26(1), 73-80.

Jeter, K. & Sussman, M.B. (1985). Each couple should develop a marriage contract suitable to themselves. In H. Feldman & M. Feldman (Eds.), *Current Controversies in Marriage and the Family*, pp. 283-292. Beverly Hills: Sage.

Larzelere, R.E. & Klein, D. (1987). Methodology. In M.B. Sussman & S.K. Steinmetz (Eds.), *Handbook of Marriage and the Family* (pp. 125-155). New York: Plenum Press.

Malinowski, B. (1922). *Argonauts of the Western Pacific*. London: Routledge & Kegan Paul.

Marciano, T.D. (1991). A Postscript on wider families: Traditional family assumptions and cautionary notes. In T.D. Marciano & M.B. Sussman (Eds.), *Wider Families: New Traditional Family Forms* (pp. 159-172). New York: The Haworth Press, Inc.

Marciano, T.D. & Sussman, M.B. (Eds.). (1991). *Wider Families: New Traditional Family Forms*. New York: The Haworth Press, Inc.

Mauss, M. (1954). *The Gift*. I. Cunnison (Trans.). New York: The Free Press. (Original work published 1925).

Moran, M. Personal Communication, October 30, 1985.

Noddings, N. (1984). *Caring: A Feminine Approach to Ethics and Moral Education*. Berkeley: University of California Press.

Noddings, N. (1988, Feb.). An ethics of caring and its implications for instructional arrangements. *American Journal of Education*.

Plummer, W. & Marx, L. (1985, May 27). An act of love or selfishness? *People*, 100.

Post, S. (1988). An ethical perspective on caregiving in the family. *Journal of Medical Humanities and Bioethics*, 9(1), 6-16.

Pratt, C.C.; Schmall, V.; & Wright, S. (1987). Ethical concerns of family caregivers to dementia patients. *The Gerontologist, 27*, 632-638.

Roswell Gilbert, Appellant, v. State of Florida, Appellee, Case No. 88-2662, Court of Appeal of Florida, Fourth District, January 31, 1990.

Sussman, M.B. (1983). Family-organizational linkages. In H. Harbin (Ed.), *The Psychiatric Hospital and the Family.* Spectrum, Inc.

Treas, J. & Bengtson, V. (1987). The family in later years. In M.B. Sussman & S.K. Steinmetz (Eds.), *Handbook of Marriage and the Family* (pp. 625-648). New York: Plenum.

Varon, J.A. Personal communication, January 17, 1992.

Weitzman, L. (1981). *The Marriage Contract: Spouses, Lovers, and the Law.* New York: The Free Press.

Reproductive Technologies and the Law: Norplant and the Bad Mother

Margot E. Young

On December 20, 1990, the American Food and Drug Agency approved Norplant Contraceptive System, hormonal implants that provide long-term contraceptive protection for women.[1] On January 1, 1991, Darlene Johnson, a 27-year-old African-American woman, was sentenced to three years on the contraceptive.[2] Within one year of its introduction onto the American market, Norplant moved from marking the increased freedom of women from the routine and uncertainty of birth control to facilitating state intervention in the reproductive choices of certain women.

Darlene Johnson's case is unremarkable but for the sentencing options she faced. Pregnant, already a mother of four who supported herself and her children on welfare, Ms. Johnson was convicted of several counts of felony child abuse. Presented with two sentencing options by Judge Harry Broadman, she could opt to spend one year in prison with three years on probation or choose four months in prison, followed by three years on probation while also using Norplant.[3] Without her lawyer present, Ms. Johnson chose the Norplant option. And, although she later changed her mind and her lawyer requested that the order be rescinded, the judge stuck with the initial sentence.[4]

Margot E. Young is Assistant Professor of Law at the University of Victoria, British Columbia, Canada. This article was written when the author was at the University of California, Berkeley.

The author would like to thank Sandy Tomc, Lisa Phillipps, Marlee Kline and Hester Lessard for helpful comments and encouragement.

[Haworth co-indexing entry note]: "Reproductive Technologies and the Law: Norplant and the Bad Mother." Young, Margot E. Co-published simultaneously in *Marriage & Family Review* (The Haworth Press, Inc.) Vol. 21, No. 3/4, 1995, pp. 259-281; and: *Families and Law* (ed: Lisa J. McIntyre, and Marvin B. Sussman) The Haworth Press, Inc., 1995, pp. 259-281. Multiple copies of this article/chapter may be purchased from The Haworth Document Delivery Center [1-800-3-HAWORTH; 9:00 a.m. - 5:00 p.m. (EST)].

This case is not anomalous. Since Judge Broadman made his sentencing order, there have been at least two other instances of court-ordered use of Norplant.[5] Politicians have also been eager to exploit Norplant as a means of responding to "problem mothers." Thus, some legislators have considered the question of mandating Norplant use for all women convicted of serious drug offenses.[6] Others have proposed Norplant as a solution to what they perceive as the problem of excessive family size of welfare mothers.[7] And public opinion polls indicate support for this judicial and legislative appropriation of Norplant technology.[8]

Why has Norplant so engaged the legal, political, and popular imagination? This paper examines some of the mechanisms by which this new technology has created the opportunity for an already present concern about the reproductive choices of certain women to take this particular punitive and regulatory form. I examine two related ways of understanding the connection between the introduction of this new reproductive technology and the increase in calls for reproductive regulation of at least some women. Both accounts are relevant not only to Norplant but also to reproductive technologies in general. The first section looks at how technologies *affect* and, at the same time, *reflect* their social environments. New technologies disrupt dominant conceptual orderings of the social and political world. Yet, these technologies are also products of their environments and, importantly, owe their particular development and use to existing cultural and social structures and assumptions. This section examines how these two characteristics of technology interact to facilitate a conservative politics of technological "progress."

The second section speaks more specially to the law's adoption of Norplant as a response to certain dilemmas. Because legal discourse is particularly receptive to adoption of new techniques of regulation and normalization, technological developments are often too eagerly incorporated into legal responses to older problems. Women whose procreative activities invoke traditional population control concerns represent one such "problem." This section, then, looks at how the politics of reproductive technologies generated by the characteristics of technological innovation described in the first section can be inscribed into and reinforced by legal discourse.

TECHNOLOGICAL "INNOVATION"

The introduction of new technology has certain destabilizing as well as reinforcing effects on relevant systems of political and social norms. My discussion is structured first in terms of how new technologies, and specifically Norplant, threaten disorder of existing conceptual systems. I then discuss how Norplant also exemplifies technology's tendency to bear the marks of the political environment from which it comes and thus to reinforce existing order. I conclude by examining how these two characteristics combine to make recent use of Norplant's technology particularly politically disturbing. Through this argument I hope to illustrate how "reproductive technology (becomes) reproductive ideology" (Beck-Gernsheim, 1989, p. 38).

New technologies disturb pre-existing forms of social order by fragmenting or disassembling previously unitary objects, processes, or social relationships.[9] This, in turn, results in fragmentation of the social arrangements that surround and depend upon the original object, process, or relationship. Assumptions about the order of things, about the arrangement of social and natural "facts" depend upon certain perceived "unities" (Shapiro, 1990, p. 335). When things are rearranged or disarranged, our patterns of thinking or meaning–what one commentator calls "our ideological capital"–disappear (Shapiro, 1990, p. 335). Society is forced to think more explicitly about how the newly deconstructed object, process, or relationship ought to be restructured, how our conceptual systems are to be reshaped so as to take into account these new "factual" arrangements. In such a manner do technological developments unsettle our sense of the world: by challenging with new visions of reorderings of the freshly created parts, by highlighting old forms of ordering that suffer from the exposure, or, at least, by making apparent old forms that were, because of their "givenness," operating less visibly.

Reproductive technologies are particularly controversial because, for many of the new relations they make possible, society has yet to generate a conceptual framework that, for most individuals, smoothly, unquestionably codes for recognition and assessment of the new processes and their participants. Old conceptual patterns–say, the notion of the family–fail to comprehend the new technology-spurred situations (Shapiro, 1990, p. 343). We are forced either to rethink what we want maternal relations, for example, to signify or to attempt to force newly configured processes into older, ill-fitting social frameworks. Only so can we deal with our "conceptual agoraphobia" (Shapiro, 1990, p. 341).

Reproductive technologies that separate heterosexual sex from procreation are good examples of this phenomenon. Disassociation of heterosexual sex and parenthood, the disruption this represents of biological processes previously conceived of as unitary, similarly refracts the social relations that have traditionally made sense of and given meaning to these events. So, for example, hormonal intervention into the female reproductive process enables heterosexual sexual behavior that is clearly not also potentially reproductive behavior. It removes the reproductive element from this form of sex. And, techniques of alternative insemination challenge traditional connections between sex, parenthood, and marriage.[10] Here, procreation is rendered possible without sex. The social relations configured in part by artificial insemination technologies permit different assumptions about the significance or import of such things as sexual intimacy, shared genetic parenthood, and marital status.[11] And we begin to think differently about what we might want reproductive choice, responsibility, and rights to mean.

Yet, technologies must also be understood in terms of the social and political contexts from which they arise (Stanworth, 1087, p. 18; Feenburg, 1991). This notion of technology stands in opposition to that account which sees technology as simply a value-free means, indifferent to the variety of ends to which it can be put. From this latter perspective, technology assumes no necessary structure of social life; its use, not design, is at issue (Feenburg, 1991, pp. 5-8). In contrast to this argument, I want to argue that technology is inevitably socially and politically contoured.

Feenburg suggests a useful way of thinking about technological development. Individual technologies are built up from different combinations of "technical elements." Things like the spring, the lever and the electrical circuit are general examples of what is meant by technical elements. More specific to the topic at hand are such things as individual surgical techniques and techniques of biochemical manipulation. These elements, while themselves relatively neutral[12] with respect to most issues of political struggle, are strung together or collectively configured to form individual technologies that reflect various "social criteria of purpose." In this manner, the social environment of the technology determines how individual technical elements are combined. Technologies thus "fit" their environment: new technologies reflect the specific goals or needs a particular society (through its scientific community) articulates (Feenburg, 1991, p. 81).

So, technological development is the result of diffuse and multiple social practices, each located in specific contexts and peopled by specific actors. These practices represent outcomes of struggles for social control and are determined by the distribution of power and resources in society. And, thus, social relations, and assumptions about such things as race, gender, and class, form an influential element of the construction and employment of any technology. "The design of technology is . . . an ontological division fraught with political consequences" (Feenburg, 1991, p. 3; Wajcman, 1991; Marcuse, 1968, pp. 223-24).

This means we must see reproductive technologies as confirmations of dominant social conclusions about gendered and ethnic reproductive behavior and norms. Assumptions about the importance of reproductive activity to women's identity and life potential as well as less gender-specific but politically-loaded notions of individual autonomy and culpability structure ongoing development of medical intervention in the reproductive process.

The *in vitro* fertilization (*IVF*) industry provides illustration of this point. This technology addresses the problems of infertility not as instances of wider societal problems of environmental contaminants, problematic methods of birth control, or social constraints on the combination of work and childbearing for women, but as individual physiological failures. And the technology does so from within a framework that views infertility as primarily a female problem, even though significant numbers of couples who become involved in *IVF* programs do so because of low male fertility. As a result, the techniques assembled to enable *IVF* focus on manipulation and restructuring of the female reproductive capacity. And, not only does this clustering of techniques embody assumptions about the centrality of reproduction to women's lives, it enforces such a preoccupation, as the procedures themselves so intrude into the woman's other activities as to render concentration on other tasks both temporally and psychologically difficult. This is not to say, of course, that *IVF* procedures do not address infertility problems, but that the way in which they do so is sensible only within a specific social context (Feenburg, 1991, p. 82).

To summarize this last discussion, I have argued, using reproductive technologies as specific examples, that technologies have both a disruptive and reinforcing effect on their social environments. I want now to put aside for the moment the current political consequences of such a mix of characteristics and discuss more specifically how Norplant's development reflects these observations. As a new technology, Norplant unsettles norms constructed around use of both oral contraception and sterilization, yet, at the same time, it reflects prevailing gender- , race- , and class-structured assumptions about who should be contracepting and why many women's contraceptive behavior is less than ideal.

With respect to the first of these qualities–its disruptive effects–Norplant unsettles current norms of birth control by "reshuffling" the contraceptive options available. It does this by selectively combining qualities of both the birth control pill and sterilization. Like both techniques, Norplant is a highly reliable form of contraception.[13] But, like the birth control pill and unlike sterilization, Norplant provides temporary contraception, is not extremely physically invasive, and demands a lower initial financial outlay. And like sterilization, but unlike the birth control pill, Norplant does not rely upon the active, ongoing involvement of women in the contraceptive process.

As I argued more generally earlier, this separation and remixing of birth control processes affect how society thinks about contraceptive practices. The temporary, physically unobtrusive, yet reliable nature of birth control offered by Norplant makes previously discounted birth control policy less obviously objectionable. American law has, since 1942, enjoined against state-coerced sterilization, at least absent very strict due process and equal protection considerations.[14] But Norplant sufficiently changes what such "sterilization" need involve, rendering a state-ordered procedure possibly more legally and socially palatable. Unlike the sterilization procedures at issue in those instances where the court has condemned forced sterilization, mandated Norplant use does not mean that the individual "is forever deprived of a basic liberty." It is not true that "[t]here is no redemption for the individual whom the law [so] touches" (*Skinner v. Oklahoma*, 1942). Norplant is, after all, only a temporary method of birth control.[15] But, unlike other temporary birth control techniques, Norplant is more suited to coercive application because of its independence from active user cooperation.

I do not mean to imply that coerced sterilization in the United States stopped as a result of a 1942 court decision. Quite the contrary. Widespread sterilization abuse was "discovered" in the 1970s and a pattern of coerced sterilizations for women of color and low income women emerged. Medical residents honed their surgical skills by performing tubal ligations on Hispanic women who were unaware of the nature of the procedure. Radical hysterectomies were performed on Native American women without their consent. African-American women on welfare had their babies delivered only on the condition they also consented to sterilization (Nsiah-Jefferson, 1989, p. 46; Nsiah-Jefferson and Hall, 1989, 103-104). The result of such a history is that women on welfare have a sterilization rate 49% higher than that of other women. Women of color are also disproportionately sterilized as the following sterilization rates indicate: 20% African-American women, 24% Native American women, 37% Puerto Rican women, and 16% white women (Blank, 1990, p. 128). Formal judicial pronouncements against non-consensual sterilization simply ensured that these procedures were deployed extra-legally, by other mechanisms of social control. My argument is that Norplant, by removing those elements that made coerced sterilization problematic within formal legal discourse, creates the political moment for the motivation informing this "secret" program of sterilization to make a more public appearance and argument. It may no longer be necessary that forced sterilizations–at least those that use Norplant technology–be hidden within the administrative interstices of the state and the medical profession.

So Norplant presents a birth control option that re-raises the question of contraceptive regulation through court order. Judges and legislators may be more comfortable limiting women's reproductive options by means of Norplant. Norplant offers what makes surgical sterilization legally practical—easy enforceability and certain results—without the attendant drawbacks of irreversibility and extreme physical invasion.[16]

Yet Norplant also reflects its social and political environment. It is significant in this context that Norplant is a female contraceptive,[17] that it provides a medical solution to the problem of unwanted pregnancies, and that it operates by way of interference in a woman's biological hormonal processes.[18] Moreover, Norplant allows for a situational and chronological separation between contraception and sex. Cultural factors that make women uncomfortable touching their genitals or interrupting "spontaneous" sexual activity to insert or apply contraceptives recommend birth control methods that allow for "hands-off," detached contraception. Unease about sexual activity, the desire for "normal" uninterrupted heterosexual sex in which men are active and women overcome, does not favor contraceptive technologies that require "on-site" female skill, attention, and will (Wajcman, 1991, p. 77). Norplant conforms with both of these dominant cultural constructions of heterosexual activity.

What is most interesting about Norplant, however, is the way these two characteristics I have just detailed—Norplant's disruptive effects on existing formal consensuses about state-ordered or encouraged sterilization and Norplant's reflection of traditional fears about women's reproductive autonomy—combine to position Norplant as useful to conservative reproductive politics. And here I want to return to my previous comment that the two characteristics of technological development I have discussed can combine in politically dangerous ways.

My argument is that while the disruptive effects of technology might appear to promise at least a reexamination, if not a reworking, of dominant assumptions about proper or necessary social orderings, the cultural character of technology operates often to mute and conservatively channel this radical potential. The options made apparent by the fragmentation characteristic of new technology are already prefigured by the very social relations that they seem to be challenging. So that while new technologies do in some way threaten dominant assumptions of social ordering, they do so from within a larger ideological framework that is consistent with the very norms apparently under fire. As an example of this process one might consider contractual motherhood. This practice disrupts the institution of motherhood as it has been traditionally understood, at least within white western societies. But it does so still in terms of a technological agenda that, like the tradition it disturbs, stresses the importance of paternal biological connections and undervalues and de-emphasizes the reproductive labor done by women. It is necessary both to acknowledge the potential of new forms of technology to force alteration of the existing dominant conceptual frameworks that "map" the social world for many of us, and to recognize the extent to which such challenges themselves come ideologically loaded.

I want to emphasize the importance of the last caveat because it is in our failure to assert this with respect to reproductive technologies that we often encourage what I have previously called a conservative reproductive politics. We do so in two ways. The first is relatively straightforward. We fail to capitalize fully on whatever progressive possibilities might lie with a particular technological reform by not guarding adequately against their cooptation by the dominant ideological field that accounts in a more subtle way for the very appearance of the new technology. Again, I offer another example. Although not a new technology, alternative insemination, initially informed by concerns of reproduction within monogamous, heterosexual relationships, now, in combination with new techniques of semen storage and delivery, allows for non-sexual procreation by individuals located outside such traditional relationships, say, a lesbian couple. Yet, the technology's sanctioned social use remains tightly structured by prevailing assumptions about parenthood that emphasize the monogamous, heterosexual couple. The most dramatic modern innovation this technology has enabled is the commercialization of "surrogate motherhood": a practice, as noted, replete with the biases of traditional family ideology. We may be led to acknowledge a radical widening of possibilities for motherhood, but this has been almost instantaneously muted by reassertion of dominant paradigms through such language as "surrogate mother" and through traditional custody arrangements. Whatever re-thinkings of parenthood traditions alternative insemination made possible have been more than countered by the technology's enlistment in aid of a rearticulation of traditional frameworks of family structure. Perhaps more forceful awareness of the ideological locatedness of technology might serve to give warning about this sort of political capture.

Failure to recognize the political character of technology also, secondly, helps facilitate legitimation of ongoing conservative political programs. When we acknowledge the shaking-up of dominant understandings of particular social relations but do not attend to the politics that structure such destabilization, we allow for the appearance of reform without the substance of change. We interpret the fragmentation effected by technology as creating the impetus for political change. Yet, we ignore how the manner of fragmentation and the possibilities it reveals or, indeed, leads to are themselves politically determined. These politics remain invisible, masked by the change technology seems to herald. So, the fragmentation effects of technology function to obfuscate reassertion of old norms. The rhetoric of change helps legitimate the continuance, albeit in new forms, of dominant ideologies.

This error is not infrequently made by legal scholars in their analysis of new technologies and implications for legal regulation. For example, Maguire Shultz, in an interesting article on intent-based parenthood, illustrates this failing. In this piece she commends the new parental possibilities made feasible by contractual motherhood arrangements and argues that it is through permissive legal regulation of alternative parenting combinations that we might see a desirable rethinking of paternal child-care responsibilities. "Developments in reproductive technology have created new biological and social options that in turn challenge old assumptions and pose new dilemmas for legal doctrine and policy" (Shultz, 1990, p. 300). Yet, by failing to give adequate notice to the power of traditional arrangements and how traditional assumptions have prestructured commercial contractual motherhood arrangements, Shultz allows a rhetoric of social progress to mask a reality of affirmation of traditionalism.

I want to return to consideration of Norplant to demonstrate how a similar process is at work in relation to the new contraceptive practices Norplant makes possible. In particular, I want to discuss in more detail the implications of Norplant for women's reproductive agency: the interaction of the contraceptive's destabilization of contraceptive options and its political heritage.

Norplant renders women's willful action with respect to birth control or other technological means of ordering reproductive choice or behavior less important.[19] Some sort of positive will is necessary with respect to implantation of the Norplant rods, but, other than this initial action, a woman's continued involvement with the contraceptive is passive. So, unlike the birth control pill–the other temporary contraceptive with similar rates of pregnancy prevention–Norplant does not require daily application. A woman cannot simply forget to continue to use Norplant. There are no monthly prescriptions to fill, no daily pill-taking. Once implanted, Norplant can be forgotten about and its contraceptive abilities remain unaffected. It requires an active birth-control decision only once every five years.

This reduction in emphasis on women's contraceptive agency echoes at least two background concerns currently structuring development of birth control techniques. The first concern is less ominous; it reflects a desire that birth control be made as least onerous for its users as possible. Norplant, in this light, represents an advance in convenience, a gesture towards women who find daily pill-taking or monthly prescription-paying hurdles to effective contraception.

The darker side to this convenience is that it also responds to a larger political and social concern about women whose reproductive agency when expressed in pregnancy is a problem. And these women are not the same women whose complaints of convenience occupy researchers. This second group of women are women of color (particularly African-American women, Native American women, and third world women), low-income women, and single mothers; all of whom serve as sites of concern about questions of social, political, and economic control.[20] These are the women whom dominant, traditional ideologies of population control, eugenics, and family do not trust to exercise their reproductive agency in socially desirable ways.[21] From this perspective, also, Norplant commends itself as a method of birth control. Once the initial implantation of Norplant has taken place, it is the discontinuance of Norplant that requires conscious applied action: to end use of Norplant, a woman needs medical assistance.[22] For many women–often members of the groups targeted for coercive Norplant use–the expense and inconvenience of medical services may be enough of a disincentive to disincline them to seek to have Norplant removed.[23] Thus, unlike other temporary methods of contraception, once implanted, Norplant's continued use is aided, not damaged, by such factors as neglect, poverty, and apathy. Viewed from this perspective, Norplant represents a sinister solution to the problem as it is seen from traditional reproductive and family politics. While the more positive aspects of Norplant permit the envisioning of a new era of easy, reliable birth control–an increase in the agency individual women exercise over their reproductive fates–the negative agenda of Norplant development paints a bleaker picture of enhanced coercive regulation of some women's reproductive decisions.

The trick is to realize that both of these scenarios are real. For some women–notably, white, affluent women–Norplant could offer some increase in current contraceptive options. But for other women–African-American mothers on welfare, say–Norplant is more likely to represent an increase in the control others are able to exercise over the women's reproductive capacities. I want to emphasize the latter situation, both because I think the "positive" effects of contraceptive development for privileged women are themselves more complicated and because the treatment of Norplant as a new and liberating birth control choice for women runs the danger of eclipsing this more negative side of the technology. The emancipating picture of Norplant needs to be counterbalanced by a more nuanced understanding of the impact of the technology on American contraceptive politics. We need to insist that the consequences of particular uses of individual technologies shape our assessment of that technology, that technologies do not stand apart from their social and political deployment.

To summarize and conclude this first section, then, my argument is that the facilitation of conservative reproductive politics, such as we see happening with Norplant, is not simply the result of political opportunism but, rather, is prefigured by the pattern of current reproductive technology development itself. And, we facilitate such a conservative agenda when we treat technology as an uncomplicated harbinger of progress, or of social destabilization, and fail to attend to the politics already embedded in and affirmed by any particular technological development.

LEGAL DISCOURSE

In this section, I want to discuss one aspect of legal regulation that follows from the kind of technological development I have outlined above. I focus on legal discourse not because it is the most significant discourse of control in women's lives but because it is often among the most publicly articulated and as such has certain symbolic importance (and, of course, material consequences for those individual women it concerns directly). Thus, the focus of my paper returns to the example with which it began– Darlene Johnson's Norplant probation order–as an instance of one form of law's interaction with technological reform.

First, however, I want to set up the discussion that follows by considering the notion of "bad mothers" briefly alluded to in my first section. I do so at this stage because the notion of bad mothers is a category of deviance, the solution to which is increasingly looked at in terms of the sort of legal regulation of women's reproductive capacities that Norplant's technology can facilitate. Recall that I discussed those women whose motherhood practices serve as foci of concern for traditional theories of political and social control: women of color, women on social assistance, single mothers. These are the women coercive sterilization practices target; these are the mothers dominant politics codes as "bad mothers." Since the nineteenth century regulation and control of women within western cultures have been structured in terms of an idealized notion of the family. Women are ideally represented as mothers; real women as either good or bad mothers, women whose maternal activities conform with or deviate from the idealized maternal figure of white, middle-class family life (Maher, 1992, p. 161; Handler and Hasenfeld, 1991, pp. 22-3). And, deviant mothers have become symbols of social disarray. It is argued that it is in their failure to conform with traditional patterns of mothering–in raising children outside of heterosexual relationships, in extended kinship relationships, in impecunious circumstances–that the root of such things as violence, poverty, and social anomie lie[24] (Davin, 1978; Moynihan, 1965).

Armed with this formula of proper motherhood, legal, political, and welfare agents have participated in the regulation and penalization of women whose mothering activities contradict the dominant ideal. The notion of the "bad mother" is thus an example of what Foucault means by anomalies in the social body: a category of social deviance both created and addressed by a variety of techniques of discipline and normalization, including law (Foucault, 1980, 1979; Dreyfus and Rabinow, 1983, p. 195; Smart, 1989). Thus the idea of the "bad mother" provides the context for the blending of legal and disciplinary discourses I wish here to document: a blending which constitutes a "gender specific form of punishment and regulation" (Maher, 1992, p. 156).

Darlene Johnson's case may seem at first to be an inappropriate example of this process. Her appearance before the law was, after all, the result of what was reported as a severe physical beating she had given two of her children. But my argument is not that such abuse is not problematic and, probably, rightly a cause of some concern. It is that this concern had certain punitive consequences for the mother that had at least as much to do with Johnson's skin color, gender, and social class as it had to do with how she chose to discipline her children. That the first woman to be subject to mandated Norplant use should be African-American, on welfare, and already the mother of a large family is not simple coincidence. The fit between this case and the history of the regulation of motherhood is too striking to ignore.

To return, however, to the main argument of this second part of the paper, I wish to use Foucault's notions of juridico-discursive power and disciplinary power to discuss one of the mechanisms by which the social figure of "bad mothers" is addressed in law. In so doing, I hope also to demonstrate how reproductive technologies figure in the symbiotic interaction of legal discourse and the "sciences of normalization," and in the ability of legal actors to structure their responses to what they perceive to be female culpability through regulation of the female body. More concretely, it is possible to see in the establishment of Norplant use as a term of punishment for "bad mothers" an example of the particular interaction of legal discourse, regulation, and technology I have introduced previously.

Foucault describes the power that characterizes the modern episteme as creative and technical. It is power less concerned with negative sanctions and more with techniques of normalization. Smart argues that traditional legal discourse–what Foucault terms juridico-discursive power (the discourse of rights)–exists in tandem with this other mode of power–disciplinary or regulatory power. These "two parallel mechanisms of power" are less distinct in practice than their analytics imply. Law and legal discourse often provide the institutional justification and environment for regimes of disciplinary power while technologies of normalization are frequently the means by which law extends its own power[25] (Smart, 1989, p. 8).

So, in this paper, I am assuming an interaction of juridical and disciplinary modes of power which can result in the colonization of disciplinary techniques by legal apparatuses. Law channels the exercise of political power through declarations of rights and penalties. This process is supplemented by law's adoption or incorporation into its own rituals, medical, psychiatric, social work, and other professional discourses. What occurs is a "conflation of old and new contrivances of power" (Smart, 1989, p. 14). Law thus extends its authority, "not just in terms of discovering new objects for scrutiny, but in terms of new methods of application" (Smart, 1989, p. 96).

One way law accomplishes this is by translating concerns of welfare into the language of rights. Once an interest is transformed into a rights claim, the court can exercise its traditional powers to coerce or regulate in the name of such rights. In so doing, the court becomes able to exercise power in areas it would otherwise be forced to concede to more straightforward regulatory discourses or practices (Smart, 1989, pp. 19-20). In this way, does law extend or, at least, maintain its reach. And, while the law often appears and claims to be more measured and responsive in its substitution of traditional criminal penalties by more innovative, regulatory strategies, we should not assume that these new responses are less oppressive. They may be equally intrusive and inspective of individual lives (Smart, 1989, p. 97).

One can see this process of translation at work in those instances where Norplant use has been suggested as a solution to the problem of abusive mothers. There is something distinctly odd about one way the argument for mandatory or financially-encouraged use of Norplant is frequently framed. It is set up as a conflict between the state's responsibility in protecting the interests of future children and the mother's interest in control over her own reproductive life.[26] Thus, Judge Broadman, in an interview after his sentencing of Darlene Johnson, defends his order in the following way:

But what you have to do as a judge is you must balance conflicting
constitutional rights. Here, what I did was I found that there were
constitutional rights of the children, the born children and her unconceived children. And I balanced their rights against her rights and
they won. (*American Political Network Abortion Report*, November
12, 1991)

Now, obviously, this is neither a legally authoritative nor substantively
impressive rendering of American constitutional argument but it does
communicate the kind of imagery the Judge publicly uses to justify his
decision to mandate Johnson's Norplant use. Even in a more obvious
regulatory environment, rights discourse appears. Kansas State Representative Patrick used a similar justification for his proposed legislation providing financial encouragement for welfare women to use Norplant:

. . . it's time we stopped worrying about the rights of the mother and
started worrying about the rights of the children she's bringing into
the world. (Rees, 1991)

This extension of legal recognition, the creation of new rights-bearing
entities, is not an unusual phenomenon. It is, after all, what has happened
in the abortion debate: claims of foetal rights now share center stage with
women's claims to reproductive freedom. And, in state articulation of
other duties owed by pregnant women to their foetuses, we see a similar
grant of state recognition of foetal interests. Nor is it novel to criticize this
increasing assumption of situational tension between the pregnant woman
and her foetus (Stanworth, 1987; Petchesky, 1987).
    But what is unique about the Norplant situation is the extent to which
legal and political actors have gone to locate some innocent child's interest, in whose name the state can restrict otherwise formerly inviolate
female reproductive interests. Distinct from other scenarios where this
imagery of foetal and maternal conflict is more familiar, the Norplant
situation has two peculiar characteristics. The first is that the entity the
state seeks to protect does not as yet exist. Unlike the foetuses whose rights
anti-abortion crusaders champion or courts invoke in prosecuting pregnant
drug-using women, this entity has no actual physical existence or presence, of any sort. Moreover, and this is the second peculiarity, if the courts
are able to force women to use Norplant, then this creature, whose rights
justify the coerced sterilization of its potential mother, will never exist. So,
it seems, our protection of these future children is achieved by ensuring
that they and their potential interests never materialize. We express our
respect for the rights of these children by not allowing them to be con-

ceived and thereby ensuring that there is no real entity to whom any recognition can be owed. Thus, to respect them, we have to negate the very potentiality that, in the first place, dictated they be recognized.

Such rhetoric is, however, functional. The kinds of restrictions on women's reproductive autonomy represented by judicially-ordered or legislatively-incited use of Norplant are less easy to justify in terms of political imagery. In order to cast the issue as one of conflicting rights, the state must set up a fictive bearer of legal interests. Only so can it create a rights-based justification for the coercion of a real bearer of legal interests. So, actual women's rights are trumped by the assigned rights of imaginary persons.

What motivates this rhetoric is a desire to avoid at least the appearance of instrumentalization of the woman, of disciplining her in aid of some larger social project, a concern about population control. Power, after all, "is tolerable only on condition that it mask a substantial part of itself. Its success is proportional to its ability to hide its own mechanisms" (Foucault, 1980, p. 86). The woman is not to be seen as a means to an end but as an actor whose agency is compromisable only in relation to concerns which are themselves concerns of human dignity and autonomy. The legal rituals of protecting rights and coercing obligations situate and legitimate political dominations (Foucault, 1971; Leonard, 1990). By casting the issue as one of competing rights, otherwise operative constraints on limiting women's reproductive autonomy are bypassed.

But what becomes apparent once the speciousness of the figure of the unconceived child is exposed, is precisely the instrumentalization and objectification of the woman. She is after all not treated as an end in herself but rather as a means of addressing a larger social concern–even though, ironically, it is precisely the insistence upon her autonomy in the first place (her criminal culpability) that allows so singular a placement of blame, despite obvious situational factors of racism, sexism, and poverty, on her head. So mandated Norplant use, then, isn't best understood as a response structured by concerns of individual rights–despite the rhetoric of judges or commentators. Rather it is about policy concerns: concerns of social control, economic cost, and population composition.[27] To repeat my early remarks, the discourse of rights is used as, or at least functions as, a cover for a discourse of social control.

What gives this process certain gender-specific consequences is the fact that, historically, the notion of female culpability in law has been mediated through the construction of women's bodies as sites of legal jurisdiction. And women's corporeality has traditionally been framed in terms of their bodies' reproductive capacities (Maher, 1992, p. 67; Smart, 1989, pp. 92-3).

While this historical aspect of law has diminished somewhat–Smart notes that women's bodies no longer constitute bars to entering professions or exercising contractual will–it remains a significant force still in the area of criminal law and in modern law's selective deployment of recent mechanisms of surveillance and normalization. "Having a female body becomes a *conduit of disqualification,* no less significant because it does not always have the same effect in all areas of law and legal activity" (Smart, 1989, p. 96).

And as technological discoveries provide more knowledge about women's bodies and their reproductive capacities, as they render such capacities more manipulatable, the potential reach of legal regulation correspondingly expands (Smart, 1989, p. 97). So, for example, technological advances in fetal monitoring–such as ultrasonograms or chorionic villi sampling–increase the "visibility" of the fetus, rendering the issue of fetal health fertile terrain for increased regulation of women. Such "panoptics of the womb" have created another field for legal surveillance and intervention (Petchesky, 1987, p. 69; Smart, 1989, pp. 96-7; Maher, 1992, pp. 170-1). So, too, the introduction of Norplant has created another means by which law can exercise control over women's bodies.

And it bears repeating that such technological innovation itself is by no means neutral. Rather, as I have argued in the first part of this paper, technology comes imprinted with its own political agenda, an agenda that, in the case of reproductive technologies, shapes how the law is able to increase and make possible forms of access to women's bodies and what assumptions about women's sexuality and reproductive behavior are expounded by the law. It is in this manner that the law is often complicitous in the propagation of the gender, race, and class politics that have shaped the development of reproductive technologies. Moreover, the same social forces that dictated the particular paths technological development has taken are often also present in the assumptions that structure the discourses of normalization that structure law's use of technology. Thus, the insertion of reproductive politics into legal discourse happens at, at least, two levels: by means of the opportunities technologies themselves offer and in the assumptions that inform the concerns of the regulatory discourses that can structure the law's incorporation of these technologies.

CONCLUSION

This, then, is the particular interaction of legal discourse, regulatory norms, and technology I asserted was exemplified by recent legal appropriation of Norplant technology. A technological means of temporary sterilization that de-emphasizes women's reproductive agency, linked with social welfare concerns about those women whose demographics and reproductive behavior qualify them as "bad mothers," and added to the ability of legal discourse to frame the issue as a conflict of rights where the other party has the perfect innocence of the unconceived child, results in a new manifestation of law's traditional regulation of women's bodies.

NOTES

1. Norplant consists of six silicon (Silastic) capsules, each 34 mm long and 2.4 mm wide and filled with 36 mg of levonorgestrel, a synthetic progestin widely used in oral contraceptives. The capsules are implanted under local anesthetic in a fan-like fashion along the inside of the upper arm or forearm. The levonorgestrel is released from the capsules gradually and provides contraception for at least 5 years. A second version, Norplant-2, is also available and consists of 2 capsules providing protection for at least 3 years. Norplant works primarily by suppressing ovulation. As well, it effects cervical mucous, reducing and thickening it and thus impeding sperm mobility. It also suppresses development and growth of uterine endometrium, possibly preventing conception by limiting progesterone secretion during the luteal phase of the menstrual cycle (*Journal of American Medical Association, 1992*, p. 118).

2. *People v. Darlene Johnson*, No. 29390 (Cal. Sup.Ct., Tulane County, 1991).

3. Additional terms of probation included counselling and parenthood classes.

4. The sentencing order was appealed by Ms. Johnson's lawyer, and stayed pending the outcome of the appeal. Before the appeal was heard, Ms. Johnson violated the terms of her probation by using cocaine and was sentenced to prison. The trade-off between incarceration and temporary contraception no longer relevant, the issue was declared moot and the appeal was dismissed by California's 5th District Court of Appeal on April 13, 1992 (*New York Times*, 1992).

5. Both instances occurred in Texas. In March 1992, Ida Jean Tovar, following conviction for child abuse of her son, agreed to trade a prison sentence for implantation of Norplant and probation (*American Political Network Abortion Report*, 1992). In the fall of 1991, Cathy Lanel Knighten, charged with deliberately smothering her infant daughter, was sentenced to Norplant use for five years as part of a plea bargain agreement (*United Press International 1991*, 1991). In at least two other cases, arguments have been made that Norplant should similarly be ordered. In September, 1992, the attorney of a farm worker convicted of second-degree murder of her new-born son argued for a sentence of probation and forced contraception (*Los Angeles Times*). And in November 1992, a Florida Judge has allowed a child advocacy group (Valuing Our Children and Laws) legal participation in an upcoming child custody hearing so that it can pursue a contraceptive request (*United Press International 1992*).

6. In February of 1991, Kansas State Representative Kerry Patrick (R) introduced legislation that would require women of childbearing age who have

been convicted of felony possession or distribution of cocaine, crack, or heroin to use Norplant. The bill requiring Norplant use for women convicted of drug felony has been put on hold while the state's sentencing guidelines are rewritten (Rees, 1991).

7. Kansas State Representative Patrick has also introduced legislation offering poor women a single payment of $500 upon implantation of Norplant, followed by annual payments of $50 for continued use. This bill was defeated, 77-27. Other unsuccessful attempts include Louisiana State Representative David Duke's (R) sponsorship in April 1991 of legislation proposing that welfare women be offered $100 a year for Norplant use. The bill was amended to remove the cash incentive and now simply proposes to add Norplant to the list of contraceptives social and health care workers must discuss with welfare mothers. Approved by the House, the bill remains in the Senate Health and Welfare Committee (Rees, 1991). The Mississippi State Assembly has also refused to adopt legislation mandating use of Norplant by welfare recipients (McNichol, 1992). More recently and successfully, Tennessee State Representative Steve McDaniels (R) sponsored a bill (approved April 1992 by the Tennessee House Health and Human Resources Committee) that establishes $500 grants for welfare mothers who use Norplant and for men on Medicaid who have vasectomies. Originally, the bill proposed only the cash grant to welfare women but was revised to reflect criticism that it was racist and sexist (*Chicago Tribune*, 1992). Governor William Schaefer of Maryland in his seventh annual State of the State address called for consideration of requiring men to have vasectomies and women to use Norplant "if they're on welfare and have a certain number of illegitimate children" (*The Washington Post*, 1993).

8. A July 1991 reader poll done by Glamour magazine found that 47 percent of its respondents felt that welfare women should be offered economic incentives to use Norplant. The poll also found that 55 percent favored mandatory Norplant use for women convicted of child abuse (Rees, 1991). An *L. A. Times* survey canvassing Californian residents, reported May 27, 1991, found that 47% strongly approved of making Norplant mandatory for drug-abusing women of childbearing age. An additional 15 percent of the respondents replied that they "somewhat" approved. Sixty percent of African-American respondents strongly or somewhat approved. Women were more likely than men to approve of the measure (*American Political Network Abortion Report*, May 29, 1991).

9. So, for example, organ transplant technologies render less absolute the physical separateness of individual human bodies, genetic technology allows the reproductive process selectively to produce female or male children, and steroid or growth-hormone therapy separates physical development from its traditional context and purpose. For a more detailed discussion of these examples and how technologies function as a tool of fragmentation and reassembly, see Shapiro, 1990.

10. Thus, some commentators express concern about the "assaults on marriage and the family, to say nothing of the subtle devaluation of sexual intimacy" they

believe such technologies trigger (Hellegers and McCormick (1978), 77, as quoted in Stanworth, 1987, p. 23).

11. A similar separation between genetics and gestation has occurred with the development of *in vitro* technology. An ovum, fertilized either inside the woman who has donated it or outside in a petri dish, can be implanted and brought to term within a second woman. What was once conceived as a continuous biological process is now broken up into a number of parts: for example, egg maturation, egg "harvesting," fertilization, implantation, gestation. This fragmentation of biological processes is mirrored by a corresponding "conceptual and relational fragmentation." So we are, for example, presented with a multiplicity of mothers-genetic, gestational, and custodial mothers (Shapiro, 1990, p. 335) (not to mention genetic grandmothers who are also gestational mothers, etc.). The significance of each of these roles, relative to the others and even on its own terms, is as yet unclear.

12. I say only "relatively neutral" because I think that such technical elements also reflect assumptions about what is useful to do and what the objects or subjects of scientific research are. However, for the point I want to make here, it is not necessary to politicize these foundational techniques.

13. Norplant is one of the most effective contraceptives available; it has a failure rate of 0.3% to 0.6% in 1 year and 1.5% for 5 years. Its effectiveness is due both to the constant serum levels of levonorgestrel achieved and to a necessary compliance rate of 100% if the capsules remain in place (Requirements, 1992, p. 1818).

14. See *Skinner v. Oklahoma* (316 U.S. 535; 62 S. Ct. 1110) in which the United States Supreme Court held unconstitutional an Oklahoma statute providing for the sterilization of habitual criminals. In its judgement, written by Douglas, J., the Court characterized procreation as "one of the basic civil rights of man (sic)" (at 541), thus justifying a standard of strict scrutiny with respect to any classifications a state makes in sterilization law.

15. This is clearly an important factor. For example, the prosecutor in the Cathy Lanel Knighten case (see *supra*, note 4) said in relation to the judge's order of Norplant use: "It was a question of whether someone like this goes to prison and gets out and reproduces, or do we do something like this. We've got a chance to make a difference, and it's not irreversible" (*United Press International 1991*, September 6, 1991).

16. As well, Norplant implantation is, at least in thin women, visible beneath the skin, thus allowing for easy identification of many users (Yanoshik and Norsigian, 1989, p. 84).

17. Most contraceptive research is done by men into methods for use by women. Few techniques are developed for use by men. In 1983, only 7% of world expenditures on research and development of contraceptives went towards developing male methods. This reflects, in part, the assumption that reproduction is a woman's concern (Yanoshik and Norsigian, in Ratcliff, 1987, p. 71). And, where such techniques are developed men have been reluctant to participate in their experimental use, so much so that the World Health Organization has recently de-

cided to forego funding research on male contraceptives given the shortage of
male volunteers even to try new methods (Newman, 1985, p. 141-2). Moreover,
technologies developed for male use tend to be less attractively packaged: their
side effects are emphasized more than comparable female technologies (Wajcman, 1991, p. 77).

18. Sixty percent of spending on research and development of contraception
went towards "high-tech" methods (Yanoshik and Norsigian, 1987, p. 84). It has
been argued that the emphasis on hormonal contraceptives rather than barrier
methods can be explained by the following reason. Hormonal contraception–the
Pill–is favored because it demands relatively little skill and time–for either the
physician or user–in application, yet retains medical control over contraception
(Wajcman, 1991, p. 76).

19. It is interesting to use the notion of reproductive agency to contrast the acceptability of Norplant as a suitable form of contraceptive with that of RU486 (the
new French abortifacient)–a drug that arguably enhances rather than diminishes
the relevance of women's reproductive agency.

20. Because of current racial, class, and social patterns, these features tend to
overlap. For example, in America, poor women are disproportionately African-
American women, African-American families have a high percentage of single
women-headed households, and often women receiving welfare are single parents
(Roberts, 1990, p. 1432, fn. 60; Fineman, 1991, p. 274).

21. Teenage mothers represent a similar "social problem" and already, health
officials are starting school-based clinics for distribution of Norplant to teenage
girls in areas with high rates of teen-age births. Such programs are underway in
Baltimore and the District of Columbia (*Boston Globe*, December 1992; *Christian
Science Monitor*).

22. Both insertion and removal of Norplant implants require local anesthetic,
sterile environment, and trained medical personnel. The procedures are far from
simple. Insertion must be done by skilled personnel; the rods can travel in the arm
muscles making removal tricky. In fact, removal is often rather difficult and painful. The capsules become embedded in a layer of fibrous tissue that needs to be
cut away. One clinical trial done in Ecuador reported that high continuance rates
may be more reflective of women's fear of removal than of satisfaction with the
contraceptive method (Yanoshik and Norsigian, 1987, pp. 83-4).

23. As well, medical personnel may be reluctant to remove Norplant, at least
for some women. An example of such a barrier to removal has been documented
in Indonesia, where it took a government declaration of the right to "removal on
request" to solve such a problem (Foreman, 1992). In the United States, there are
reports of dozens of native American women being implanted with Norplant without being told of the side effects associated with the contraceptive. Many who
sought to have the capsules removed, had their physicians discourage or refuse
removal (*Boston Globe*, December 1992).

24. For example, Rhodes Boyson, a conservative M.P. in Britain, has argued
that the procreative habits of single parents are responsible for "violent crime,
football hooliganism, mugging and inner city revolt" (Stanworth, 1987, p. 28).

25. Although Foucault's emphasis is more on the increasing irrelevance of juridico-discursive discourse to modern deployments of power, I think it is possible to argue that Smart's formulation is at least compatible with Foucault's own description of the mechanisms of power (Foucault, 1980; c.f. Leonard, 1990; Smart, 1989).

26. This is also the tension articulated in cases of punishment of women using drugs during pregnancy. The assumption of a conflict of interests between a pregnant woman and the fetus she carries is a recent legal innovation (Roberts, 1991, p. 1442).

27. State Representative Kerry Patrick (see note 6) conflates his concern for the "rights" of children with economic arguments: "Reproductive freedom is an important right but a child's right to be born healthy is paramount over a woman's right to bear a drug-impaired baby. And we, the community, have a right to be spared unnecessary costs. Simply to provide welfare payments and education from kindergarten through the 12th grade for a healthy child costs $205,000 in Kansas, a figure that climbs astronomically if that kid is born drugged" (Kramer, 1991).

REFERENCES

Alexander, J. Mobilizing Against the State and International "Aid" Agencies: "Third World" Women Define Reproductive Freedom. In M. G. Fried (Ed.), *From Abortion to Reproductive Freedom: Transforming a Movement.* Boston: South End Press, 1990.

American Political Network Abortion Report. California: Constitutionality of Requiring Norplant. November 12, 1991.

——— California: Wilson Will Help Clinics Circumvent Ruling. May 29, 1991.

——— Texas: Child Abuser Chooses Norplant Over Prison. March 12, 1992.

Babington, C., Tapscott, R. Schaefer Talks Tough On Welfare; Forced Birth Control Measures Suggested. *The Washington Post.* January 15, 1993.

Beck-Gernsheim, E. From the Pill to Test-Tube Babies: New Options, New Pressures in Reproductive Behavior. In K. S. Ratcliff, *Healing Technologies: Feminist Perspectives.* Ann Arbor: The University of Michigan Press, 1989.

Blank, R. *Regulating Reproduction.* New York: Columbia University Press, 1990.

Chicago Tribune. Birth Control Incentive. April 26, 1992, Womenews, p. 11.

David, A. Imperialism and Motherhood. *History Workshop*, 1978, 5, 9-65.

Dreyfus, H. L. and Rabinow, P. *Michel Foucault: Beyond Structuralism and Hermeneutics.* Chicago: University of Chicago, 1983.

Feenburg, A. *Critical Theory of Technology.* New York: Oxford University Press, 1991.

Fineman, M. L. Images of Mothers in Poverty Discourses. *Duke Law Journal*, 1991, 2, 274-295.

Forman, J. Women's Right vs. Birth Controls; on Eve of Rio Summit, an Old Feud Re-erupts. *The Boston Globe.* May 25, 1992.

Foucault, M. *The History of Sexuality, Volume I: An Introduction.* Robert Hurley, trans. New York: Vintage Books, 1980.

———— Nietzsche, Genealogy, History. In P. Rabinow (Ed.), *The Foucault Reader.* New York: Pantheon, 1971, 76-100.

Gardner, M. Paying Teenagers Not to Have Babies. *The Christian Science Monitor.* January 14, 1993.

Handler, J. and Hasenfeld, Y. *The Moral Construction of Poverty: Welfare Reform in America.* Newbury Park: Sage Publications, 1991.

Hellegers, A. E. and McCormick, R. A. Unanswered Questions on Test-Tube Life. *America*, 1978, 139, 77.

Jacobs, S. Norplant Draws Concerns Over Risks, Coercion. *The Boston Globe.* December 21, 1992.

Kramer, M. The Political Interest: Who Owes What To Whom. *Time.* October 14, 1991.

Latour, B. *Science in Action.* Cambridge: Harvard University Press, 1987.

Leonard, J. D. Foucault: Genealogy, Law, Praxis. *Legal Studies Forum*, 1990, 14, 3-25.

Maher, L. Punishment and Welfare: Crack Cocaine and the Regulation of Mothering. In C. Feinman (Ed.), *The Criminalization of a Woman's Body.* New York: Harrington Park Press, 1992.

McNichol, D. Wisconsin Reform Included in Welfare Debate. *State News Service*, June 4, 1992.

Moynihan, D. P., The Negro Family: The Case for National Action. Washington, DC: U.S. Government Printing Office, 1965.

New York Times. Birth Control Order is Declared Moot. April 15, 1992, 23.

Newman, E. Who Controls Birth Control? In W. Faulkner and E. Arnold (Eds.), *Smothered By Invention: Technology in Women's Lives.* London: Pluto Press, 1985.

Nsiah-Jefferson, L. Reproductive Laws, Women of Color, and Low-Income Women. In N. Taub and S. Cohen (Eds.), *Reproductive Laws for the 1990's.* Clifton, New Jersey: Humana Press, 1989.

Oberman, M. The Control of Pregnancy and the Criminalization of Femaleness. *Berkeley Women's Law Journal*, 1992, 7, 1-12.

Petchesky, R. Foetal Images: The Power of Visual Culture in the Politics of Reproduction. In M. Stanworth (Ed.), *Reproductive Technologies: Gender, Motherhood and Medicine.* Minneapolis: University of Minnesota Press, 1987.

Postman, N. *Technopoly: The Surrender of Culture to Technology.* New York: Alfred A. Knopf, 1992.

Purvis, A. A Pill That Gets Under the Skin; Norplant Could Spur Birth Control and Stir Controversy. *Time.* December 24, 1990.

Ratcliff, K. S. Health Technologies for Women: Whose Health? Whose Technology? In K. S. Ratcliff (Ed.), *Healing Technologies: Feminist Perspectives.* Ann Arbor: The University of Michigan Press, 1989.

Reed, M. Judge Sentences Mother of Slain Baby to Prison; courts: Francisca Maria Sanchez Jimenez Will Serve 15 Years to Life Dumping Her Newborn into a Portable Toilet in a Saticoy Onion Field. *Los Angeles Times.* October 8, 1992.

Rees, M. Shot in the Arm: The Use and Abuse of Norplant: Involuntary Contraception and Public Policy. *The New Republic.* December 9, 1991, 205.

Requirements or Incentives by Government for the Use of Long-Acting Contraceptives. Board of Trustees Report, *Journal of American Medical Association*, 1992, 267, 1818-1821.

Roberts, D. E. Punishing Drug Addicts Who Have Babies: Women of Color, Equality and the Right of Privacy. *Harvard Law Review*, 1992, 104, 1419-1482.

Shapiro, M. H. Fragmenting and Reassembling the World; Of Flying Squirrels, Augmented Persons, and Other Monsters. *Ohio State Law Journal*, 1990, 51, 331-374.

Shultz, M. M. Reproductive Technology and Intent-Based Parenthood: An Opportunity for Gender Neutrality. *Wisconsin Law Review*, 1990, 298-396.

Smart, C. *Feminism and the Power of Law.* London: Routledge, 1989.

_____ Law's Power, and the Sexed Body, and Feminist Discourse. *Journal of Law and Society*, 1990, 17, 194-210.

Stanworth, M. Reproductive Technologies and the Deconstruction of Motherhood. In M. Stanworth (Ed.), *Reproductive Technologies: Gender, Motherhood and Medicine.* Minneapolis: University of Minnesota Press, 1987.

United Press International 1991. Contraceptive Device Part of Plea Agreement. September 6, 1991.

United Press International 1992. Judge Finds No Legal Precedent for Ordering Contraception. November 14, 1992.

Wajcman, J. *Feminism Confronts Technology.* Cambridge: Polity Press, 1991.

Walsh, V. Contraception: The Growth of a Technology. In L. Birke, W. Faulkner, B. Best, D. Janson-Smith, K. Overfield, (Eds.), *Alice Through the Microscope: The Power of Science Over Women's Lives*, 1980.

Yanoshik, K. and Norsigian, J. Contraception, Control, and Choice: International Perspectives. In S. K. Ratcliff (Ed.), *Healing Technologies: Feminist Perspectives.* Ann Arbor: The University of Michigan Press, 1987.

Deborah:
Archetypal Federal and Family Judge

Kris Jeter

In October 1991, my husband and I were in Washington D.C. participating in the wedding celebrations of his youngest daughter. In between
family functions, we attended the opening day of the "Circa 1492" exhibit
at the National Gallery. We were amazed at the small turnout for such an
unprecedented display of African, American, Asian, and European objects, many considered national treasures, all dating from the time of
Columbus's voyage to the Americas, gathered together for just three
months in this one location only. In a city continually riveted with news-
making political events, mostly accepted without much concern by the
general public, a Congressional hearing was deemed much more important
than the opening of an exhibition.

As we traveled around the city, each apartment house reception area,
home, hotel lobby, restaurant, store check-out counter, and taxi cab had a
radio or television turned on loudly. There were no questions or complaints about the intrusion of media upon personal lives. We each were
held spellbound with the proceedings of this particular United States Congressional hearing. Attorney and Professor of Law, Anita Hill, was testifying before the Senate Committee determining if Clarence Thomas should
be confirmed as a Supreme Court Justice. The testimony of Anita Hill
before a committee of male senators will long be remembered and has
already become a catalyst for change in the political and judicial structure
of the United States.

Kris Jeter is a Principal, Beacon Associates LTD, Newark, DE.

[Haworth co-indexing entry note]: "Deborah: Archetypal Federal and Family Judge." Jeter, Kris.
Co-published simultaneously in *Marriage & Family Review* (The Haworth Press, Inc.) Vol. 21, No. 3/4,
1995, pp. 283-305; and: *Families and Law* (ed: Lisa J. McIntyre, and Marvin B. Sussman) The Haworth
Press, Inc., 1995, pp. 283-305. Multiple copies of this article/chapter may be purchased from The
Haworth Document Delivery Center [1-800-3-HAWORTH; 9:00 a.m. - 5:00 p.m. (EST)].

Eight months later, in June 1992, the Supreme Court decision regarding the Pennsylvania abortion law again focused the attention of women on women's rights and powers. Are male attorneys, governors, lawmakers, and judges qualified to decide the fate of a woman's body and thereby the fate of a nation's families?

The Anita Hill testimony and the Supreme Court decision on abortion are just two of the legal events recently receiving high media attention. They raise the issue regarding the impact of law on women, the family, and the country. Likewise, they challenge citizens to take action to increase the low number of females who may influence the content of legislation and work with the law and its legal systems.

Family Law has, in the main, across cultures and eras, been biased toward masculine interests, an expression of gender power. Judicial systems are primarily masculine institutions with male attorneys pleading cases before male judges. The legislatures, the lawmaking bodies, are overwhelmingly composed of males.

As the complexion of legal and political systems changes, ancient archetypes of the female judge may be of value and interest to women lawyers, judges, politicians, and social artists. Although history is written primarily by men, a few women archetypes have survived the millennia of oral histories and written texts, revisions, and commentaries.

PURPOSE

In this analytic essay, I tell the story of Judge Deborah. Deborah is an archetype deep within the psyches of Western peoples and a role model for today's woman wishing to be an advocate in the legal system. The stories of the Hebrew scripture are rich, providing varied characters, role models, and prototype options for living. Immersed in the depths of the human psyche is the universal, primordial, collective unconscious inhabited by archetypes, internal forces of energy which seek to organize the psyche's varied interactions and to sustain the endurance of the ego consciousness. These archetypes are spontaneously expressed cross-culturally as vital life forces and archetypal images in art, fantasies, dreams, fairy tales, and myths. It is through the archetypal images that the human being reveals profound unconscious longings and yearnings (Jung, 1969).

Jewish rituals, as well as Christian and Jewish art forms honor Deborah. Deborah's story is told in two parallel narratives in the Book of Judges in the Hebrew scripture. Judges Four is in literal prose and Judges Five is an exhilarating ballad ascribed to Deborah. This Song of Deborah is one of the oldest pieces of literature in the Hebrew scripture (Meyers, 1988, 59).

Throughout the year, Jews read the entire Torah (Genesis, Exodus, Leviticus, Numbers, and Deuteronomy), each week studying a section plus Haftorahs (corresponding readings from the Hebrew scripture). The Song of Deborah is read during the sixteenth week, after Moses' Song by the Sea, Exodus XV (Hertz, 1990). These Songs are parallel in tenor, timbre, and tone.

From one generation to the next, Kurdistani Jews have repeated an ancient Aramaic epic chant about Deborah. Over the centuries and even today, pilgrims venerate the tombs of Deborah and the protagonists in her story, Jael, Heber the Kenite, and Barak Ben Abinoam. The four are buried in the beautiful foothills of the mountains on the frontier of northern Israel near Lebanon (Lanboy, 1972, 1889 and *Our Ancestors*, 1989). Contemporary Israelis dance to folk songs about Deborah written by Uri Givon and Sara Levi-Tannai.

Deborah has been celebrated in Christian visual, musical, and poetic arts. Church decorations, such as those in the Ulm Cathedral and Madrid's San Andres Church; manuscript illustrations, such as the *Psalter of St. Louis* and *Queen Mary Psalter*; oratorios, such as Baldassare Galuppi's *Jahel*, Handel's *Deborah*, Porsile's *Sisara*, and G. Fr. Rubini's *dialogo Debora*; operas, such as Josef Foerester's *Debora* and Pizzetti's *Debora e Jaele*; paintings, such as Lucas Cranach's; pen drawings, such as Rembrandt's *Jael*; poetry, such as Guy Le Fever de la Bodrie's epic, *La Galliade*; tapestries such as Gobelin's; plus wood-engravings such as Lucas van Leyden's have kept this story alive in human memory (*The Bible in Art*, 1956; *The Jewish Encyclopedia*, 1901-1906; Levy, 1936; Maus, 1954).

The archetype of Deborah is deep within human consciousness, ready to be tapped as a role model of an honored woman judge, as well as successful financial investor, plus revered prophet, poet, philanthropist, prophetess, warrior, and wife. In this analytic essay, I tell the story of Deborah, reconstructing her life in light of recent research on family and civic life in pre-monarchic Israel and Judah. I then suggest ways that Deborah's life can serve as a positive archetype, prototype for contemporary Family Law Judges.

THE DECALOGUE AND THE MOSAIC LAW

Deborah, the Judge, utilized as the basis of her work, the original ten laws, the Decalogue and the Mosaic code which developed from it. An age-old story tells about the presentation of the law.

Once upon a time, all humans lived in a dim, murky darkness (Torah and Haftorah, 1990, 400-406). The Omnipotent One traveled from east to west, from south to north, offering a Decalogue, a simple list of just ten laws, only 120 words, to one kinship group after another. Each group would find fault with one or another of the laws and reject the entire package.

Alas, for the children of Israel, the world was especially dim and murky. For 400 years, they had toiled as slaves in Egypt. However, one spring, during the full moon, God with Moses, Miriam, and Aaron acting as human intermediaries, freed the Hebrew slaves from bondage. Each family, each individual quickly left Egypt. Upon arriving at the Red Sea, each wondered how this liquid yet very real frontier could ever be crossed. Miraculously, the Red Sea opened and each Israelite emerged, as if reborn anew each from the red sea of her or his own mother's womb.

The children of Israel walked in the vast desert, a universal, archetypal wasteland. At an oasis, Mt. Sinai, they made camp, rested and contemplated their future. Here, at a small wellspring in the middle of the immense wilderness, the dim, murky darkness was pierced by a thunderbolt of lightning that even today illumines the sky.

Gathered together at the base of Mt. Sinai was every person who already has or will ever accept the ten laws. All nature was quiet, in reverence of God and the possible consequences of such a gift. One-to-one, face-to-face, the Omnipotent One presented each of the ten laws. Every attendee was accorded intimacy with the source, the wellspring. The revelation of the law, the vision of an ordered life was awe-inspiring. Life was imbued with a sense of certainty, confidence, and conviction. All bodies, hearts, minds, souls, spirits, were enlightened and charged to act in accordance with the ten laws.

Without the adoption of these laws, the history of the Children of Israel would have been reduced to a hieroglyph on an Egyptian register, a potsherd in the archaeological record. The Covenant infused and animated the Hebrew tribes with a challenge, a purpose, a blueprint for life, a light to illumine the darkness. The Decalogue has become the basis for much of Western civil and criminal law.

Three thousand, three hundred years later, scholars have delved into the origins of the Decalogue. Other legal documents of related eras and cultures including the Laws of Eshnunna of 2000 BCE area near Bagdad, The Code of Hammurabi of 1728-1686 BCE Old Babylonian (Amorite) Kingdom, Mesopotamian Legal Documents of 1500 BCE Nuzi on the Tigris River, and Aramaic Papyri from Elephantine on the Upper Nile have been identified (Pritchard, 1958).

The Code of Hammurabi discovered in Susa, Iran by French archaeologists in 1901 has been hypothesized by some researchers to have been an influential predecessor to the Decalogue. Although 24 similarities have been identified between the Code of Hammurabi and the Mosaic Code, differences in the context, philosophy, and practice are most evident. Babylon was a complex society ruled by a king and bureaucracy intent on coordinating agriculture, business, commerce, and industry. The children of Israel were a nomadic pastoral people with no central government.

Hammurabi's Code concludes with the judgement of the removal of an ear of a slave who wants to be free. Several hundred years later, the Mosaic Code is written and commences with the case of the slave who, after six years of service is granted and refuses freedom (Exodus 21:2-6). A hole is to be pierced in the ear as a symbol of shame.

The Decalogue and the ensuing Mosaic Code promote the freedom of the individual to live peacefully, ideally, to "live and let live." Every human, every animal, every plot of land is to be at rest every seventh day, every seventh year. The indigent are to be provided assistance, preferably before they become afflicted.

Israel was surrounded by kings who dictated and enforced laws to sustain their bureaucracies. Subjects had the choice of senseless submission or rash revolt. However, royalty and commoners alike made sacrifices to their kingdom's pantheons, in hope that the offerings would influence the unaccountable, thus, deified forces of nature.

Meanwhile, the legal system of Israel indicates that each person is a responsible being who may or may not choose to conform to the laws. The consequence of non-compliance is chaos. The monotheistic deity is possessive and exclusive, creating order out of chaos when humans adhere to the law. When leaders are needed to solve social and military crises, individuals are chosen according to natural attributes, experience, and prominence.

For forty years after receiving the Decalogue, the children of Israel wandered in the desert (Harper, 1987, 50). Major portions of Exodus, Leviticus, Numbers and Deuteronomy tell of this journey within the context of history. In time, wandering nomadic tribes were transformed into a sedentary unified nation. The Hebrew scripture relates the policies and procedures of the law, religion, and government. Moreover, we see how during drought, famine, and wandering, the desires of individuals for a balanced emotional, physical, social, and spiritual life are sensed with an all-inclusive empathy and set into a code of laws for the human community.

The Israelites brought to Canaan an exceptionally unadulterated and hopeful conceptualization of democracy. For instance, all persons and all tribes had equal standing with their counterparts. The community of law-abiding citizens, the government itself acknowledges that the legal system exists because time has demonstrated that laws are above ethical and practical demands (Davis, 1976, 1988, 133-135).

A new generation, free of the slave mentality, was born, eager to enter the Promised Land. James Harpur (1987, 50) indicates that the hillsides of Israel were uninhabited and available for occupation. However, along the Mediterranean Coast and in the lowlands of the Jezreel valley and Lake Kinnerit, the Canaanites lived in Ai, Hazor, Jericho, and other walled city-states, fortified with extensive military armies and weaponry.

The Canaanites were composed of Hurrian, Indo-European, Philistine, and Semite peoples. Acknowledging this diverse population, urban temples included worship of international deities as well as their own goddesses, *Ashtaroth* and their gods, *Baalim*. They harvested produce, such as grains and timber, processed oil and wine, and herded cattle. The Canaanites were accomplished at ivory carving, metallurgy, and textile manufacturing. In fact, the name, Canaanite, may be derived from the purple fabric dye, *kinahhu*, for which they were famous. The wealth of Canaan was evident to all. Goliath was pictured with a magnificent armor (1 Samuel 17:5) and the King of Hazor was told to have at his disposal 900 iron chariots (Judges 4:3).

DEBORAH'S LIFE

The woman, Deborah, lived in twelfth century BCE during the earliest times of Israel. Carol Meyers (1988), through in-depth studies of anthropology, archaeology, Hebrew scripture, and sociology, has reconstructed the social organization and familial roles of pre-monarchy Israel and Judah, the Iron I period dated twelfth and eleventh century BCE. The twelve tribes of Jacob were the larger, political-social units. Each tribe was composed of fifty clans. The clan (*mispahah or 'eleph*) was the social and political unit which addressed such issues as land allocation, grants, and defense. This was also the group from which endogamous mates were selected for marriage.

The household (*bayit*) or extended family (*bet'ab or bet'em*) was a self-sufficient co-residential social unit consisting of a dozen familial and non-familial members. Intermarriage with women from surrounding nations was common in early Israel. The talents of each member of the family were valued. The worship of a wide variety of deities was accepted by the foreign-born wives. Divine assistance from any realm was welcomed. Crops were grown using subsistence farming techniques. Domesticated animals were herded in the hills and corralled on the ground floor of their owner's home. In the courtyard, there were kitchen, workshop, and storeroom areas. On the second floor were the dining, living, and sleeping areas. There is no evidence of public facilities for trade, water utilities, or worship.

Meyers proposes that tasks were delegated according to age and season. Each job was essential to the survival of the household. Thus, members were interdependent upon each other. Women were active and were valued in generating, apportioning, and processing foodstuffs. They also produced for their own personal use, as well as for sale and trade, fabric, clothing, perfume, and perhaps, pottery.

In Proverbs, the roles of both parents are delineated; the primary task for each parent was to educate their children. Hebrew was the first language in the Near East to have an alphabet with a reduced number of letters, thereby the reading and writing an alphabet with only 22 letters was a skill any person could acquire.

The word for husband (*ba' al*) also means owner. Descent was patrilineal. An estate of rocky, hilly land required a particular knowledge of how to survive utilizing to best advantage the available water supply while adapting to each change of temperature, wind force and direction. This specific information was passed on from father to son.

Exogamy encouraged women to be autonomous, yet adaptable; independent while interdependent. Women were responsible for the future generations of the household, family, tribe, and nation. The inclusion of stories about prophetesses and wise women in the Hebrew scripture indicates that they did indeed exist and were valued. Wisdom (*hokma*) was depicted as a woman, a colleague of God, source of education, enlightenment, morality, and veracity.

Intermarriage and acceptance of the foreign partner's religion was a tradition through many centuries. *Teraphim* were female statues used by the Babylonians and Israelites for divination (Ezekiel 21:21; Judges 17:5; 18:14-20). Rachel and Micah felt it was important to keep *teraphim* in their possession (Genesis 31; Judges 17:1-13; 18:1-31). It was only in 658 BCE that King Josiah destroyed all profane altars and cult objects from the Temple and outlawed heathen shrines (II Kings 23).

By 538 BCE, intermarriage was decreed illegal. Jews returning from exile in Babylon were ordered by Ezra, the Hebrew priest and scribe, to divorce "foreign wives" (Ezra 10:10-11).

Law is integral to the history and life of Israel. Most of the Pentateuch and much of the earlier Hebrew scripture presents laws for behavior. For instance, children are commanded to honor their parents; love was not mandated because at times, this could be difficult (Kaspi, 1993). Legal principles governing conduct are joined to spiritual belief and righteous behavior. Family law is closely linked to national law. Marriage, divorce, and adoption affect dominion over resources. In essence, the Decalogue aims to safeguard both parents and the family.

Tikva Frymer-Kensky (1992) has analyzed the shift from Near Eastern polytheism to Hebrew monotheism. Frymer-Kensky contends that as belief in one deity became the norm for the children of Abraham, the convictions about creation of the world and universe, intellectual and aesthetic training, social and legal organization, and humankind radically changed. Human beings developed skills that could successfully manipulate their environment. The utilization of these skills decreased human dependence on varied gods and goddesses.

DEBORAH THE JUDGE

Deborah lived in this intermediate time between the Israelite settlement of the highlands and the ascent of the monarchy (Harper, 1987, 62). The Israelites consisted of family units associated with tribes. There was no city-state or bureaucracy. These ancients could be considered pioneers attempting to live in the wild frontiers of the hinterlands. In the Book of Judges, we meet rural Israelites attempting to live in peace with their urban Canaanite neighbors. These neighbors had conflicts, but also agreements and treaties.

During critical junctures of unrest, leaders arose to guide the tribes through the crisis. Leaders, such as Gideon and Samson were called *shofeim*, judges. Today, we moderns would call these leaders heroes, military commanders, or prophets. However, one of the *shofeim* or judges was actually an administrator of the law for individuals, families, tribes, and the nation Israel. In contemporary, western nations this *shofeim* would be equivalent to a judge of the family court. One such judge was Deborah (Judges 4:5). Confidence in her judicial decisions is evident by Israel's choice and acceptance of her as a leader during war and peace.

DEBORAH THE WARRIOR

We read that for twenty years Jabin, King of Canaan who was seated in Hazor, had persecuted the Israelites. He severely limited both commerce and travel, thereby intensely restricting intra- and inter-tribal communication. The knowledge of Jabin's military strength, complete with 900 swift chariots, intimidated the Israelites.

Accordingly, Deborah dispatched Barak, son of Abinoam, of the tribe of Haptali to whom she revealed Yahweh's military plan. Barak was to enlist 10,000 troops and camp on the Mount Tabor, a consecrated peak where Israelites had traditionally tendered prayers and made sacrifice (Deuteronomy 33:19). Deborah prophesied that the Israelites would meet and win victory over Sisera, Jabin's military commander and his army of chariots and soldiers at the Torrent of Kishon. Barak was reluctant and not confident that he would discern the exact time and place from which to attack. When Barak asked Deborah to escort him, she conceded. However, she indicated that because of his insecurity, the resulting triumph would be accorded to her.

Deborah, Barak, and their 10,000 troops made camp on Mount Tabor. At Deborah's command, they proceeded southward to the plain of the Torrent of Kishon. Deborah, in synchronicity with nature, issued her orders to coincide with an extraordinary rainstorm. The Torrent of Kishon flooded, causing the chariots to be mired in the soggy plains. The 40,000 Canaanites with their 9,000 chariots were utterly surprised, quickly in disarray, and easily delivered to the Israelites. Sisera escaped and ran east to the camp of a Canaanite ally, Heber the Kenite. Heber's wife, Jael, provided him nourishment and shelter. Confident that he was safe, Sisera slept. However, Jael victoriously consummated the battle by thrusting a tent-peg into the forehead of Sisera.

Never before had the varied autonomous tribes of Israel gathered together to attack the Canaanites. Slings with stones, plus swords, overpowered a sophisticated, mighty war machine. This story imprints humankind's collective unconscious with the knowledge that victory by the underdog following the prophecy of a woman judge with the blessing of the Omnipotent One is possible. Deborah and Jael rose to be archetypes of strong women.

Susan Niditch (1989, 53) has studied the alliances between passion and expiration, lust and war, love and hate expressed in the story of Jael and Sisera. The woman warrior is presented as a complete, complex human; "the tale is rich in images of directed action, self-assertion, and consciousness on the part of the underdog."

Women warriors are discussed in the Song of Songs (1:9; 4:4; 6:4,10; 7:4; 8:9,10); their dynamic strength is associated with the mighty power of animals. Deborah is accomplished as a warrior in the rigorous discipline of an ancient Greek form of martial arts. Through meditative concentration, she practices the freedom of choice and the action of spontaneity. She maintains her center of gravity in the midst of dynamic movement. Deborah considers each person, from adversary to supporter, with sympathy and facilitates that person's free autonomous expression. Deborah propels when pulled and pulls when pressed. Conflict, like love, is an expression of intimacy.

DEBORAH THE POET

The Song of Deborah holds a high place among Triumphal Odes in the literature of the world. It is a work of that highest art which is not studied and artificial, but spontaneous and inevitable. It shows a development and command of the resources of the language for ends of poetical expression which prove that poetry has long been culti- vated among the Hebrews.

–G. F. Moore (*Hertz,* 1990, 283-284)

Biblical researchers have proposed varied dates for the actual writing of the Song of Deborah (Harper, 1987, 62). Most consider the Song to be the oldest Hebrew poem or among the oldest of this genre (C. G. Montefiore and H. Loewe, 1974, 557). Many believe that the Song of Deborah was composed at the time the events took place. Some suggest that it was written in the ninth century BCE. The Song of Deborah is tripartite in structure. There is the introduction, poem, and the conclusion.

The introduction (Judges 5:2-11) is similar to Canaanite writings of fourteenth century BCE Ugarit as well as Hebrew scripture such as the Blessing of Jacob (Genesis 49), the Song of Miriam (Exodus 15), and Psalm 68. Yahweh is acknowledged and called forth. Such introductions indicate that they may have been sung during rituals in which the covenant was reestablished, and, later, at the Temple in Jerusalem to remind listen- ers of Yahweh's deliverance of Israel from her enemies.

The body of the poem (Judges 5:12-30) tells the story. The war is pro- claimed. Some tribes choose to fight; the remaining are chastised. The battle is fought with Yahweh and the stars on the side of the Israelites. Jael's killing of Sisera is described and her courage is acknowledged. Sisera's mother futilely awaits her son's homecoming with the plunder of war.

Two especially exquisite passages relate the course of human events to the heavens. The "stars" (Judges 5:20) are their allies; the rainstorm creates the quagmire which makes the Canaanite assault and escape im- possible.

The dramatic conclusion (Judges 5:31) also contains reference to the heavens. The love for the Omnipotent One and the Law is aligned to the brilliance of the unconquerable sun which nullifies nighttime's darkness, and indeed, the dim, murky darkness of human existence. We read the conclusion, seeing prophecy revealed into actuality, inspired by the beauty and message, happy that forty years of peace follows.

Recent anthropological research on the poetry of the Yemenite Jews may give us ideas on the importance of the role of the poet in community life, especially for a judge, prophetess, and warrior, such as Deborah. Between 1949-1950, S. D. Goitein (1988) studied the Yemenite immigrants who traveled on the "Magic Carpet" from Yemen to Israel. Yeminite males write and read their religious songs in Hebrew. Yeminite women create oral poems at the moment of presentation in the vernacular Yeminite language. The poems are secular, yet acknowledge God as being present and listening. Formal poetic verses and Hebrew phrases may be entwined with the latest news.

Goitein contends that Yeminite women echo genres found in the Hebrew scripture which may well have been written by women. Before mass media, it was the women who announced the news. They met the soldiers, welcoming them back home, cheering and praising the warriors. Sacrifices were made, thankfulness expressed. They celebrated, feasting and dancing to compositions for brass, rhythm, and string. The enemy was ridiculed and taunted; the Song of Deborah is a prime example of this genre.

DEBORAH THE JUDGE-PROPHET

According to J. R. Porter (1982), of all the judges in the Hebrew scripture, only Deborah and Samuel are called nabli' or judge-prophet. Deborah was a judge because she was a prophet. Of all the judges named in the Hebrew Bible, Deborah is the only judge who actually judged! Her keen abilities to see the present and future, predict events, administer laws, mediate, and speak poetry were deemed so important to the war effort that she became commander in chief.

Deborah's attributes and family have been constructed in the *Aggadot* (legends or post-Biblical writings contained in the Talmud and Midrash). The *Aggadot* refer to Deborah as a wealthy philanthropist. From the Hebrew scripture, we know Deborah's husband, Lappidoth, by name only. The *Aggadot* indicate that the word Lappidoth is derived from the Hebrew word *lappid*, which means torch, and thus, he was a candle maker for religious celebrations. Otherwise, Lappidoth is considered in the *Aggadot* to be less intelligent than Deborah.

Deborah is assumed to have been a mother but this is not mentioned in any text. Childbearing was encouraged and parenting roles were incorporated into everyday life. The Hebrew scripture tells us of women who have borne children late in life, such as Sarah, and who pray for children, such as Rachel and Hannah. Thus, because the infertility theme is not incorporated into the story of Deborah, it is postulated that she indeed had children and a family.

Carl Meyers believes that the head of the household could act as a diviner, an oracle for the household; the title for this person would be "father" or "mother." At Yahweh's charge, Deborah "arose as a mother in Israel." This title refers to her keen talent to listen to the Lord and to speak prophesies for her household and also the nation.

In fact, Deborah may be a title rather than a name. The title relates both to the role of Judge and to the role of the Queen Bee. Both administer over the production of consumables, such as honey and wax. Both can sting the opposition to defeat. Deborah's husband, Lappidoth, utilizes the bee's wax to manufacture candles.

Rabbinical expositions indicate that Deborah was given an unbecoming name of Bee because of her hubristic military command and pretentious poetry about her actions in the campaign. Actually, the bee goddess and her priestesses had been revered for millennia. The bee is portrayed as a goddess in vase painting of 6400-6200 BCE Thessaly; pot shard of 6000 BCE Hungary; bone carving of the 4000 BCE Ukraine; gold filigree of 2000 BCE Crete; and a gold plaque of 700 BCE Rhodes (Gimbutas, 1982, 181-190; Jeter, 1992). The bee was a symbol of proliferation and renewal. Its antennae are shaped like the crescent moon. Honey was known as the food of the deities, a sweet intoxicant, a stimulant for well being and long life. Minoan art depicts the knowledge and practice of apiculture on Crete. As apiculture spread, humans no longer had to rely on searching for wild honey. Rather, bees could be kept and their honey collected on a regular basis.

Helmer Ringgren (1982) has reviewed Near Eastern prophecies. Letters from Ebla, palace texts from Uruk, Neo-Assyrian documents, and Deir 'Alla inscriptions are prophecies given voice by goddesses and women.

In the Artemisium of Ephesus, one of the seven wonders of the ancient world, rosettes decorated with headless bees have been found; it is hypothesized that they were amulets to deflect the evil eye (Ramsome 1937: 110). The bee was the title given in Eleusis to the Priestesses of Demeter and in Delphi to the oracles (Tuebal, 1990, 25; Keller, 1988). Erich Neumann (1972; Tuebal, 1990, 28) proposes that the bee priestess was unmarried and engaged in sexual relations only once. Tuebal theorizes that the mythological term and ancient practice, *heiros gamas* or the sacred marriage, may well be modeled after the sex life of the Queen Bee.

In Delphi, Eleusis, Ephesus and other oracular centers, the priestess and priest were considered to be emissaries for the deities. Advice was sought from the priestess and priest about the present and future, the mundane and the important, the personal and civic. Voices were heard, visions seen, smells analyzed, bodies touched, spices tasted, intuition acknowledged, dreams interpreted.

Teubal (1984) believes that the Hebrew matriarchs were actually priest-esses, skilled at foretelling the future. Their names are honorary titles for Mesopotamian goddesses: Sarah, the Princess; Leah, the Wild Cow; Rachel, the Ewe. For instance, Sarah's services were sought by the Pharaoh of Egypt and the King of Gezer. Sarah resided most of her life in Mamre, a grove of sacred terebinth trees and oracular center. Leah and Rachel inter-preted their husband's dream, instilling in him courage to leave their father's home. Rachel carefully took the statues of the goddess with her, hiding them under her skirts. When her father came to look for the house-hold deities, she told him that it was her menstrual period, thus, being the first woman recorded to use the menstrual period as an excuse.

Two other prophetesses are discussed in Hebrew scripture. During the late monarchy in seventh century BCE, Huldah, whose name means wea-sel, was sought for consultation by King Josiah (I Kings 22:14-20, II Chronicles 34:22-8). After the return from exile in Babylon, Noadiah (whose name means "revealed by God") was hired by Tobiah and Sanbal-lat, leaders in neighboring territories, to discourage King Nehemiah from completing the work of rebuilding the walls of Jerusalem (Nehemiah 6:14).

Through prophecy, we learn that God spoke to women and men; their messages, often presented as charismatic poetry, were valued by the entire community (Bird, 1974, 41-88). Miriam (Numbers 12:1-2, 76) preceded Deborah. "Service women" (Exodus 38:8, 1 Samuel 2:22) are thought to be prophets. Later, in the Second Temple in Jerusalem, female singers are acknowledged (Ezra 2:65; Nehemiah 7:67; I Chronicles 25:5; Bird, 1974, 68). Parallel to the prophets were magicians (I Samuel 28:7; Exodus 22:18; cf. Deuteronomy 18:10; II Chronicles 33:6; Bird, 1974, 78). The wise woman (II Samuel 14:2; 20:16) was sought for advice. Anna, a woman oracle, was present at the circumcision of Jesus (Luke 2).

Cheryl Anne Brown (1992) has analyzed the story of Deborah written by Jewish authors of the first century CE. For instance, in *Jewish Antiqui-ties*, Flavius Josephus devotes only ten paragraphs to Deborah. Josephus discusses Deborah's duties as a prophet and ignores her roles as a judge, leader, poet, or warrior.

However, Brown finds that in *Biblical Antiquities*, Pseudo-Philo elabo-rates upon the position of Deborah. Deborah, as Moses before her, was sent by God as a testimony of the divine care for the human condition.

Deborah and Moses were to govern and emancipate the people. Moreover, she was to "enlighten," to teach the Torah within the wisdom tradition. Pseudo-Philo translates 'eseth lapidoth (Judges 4:4) to mean a woman who enlightens the mind, rather than the wife of a torch or candle maker. Deborah is placed among other notable instructors including Moses and Samuel.

Deborah is described by Pseudo-Philo as having power over the angels, stars, and the world, abilities accorded to the Egyptian goddess Isis and Biblical heroes, Joshua and Moses. After the military victory, Deborah proclaimed the ultimate atonement of humans with God. Pseudo-Philo concludes with a discussion of Deborah's death. The community mourned for seventy days, the number of days they grieved for Jacob. The memorial statement (Brown, 1992, 69-70) described Deborah as a "mother of Israel," "holy one," and "leader of the house of Jacob" who "firmed up the fence about her generation."

In the Hebrew scripture, Deborah is one of only two nabli' or judge-prophets and the only judge who truly judged. A careful reading of the Hebrew scripture, the Aggadot, Jewish Antiquities, and Biblical Antiquities cross-referenced with interdisciplinary studies indicates that Deborah was a judge precisely because she was a leader, mother, poet, prophet, teacher, and warrior.

DEBORAH THE ARCHETYPE

James Hillman (1985) has written that if you want to know the archetype, the place of the archetype must be studied. By understanding where the archetype is in the order of the universe, we may begin to learn where the archetype is within the order of our psyche. Deborah the Judge is primarily associated with two geographical sites: Bethel and the Naphtali Mountains. An investigation into these places, indeed, reveals significant information about the identity of Deborah.

Reading Judges 4, we meet Deborah sitting under a palm tree near Bethel, a few miles north of Jerusalem. The palm tree has long been known as the "birth tree" in the near east, as well as the source of both "milk and honey" (Numbers 14:7-8). Deborah the Judge sat near the burial site of Deborah the Wet-Nurse who escorted the second matriarch Rebekah from her parents' home in Mesopotamia to meet and marry her cousin, Isaac. Deborah died at an unspecified time during the twenty years between Rebekah's marriage and the birth of her twins. She was buried under the Allon-bacuth, the Oak of Weeping (Genesis 35:8). The Hebrew word allon has two meanings: oak tree and power (Bar-Moshe, 1993).

Thus, this tree was known to be an oracular oak tree as well as a tree under which Deborah, the Wet-Nurse was buried.

Today, Bethel is both an archaeological site and a town located twelve miles north of Jerusalem in what is today called the West Bank of the Jordan River. Four thousand years ago, Bethel was an important trading center for caravans (Albright, 1968, 35; Teubal, 1984, 89). After a visit by an oracle, Jacob named the town the "Home of El Shaddai," the God who transported Sarah and Abram to Israel and promised the land to them and their descendants (Genesis 35:11). El Shaddai has been defined as God Almighty (Hertz, 1990, 130) and even God of the Mountains, God of the Breasts (Tompkins, 1993).

In the desert the tree, providing nourishment and shade, was long considered holy. A "stylized . . . date palm" was the symbol of the Goddess Asherah (Olyan, 1988, 1). Today, pillar statues of female faces firmly integrated upon tree trunk-appearing torsos are archaeological artifacts found all over the Middle East. It was not until King Josiah's rule from 640-609 BCE, that worship of Asherah was prohibited and her sacred trees and cult symbols destroyed (Deuteronomy 7:5; 12:3; 16:21; II Kings 21; 22; 23).

Deborah, the Judge, presided over her court of law in Bethel, an ancient oracular center for the long-worshipped bee goddess and the more recent god, El. She sat under a palm tree and near an oak tree, living reminders of the ultimate power of the cycle of birth and death.

The second site with which Deborah the Judge is associated is the Naphtali Mountains towering above the Hula Valley. To the west of *Metzudat Yesha* or Salvation Junction, among groves of apple, olive, and oak trees stands an ancient *elah* tree; its seven-leafed branches spread over one thousand square feet of area. The Hebrew word *elah* has two meanings: terebinth or oak tree and goddess (Bar-Moshe, 1993).

Nearby are the graves of Deborah, Jael, Heber the Kenite, and Barak Ben Abinoam. Red poppies, yellow daisies, plus wild flowers and grasses of other hues create the appearance of a rich oriental carpet. The well-worn path to their cemetery as well as candle wax on their tombs is evidence of the remembrance of Deborah's story even today. Here in these groves the spirit of Deborah is ever present. The site itself inspires pilgrims to rise to a higher nature, to live with integrity within the family and community, to work toward a just world of equity for all.

Just eight miles north of Salvation Junction on the mountainous rim of the Hula Valley is Abel Beth-Maachah. Abel Beth-Maachah or the Meadow of the House of Maachah is referred to in the Hebrew scripture; the archaeological site has been identified just north of Kibbutz Kefar Gil'adi (Kaplan, 1977). Abel Beth-Maachah was a center for oracles. It was referred to as "a mother in Israel" (II Samuel 20:14-22). Here, Tekoah, a "wise woman" resolved a crisis involving David's general, Joab (II Samuel 14:1-24).

Both sites associated with Deborah, Bethel and the Naphtali Mountains, are in the higher elevations of Israel; pointed peaks are unequivocal expressions in nature of maternal breasts. Here, grow majestic oak trees; their very names also mean power and the goddess. The tree's branches spread out to provide a protected outdoor courtroom as well as sacred space in which Deborah could work as a prophet-judge. Bethel and Abel Beth-Maachah are cities where women oracles were respected.

I recently was a participant-observer at two pilgrimages which have provided me with insights on Deborah, the bee, and Deborah, the judge. I spent the day preceding a New Moon at Rachel's Tomb in Bethlehem. Crowds of religious and traditional Jewish women come each month on this day to pray for the well-being of their families. Each woman reads the Psalms and prayers in a hushed voice. The discrete voices merge together to create a sound not unlike the humming of a beehive. A pilgrim, listening to the unison of prayers, to the beehive of activity, may well feel propelled into movement. With the archetypal beehive swarming behind her, anything is possible.

At the Tomb of Rabbi Mier Baal Haness in Tiberias, I observed a young religious Jewish woman (whom I shall call Deborah) give blessings. For almost four hours, women swarmed around Deborah, as if she was a queen bee. The crowd strains to hear each word. Despite the movement of the crowd, Deborah is quite grounded. Never is she far away from the tomb of Rabbi Mier Baal Haness, the Miracle Maker.

She listens carefully, one at a time, to each woman. The words may be confidential whispers to her ear or public proclamations before the group. Holding the woman's hand against her heart and with her eyes closed, Deborah pronounces a blessing for the person and her family. Then she looks directly into the woman's eyes, recommends particular prayers, points upwards, and speaks lovingly of the abundant blessings available to all. The recipient often expresses emotions, releasing tears or smiling happily. Deborah accepts no payment. She says that she is simply acting as a conduit and that she also is being blessed by the exchange. Then, in thankfulness, the woman kisses her hand and Deborah kisses her in return or they exchange hand caresses and kisses on each other's cheeks.

This modern day Deborah stands erect, bending at her waist to attend intimately to each person. Deborah's demeanor is direct. At times, her voice shocks individuals to new insights and behaviors. She is assertive, confident, empathic, and expressive. Deborah is dressed very properly; a long-sleeved, white lace blouse covers much of her ankle length dark blue skirt. A white silk bun conceals her hair fully and highlights her red cheeks. With each exclamatory nod of the head, the bun slips, and women rearrange it properly again upon her head. Deborah's right front tooth is missing. In her right hand, she holds a prayer book.

Some men bring their infirm women relatives to Deborah for a blessing. They leave Deborah thankful for the encounter. There were, however, two religious men who stood watching, veritably open-mouthed in judgement. When they confronted Deborah, she answered calmly, directly, without any hesitancy or defensiveness. As I observed this contemporary extemporaneous, informal ritual, I marveled to think that many of the behaviors may well have been behaviors exhibited almost three thousand years ago by Deborah, the prophet-judge.

Scholars have analyzed the significance and nature of the bee in the story of Deborah. Ignaz Goldziher (1967, 430) has proposed that Biblical literature is based on solar mythology. He contends that the ancients knew Deborah, the bee, and Jael, the wild goat, to be clouds that stimulated lightning. In the tradition of the thunder deity, General Barak assumed the warrior role.

Hilda M. Ramsome (1937, 67) has interpreted Deborah and Barak to be natural phenomena. The war effort was ignited by lightning striking a sacred tree in which a revered swarm of bees live.

There are just a few references to the bee in the Hebrew scripture; however, there are almost fifty references to honey (Young, 1879). The Psalms relate God's judgements to be "sweeter than honey and the honeycomb" (19:10). In the Song of Solomon, honey and the honeycomb are associated with the bride and bridegroom.

CONCLUSION

My bride, my sister, I have come
To gather spices in my garden,

To taste wild honey with my wine,
Milk and honey with my wine.

Feast, Drink–and Drink Deeply–Lovers!

–The Song of Songs, 18 (Falk)

Deborah gives voice to her feelings and knowledge, acts in consonance with her emotions and thoughts. Her song is one of the earliest written works in the Hebrew scripture. Deborah was not shy. She told her own story, wrote her own press.

Research on the matriarchs is akin to the restoration of a poorly preserved 3,800-year-old tapestry. The golden strands in the Hebrew scripture and silver threads of post-Biblical texts are carefully woven with the multi-colored threads gleaned from an ever-expanding body of interdisciplinary research. This tedious, cross-cultural work can provide us with a more fully human portrait of Deborah. In today's terminology, Deborah is a "super woman" who "has it all." It is precisely this breadth of experience, extension of empathy, that makes her a judge written into history and esteemed over the ages.

I like to imagine that Deborah lived in a happy marriage, a healthy supportive relationship. A tangible connector between Deborah and Lappidoth, literally the bee and the candle maker—wax—may illustrate an interdependence between the spouses. Deborah produced wax which was recycled by her husband to lighten sacred areas. The methodology to produce and retain a light in the dark of the pre-conscious, in the dark of the sacred area, was considered awe inspiring, enlightening. With the introduction of torches, hours of daylight were lengthened, animals were subdued, life seemed almost controllable with wax torches. The eternal light of the altar was a memorial to ancestors, an eternal lamp of hope in the ultimate meaning of life. Both Deborah and Lappidoth sought to replace darkness with light, the profane with the sacred, fear with courage.

Deborah follows in the proud line of the matriarchs who are also priestesses, respected for their wisdom of the sacred. Deborah may have, in the tradition of the Eastern priestesses, engaged in sexual relations only in the context of the sacred marriage or *heiros gamas*, with a king to insure the fertility of the land. However, I like to imagine that Deborah followed the injunction repeated often in the Hebrew scripture, "Be fruitful and multiply." Moreover, I propose that Deborah's children were so well-adjusted and happy, family life so loving and healthy, that it was a role model for the community. Deborah's admirable leadership skills so exemplary in her home were desired for the community at large.

Deborah follows the Jewish tradition of Sarah, Rebecca, Rachel, and Leah, *zaddikot*, which is translated from colloquial Hebrew to mean righteous women and our mothers. Of these four "mothers," Sarah, Rebecca, and Rachel have delayed childbearing and only Leah has more than two children (Genesis 11:30; 25:21; 29:31; Frankiel, 1990, 5). Tamar Frankiel (1990, 6) has associated the essence of the woman, the mother, with the role of the prophet. The archetypal mother has the dual abilities to perceive an immediate apprehension or cognition and, moreover, to act upon this second sight, this sixth sense in a manner which creates the best future for herself, her children, and their children. She entwines these heightened skills into the role, indeed, status we call prophetess!

Frankiel (1990, 46-47) contends that the archetypal Biblical woman is accessible and amenable; moreover, she is highly effective because rather than investing resources into hierarchical power struggles, she negotiates informal networks with a sophisticated finesse.

Furthermore, the *zaddikot* are engaged in authentic intimacy (Frankiel, 1990, 48) with their inner selves, the deified, the sacred, their family and community. They deliver children; guard, nurture, and protect the family. Deborah, as an exemplary *zaddikot*, bravely accepts challenges and creates ventures, atoning the life force of not only her family, but the community at large.

Deborah leads a well-balanced life, creating harmony between her intuitive and rational functions. She is an orator and writer, a poet and military strategist, a prophetess and a judge. She lives in the present, mindful of the past, and conscious of the future.

Deborah sits on the ground, as if grounded to the earth source. She sits in a grove of trees, sacred to the oracle. The tree that not only survives but flourishes rooted in sand, pebbles, and rocks can teach us valuable lessons. A keen advisor can relate how a tree which continues to thrive and even bear fruit will live under a scorching sun, pale moon, and arid climate. Sitting under the palm of birth and the oak of weeping reminds Deborah and her following of the reassuring cycle of birth, death, and birth, perhaps even re-birth. Deborah's astute relationship with the ancient goddess Asherah and the newer god El Shaddai allows her to be the standard-bearer of the past and the leader of the future.

In today's world, where the public views the law as a lucrative approach for equal opportunity, professional malpractice, and sexual harassment suits; a gigantic courthouse for child abuse, custody, and divorce hearings; it is comforting, indeed, to be able to call forth an ancient positive archetype. Deborah teaches us that a Family Judge can lead a well-rounded personal life and be an effective, honest, respected professional. Perhaps, though, environment is the contextual pattern to be examined.

Deborah was a leader who reflected the values and life ways of her constituency. A psychological profile of both Deborah and the society indicates a balance of activities. The talents of women and men were both needed for the family and society to survive. Exogamy was practiced and men welcomed the foreign women and their deities, knowing that each deity was actually an outgrowth of a particular understanding about a phenomenon of nature. The rituals were acknowledgements of how humans can best work within the rhythms of nature.

People worked diligently and rejoiced often. Shabbat was already a well instituted practice. For 25 hours, from before sundown Friday through nightfall Saturday, the entire household rested. Families told each other the story of how God created the world in six days and then had rested. They recollected that their ancestors had been slaves in Egypt when Moses had proved to the Pharaoh that people are most productive when they have one day's rest out of seven. Moreover, household members– Jewish and non-Jewish–observed the commandment to keep Shabbat holy. They feasted, made love, rested, studied, worshipped. All persons were to have three meals on Shabbat, to experience the satisfaction of a full stomach.

Slowly, over the following centuries, the concept of a regularly scheduled day of rest was adopted by other cultures; it was observed that work can be accomplished much better when there is rest. However, the Jewish practice of Shabbat was not simply to unwind, shed bone-weariness and physical exhaustion. Shabbat provided a time for the common family to communicate with one another, to honor and thank a greater power for the gift of life, and to enjoy religious study and intellectual pursuits.

Throughout the year, people followed the rhythms of the seasons. New moons that cooled the desert were welcomed with prayers. The varied harvests were occasions for dancing, sleeping, eating in the fields.

Deborah's charge was a poem, a song–not a boring policy paper or political rhetoric. Poets and minstrels distill words into exciting songs, moving messages which radiate confidence in the audience. Deborah grew out of a milieu where persons were artists, where poetry and songs were the common way of communicating between persons doing everyday work. Deborah–the archetypal Family Judge–teaches us to develop a multitude of personal skills, to live boldly within the varied traditions, to act with confidence for life in peace.

REFERENCES

Albright, W. F. (1968). *Archaeology, Historical Analogy and Early Biblical Tradition*. Baton Rouge LA: Louisiana State University Press.

Alter, Robert. (1991). *The World of Biblical Literature*. New York NY: Basic Books.

Aschkenasy, Nehama. (1986). *Eve's Journey: Feminine Images in Hebraic Literary Tradition*. Philadelphia PA: University of Pennsylvania Press.

Bal, Mieke. (1988). *Murder and Difference: Gender, Genre, and Scholarship on Sisera's Death*. Translated from the French by Matthew Gumpert. Bloomington IN: Indiana University Press.

Bar-Moshe, A. S. (24 May 1993). Private Communication. Jerusalem, Israel.

Biale, David. (1987). *Power and Powerlessness in Jewish History*. New York NY: Schocken Books, 12-13.

The Bible in Art: Miniatures, Paintings, Drawings, and Sculptures Inspired by the Old Testament. (1956). New York NY: Phaidon Publishers, Inc., 142-147.

Bird, Phyllis. (1974). "Images of Women in the Old Testament." *Religion and Sexism: Images of Woman in the Jewish and Christian Traditions.* Rosemary Radford Ruether, editor. New York NY: Simon and Schuster, 41-88.

Boling, Robert G. (1964). *Judges: Introduction, Translation, and Commentary.* The Anchor Bible. Volume 6A. Garden City NY: Doubleday and Company, Inc.

Brown, Cheryl Anne. (1992). "Deborah." *No Longer Be Silent: First Century Jewish Portraits of Biblical Women: Studies in Pseudo-Philo's* Biblical Antiquities *and Josephus's* Jewish Antiquities. Louisville KY: Westminster/John Knox Press, 39-92.

Buber, Martin. (1968). *On the Bible: Eighteen Studies by Martin Buber.* Edited by Nahum N. Glatzer. New York NY: Schocken Books.

Burney, C. F., editor. (1920). *The Book of Judges with Introduction and Notes.* Second Edition. London, England: Rivingtons, 78-176.

Chrisman, Robert and Robert L. Allen, editors. (1992). *Court of Appeal: The Black Community Speaks Out on the Racial and Sexual Politics of Thomas vs. Hill.* New York NY: Ballantine.

Comay, Joan. (1980). "Deborah." *Who's Who in the Old Testament Together with the Apocrypha.* Volume I of Who's Who in the Bible. New York NY: Bonanza Books, 102-103.

Davis, O. B. (1988, 1976). *Introduction to Biblical Literature.* Second Edition. Portsmouth NH: Boynton/Cook Publishers, Heinemann.

Eliav, Arie Lova. (1988). *New Heart, New Spirit: Biblical Humanism for Modern Israel.* Translated from the Hebrew by Sharon Neeman. Philadelphia PA: The Jewish Publication Society.

Falk, Marcia, translator. (1990). *The Song of Songs: Love Lyrics from the Bible.* San Francisco CA: Harper.

Florenza, Elisabeth Schussler. (1992). *But She Said: Feminist Practices of Biblical Interpretation.* Boston MA: Beacon Press.

Frankiel, Tamar. (1990). *The Voice of Sarah: Feminine Spirituality and Traditional Judaism.* San Francisco CA: Harper.

Frymer-Kensky, Tikva. (1992). *In the Wake of the Goddesses: Women, Culture, and the Biblical Transformation of Pagan Myth.* New York NY: Free Press.

Garsiel, Moshe. (1991). *Biblical Names: A Literary Study of Midrashic Derivations and Puns.* Phyllis Hackett, translator. Ramat Gan, Israel: Bar-llan University.

Gimbutas, Marija. (1982). *The Goddesses and Gods of Old Europe: Myths and Cult Images.* Berkeley CA: University of California Press.

Goitein, S. D. (1988). "Women as Creators of Biblical Genres." Michael Carasik, translator. *Prooftexts*, 1-33.

Goldziher, Ignaz. (1967). *Mythology Among the Hebrews and Its Historical Development.* Translated from the German by Russell Martineau. New York NY: Cooper Square Publishers, Inc., 430.

Graves, Robert. (1948). *The White Goddess: A Historical Grammar of Poetic Myth.* New York NY: Farrar, Straus and Girous.

Haik-Vantoura, Suzanne. (1991). *The Music of the Bible Revealed.* John Wheeler, editor. Dennis Weber, translator. Second Edition. Originally published in French in 1978. Berkeley CA: BIBAL Press.

Harpur, James, editor. (1987). *Great Events of Bible Times: New Perspectives on the People, Places and History of the Biblical World.* Garden City NY: Doubleday and Company, Inc.

Henry, Sondra and Emily Taitz. (1985). *Written Out of History: Our Jewish Foremothers.* Second Edition Revised. Fresh Meadows NY: Biblio Press.

Hertz, J. H., editor (1990). *Pentateuch and Haftorahs.* Second Edition. Brooklyn NY: Soncino Press Limited.

Hillman, James. (1985). *Archetypal Psychology.* Dallas TX: Spring Publications, 36-37.

The Holy Bible (-). King James Translation. New York NY: American Bible Society.

Jacob, Benno. (1970). "The Jewish Woman in the Bible." *Woman.* Volume Three of the Jewish Library. Leo Jung, editor. London, England and New York NY: The Soncino Press, Page 10 (1-16).

James, Fleming. (1951). "Deborah." *Personalties of the Old Testament.* New York NY: Charles Scribner's Sons.

Jeter, Kris. (1992). "The Spirit of Home." *The Journal of Couple Therapy,* 3:1.

The Jewish Encyclopedia. (1901-1906). New York NY: Funk and Wagnalls Company.

Johnson, Buffie. (1988). *Lady of the Beasts: Ancient Images of the Goddess and Her Sacred Animals.* San Francisco CA: Harper and Row, 1988.

Kaplan, J. (1977). "Kefar Gil'adi." *Encyclopedia of Archaeological Excavations in the Holy Land.* Avi-Yonah, Michael and Ephraim Stern, editors. Volume III. Englewood Cliffs NJ: Prentice-Hall, Inc., 708.

Kaspi, Mordecai. (17 May 1993). *A Midrashic Portrait of the Patriarchs and Patriarchs.* Jerusalem, Israel: The Center for Conservative Judaism.

Keller, Mara Lynn. (1988). "The Eleusinian Mysteries of Demeter and Persephone: Fertility, Sexuality, and Rebirth." *Journal of Feminist Studies in Religion,* 4:1, 33.

Lanboy, Bezelel. (1972). *The Trip to Meron with Pictures of Holy Places.* Originally published in Jerusalem in 1889 under anonymous author. Jerusalem, Israel: P.A.I.H.K. (Hebrew. Rina Ben-Ari, Translator.)

Levy, Clifton Harby. (1936). *The Bible in Art: Twenty Centuries of Famous Bible Paintings.* Garden City NY: Garden City Publishing Company, Inc.

Maus, Cynthia Pearl. (1954). *The Old Testament and the Fine Arts: An Anthology of Pictures, Poetry, Music, and Stories Covering the Old Testament.* New York NY: Harper and Brothers Publishers, 227-229.

Mazar, Amihai. (1990). *Archaeology of the Land of the Bible 10,000-586 B.C.E.* New York NY: Doubleday.

Mendelsohn, I. (1948). "The Family in the Ancient Near East." *The Biblical Archaeologist* (XI: 2) 24-40.

Meyers, Carol. (1988). *Discovering Eve: Ancient Israelite Women in Context.* New York NY: Oxford University Press.

Montefiore, C. G. and H. Loewe. (1974). *A Rabbinic Anthology.* New York NY: Schocken Books, 557.

Morrison, Toni, editor. (1992). *Race-ing Justice, En-gendering Power: Essays on Anita Hill, Clarence Thomas and the Construction of Social Reality.* New York NY: Pantheon.

Neumann, Erich (1972). *The Great Mother: An Analysis of the Archetype.* Translated by Ralph Manheim. Princeton NJ: Princeton University Press.

Niditch, Susan. (1989). "Eroticism and Death in the Tale of Jael." *Gender and Difference in Ancient Israel.* Edited by Peggy L. Day. Minneapolis MN: Fortress Press, 43-57.

Olyan, Saul M. (1988). *Asherah and the Cult of Yahweh in Israel.* Atlanta GA: Scholars Press.

Our Ancestors: A Guide for the Sacred Places in the Galilee. (1989). Second Edition. Jerusalem, Israel: Committee for the Conservation of the Ancestors' Tombs in Israel. (Hebrew. Translated by A. S. Bar-Moshe and Eynat Guttman.) 48-51; 358.

Pardes, Ilana. (1992). *Countertradition in the Bible: A Feminist Approach.* Cambridge MA: Harvard University Press.

Porter, J. R. (1982). "The Origins of Prophecy in Israel." *Israel's Prophetic Tradition.* Edited by Richard Coggins; Anthony Phillips; and Michael Knibb. New York NY: Cambridge University Press, 12-31; 14.

Pritchard, James B., editor. (1958). "Legal Texts." *The Ancient Near East: An Anthology of Texts and Pictures.* Volume One. Princeton NJ: Princeton University Press, 133-172.

Ramsome, Hilda M. (1937). *The Sacred Bee in Ancient Times and Folklore.* Boston MA: Houghton Mifflin Company.

Ringgren, Helmer. (1982). "Prophecy in the Ancient Near East." *Israel's Prophetic Tradition.* Edited by Richard Coggins; Anthony Phillips; and Michael Knibb. New York NY: Cambridge University Press, 1-11.

Ruffins, Paul. (16-22 November 1992). "Thomas, Hill and the Anger of Black Voices." *The Washington Post National Weekly Edition*: 10:3.

Steinsaltz, Adin. (1984). "Deborah: The Political Prophetess." *Biblical Images: Men and Women of the Book.* Yehuda Hanegbi and Yehudit Keshet, translators. New York NY: Basic Books.

Stowe, Harriet Beecher. (1990). "Deborah the Prophetess." *Woman in Sacred History.* Originally published in 1873. New York NY: Portland House, 83-90.

Teubal, Savina J. (1990). *Hagar the Egyptian: The Lost Tradition of the Matriarchs.* San Francisco CA: Harper and Row.

Teubal, Savina J. (1984). *Sarah the Priestess: The First Matriarch of Genesis.* Athens OH: Swallow Press.

Tompkins, Helen Stark. (18 April 1993). Private Communication. Kennett Square PA.

Young, Robert. (1879). *Analytical Concordance to the Bible.* Peabody MA: Hendrickson Publishers, 489, 80.

Index

A mensa et thoro, 6
A vinculo matrimonii, 6,7
Abbott, G., 218-219
Abel Beth-Maachah, 297-298
Abortion
    rights of children, Supreme Court
        decisions, 130-131
    rights of fathers, 40-42
    spousal consent regarding, 41
    Supreme Court decision on, 284
Absolute divorce, 7
Abuse
    spousal
        in early England, punishment, 9
        men's rights regarding, 42-43
    sterilization, 264
Achtenberg, R., 69
ACLU. *See* American Civil Liberties
    Union
Adams, A., 13-14
Adams, J., 13-14
Adoption
    in gay and lesbian relationships,
        63-64
    rights of unwed fathers regarding,
        39-40
    by stepparents, 176-177
Adultery
    divorce due to, 101
    in early England, punishment for,
        7-8
AFDC. *See* Aid to Families with
    Dependent Children
African American(s)
    marriages among, in
        post-Revolutionary
        America, 21-22
    unemployment rates for, 87-88
African American family

black matriarchy in, 80-81
child care issues, 92-93
controversial issues in, 80
credit issues, 88-89
divorce in, 80
employment issues, 87-88
housing issues, 89-92. *See also*
    Housing, in African
    American families
illegitimacy in, 80,81-82
inequality of, in United States,
    79-80
negative view of, 80
non-traditional unions, 82
public welfare in, 80
single-parent, 77-93. *See also*
    African American family,
    and U.S. legal system
    AFDC for, 83-87. *See also*
        AFDC (Aid to Families
        with Dependent Children)
    employment issues, 87-88
    historical rationales for, 81-82
    housing issues, 89-92
    Legal Aid for, 82-83
    legal services benefiting, 83
    poverty rate, 87
    prevalence, 87
    segregation of, 90
    Social Security cuts effects on,
        84-85
    welfare for, 83-87
and U.S. legal system, 77-93. *See*
    also African American
    family, single-parent
    common law marriages, 82
    economic issues, 83-87
    lack of support, 82
    slavery and, 81-82